Indian Political Thought

K.S. Padhy
Former Professor and Head
Department of Political Science
Berhampur University
Berhampur (Orissa)

PHI Learning Private Limited
New Delhi-110001
2011

₹ 350.00

INDIAN POLITICAL THOUGHT
K.S. Padhy

ISBN-978-81-203-4305-4

The export rights of this book are vested solely with the publisher.

Published by Asoke K. Ghosh, PHI Learning Private Limited, M-97, Connaught Circus, New Delhi-110001 and Printed by Multi Colour Services, 92a, DSIDC Sheds, Okhla Industrial Area, New Delhi-110020.

Contents

Preface

This book is the outgrowth of my many years of teaching students of Political Science about the various Indian political thinkers at Berhampur University, Orissa. It is also the result of the feedback I have received from many of my students and my academic colleagues on the subject. There are hardly any up-to-date book available today in the market which deals comprehensively with the political thought of the thinkers discussed in the book. This book is meant to fill that vacuum and addresses the felt need for a comprehensive book on the subject.

Many people identify political thought with western political thought which deals with thinkers such as Plato, Aristotle, Bentham, Hegel, Mill and Marx. While their contribution to world political thought is immeasurable, there is also a body of Indian thinkers—both ancient and modern—who have contributed substantially to the political and social thought of India. In this book, I have endeavoured to describe their thought in a succinct and clear fashion.

The book is divided into 22 chapters. Chapters 1–4 deal with the political thought of Manu, the lawgiver, who gave an elaborate classification of the different castes in India and the duties they are supposed to perform; Kaultilya, the author of the famous *Arthashastra*, who describes the four stages of life and the duties of the King; Raja Ram Mohan Roy, who took upon himself the onerous responsibility of reforming the Hindu religion; and Swami Dayananda Saraswati, the religious reformer, who set up the Arya Samaj and was highly critical of untouchability and discrimination against women.

Chapters 5–8 discuss about the political thought of Swami Vivekananda whose rousing speech in the Parliament of Religions in Chicago was highly appreciated; Bala Gangadhar Tilak, Gopal Krishna Gokhale and Sri Aurobindo, the great writer whose sublime thoughts are crystallized in such works as *Savitri*.

Chapters 9–16 focus on the modern Indian leaders whose political and social thought has had enormous influence on generations of Indians and even non-Indians. These thinkers include Mahatma Gandhi, the Father of the Nation, whose ideas of *Satyagraha*, *Ahimsa* (Non-violence), *Panchayati Raj*, *Swadeshi* and *Swaraj* caught the attention of the whole nation and who galvanized the nation to free it from the British rule and achieve Independence; Jawahar Lal Nehru, the first Prime Minister of India, who built modern India and was a key figure in establishing the socialist, democratic Republic of India; Subhash Chandra Bose, the great revolutionary; JP (Jaya Prakash Narayan), the pioneer of the socialist movement; and Bhimrao Ambedkar, the Architect of the Indian Constitution and a great social reformer, who fearlessly championed the cause of the scheduled castes, and other underprivileged and marginalized sections of the society.

Chapters 17–22 deal with such other Indian thinkers as Sir Sayyad Ahmed Khan; Muhammad Ali Jinnah, the creator of Pakistan, Lala Rajpat Rai; Ram Manohar Lohia, the great socialist; Vinayak Damodar Savarkar, and Mahatma Phule.

The book is written in a student-friendly fashion, with summary, questions, and notes at the end of each chapter. It is intended as a text for undergraduate and postgraduate students of Political Science. Also, any reader who would like to have an idea about the political thought of the thinkers discussed in the book will find the book quite useful.

A number of people have inspired me and helped me in writing this book. Many of my teachers and academic colleagues have been a source of inspiration and encouragement in writing this book. Besides, quite a few of my friends and my students have motivated me in this endeavour. I am grateful to all for their cooperation during the preparation of this book. I wish to thank Mr. Surya Prakash (Babbi) for computer setting of the entire manuscript. Finally, I wish to thank the Publisher, PHI Learning, especially the editorial and production team, for the careful processing of the manuscript.

Any comments and suggestions for improving the contents will be highly appreciated.

K.S. Padhy

1

Manu

INTRODUCTION

A descendant of self-existent Brahman, son of *Swayambhu* (God), Manu is said to be the Lawgiver as well as the Creator of the Universe and all living beings. Invoked at the sacrifices (*Yajnas*) as *Prajapati* and identified with the Brahman Himself, he is said to be an incarnation of God and a deity residing in heaven. Son of Aditya (Vivaswan), he belongs to both the worlds: the deities and human beings. The *Taittiriya Samhita* speaks of him as the father of a family who has divided his estates among his sons, while the *Satapatha Brahmana* describes him as an orthodox strictly following the daily customs of men.

The Rig Veda repeatedly calls him "Father Manu". Father progenitor of mankind, creator of the tribes, races of men, etc., he is their ruler. Founder of the social and moral order, he is the inventor of sacrificial rites and of the *Sraddhas* or funeral sacrifices. Author of laws, rules and legal maxims, he has revealed the *Mantras*. It is said that God Himself created the sacred laws and taught those laws to Manu who, in turn, taught the same to Mariki and other sages like Atri, Angiras, Pulastya, Pulaha, Kratu, Pracetas, Vasistha, Bhrigu and Narada. He composed the laws in order to clearly settle his duties and those of other castes.

WHO IS MANU?

A pertinent question arises here: who is Manu or what is he? Is he a saint, a hermit, an ordinary living human being with a family of his own, a deity, an incarnation of God, or God Himself? Scholars differ in their opinion in this regard. While Govindaraga considers him as a great sage, Medhatithi treats him as a particular individual perfect in the study of the Veda and in the performance of his precepts. Others consider him as God, the Supreme Soul; the Creator of the Universe and, at the same time, He is His Creation, an ordinary human being gifted with extraordinary qualities and a brilliant lawgiver.

SIX MANUS

Besides Manu, there are also six other Manus who created the universe at different times. Each Manu, in its own Epoch, created and pervaded this whole universe, moving and the unmoving. The lifespan of a deity is around twelve thousand years; when it is multiplied by seventy-one, it is called an Epoch of a Manu. The Epochs of Manu are countless, and so are the creations and destructions of the universe.

ETYMOLOGY OF THE NAME

'Manu' means 'the wise one' and it is the name of a king who is said to be the mythological ancestor of the human race. He is the Indian Adam. Thus *Manava* (descended from Manu) is a common word for 'human'. *Manava* also means 'of the human race'.

TEXT OF MANU

The text of Manu, to many, contains the works of several authors including Bhrigu and a considerable amount of popular wisdom. However, it is attributed to someone named Manu. When it is called Manu's laws, it is distinguished from, for instance, Gautam's laws, or Yajnavalkya's laws. But these are all said to be mythological or legendary figures.

AGE OF MANU

Manu's *Smritis* or *Dharmashastras* influence either directly or indirectly every aspect of Indian life in one way or another. But it is not easy to ascertain the date of their origin. Therefore, controversy surrounds them. Similarly, it is not easy to say exactly to which period Manu belonged. Historians differ on this point. To Sir William Jones, Manu lived in 1200 B.C., while to others, he belonged to the twelfth or the thirteenth century A.D. To Hopkins, he lived in the beginning of or even before the Christian era, while Jolly thinks that he cannot be earlier than the second or the third century A.D. Buhler concluded that *Manusmriti* existed in the second century A.D. All these arguments indicate that the era of Manu has not been clearly defined or identified by the historians.

MANUSMRITI

Manusmriti reflecting the ideas of Manu is said to be the most important and authoritative work as it contains the essence of the Veda. According to Brihaspati, *Smritis* and religious scriptures will not be recognized if they differ from Manu's work. The latter, based on the *Manava-Dharmashastra*, revolves around the kings and other such personages. To Manu, life will be happy, good and noble, if it is devoted to *Artha* (finance), *Dharma* (spiritual deeds) and *Kama* (desire). One should, therefore, strive to achieve them. He should earn money; spend it on good deeds like performing *Pujas* and *Tapas* and on developmental activities so that he can attain salvation (*Moksha*).

Comprehensive and encyclopaedic, Manu's text contains twelve chapters with 2,685 verses. It is evident from the translated works of C. Buhler, Wendie Doniger, Brian K. Smith and Arthur Coke Burnell as well as from the available text itself. The following table reflects it:

Chapter	*Number of verses*	*Content*
1	119	Origin of the universe, etc.
2	249	Sources of law, the first stage of the Brahman's life, i.e. the studentship.
3	286	The second stage of life, the householder and his religious studies.
4	260	Subsistence and private morals of the Brahman householder.
5	169	Food-ceremonial purification, duties of women.
6	97	The third and fourth stages of life.
7	226	The king's duties, the second caste, etc.
8	420	Civil and criminal laws.
9	336	Civil and criminal laws continued; the third and fourth castes.
10	131	The mixed castes and classes, procedure in time of need.
11	266	Penance, expiation, etc.
12	126	Exposition of philosophical principles, acquisition of final happiness.

Manusmriti covers the following topics:

- Social responsibilities, obligations and duties of various castes and individuals in different stages of life.
- The way a perfect and righteous king rules and punishes the criminals and transgressors of law in his kingdom.
- Social relations between men and women of different castes, and of husbands and wives in the privacy of the home.

- Birth, death and taxes.
- Cosmogony, karma and rebirth.
- Ritual practices.
- Error and restoration or redemption, etc.

In his work, Manu discusses the following:

- Origin of the universe and the rules for the rituals.
- Keeping promises and attending a teacher.
- Marriage and the kinds of marriages.
- Regulations for great sacrifices and the obligatory rule of the ceremonies for the dead and for questioning witnesses.
- Various means of livelihood, vows of a Vedic graduate, kinds of food to be eaten and not to be eaten, purification and cleansing of impurities.
- Duties of women, of a king, of husband and wife, heretics, etc.
- Freedom and renunciation.
- Partition of property, gambling, and 'cleaning out thorns'.
- Attendance by commoners and servants, and origin of confused classes.
- Religious duties of all classes in extremity, and rules for restoration.
- Three-fold course of transmigration that arises from the effects of past actions.
- Supreme good, and examination of the virtues and vices of the effects of the past actions.
- Obligatory duties of (particular) countries, castes, and families, etc.

The text of Manu centres around life: how is it and how should it be? It is a model of and for life. It is about *Dharma* which covers concepts like religion, duty, law, right, justice, practice and principle. It discusses religion in its entirety, good and bad effects of the past actions and the external code of conduct of four classes of people. The code is the highest law and it is described in the revealed canon and in tradition. Therefore, a twice-born person, who is self-possessed, should always practise it. He who fails to do so does not reap the fruit of the Veda. Its strict adherence ensures full enjoyment of the fruit.

Manu's text, though ancient, cannot be ignored for its comprehensiveness. It covers family life, psychology, human body, sex, relationship between humans and animals, attitude to money and material possessions, politics, law, caste, purification and pollution, rituals, social practices and ideals, world renunciation and worldly goals. As discussed earlier, it is known by two different names: *Manusmriti* and *Manava-Dharmashastra*. The title, therefore, poses a problem partly because the first title does not contain the key term *dharma*, while the second one includes it. Moreover, *Smriti* designates a traditional sacred text like the Veda, while *Sastra* refers to 'laws', which regulate human behaviour.

Manu's teachings inspire one to fulfil his promises and liberate himself from the consequences of his past deeds. He not only purifies himself of all his sins but also helps his predecessors and successors up to seven generations in achieving salvation. Thus, the Laws of Manu wash away one's sins and give salvation to him, his ancestors and successors. They promote well-being, increase intelligence and lifespan, confer name and fame, and bring him the supreme good and happiness.

The priests, who are gifted with knowledge and wisdom and who are wise and enlightened, should read Manu's text very carefully and explain it diligently to their pupils. Kshatriyas and Vaisyas can also read it but cannot teach it. He, whose sacramental course of life from conception to cremation has been influenced by *mantras*, is authorized to read it. Males of the three Aryan *varnas* can read this text if they satisfy this condition. The sacraments may also be performed for women and Sudras, but without the recitation of *mantras*.

Manu's Laws are found in the Veda. Similarly, whatever *dharma* he has suggested for anyone is also in the Veda. It is an embodiment of all knowledge. And the Veda also contains the supreme knowledge.

MANU'S WORK ENLARGED AND 'POLLUTED'

It is very sad to comment that the content of Manu's text has undergone, over the years, drastic changes since its first publication. At least thirty handwritten texts on it are found in different libraries. Every succeeding work is more voluminous than the preceding one as it contains a larger number of verses. Undoubtedly, Manu's text, based on Veda, is objective, fundamental, original and free from biases and prejudices. But it seems that the original work has been 'polluted' by commentators and critics who spoiled its sanctity by adding or incorporating into it new verses. They are at many places opposed to one another. Commentators and scholars of eminence like Kullukabhatta, Buhler and Maharashi Dayananda Saraswati have admitted this. To Kullukabhatta, 170 new *slokas* are added to the original work. To Priyabrata Das, the number is as high as 1506. Things which are pervert and unethical have made an unashamed and unabashed entry into Manu's work, thereby undermining its spirit, substance and significance.

Manu's original work is, thus, enlarged because

- Manu was considered as the creator of the universe by his followers and disciples;
- *Manusmriti* was treated as the creation of Lord Brahma or Lord Prajapati;
- disciples of Bhrigu wanted to make their master more popular and, hence their attempts to rename *Manusmriti* as *Bhrigusamhita*;
- *Tantriks* and *Saktas* justified slaughtering of animals;
- later Vedantics argued that Lord Brahma was born out of an egg, and from Him came out the whole universe;
- individual's birth, not his role, determined his caste; Brahmins monopolized the study of scriptures and denied this opportunity to others;

- new social values like child marriage, polygamy, etc. were upheld and justified;
- pervert principles opposed to the Veda were rationalized and upheld. Performance of funeral rites after death, offering meat to the deceased, penance for different sins and misdeeds, etc. were considered as ethical and not contrary to the Vedic principles.

MANU IN VEDA

Eminent scholars and commentators like Raghavananda, Kulluka, Medhatithi have highly acclaimed the text of Manu because the word 'Manu' is mentioned in the *Vedas, Mahabharata, Brihaspati-smriti,* etc. References like "Whatever Manu said is curative", "Manu divided his property among his sons", "A *smriti* opposed to Manu is not approved" have encouraged a few European and Indian scholars to make Veda the source of Manu's origin and his history. In other words, attempts are made to discover Manu from it. But nowhere it mentions the name of any person, nor is there any reference in it to geography or history of any area, of any person, country, or civilization. It has given to the mankind eternal and sublime knowledge so that man can live and lead an ideal life. It is the source of each and every branch of knowledge: science, philosophy, art, literature, etc. A *Mantra* in the Rig Veda reads thus: "*Ahascha Krishna-mahararjunam cha*". This means that when one comes across these two names, i.e. Krishna and Arjuna, he may think that these are the names of Lord Krishna and Arjuna who lived during the age of Mahabharata. But by thinking so, he is mistaken. Here 'Krishna' means 'night' and 'Arjuna' refers to 'day'. In the Rig Veda, the word 'Manu' is mentioned in the following *Mantra*: "*Jamatharba Manuswita Dadhyaom Dhiyamantrat*". Here the word 'Manu' means the 'sage', the *rishi* who has controlled his senses. The word 'Manu' referred to in another *Mantra* in it reads thus: "*Jani Manurabrunit*". It means the medicines which Manu recognized. Here 'Manu' means 'Vaidya' (doctor). In the Yajur Veda, the term 'Manabe' means 'knowledgeable person'. In another *Mantra*, "*Jebhyo Hotram Prathamamayeje Manuh*", the word 'Manuh' means 'considerate'. It is, therefore, against the Vedic principles to find out any proper noun, i.e. a name of any particular person in Veda.

Medhatithi, a very senior ancient commentator on Manu's work, rightly said that Manu, a person, became very famous by reading, knowing and understanding the Veda and by performing *Yajna* and *Tapas*. Highly spiritual, he knew the spirit and substance of *Dharma*. To Medhatithi, the *rishis*, saints and sages have disseminated knowledge from different Vedas, i.e. Rig, Yajur, Sam and Atharva. But Manu was the propounder of the *Smartha Dharma*, i.e. whatever he said was inspired by and in accordance with the canons of Veda.

SRUTI (HEARD) AND *SMRITI* (TRADITION)

The roots of religion are the entire Veda, the traditions and customs of those who know the Veda, the conduct of virtuous people and what is satisfactory to them. The Veda is known as the revealed canon (*Sruti*: heard) and the teachings of religion as the tradition (*Smriti*). Religion arose out of these two: *Sruti* and *Smriti*. He who disregards them and relies on the logic is an atheist and a reviler of the Veda. Virtuous people should, therefore, excommunicate him. *Smritis* are surrounded by fictitious traditions and mythological legends grow up either spontaneously as the real origin had been forgotten or fabricated intentionally to show that these works possess divine authority.

What is more important is that such legends or portions of them have been introduced into the text to obscure the real character of the *Smritis*. These peculiarities are particularly marked in the *Manava-Dharmashastra*. Its opening four verses narrate how the great sages approached Manu and requested him to explain the sacred laws and he explained them about the creation of the universe as well as of his own origin from the Brahman. He said that he learnt the Sacred Law from the Creator Himself who enacted them. Teaching them to ten sages including Bhrigu, he then asked Bhrigu to expound them. The latter completed his task by explaining the seven *Manvantaras*, the *Yugas*, and other divisions of time and by describing the order of the creation. He completed his work with an observation that he did his job 'exactly as it was revealed to him'. This is how *Manusmriti* has originated.

ORIGIN OF THE UNIVERSE

Once the great seers, sages and saints approached Manu and with utmost humility, they requested him to explain them about the origin of the universe and caste. Moved by their requests, he answered them:

> It was dark. There was nothing but darkness. Nothing could be visible and seen. Nothing could be discovered and knowable. It seemed as if everything was asleep. Then the self-existent Lord became manifest and with this manifestation the darkness was removed. Lord who is subtle, eternal, indiscrete and can be known by supra-sensual, consists of all elements and became manifest of Himself.

God produced different beings from His own body. First, He created water and laid a seed in it. That became a golden egg from which Lord Brahma, the grandparent of the entire world, was born. After His birth, the egg was split into two parts. And with these two shares Lord Brahma formed the heaven and the earth; in the middle, the sky and the eight regions, and the perpetual place of waters. From Himself, He created mind and from mind egoism. Brahma created all beings of the world either by Himself or through His agents. Thus, this non-eternal universe arose from the eternal.

Lord Brahma created divine beings, time and its divisions, the lunar zodiac and planets; rivers, oceans, rocks, plains, and uneven ground; desire, anger, austerity, speech, and sexual enjoyment; and desiring to create these beings and things, He created this creation.

For the prosperity of the worlds, He created from His mouth, arms, thighs and feet the Brahman, Kshatriya, Vaisya and Sudra, respectively.

The Lord divided His own body into two. He became a male by half, and half a female. The female portion of the Lord gave birth to Biraj, who after practising austerity, spontaneously produced Manu and the latter created beings. But before that He created ten seers: Marichi, Atri, Angiras, Pulastya, Pulaha, Kratu, Pracetas, Vasistha, Bhrigu and Narada. They remained in charge of producing other beings—Yakhyasas, Rakhyasas, Pisachas, Kinnaras, Gandharvas, Apsaras, Asuras, Nagas, Serpents and Eagles. They also produced lightning, thunderbolts, clouds, Indra's bent and unbent bows, meteors, comets and various luminaries; men, apes, fishes, and all kinds of birds; cattle, deer, and beasts of prey and animals with two rows of teeth; worms, and winged insects, lice, flies; and bugs, with all biting gnats, and innumerable things of different kinds.

All these things and beings, stationary and movable, were created by those great beings who were under the command of Manu.

SOCIAL ORDER

Castes and Their Functions

To preserve His creation, the Lord assigned separate duties to those who sprang from His mouth, arm, thigh and feet. For Brahmans, He ordered teaching, study, sacrifice (*yajna*), giving and receiving gifts, etc. A Brahman exists for the sake of Dharma; he explains and protects the Veda. A Kshatriya was to defend the people, study, sacrifice; to give alms, and he should not have any attachment to sense objects. A Vaisya was ordained to tend the cattle, produce crops, study, sacrifice, undertake trade and commerce, etc. One duty the Lord assigned to a Sudra — service to those (Brahman, Kshatriya and Vaisya) classes, without any grudge.

The Mixed Castes and Classes

The Brahman, Kshatriya and Vaisya are the three twice-born castes, while the fourth one, the Sudra, has only one birth. He does not have the second birth by putting the sacred thread on the body. The members of the first-three twice-born castes, while looking after their respective occupations, should read the holy texts. But among them, a Brahman only should explain these texts, and understand other castes. His origin, his upbringing, his pre-eminence and exposure, his knowledge, his conduct and character — all these have made him virtuous and the lord of the castes. Castes get mixed up when pure castes commit adultery by marrying those who should not have married, and when men desert their respective occupations.

If someone belonging to a low caste performs by greed the functions assigned to upper castes, his property should be confiscated by the king and he should be banished from the kingdom. It is better to be imperfect in one's duty rather than doing well the duties of another. By doing so he falls from his caste at once. If a Vaisya is not able to perform his own duties, he can perform those of a Sudra. He must engage himself in what ought to be done and stop this as soon as he feels confident of joining his own profession. When a Sudra cannot serve the twice-born, and faces a situation when his son and wife are dying, he may work as a manual labourer. A Brahman, who is in dire need, may take gifts from everybody and by doing so he does not become impure.

One can eat any type of food from any one when he is on the verge of death. By doing so, he does not commit any sin as the air is not soiled by the dirt. A Brahman may accept grains and fruits from any one when he cannot otherwise support his life. Doing so is better than receiving presents and picking up kernels is even better than that. A Sudra may serve a Kshatriya or a Vaisya. But he should serve the Brahmans for the sake of heaven, or for the sake of both (heaven and livelihood).

FOUR ORDERS OR STAGES OF LIFE

First Order or Stage of Life

Every individual seeks to achieve something in his life. For example, a Brahman seeks divine knowledge, a Kshatriya has a desire for power and a Vaisya has an urge for wealth. This can be possible only with right education. For a Brahman education begins in his fifth year; for a Kshatriya it is the sixth year and for a Vaisya it is the eighth year. A Brahman should learn about the *Gayatri Mantra* before the sixteenth year, a Kshatriya before the twenty-second year and a Vaisya after the twenty-fourth year. They should be taught customs, ceremonial purity, attending to the sacred fire and the *Sandhya* devotions. As long as they are students, they should do the following:

- Wear skins of black deer or deer, or of goat.
- Go for alms (begging).
- Collect fuel, sleep low on the ground, do what pleases their teacher.
- Read what their teacher wants.
- Lead a very simple, austere life however rich their parents may be.
- Not to utter the name of their Guru.
- Remain away from all sensuous and seductive objects.
- Pay respect to Guru's worthy sons and kinsmen.
- Not to salute the youthful wife of Guru if she is twenty-year-old.
- Go to bed after sunset and get up early in the morning before sunrise.

A man gets water by digging with a spade. Similarly, an obedient student attains divinity only by serving his Guru.

Second Order or Stage of Life

In one's second stage of life when his education is over, he marries and becomes a *Grahastha* (householder). He should honour the seers by studying the Veda, the deities by offerings, the manes (members of the family who are dead) by funeral obligations, men by food and beings by offerings. He should offer food to the guests first and then give alms to beggars. A guest coming in the evening after the sunset should not be allowed to leave the house in night and be properly treated by the householder. Hospitality rendered to a guest brings prosperity to the latter.

A Householder's Duty as Regards Subsistence and Private Morals

A Brahman, after spending the first quarter of his life with a Guru, should

- stay with his wife in his house in the second quarter of life without doing harm to any one;
- earn wealth without taking much pain, as it is necessary for his survival;
- not cheat or deceive others, be free from fraud, and lead a pure life, perform his duty as prescribed by the Vedas, as by doing this he gets maximum happiness.

If a Brahman, after returning from his Guru's *Ashram*, does not get money to live on, he may seek wealth from a king, or from someone who performs rites or who makes *Puja*, or from a pupil, but not from any other. If he has property, he should never put on dirty clothes. He must trim his hair, nails and beard and devote his time to study the Vedas. He should not look at the rising sun or the sun when it sets or when it is eclipsed, or when it is at the zenith. He should not run when it rains, nor see his own image in water. During the four days of menstruation of his wife, he should not touch her with passion, nor should he share a common bed with her. If he does so, his learning, glory, strength, sight and longevity are destroyed.

A twice-born householder must not

- have a craze for too much wealth, try to amass wealth through dubious means and crooked measures;
- be lustful and sensuous;
- possess wealth if it distracts his attention from reading the Vedas and discharging his obligations.

It is his duty to teach the Vedas; wear his clothes, exercise his intellect and deliver his speech commensurate with his age, calling, wealth, knowledge and family, and give alms to beggars.

One should not

- eat or sleep when the sun rises or sets in;
- share his food with his wife, look at her eating, sneezing and yawning (opening the mouth wide with a deep inhalation as a result of fatigue, drowsiness, or boredom);
- take naked bath;
- pass his urine on road, on ashes, on cultivated ground, on a mountain, in a ruined temple, on anthill, in pits with living beings in them, when walking or even standing, when sitting on river's bank, on the top of mountain;
- excrete while beholding the fire, wind, Brahman, sun, water, or cattle;
- discharge urine or ordure, or unclean things — poison or blood into water;
- look at a naked woman;
- talk with a woman in her courses (during the period of menstruation);
- sleep alone in an empty or deserted house;
- go to a feast uninvited;
- awaken a person who is asleep;
- cut his nails by his teeth, talk scandal, ride on the back of a camel, enter a house except by the gate and to be too close to the roots of trees;
- bathe after taking food, at midnight, in an unknown pond, or pool;
- honour his enemy, an enemy's companion, a vicious person, a thief, or the wife of another person;
- hate a Brahman, a Kshatriya, a snake, however mean they may be;
- speak what is unpleasant;
- have fruitless enmity or disputes with any one;
- find fault with those who are deformed, invalid, ignorant, illiterate, old and aged, ugly, poor and born in low castes;
- be rude to old men (if they come), pay disrespect to them, hurt their sentiments, unseat them from his seat;
- practise cruelty, hatred, pride and anger;
- tolerate the mistakes of his children or pupils.

A sadist and a vicious man, who has earned wealth through unjust means does not get real happiness. One may suffer for his virtues. But he should not be motivated to adopt corrupt means to enrich himself and feel frustrated by observing the prosperity and glory of the wicked ones. Vice practised in the world does not at once bear fruit like the earth, but, proceeding by degrees it tears up the roots of the doer. One is punished for his misdeeds today; if not today, tomorrow; if not tomorrow, a day after; a must; if not he, his son suffers and if not his son, his grandson, a must.

A householder should have control over his speech, sex, arms and belly; admire truth, virtues, noble customs and purity; avoid quarrel with a priest, a Brahman, a child, a teacher, a maternal uncle, a student, a guest, a dependent, an old and sick person, a physician, a relative, and with those people who are related through mother. Again he should not have any dispute with his mother, father, brother, son, wife, daughter and servant. He should cultivate virtues by degrees. For in the next world neither father nor mother will be there as helpers; nor son, nor wife, nor kinsmen to help him in any way. Virtue alone will be there to help him. Each being is born alone, also dies alone; alone each one enjoys his good deeds; alone, also, his bad deeds.

He gets name, fame, prestige, wealth, wisdom and glory if he recites the Vedas before the sunrise and sunset.

Third and Fourth Orders or Stages of Life

When a householder sees wrinkles and grey hair on himself and sees the child of the child (grandson or granddaughter), he should go to the forest either alone or with his wife. In the forest he should lead a very simple life; live like a hermit; offer *puja*; and do meditation. He should eat roots, fruits and herbs; wear a skin or bark; bathe in the morning and also in the evening; have long hair, beard, and nails; recite the Vedas; honour those who come to see him; offer alms to the poor; and treat his guests properly. He should control his mind; subdue his senses; be composed, well disposed and subdued; become a giver and not a taker; and be compassionate to all beings.

After living in the forest for sometime and having spent the third part of his life in the forest by observing austerity, he should, in is last stage of life, visit different places of spiritual importance. During this period he should tolerate abuse. He should not have any one as companion, should not enter into any dispute with any one, speak false or untrue speech or words and be angry. When he becomes harmless, controls sense organs and conquers passions, he becomes immortal. By making himself free from all kinds of emotions and bondages, he enjoys bliss and eternal happiness. This becomes possible only when he follows strictly the ten-fold laws: resolution, patience, self-restraint, honesty, purity, restraint of the organs, devotion, knowledge (of Veda), truth and absence of danger.

THE KING

Who is He and What is He?

According to Manu, Lord, the Almighty, created the king taking eternal particles of Indra, Wind, Yama, Sun, Fire, Varuna, Moon, and Kubera. The king, therefore, surpasses all created beings in lustre. Hence, no one should look at him. He is a deity in human form, a divine reincarnation, learned and cultured; well-versed in all branches of knowledge, a perfect man of intellect, calibre and moral character. He follows the advice of the Brahmans who are learned in the Vedas; constantly worships and acquires the knowledge of the Supreme Soul. Since he has full control over himself, he proves to be a successful administrator. If he does not have these qualities, he goes to hell after his death and he is not a man of worth to be worshipped, respected and honoured by his subjects.

Hunting, gambling, sleeping during day time, drunkenness, spending maximum time with women, inordinate love for dancing, singing and music, and useless travel are the ten-fold set of vices springing from the instinct of love or pleasure. Treachery, slandering, violence, envy, reviling, unjust seizure of property and assault are the seven-fold set of vices produced by wrath or anger. The king should remain far away from these vices. He should not be greedy. Let him conquer it. He should know that drinking, dice, women and hunting happen to be the most pernicious vices. Since it is better to die than to live with vices, he must, therefore, conquer his senses. Then only he can keep his subjects in obedience. He must shun all the vices which originate from the instinct of pleasure and which proceeds from wrath and which ends in misery. He should not waste his time on sensuous pleasures. He loses his health, wealth and virtues if he spends his time with wine and women.

The king can be good, pure, pious, honest, truthful and prudent if he gets up early in the morning and worships the Brahmans, who are well-versed in the three-fold sacred science and learned (in polity), and strictly follow their advice. He should also worship aged persons. Let him be modest and be an embodiment of modesty. Because a modest king never perishes. Without modesty he will perish as has happened with many kings like Nahusha, Sudas, Sumukha and Nemi.

The incarnation of God, he behaves in various ways which resemble the ages of the world, i.e. the *Krita, Trita, Dvapara* and *Kali*. He is also identified with them. While he is asleep, he represents the *Kali* (iron age), walking the *Dvapara* (or brazen age), ready to act, the *Trita* (or silver age), but moving (actively) the *Krita* (or golden) age.

Let the king imbibe and emulate the qualities of Indra, Sun, Wind, Yama, Varuna, Moon, Fire and Earth. The Lord Indra gives us water by sending copious rain during the four months of the season. Similarly, like Indra, the king should also shower gifts and confer benefits on his people. As the Sun draws the water during the hot summer, the king should also draw his taxes from his subjects. The Wind is all-pervading. Without it, no living creature can survive. In the shape of vital air it enters into all creatures. Like the Wind, the king should also penetrate everywhere through his spies. Here he resembles the Wind. Yama, the Lord of Death, does not spare anyone, be he is His friend or foe. Everyone has to die one day. No one can escape from His jurisdiction. Like Yama, the king also exercises his power over everyone living in his kingdom and the latter is subject to his laws. Varuna punishes a sinner by binding him with ropes. So also the king should punish the wicked. No crime should go unpunished in his kingdom. People feel happy to see the Moon, so also they should feel happy when the king appears before them. Like Fire, the king should destroy his enemies and criminals. Endowed with brilliant energy he destroys wicked vassals. The Mother Earth supports all created beings equally by nurturing them and feeding them. Like Her, the king should also support all his subjects without any discrimination.

A deity in human form, created by God containing elements of various deities, the king should not be criticized and hated by any one. He should not be considered as a mere mortal. Fire destroys if one becomes careless. So also the king when he becomes angry. No one can escape from his anger, however big he may be. He knows his purpose for which he has been created. He assumes by turn different shapes for the attainment of complete justice. Padma, the Goddess of Fortune, always favours him, victory dwells in Her valour and Her anger causes one's death. It is, therefore, rightly said that he contains the lustre of deities.

Being always pure, he is not tainted by impurity at any time. He is pure like Brahman. He also wants that all his ministers, officers and servants should remain pure. He is never impure because he is an embodiment of the virtues possessed by the deities.

Duties of the King

As a Protector

God created the king, a Kshatriya by caste, to protect the people, the creatures as well as the whole world. He is bound to protect those who are good and virtuous. It is his most commendable job. He enjoys power, position and prestige. He is rich, resourceful and commands respect. Subjects look at him with awe and reverence. Hence he should behave like a father towards them. If he fails in his duty, he certainly goes to hell. If he receives one-sixth of the agricultural produce as tax but fails to serve them, he incurs their curse and displeasure. If he becomes weak and fails to punish the thieves and criminals, the administration is paralysed and the consequence is anarchy, disorder and lawlessness. He is solely responsible for this and loses his heaven after his death. He is, therefore, divinely ordained to protect those who are good, virtuous, innocent and simple and punish those who are criminals, anti-socials as they are dangerous to the society.

The king shall protect the inherited as well as other property of a minor, until he becomes a major or as long as he is in his teacher's house for his studies; those women who are not blessed with children or those who are helpless and there is none to take care of them or those who suffer from incurable diseases, or those who are widows; the harlots or prostitutes and those whose husbands are absent. He shall protect them from all kinds of apprehension and sufferings. If he fails to do so, he shall be deprived of his life and kingdom. When the bodies of living creatures are tormented, they are destroyed. Similarly, the life of a king is destroyed when he oppresses his kingdom. When his subjects are robbed or kidnapped from his kingdom and are not rescued by him and his officials, he is no more a living king as he is dead and gone.

The king proves his worth and is honoured if he ensures safety of his subjects. In doing so he receives from them one-sixth of their spiritual merit. And in case he fails, he gets the same amount of demerit from them. But an ordinary person gains *Punya* by reading the Veda, making charitable gifts or worshipping Gurus and Gods.

Thus, a king, who fails to protect his subjects and at the same time collects taxes, tolls, duties, daily presents and fines, certainly goes to hell after his death, takes all the foulness of his subjects and sinks low after his death; but he goes to heaven if he ensures their safety and protection. He should not forget that this is his most important job for which he has been created by God.

To Punish the Wicked

The king performs all his functions sincerely, and while doing so, he punishes wherever it is necessary. It is the fear of punishment that forces everyone to obey him and not to deviate from his duties. The whole world is kept in order by force or fear of force. There is no doubt that only a few people are good and noble while others are ignoble, base and mean and commit wrongs and errors. It is through the fear of punishment their actions can be controlled and regulated. Every one fears him and obeys him only when he is tormented. The king, who acts according to the canon and who is wise, truthful, considerate, virtuous and conversant with virtue, pleasure and wealth, is a just inflictor of punishment. But he himself perishes with the same force if he is vicious, voluptuous, partial, deceitful, whimsical and prejudiced. When he deviates from his assigned path by not performing his divine-ordained duties, he is struck by the same force which he uses to deal with the crimes and criminals. It is not only the king who is punished but also the whole world including the deities and sages. No one including the father, the mother, the friend, the wife, the son, the domestic priest, is exempt from the king's might.

Inflict of punishment after due consideration and without any haste makes people happy. But violation of this principle invites doom. If the king does not punish the culprits and offenders, the stronger would attack the weaker and let loose the reign of terror. The weaker ones may also enter into alliances to defeat the strong ones. In such situations, law of jungle, i.e. might is right operates.

Punishment or fear of punishment helps the king to maintain order and discipline in the society, promote unity and integrity of the nation and ensure safety and security of everyone. Being the creation of God and His direct representative, he gives protection to those who deserve it. Fear of force or punishment forces everyone to fulfil his obligations. King's mode of application of force determines and decides the fate of the individual and the community. Partiality, deceitfulness, cruelty, greed, ignorance, self-indulgence, etc. can be punished. He has unlimited jurisdiction over offenders irrespective of their rank or status. He is supposed to administer criminal justice with strict impartiality.

Catching hold of the thieves: The kingdom prospers and the king's fame spreads when he punishes the thieves and wicked ones and rewards and favours the virtuous. He should check the activities of the culprits and anti-socials and criminals by imprisoning them, putting them in fetters and awarding corporal punishment. He can maintain public security if he catches hold of two classes— open and secret — of thieves with the help of spies. The former consists of those who extort bribes and other types of cheats, rogues, gamblers, fortune-tellers, sanctimonious hypocrites, high officials and physicians guilty of improper conduct and so forth. The latter comprises burglars, foresters and so forth. The king should arrest them with the help of spies who should disguise themselves and pretend to follow the same occupations and instigate the thieves to commit offences so that they can be arrested. The king then shall punish them accordingly. These evil-minded thieves, who are cruel, wicked and notorious scoundrels, cannot be reformed without being punished.

With the help of reformed thieves the king can catch hold of rogues and thieves. Under various pretexts like introducing them to Brahmins, offering them various gifts and incentives and on the pretext of showing them feats of strength, the spies would persuade the thieves to meet the officers of justice. A thief will be put to death when found with stolen goods and implements of burglary. Anyone providing him shelter or helping him in hiding his instruments of burglary, may also be put to death. Criminals as well as abettors of crime should be given the death punishment. A robber loses his hands for his crimes. On the first conviction, he loses two fingers only; on the second, one hand and one foot; on the third, he shall be given death punishment.

Punishments for crimes: Manu prescribes punishments for crimes and misdeeds causing injury to the public such as destroying bridges, cutting the water supply, adulterating commodities, damaging dams or tanks, wrong treatment of patients, dishonest dealing with customers, practising incantations for destroying life, dishonest behaviour by goldsmiths as well as theft of agricultural implements and medicines. Royal officers and vassals, who do not take any action during attacks or who do not come to rescue the victims when they are looted or when a dyke is destroyed or a highway robbery committed, are punished.

An offender, who damages a man or a tank, gets death punishment from the king or shall be killed by drowning him in water or asked to repair the damage. If he breaks open into a royal storehouse, an armoury or a temple, or steals elephants, horses or chariots shall be slained by the king without hesitation. If he steals or takes away the water of a tank or cuts off the water supply to his own advantage must be asked to pay the lowest fine. He who spits on the royal road must be asked to remove the same and pay two *Karshapanas*. But if he is an old and ailing man, or if the offender is a woman, they shall be asked to simply remove the filth without paying any fine. If he destroys a bridge, the flag of a royal palace or a temple, or images, he is asked to repair the whole and pay five hundred *Panas*. If he adulterates the unadulterated commodities or breaks the gems or bores them improperly, he may lose two fingers. But if he cheats or behaves dishonestly with honest customers, he shall meet the same punishment or get the higher one by losing one hand and one foot. If he destroys the wall of a town or breaks a town gate, he must be immediately banished. A goldsmith gets more severe punishments if he misbehaves dishonestly by cheating his customers. The most poisonous, bitter and innocuous of all the thorns, he should be cut into pieces with razors. All the prisoners and offenders should be placed in a prison near a high road so that they can be seen by others. This will certainly deter others from committing the crimes.

Measures to prevent and punish the crimes: The king should see that no crime goes unpunished and be very firm while dealing with criminals. *Danda* or chastisement should be firm. Otherwise, crimes would rise in the society. He should control and watch particularly the traders who always try to cheat the consumers. To prevent this, he should take steps or fix the prices of all marketable goods, mark the weights and measures and re-examine them every six months. The state should supervise all those who are engaged in different occupations. Mechanics and manual workers also come under state supervision. Doctors who neglect their patients must be fined.

King: not to acquire culprit's property: A good, noble and virtuous king must not try to acquire for himself the property of a man found to be guilty of misconduct. But if he does so, out of greed, he is tainted by that guilt which the offender has committed. If acquired by mistake from such persons, he should throw the same into the water thereby offering the same to Varuna, the Lord of Punishment holding His sceptre over the kings. Or he may donate the same to a Brahman, who has learnt the whole Veda and, therefore, is the lord of the whole world. Men live for a long period, infants do not die, deformed children are not born and crops abundantly grow in a country where the king does not grab the property of the sinners.

To Appoint Ministers and Other Officials (King's Executive Power)

The king should appoint a Brahman as his royal priest and seven or eight ministers whose ancestors should have been royal servants. They should hail from noble families, be well-versed in the sciences, and be heroes having skills in the use of weapons. He should consult them, first individually and then collectively, everyday on various subjects like peace, war, finance, endowments and general administration. But the final decision lies with him. An eminent person should be appointed as foreign secretary to deal with 'foreign affairs' of the state, to conclude treaties and alliances with other states and act like an ambassador. The king also appoints other officers in mines, storehouses, revenue, manufactures, etc.

Minister's qualification: Manu also discusses the qualifications of the ministers. The king may be highly learned, a great expert in all branches of knowledge, a perfect man. But alone he cannot perform his duties sincerely, because it is not an easy job to run the administration smoothly. Hence, he has to depend upon his ministers for the smooth conduct of official business. It is, therefore, natural that ministers and officers should be highly qualified. The king should appoint as many persons as is required by him in running the administration. They must be firm, wise, skilful, brave and men of character and integrity. Among them, those who are brave, the high-born and honest should be appointed in the revenue department, in mines, manufacturers, and storehouses. But the timid should be given appointment in the king's palace.

Appointment of ambassador: The ambassador should be well-versed in all sciences, able to understand hints, facial expressions and gestures. Honest, skilful and hailing from a noble family, it is he who alone makes king's allies and separates them. He transacts that business by which kings are united or disunited.

Appointment of priests: The king should also appoint a domestic priest and choose officiating priests.

King's Interaction with His Subjects

The king receives his subjects when they come to meet him, shares their sorrows, consoles them, extends cooperation to them and tries to solve their problems. Once this meeting is over, he retires with his ministers for consultation. He goes with them either to a hill or sits with them on the terrace. The place should be lonely and solitary so that there is no disturbance. Only a few deserving people know about this and his secret mission should not be disclosed to unwanted and undesirable people. During consultation, people who are idiots, dumb, deaf, blind, aged, sick, deformed should not be allowed to be present. Women and barbarians should also be asked to leave from such place as they cannot keep the secrets to themselves. The king, therefore, should be very careful about them.

King's Discussion with His Ministers

At midday or midnight, when he feels relaxed and his mental and bodily fatigues are over, let him think alone or discuss with his ministers matters relating to

- pleasure, wealth and virtue;
- his daughter's marriage;
- preventing his sons from committing any harm to his subjects;
- sending ambassadors;
- completion of his projects (already begun);
- behaviour of women in his harem;
- activities of his spies;
- eight-fold business (it consists either of 'conciliation, division, employment of force and gifts' or 'of agriculture, trade, building bridges, embankments, fortresses or repairing them, catching elephants, digging mines, settling desert districts and cutting down forests', or 'of collecting revenue, expenditure, dismissing bad servants, prohibiting bad conduct of the castes and orders deciding difficult points in one's own affairs, deciding legal cases and punishing and imposing penances');
- the goodwill or enmity of his neighbour kings, and of the neutral king and of his enemy.

To Honour the Brahmans

Manu considers Brahmans to be men of knowledge, wisdom, intellect and character. They are so powerful that they can create other worlds, other guardians of the world and deprive the gods of their divine station. The three worlds (heaven, earth and hell) and deities owe their existence to those whose wealth is the Veda. A Brahman is a great divinity. Manu has highest regards for them. Adoring them, he has said that even if they are engaged in all sorts of mean occupations, they must be respected, but not hated. Each one of them is a great deity. He advises the king not to displease them by provoking or causing an injury to them. Because by doing so, he destroys his own-self, his own army and his own vehicles.

To Undertake Developmental Activities

The king should ask his officers to work for the betterment of the people. This should be his highest duty. He should strive for increasing the wealth of his country by undertaking developmental activities. This he should do in a righteous manner. He should give food to all living beings with love.

To Acquire, Retain and Augment

The king should work hard to gain what he has not; but what he has, he must preserve it carefully; he should take measures to augment what he has preserved; and what he has augmented let him distribute the same among worthy persons and those who really deserve. He should be aware that these are four means to secure the aims of human existence and let him adopt them and employ them.

Acquisition of Power/Suppression of Enemies

To Manu, the king should take effective steps to acquire and maintain power and achieve his desired goal; constantly display his prowess, explore the weaknesses of his enemy and not to disclose his secrets; if necessary, use force to subject all creatures to himself; act without guile and never be treacherous, carefully guard himself against his enemies and know their deficiencies and shortcomings. As the tortoise hides its limbs, he should also conceal his weak points, protect his kingdom and annihilate his foes. This he does as the weeder plucks up the weeds and preserves the corn.

To Wage War

The king can wage a war, if it is a must in the prevailing situation. It can be undertaken at any time, by oneself and for one's own purposes. It can also be waged to avenge an injury done to a friend, or when an urgent matter has suddenly arisen. He should think twice before declaring a war and should not do so unless he is confident of his victory. He should resort to peaceful means to avoid any immediate injury. But when he thinks that his subjects are happy and that he himself is well-placed and enjoys an exalted position or when he knows that his army is superior to that of his enemy, he can declare war. But if his defence force like army is not strong but very weak, he must give a serious thought to it, i.e. waging the war or not or if necessary he should make a compromise with his enemy. If the enemy is stronger than him, he should divide his army and, thus, achieve his goal. If he is sure that he will lose the war because of the very powerful forces of the enemy, he should seek the support of a righteous and powerful king. He must arrange matters in such a manner that no one can challenge his authority. Neither friends, nor neutrals, nor foes can surpass him in any respect. Let him arrange everything in such a manner that no ally, no neutral or foe can harm him. It is his political wisdom that makes him successful.

If the king feels that he should declare a war against his enemy, he must attack him during the first quarter of the year (February–April). This should be done keeping in view the condition of his army. Even at other times when he has a chance of victory, or when a disaster has befallen his foe, he may attack him. But before this he must ask his spies to assess the situation. When conditions are most favourable, he should attack his enemy without fear. If he wants to avoid war, he should conquer his enemy by conciliation, by presenting gifts to him, and by creating dissensions. Once he occupies the enemy king's kingdom or defeats him, he should harass the latter's kingdom and see that everything—food, water, fuel and grass—is destroyed or spoiled. Tanks, ramparts and ditches are to be destroyed.

Once he conquers his enemy's kingdom and banishes the enemy king from the country, he should choose any relative of the vanquished king to occupy the throne and the king can impose certain conditions on the newly appointed ruler of his enemy state. He should not change the customs and should honour the newly appointed king by presenting gifts to him and his officers.

After his victory, the king should worship God and deities and honour those who are virtuous (preferably Brahmans), grant certain exemptions and declare safety for those who need his protection. He should be, however, very cautious while dealing with his friends having secret connections with his enemies.

The king's war policy should be influenced by future prospects of his country, his own-self as well as by immediate present and the good and bad aspects of all past transactions. Like a crane, he should mediate gain; like a lion, he should advance; like a jackal, he should rush on; like a hare, he should fly.

To Protect Himself

The king should take all measures to protect himself and preserve his wealth so that he can make use of it at the time of need. For the sake of his wife, he may give up all his possessions and he may give up his wife as well as his wealth to preserve himself.

Administration of Justice (King's Judicial Power)

The king is the highest court, the final arbiter of justice and the lawgiver to his subjects. When he seeks to investigate law cases, he enters along with Brahmans and experienced councillors into his court of justice. With the help of the principles drawn from the local usages and from the institutes of the Sacred Law (*Smriti*), he decides all law cases which can be classified under eighteen categories. They are as follows:

1. Non-payment of debts
2. Deposit of pledge
3. Sale without ownership
4. Concerns among partners
5. Resumption of gifts
6. Non-payment of wages
7. Non-performance of agreements
8. Rescission of sale and purchase
9. Disputes between the owner (of cattle) and his servants
10. Disputes regarding boundaries
11. Assault
12. Defamation
13. Theft
14. Robbery and violence
15. Adultery
16. Duties of man and wife
17. Partition (of inheritance), and
18. Gambling and betting.

If the king is not in a position to administer justice personally, he should appoint a learned Brahman to try the cases. A man who speaks lie in the court commits sin. Where injustice destroys the justice, falsehood the truth, and where judges become silent spectators of the crimes, they are also, sooner or later, destroyed. Justice should be preserved, never to be violated. A violator of justice is considered to be a Sudra. The only friend which follows men even after their death is justice. Everything else is lost when the body decays after death. If the king allows a Sudra to act as a dispenser of justice, he sinks like a cow in a morass. One cannot administer justice by becoming arbitrary, prejudiced and whimsical.

The king should know what is expedient or inexpedient, what is justice or injustice. After knowing this, he should examine the causes of suitors according to the order of the castes. Justice can be perfect if he is aware of the laws of castes, of districts, of guilds, and of families.

Dismissal of a case

A legal case or lawsuit brought to the court for trial or adjudication is dismissed if or when the plaintiff

- withdraws or retracts his statements;
- makes his statements confused and contradictory;
- calls a witness not present at the time of transaction;
- fails to prove what he said or does not abide by what he said;
- discusses with witnesses in a place not suitable for it;
- fails to answer a question or declines to do so;
- fails to prove his allegations; and
- leaves the court without answering the question.

The defendant loses his ground if he does not plead his case within forty-five days of filing the case.

It is unethical if the king or his servants bring lawsuits against someone or hush up the same if it has been brought before them by some one else.

When the king occupies the chair to deliver justice, he should discover what is going inside the mind of the person who appears before the court as a criminal by watching his external signs. One's internal mind or disposition gets reflected in his motions, gait, gesture, speech, changes in the eye and the face.

The importance of witness in the disposal of legal cases cannot be ignored. Therefore, when the king is engaged in judicial proceedings, he must emphasize the following:

1. Truth
2. Object of the dispute
3. The witnesses
4. The place
5. The time, and
6. The aspect.

When a complainant wants to prove that he had given an amount as loan or debt to a person and when the latter (debtor) argues that he has not taken any loan from the complainant, the latter must bring a witness or a few witnesses to prove his contention.

Householders, men with male issues, inhabitants of the country, Kshatriyas, Vaisyas or Sudras are competent to act as witnesses and give evidence. Trustworthy persons may be made witnesses in lawsuits.

The king, mechanics, actors, singers, dancers, musicians, Brahmans learned in the Vedas, slaves (by birth), one of bad fame, one afflicted with leprosy or some other bad disease, a thief, a servant for wages, a hard-hearted man, an angry man, a murderer, a low-caste man; one who performs a duty which he is not supposed to do, an aged person, an ailing patient, an intoxicated man, an extremely aggrieved person, one tormented by hunger or thirst, or desire, one oppressed by fatigue, a thief, and a wrathful man — all these are debarred from acting as witnesses in the law courts.

In the absence of qualified witnesses, evidence can be given by a woman, an infant, an aged person, a student of the Veda, a relative, a slave, or a hired servant. A judge may listen to the evidence given by the infants, aged and diseased persons, but should not take it seriously as they are apt to speak lies. A witness should depose in the court what he has seen or heard; he should speak the truth. By doing so, he goes to heaven and never loses spiritual merit or wealth. But if he misleads the judges, he goes to hell.

By giving truthful evidence, one becomes purified and his merit grows, his *Punya* increases manifold. He should remember that "the soul itself is the witness of the soul, and the soul is the refuge of the soul". Therefore, he should not despise his own soul, the supreme witness of men. Whatever bad, whatever wrong one does, it is distinctly seen by all gods. But the fools and wicked ones always believe that "no one sees them". He who speaks the truth need not take his bath in the river Ganges to get rid of his sins, nor should he visit the land of the Kurus. One starves by giving false evidence. He becomes blind and begs food even from his enemies.

If a witness, being guided by pious motives and noble desires, tells a lie, he does not go to hell as he does not commit any 'sin'. Such evidence may be called as the speech of the gods. By telling the truth if someone dies, then true evidence should not be given in the court. Here falsehood is preferable to truth. But the witness for having spoken lie in the court must go for penance by offering boiled rice to Saraswati, the Goddess of Speech. If a witness, within seven days after deposing evidence in the court, faces any misfortune through sickness, fire, or the death of any relative, he shall have to pay the debt and a fine. False evidence given out of malice, terror, distraction, covetousness, friendship, lust, wrath, ignorance, childishness, shall be dismissed and the witness is to be fined accordingly or he may be banished from the country. This should be done to restrain and prevent injustice.

At times, a situation may so arise that it would not be easy to dispense with justice because the king or his councillors are not clear about the law that is to be applied. If laws are not clear or if they are absent, justice is to be administered in accordance with what the Brahmans propound and this shall be legally binding. These Brahmans must be considered as 'Sishtas' as they have studied the Veda together with its appendages. They can also provide proofs by citing them from different texts to substantiate their arguments. They possess the revealed and sacred texts which are perceptible by the senses and which distinguish between virtue and sin. The Brahmans teach the Veda and make the revealed texts perceptible by reciting them.

Any declaration whatever made by an assembly consisting of three to ten persons becomes law. Its legality cannot be challenged or disputed. A legal assembly may consist of ten persons: three of them knowing one of the principal Vedas, a logician, a Mimansaka, one who knows the Nirukta, one who recites the sacred law, and three persons belonging to the first-three orders. Commentators and scholars differ in their opinion as to who these three persons are. To some (Govindaraga and Kulluka), they are a student, a householder, and a hermit. Medhatithi, however, argues that instead of hermit, he should be an ascetic, because a hermit is never allowed to enter the village. Other scholars are of the opinion that the word 'three persons' refers to Manu's first-three orders (i.e. the student, the householder, and the hermit). Of three members, each one of them is well-versed in one of the three Vedas, namely, the Rig Veda, the Yajur Veda and the Sam Veda. These three are competent to decide doubtful points of law.

A single Brahman well-versed in the Vedas can declare whatever to be law and it must be considered supreme legal. Manu has wanted that even thousand Brahmans, who have failed to perform their sacred duties and not acquainted with the Veda, and live only by the name of their caste, cannot constitute a legal assembly. The Brahmans must thoroughly study and then obey the ten-fold law so that they can enter the highest state of consciousness and attain salvation. The ten-fold laws are:

1. Contentment
2. Forgiveness
3. Abnegation and abstention from unrighteously appropriating anything
4. Obedience to the rules of purification
5. Coercion of the organs
6. Wisdom
7. Knowledge (of the supreme soul)
8. Truthfulness
9. Self-control, and
10. Abstention from anger.

A Brahman to Act as Adjudicator

If the king is not in a position to try the cases personally or investigate the suits, he should appoint a Brahman to try the cases. But, a Sudra cannot be appointed to adjudicate the legal cases. He is debarred from interpreting the laws though he is the dispenser of justice and lawgiver to his subjects. He cannot be irresponsible, ruthless, arbitrary and whimsical while dispensing justice. He should not do anything without consulting his ministers. Even though he is an expert in all the sciences, well-versed with the policies and principles and thorough in rules and regulations, he has to take all his ministers into confidence and accept their suggestions. If he fails to do so, his days of doom begin. He digs his own grave, brings his own ruin and soon perishes. He may also lose his state as well as his subjects. The cleverest of all his ministers should be a Brahman and upon him he should depend fully. He should be entrusted with the task of executing all the resolutions. Such a person should be declared as the prime minister or chancellor.

The King is Subject to Law

The king is not above law. He is to be fined and admonished if he violates it. He is neither pardoned nor his crimes are condoned. He gets more punishment for an offence than what an ordinary person gets for the same offence. "Where common man would be fined one Karshapana, the king shall be fined one thousand; that is the settled law". *Manava-Dharmashastra* and *Arthashastra* never place the king above the law. While the latter allowed the king to make new laws, *Manusmriti* prohibited him from doing so. Though he cannot enact substantive laws, he can pass regulatory laws.

SAPTANGA THEORY OF THE STATE (ELEMENTS OF THE KINGDOM)

Manu's kingdom contains the following elements:

1. The master (i.e. the king)
2. The ministers
3. The fort (i.e. the chief city or the capital where the king resides)
4. The territory
5. The treasury
6. The army, and
7. The ally (friend).

Interestingly, Arthur Coke Burnell and Edward W. Hopkins in their works on *Laws of Manu* have substituted 'territory' by 'people' as an element of the state.

The king should realize that of these seven elements, each one is more important than the one that follows it, in order, and its loss causes the greater disaster. For example, the king is more important than his ministers; the latter are more important than the fort; the fort is more important than the capital city. Like this, the order goes on. Ally happens to be the least important element while the king constitutes the most significant aspect of the state or kingdom.

LOCAL-SELF GOVERNMENT

The ultimate unit in local government is the village. It must be well protected. To ensure this, the king should place a company of soldiers commanded by an officer in the midst of two or three or five, or hundreds of villages so that the latter can be well protected. Each village should have a lord or headman. The king appoints the lords of ten villages, lords of twenty, lords of a hundred and lords of a thousand. The village administration is to be run vertically. The lord of one village informs the lord of ten villages about the crimes committed in the village. Similarly, the latter reports the same thing to the lord of twenty villages. The communication process, thus, goes in an ascending order. The lord of one village should collect articles like food, drink, fuel, etc. from the villagers daily and furnish the same to the king.

A town must be administered by a "superintendent of all affairs" and he must be assisted by spies who should keep an eye on the activities of the people. A minister should be in charge of this government. Royal officials' activities must be scrutinized. Though they protect the people, "they become knaves" and try to seize the property of others. If they do so, they must pay a heavy price for it. Their properties may also be confiscated and they may be banished from the country. Irresponsible ministers should be fined a thousand *panas*.

AN ESTIMATE

Manu was so much popular and his work was so much significant that the subsequent writers and social scientists were highly influenced by him and they strongly believed that whatever he has said is medicine. According to *Taitriya Samhita* and *Tandya Brahmana*, "as an individual takes medicine to cure his illness, so also a society should adopt whatever Manu has said in order to remove injustice and ignorance from it". His text is, therefore, a medicine for us. It should not be forgotten or ignored. It is because of its importance it is not only cited in other ancient Indian texts but also is still considered as the standard source of authority for everything that stands for or constitutes the Hinduism, particularly its centre piece, i.e. *Varnasrama-dharma* (social and religious duties tied to class and stage of life). Over the centuries, it has attracted nine complete commentaries.

Manu's text happens to be one of the first Sanskrit works which has been translated into many European languages. Sir William Jones, one of the founding fathers of modern Indology, who came to India to act as a justice under the administration of British East India Company, translated the text in 1794. The statue of Jones in St. Paul's Cathedral in London holds a volume of Manu in its hand. In G.C. Haghton's book *Manav Dharma Shastra*, he wrote in its preface:

> There is certainly a strong resemblance, though obscured and faded by time, between our Manu with his divine Bull, whom he named as *Dharma* himself, or the genius of abstract justice and the Mneues of Egypt with his companion or symbol, Apies, and though we should be constantly on our guard against the delusion of etymological conjecture, yet we cannot but admit that Minos and Mneues have only Greek terminations, but that the crude noun is composed of the same radical letters both in Greek and in Sanskrit.

Jones further said:

> Dara Shucuh, a lover of literature and who belonged to the Moghul dynasty (of India), was persuaded, not without sound reason, that the first Manu of the Brahmans could be no other person than the progenitor of mankind to whom Jesus Christ and Musalmans unite in giving the name of Adam.

Manu as lawgiver became so famous that the people living in various parts of the world also named their lawgivers as Manu. So if Manu was the name of person in India, in other countries it referred to those persons who enacted laws for the people. In other words, if Manu was a person in India, it was a 'profession' in other parts of the world.

Manu's influence spread far and wide. G.P. Upadhyaya in his *Manusmriti* wrote:

> The influence of *Manusmriti* spread beyond the confines of India. In Burma, two inscriptions read: we have an inscription in which occur verses, one of which is identical with Manu (2nd chapter: 36th verse) and the other is summary of Manu (3rd chapter: 37–80 verses). The Burmese are governed in modern times by the *Dharma*, that which is based on Manu.

To Madam Blavesky, Manu's text was the source of inspiration and pattern for all the codes given by various lawgivers of ancient civilization. It was adopted in one form or another in different parts of the world. While to J.D.M. Derrette, author of *Manusastravivarana*. Manu's work was one of the world's premier compositions in ancient law, more valuable in every sense than Hammurabi and able to hold its own in comparison to the convenant and priestly codes of Moses, to Mariz Winternitz, there is no work that has had such great fame and has for centuries been considered to be so authoritative as the *Manava Dharma Shastra*. Manu's work was translated into English by Jones and then translated into German, Portugues and Russian. Manu's fame spread far and wide.

The text is extremely popular because of its completeness, orderly arrangement, and intelligibility. It is meant for one and all, for those who live in this world and for those who want to live in this world. Based on the Veda, it is meant for the whole mankind as it seeks to bring an all-round development of man: body, mind and soul. This ultimately helps in establishing a society free from sufferings, miseries and sorrows. This is possible because every individual renders service to the society. And this he does according to his ability, thinking, perception and capacity. He who is willing and capable of removing the darkness of ignorance from the society by spreading knowledge and education is known as a Brahman (Brahmin); he who has courage, vigour, strength to remove injustice and exploitation from the society is a Kshatriya; those who are neither interested in scriptures nor have enough physical strength to protect the society from disturbance and aggression engage themselves in cultivation and other professions so that demands and requirements of life are met. They are the Vaisyas. And those who do not belong to any of these classes of people are called

Sudras who serve others. This is how Manu divided the society into four classes. Like Manu, Plato, a great Greek political philosopher of the fifth century B.C., also classified the people under three categories, namely, guardians, defenders and producers (of the provisions necessary for life).

It should be remembered here that Manu's concept of social structure or caste system does not rest on birth. It is not hereditary. One does not inherit it from his parents. It is one's job or role in the society that he performs voluntarily, makes him either a Brahmin, a Kshatriya, a Vaisya, or a Sudra. A son of Brahmin father need not be a Brahmin. But, unfortunately, this principle has been violated. It is because of this the society has been paying a heavy price for it.

Manu has been severely criticized for his views on women for subordinating their status to that of men, for having denied them from reading the Veda. It is certainly unfortunate. He has categorically said that women are to be honoured by all including fathers, husbands and brothers-in-law who want to progress and prosper. Where women are honoured, there the Gods rejoice. And where they are dishonoured, there all rites are fruitless. Where women grieve, the family quickly perishes and where they do not, it always prospers. Women are to be honoured at ceremonies and festivals with ornaments, clothes and food, by men who desire wealth. In a family where the husband pleases his wife and wife her husband, there prosperity flourishes. This shows that Manu had tremendous regards for women. Never had he wanted to denigrate their status or image by giving them a secondary status in the society. Whatever derogatory comments have been made against them or whatever ill has been spoken about them in Manu's text are the perverted views of critics and commentators on Manu's work. These cannot be his original ideas.

The Veda teaches man to love animals, to protect them, not to be violent towards them and to ensure their safety. It further teaches him to be completely non-violent in words, deeds and ideas. Sacrifice of animals is strictly prohibited in the Vedas. But, later, those who developed a lust for meat, fish, etc. prepared certain verses supporting the slaughtering of animals and made their entry into the original text of Manu. The result is that Manu was in favour of killing of animals. How absurd it is! He had strong faith in the Vedas, which says that animals to be considered our best friends.

Manu will go down the annals of history not only as the lawgiver but also who wanted to see the man the most wonderful creature of God — pure, complete and perfect.

POINTS TO REMEMBER

- Manu: descendant of God, son of *Swayambhu*, creator of the universe, son of *Aditya* (*Vivaswan*), an orthodox, progenitor of mankind, the lawgiver, inventor of *Sraddhas* and funeral sacrifices, founder of moral order. God taught him laws and he did the same to others.

- Who is Manu? What is he? Scholars differ in their opinion. There are six Manus.
- Meaning of Manu: the wise one, the Indian Adam.
- Manu's text contains the works, some argue, of Bhrigu and others. Influence of *Smritis* or *Dharmashastras* on individuals.
- What is the age of Manu? William Jones, A.D. Hopkins, Jolly, Buhler differ in this regard.
- *Manusmriti* contains the essence of the Veda. It revolves around kings. One should sincerely seek after Artha, Dharma and Kama. In such cases, salvation is a must. Comprehensive and encyclopaedic, it has 2685 verses and 12 chapters. *Manusmriti* covers castes and their obligations, the king's role and rule, relations between men and women, rituals, birth and death, karma and rebirth, etc.
- In his work, Manu discusses origin of the universe, keeping promises, marriage, rituals after death, means of livelihood, duties of women, freedom, renunciation, king's duties, duties of husband and wife, inheritance, gambling, duties of families and castes, etc. Manu's text centres around life. It discusses religion, effects of past actions, people's conduct. It not be ignored as it covers various aspects of life. Manu's teachings inspire one to fulfil his vows and liberate himself from past "Karmas".
- Manu's work washes away all his sins, ensures salvation, promotes well-being and brings happiness. Wise priests should teach the text to their disciples. It reflects the Teachings of Veda.
- Manu's text has been, over the years, enlarged and thereby polluted. There are various reasons for its "pollution".
- The word 'Manu' is referred to 'in different scriptures'. It does not refer to 'any person'. It means or refers to 'sage', 'doctor', 'knowledgeable person', 'considerate'. Medhatithi: Manu: a knowledgeable person and highly spiritual.
- *Sruti:* Vedas known as the revealed canon.
- *Smriti:* the teachings of religion, surrounded by fictions, its real character is obscured.
- Manu, when approached, explained the sacred laws to Bhrigu and others and requested Bhrigu to expound them. The latter did his job. Govindaraga: disciples of Bhrigu recited the work descended to him.
- Origin of the universe: in the beginning, everything was in dark. When God appeared, darkness vanished.
- Everything is the creation of God. He created castes. God is half male and half female. The female part produced Biraj. Biraj gave birth to Manu. Manu created ten seers and beings.

- Social order: people belonging to different castes perform different functions.
- The upper three castes people should purify their body, mind and soul. A Brahman is superior to a Kshatriya and a Vaishya. Castes get mixed when pure castes commit adultery.
- One can change his profession, if it is a must. But when the situation becomes normal, he should come back to his assigned profession. People perform different functions at different stages of life.
- A householder is supposed to lead a pure life. He should discharge all his obligations, be spiritual and God-oriented.
- One should not earn property through dubious means, have a craze for too much wealth. He has many duties to perform.
- When one becomes grandfather, he should leave the society and go to the forest for meditation and self-realization. At least, he should become a sanyasi. He follows ten-fold laws.
- The king: creation of God. A deity, learned, perfect. He should practise virtues and give up vices. He should be virtuous, but not sensuous. He emulates the qualities of deities; the qualities of Indra, Yama, Varuna, Wind, the Mother Earth, etc.
- Duties of the king: He protects: the subjects and their properties; the poor, destitute, harlots; the minor's property (inherited or otherwise); those women who are issueless, helpless, poor and poverty-stricken; the widows, and prostitutes.
- The king should punish the wicked, the ignoble. If he does not do so, if he gets them released, if he is sympathetic to them, he incurs the displeasure of his subjects and deities.
- Punishment needs to be harsh so as to deter others from committing crimes. Vices are to be punished and severely dealt with. The king administers criminal justice with strict impartiality.
- Severe punishments to the criminals.
- As crimes vary so also the punishments. Criminals must be severely dealt with.
- The king appoints the ministers and officials. Ministers: men of knowledge, character and integrity. He appoints qualified persons as ministers, ambassadors and priests. He interacts with his subjects and others.
- King's secret mission: his discussion with his ministers.
- The king: to honour the Brahmans; to undertake developmental activities; to acquire what he has not, and preserve with care what has acquired, retain and augment what he has preserved; to deal with the enemy; to

wage war; to conclude. He should try to acquire, preserve and distribute. He should suppress his enemy.

- Treaties with other states; the king should protect himself. To attack the enemy at the right time. One should strike the iron when it is really hot.
- The king to spoil the provisions like food, water, fuel, etc. of the enemy's state after defeating the enemy king.
- The king is the highest court, the final arbiter of justice and the lawgiver to his subjects. He decides on law cases which come under eighteen categories.
- A lawsuit can be dismissed for various reasons. He who violates law or justice is a Sudra.
- Certain persons are debarred from acting as witnesses.
- Evidence can be given by some in the absence of qualified witnesses. They are not to be taken seriously by the judge. It is a good deed to give truthful evidence. God watches all our activities.
- Members of the legal assembly can declare anything to be law. This cannot be challenged or disputed. These members are experts in different fields of knowledge.
- If the king fails to dispense justice, a Brahman appointed by him does the job on his behalf. The king consults with his ministers and accepts their suggestions.
- The king is not above law, he is subject to it. Gets more severe punishment than what an ordinary person gets for committing the same offence. He cannot make new laws.
- Village is the ultimate unit in local government. It is to be protected. Lords of villages are appointed and they are placed in vertical order. The communication is in an ascending order. A town is administered by one superintendent.
- Royal officials are subject to scrutiny. Manu's prescriptions are very effective as they are the products of a thorough diagnosis.
- Manu's text has been translated by scholars and commentators in various languages.
- Manu is a person in India, but a lawgiver in other countries. He is a source of inspiration to many and a great authority on law.
- Manu's caste structure does not rest on 'caste', but on profession. It is one's job that determines his caste. Manu is criticized (for no fault of his) for subordinating the status of women. This criticism is biased. Veda teaches to love animals. Man to be non-violent. To Manu, man is the most wonderful creation of God.

2

Kautilya

INTRODUCTION

Kautilya, the greatest authority on science of polity, was, to some, also known as Chanakya or Vishnugupta. But this view is rejected by many historians and critics like H. Jacobi, E.J. Johnston and T. Burrow. To them, Kautilya, the author of *Arthashastra*, and Chanakya, the Prime Minister of Chandragupta Maurya, the first king of the Maurya dynasty, were two different persons. They pointed out that the earliest Sanskrit literature like *Mruchhakatika* written by Sudraka (probably during the fourth century A.D.), Nandisutta of the Jains, Kashmirian Sanskrit versions of *Somadeva* and *Kshemendra*, *Bruhatkatha* of Ganadyha mentioned about Chanakya but not about Kautilya or Vishnugupta. The *Mahavamsa*, a Buddhist literature, also spoke of Chanakya and nowhere was it stated in these earlier works that Chanakya was the author of *Arthashastra*.

Chanakya, the Chancellor or the Prime Minister of Chandragupta Maurya, and Kautilya, the author of *Arthashastra*, were two different persons who not only lived in different regions of the country but also with a gap of five hundred years. To Jolly and Meyer, Kautilya belonged to the South India, while Chanakya hailed from North India. As regards Vishnugupta, it is considered to be another name of Kautilya. It has been argued that Vishnugupta was the original name of Kautilya and most likely Kautilya was the "gotra" name of Vishnugupta.

Chanakya was very famous for his works and cleverness. Probably it was because of this Vishakadatta, according to Burrow, identified him with Kautilya, who actually lived five hundred years after Chanakya. This development took place most probably after the *Arthashastra* was written. Following this identification, some one added a verse at the end of the final chapter of the *Arthashastra* stating that its author was responsible for the humiliation, defeat and destruction of the Nandas.

According to the Ceylonese Chronicle, *Mahavamsa*, Chanakya was a learned Brahman of Taxila. After his marriage, his wife was insulted by her mother as he was a very poor Brahman. Therefore, he took an oath to earn money and become rich. And with this purpose, he came to Pataliputra where he was humiliated by the Nanda king. Enraged, he promised to take revenge against the Nanda dynasty, and achieved his goal. It was overthrown and succeeded by the Maurya dynasty of which Chandragupta Maurya was the first king. And Chanakya became his Prime Minister.

Chanakya was born in the Golla Vishaya. His father, Chanaka, was a Brahman by birth but later became a Jain. It was said that Chanakya was born with full-grown teeth. At the time of his birth, the Jain saints, who were residing in his house, predicted that the new-born baby would become a king in future. His father, Chanaka, who was highly religious and spiritual, became unhappy with such prediction as he felt that the kingdom was nothing but a hell. Therefore, he removed all the teeth of his son. Following this, the saints predicted that the baby would rule over the kingdom by proxy. When Chanakya grew up, he was taught in fourteen branches of knowledge of the Jains. And he himself became a Jaina in his old age.

ARTHASHASTRA: CONTROVERSY ON THE DATE OF ITS PUBLICATION

Historians and critics do not agree with one another on the date of publication of *Arthashastra*. R. Sham Sastri, T. Ganapati Sastri, K.P. Jayaswal, D.R. Bhandarkar, R.K. Mookerji, K.A. Nilakantha Sastri, H.C. Ray, Kane, L.D. Barnett, V.A. Smith, F.W. Thomas, Romila Thapar, D.D. Kosambi and others argued that *Arthashastra* was written towards the end of the fourth century B.C. This is said to be the traditional view. To U.N. Ghoshal, it was authored during the pre-Maurya period, i.e. third century B.C. However, the opponents of the traditional view like Jolly, Keith and Winternitz are of the opinion that the *Arthashastra* is a later work produced in early centuries of the Christian era, while some of them consider it to be written in the fourth century A.D. Thus, the scholars are distinctly divided into two groups on the issue. But in the textbooks and in the teachings of Maurya history and polity in higher classes in India, the traditional view has been widely accepted.

KING–PRINCE RELATIONSHIP

Discussing the relationship between the king and his sons, Kautilya observes that a king can protect his kingdom only when he himself is protected from his enemies as well as his near and dear ones including his wife and sons. He should not allow his children to indulge in sensuous pleasures as this amounts to living death. As a piece of wood is eaten by worms so also the royal family disintegrates and suffers if the princes are indisciplined, disobedient, sensuous and pleasure-seeking. Therefore, Kautilya advises the king to take proper care of and give due attention to his children so that they can be upright, sincere, disciplined and duty-bound.

Prenatal Care

Importance should be given to prenatal care of children. When the queen is in her period of menstruation the priests should make offerings to Indra and Brihaspati. During her pregnancy, well-trained nurses should look after her. Arrangements are to be made for the nourishment of the foetus and for delivery. After the birth of the son, the priest performs the rites. The prince grows up with age under the guidance of the experts. A benevolent, people-friendly, self-sacrificing king enjoys the earth alone by becoming its master without sharing it with any other ruler.

Prince: A Trainee

Soon after the tonsure ceremony, the prince should start learning the alphabets and the arithmetic. After the thread ceremony, he should learn the three Vedas, Philosophy, Economics, Science of Politics, etc., read History, which includes *Udaharana, Dharmashastra, Arthashastra, Itivratha, Puranas*, etc., undergo training in the art of using elephants, horses, chariots and weapons, and observe celibacy till he reaches the sixteenth year and, thereafter, he should marry.

Prince: Nature and Activities

The prince should control the senses and give up vices like lust, anger, arrogance, pride, greed, and foolhardiness; cultivate his intellect by association with elders and good people, and lead a simple life; be upright and a paragon of virtues like character, integrity and honesty; and be protected by the secret agents from the worldly evils. They should see that the prince does not become a victim of wine, women, gambling and hunting. He must be prevented from attacking his father and snatch away the kingdom from him. If he is lustful and leads a life full of vices and does not care the elders and teachers, he should be imprisoned by the king even if he is the only son. If the king has many sons, he should send his unruly son to the frontier or some other region. If such a prince is brave and courageous, he should be made the Commander-in-Chief of the army. If he fails to change himself for the better or who is incorrigible, he should be killed or poisoned, provided the king has other sons. If the king has no other sons, the incorrigible prince should be confined in a place and steps should be taken to reform him.

But if the prince, who is disciplined, obedient and loyal, finds it difficult to lead a good life, he should be supported by his father, and obey him even if he is asking to perform an unworthy job. He should perform this task sincerely. However, he should not accept this assignment if his life is at stake or if this instigates the subjects to revolt against him, or if it involves a heinous sin. Even though he performs faithfully and sincerely the job assigned to him, he may incur the displeasure of the king or may not be duly awarded by the king. The latter may like another son of another wife (other than the mother of the prince). In this case the prince, disliked by the king, should go to the forest. If there is fear of death or imprisonment, he should seek the help of neighbouring prince who is just, helpful, pious and truthful. He should stay with him, accumulate wealth, organize his own army, and enter into marriage relations with princesses belonging to very powerful men, establish contact with forest chieftains and win over certain sections of the people of his father's kingdom.

If a prince, disliked by the king, wants to act alone without any external assistance, he should work in mines and factories or secretly steal the wealth of rich widows after securing their confidence or of heretical corporations, or of the temples except that to be used by Brahmans learned in the Vedas. He may also plunder the caravans and sailing vessels or conquer an enemy town to secure the help of the persons related to his mother, or with the help of his friends he may attack and kill the king.

The politics of Kautilya is thoroughly immoral and even patricide is allowed in certain circumstances.

ROYAL SUCCESSION

The eldest son of the king succeeds him (king) when the latter dies or is unable to rule any more because of his poor health. In case a king has many sons and all are indisciplined, then they may be confined in one place and he should not allow any one of them to succeed him. If his only son is not good, he should try to have a grandson. He may also ask one of his grandsons (daughter's son) to succeed him. An old or diseased king may also request his wife to go for a child and in this connection she may establish physical contact (sexual relationship) with any of her relatives or any member of his (king) family, or a virtuous neighbouring king.

Kautilya has prescribed certain norms for the royal succession when calamity befalls the king or when the king dies. In such a situation, the minister should see that the crown prince succeeds the king and then announces the death of the latter. If a well-trained prince is not available, the minister should choose a young prince of the royal family (obviously not in the direct line of succession), or a princess so that later an offspring may be begotten of her by a man of the same caste, or a pregnant queen and seek the support of the high ranking officers in favour of the emblem of sovereignty till the new prince is grown up and attains the youthhood.

The princess cannot succeed in her own right. She wields authority till her son is duly crowned. After being blessed with a child, she should not be permitted to go for another child. She cannot think of leading a married life if she wants her son to succeed to the throne. The reason being that her husband may seize it and rulership may pass into a different family.

POLICY OF COLONIZATION

Colonization of the Janapadas

The new and rural tracts should be occupied by the people who are either foreigners or who migrate from thickly populated areas. In these tracts villages are to be constructed, each inhabiting one hundred to five hundred families belonging mostly to the Sudra cultivators. Each and every village will be surrounded by boundaries so that it is well protected and the villages should grow around a town. In every village lands are granted to the priests, chieftains, preceptors, and Brahmans learned in the Vedas, who look after religion. These lands are exempted from fines and taxes. They pass to the corresponding heirs. Similarly, lands are also granted to various subordinate officials — heads of the departments, accountants, *gopas, sthanikas*, elephant-trainers, physicians, horse-trainers and couriers.

Agriculture

Kautilya advises the state to undertake the agricultural developmental activities and give the preferred fields to the tax-paying cultivators for a single generation. But the unprepared lands made cultivable by the tenants are not to be snatched away from them. He who neglects cultivation is punished. His holdings are transferred to others or to village servants and traders. The Government should pay loans and advances in the form of grains, cattle and money to the farmers who should pay back afterwards. Only such favours and exemptions are to be made which would help in increasing the state revenue.

Irrigation and Industry

The Government should irrigate the lands with natural water resources or with water brought in from elsewhere. Agriculture is to be protected from oppressors. Improvement in the field of agriculture should not take place at the cost of industrial and commercial development. The state should see that factories are set up, mines worked, forests created, trade routes opened, pastures provided and market towns and ports established.

Output Maximization and No Entertainment

The villagers should remain healthy to produce maximum output in the interest of the state. People are to be punished who do not properly look after their family members, who become ascetic without leaving any property for wife and children, and who induce women to leave home. The villagers are not allowed to have parks and places of entertainment. Dancers, musicians, actors, etc. are asked not to entertain the villagers. Kautilya is of the opinion that if these two things are followed, then the revenue of the state will increase. People are not to pay taxes if there are famines, floods, pestilences, etc.

The king should take adequate steps to protect agriculture from the burdens of fines, compulsory labour and taxes, and the cattle–hens from thieves, wild animals, prisoners as well as from diseases. All forests, irrigation works, trade routes, etc. are to be protected by the king.

Disposal of the Non-agricultural Land

The uncultivated lands are to be disposed. For grazing of domestic animals pastures are to be made; for the use of the king a hunting forest is to be created; for the performance of the *yajnas* and study of the Vedas the ascetics are to be provided with lands; a forest sanctuary is to be made for the animals and economic forests are to be set up; and an elephant preserve should be created with an adequate trained staff.

EMERGENCY REVENUE

Demands on Farmers

Kautilya has provided certain extraordinary measures to improve the financial position of the state when the king suddenly faces financial difficulties. These measures may be classified under two categories:

1. Benevolences, which are to be levied once and not twice, and
2. Miscellaneous methods.

Under the first category, the king can impose taxes on the cultivators. The cultivators of the government-irrigated lands may be asked to pay taxes. One-third or one-fourth of the produce should be paid by them to the king. In case of poor quality of lands, taxes should be proportionate with their yields.

Persons employed in material forests, colonization of waste lands, elephant forests, building forts and embankments or trade routes, or in a region small in size which is on the frontier should not pay taxes to the state.

The king should help those persons engaged in developing a new settlement by providing grains, cattle, cash and the like. He should not impose taxes on the forest products and the property of learned Brahmans. He may also purchase those products to favour them.

If the king fails to improve the financial position, he should ask the farmers to sow the fields in summer. The farmers are forbidden from taking the yields except handful of vegetables and grains plucked by hand for purposes of worship of God and manes and for charity or for the sake of cows. And they should also leave something for the mendicants and village servants. Theft should be severely dealt with and thieves may be given death punishment.

At the time of any crisis, the state should take a fourth part of grains, a sixth part of wild produce and of goods made of silk-cotton, lac, linen, barks, cotton, wood and silk, medicines, perfumes, flowers, fruits, and vegetables, also of wood, bamboos, meat, dried meat, one-half of ivory and skins.

Benevolences from Dealers

The following schedules of rates of benevolences are to be paid by the dealers:

1. Dealers in articles of wood, bamboo, stones, earthenware, and cooked rice shall pay a tax of 5 per cent.
2. Inferior craftsmen and keepers of harlots shall pay a tax of 10 per cent.
3. Traders in grasses and chief craftsmen shall pay a tax of 20 per cent.
4. Dealers in grains, liquids, metals and carts shall pay a tax of 30 per cent.
5. Dealers in yarn, clothes, copper, steel, bronze, perfumes, medicines and wines shall pay a tax of 40 per cent.
6. Dealers in gold, silver, diamonds, gems, pearls, corals, horses and elephants shall pay a tax of 50 per cent.
7. Actors and prostitutes shall pay half of their wages.

Besides the above, the skilled workers are to pay tax in cash.

Demands on Breeders of Animals

Regarding the benevolences to be paid by this last class, Kautilya in his *Arthashastra* mentions the following charges:

1. Owners of cocks and pigs shall give half of the stock, of small animals one-sixth, of cows, buffalos, mules, donkeys, and camels one-tenth.
2. Keepers of harlots should employ beautiful female servants for the king.

Miscellaneous Methods for Increasing the State Revenue

When the benevolences fail to augment the revenue of the state, the king can ask the subjects to pay donations under the pretext of performing some work. Those who pay high amounts should be rewarded with umbrellas, decoration, turbans and positions.

The king should not adopt dubious means like fraud and violence to increase the revenue of the state. However, he may resort to them in emergency cases and apply them to enemies and sinners.

STATE CAPITALISM

Nature

Kautilya was a staunch advocate of state capitalism. It is the duty of the state to extract the mineral ores, collect the forest products, convert the raw materials into manufactured goods in the state refineries and workshops and dispose them.

State Farms

Since the Vedic age, the people of India have chosen agriculture as their main mode of living. Hence Kautilya emphasizes the development of agriculture to increase the state revenue. He states that the farm workers and their officers should be well-versed in the science of agriculture and of trees and plants. This officer has to perform different functions: involving himself in the direct cultivation of the fields; collecting seeds of different varieties for cultivation; making use of the services of free labourers, slaves and convicts; collecting astronomical and meteorological data regarding rainfall, etc. and applying the same while sowing; reaping the harvests properly and thoroughly; and storing the product and grains carefully.

State to Rear Domestic Animals

Kautilya describes in detail the rearing of domestic animals by the state. Stables should be constructed for the animals like cattle, horses, asses and camels belonging to the king for their proper rearing. Two superintendents remain in charge of these domesticated animals. They maintain records regarding the birth of the babies and their age, their varieties, their colours, weights, etc., take proper care of the animals, particularly their grazing, safety, etc. The state provides rations for these animals.

Forests as Source of State Revenue

Forest-yields constitute a part or a source of the state revenue. Forests are classified under four categories:

1. Wild animals
2. Domesticated animals

3. Economic forests, and
4. Elephant preserves.

The products of economic forests consist of hard wood, the bamboo group, the plant group, *bhujapatra* manufacturing, materials for rope-making, dying materials, medicinal substances, etc. The state should go for the afforestation of the barren lands. A special superintendent and forest guards should be appointed for the economic forests. Steps should be taken to manufacture all varieties of forest products.

State Monopoly of Mines and Minerals

As the state enjoys absolute monopoly over the mines found within its physical boundary, a high-ranking officer is appointed to look after the working of the mines. He controls and supervises them. Other officers are also appointed to deal with other branches of the mining industry and trade in minerals. Being experts in their own fields and thorough in the metallurgical sciences, they find out the disused mines, and search for new ones; lease out the costly mines; bring under their direct control other mines; and look after the marketing of the finished products.

There are also other superintendents looking after other branches of the mining industry. The Superintendent of Salts exercises full control over the salt industry and trade, the Superintendent of Iron, who deals with iron and other metals like copper, lead, tin, bronze, etc., remains in charge of laboratories for processing the metals as well as their marketing, the Superintendent of Mines looks after laboratories for processing precious substances and take steps for their marketing, and the Superintendent of Gold heads laboratory where various technical processes are being carried out in connection with the working of the metals.

State Trading

The state plays a major role in regulating trade and industry and for this purpose it appoints a number of superintendents. The Superintendent of Commerce takes measures to promote the trade and commerce of the state to its best advantage, the Superintendent of Weights and Measures enforces the use of standard weights and measures, the Superintendent of Ships regulates transport by water and collects ferry dues, the Superintendent of Customs collects customs duties on commodities for internal and external commerce, and the Superintendent of Coins remains in charge of the stamped coins, while the *Rupadarsaka* examines them.

State Breweries

The Superintendent of Liquor manages the breweries and state-owned wine shops. The private breweries and liquor shops pay heavy duties to the state.

Textile Factories of the State

To Kautilya, the State should manufacture fabrics only for the needs of administration. The Superintendent of Fabrics remains in charge of spinning and weaving operations. A spinning factory should be set up for the spinning of yarns, other *Karmasalas* (factories) are to be set up for manufacture of woven fabrics. The state provides a wide variety of raw materials out of which yarn should be prepared. Female labourers should be employed for weaving on contractual basis.

BRAHMANS IN THE *ARTHASHASTRA*

Varna System

Kautilya states that the kin regulates the social order which is based on the *Varnashrama* system, divinely ordained, prescribed by and in the Vedas, and immutable. Since the state has not created this order, it cannot, therefore, alter it or modify it. Its duty is to simply maintain it and preserve it.

The rules regarding the duties and occupations of the four Varnas have been for the first time systematized in the *Dharmashastra* and the same has been elaborated in the *Smritis*. Kautilya has been very much influenced by it. To him, the king should rule over the state on the advice of the ministers; the four upper castes (Brahmans, Kshatriyas, Vaishyas and Sudras) should remain in the city (or village) and the *Chandals* should remain outside the city or the village as they are considered to be the outcastes. Kautilya differs on certain aspects from *Dharmashastra* and *Smriti* as he considers Sudras as an Arya community, which is distinguished from the Mlechhas or non-Aryan communities. The four varnas are prohibited from selling or pledging their minor children. But this is not applicable to the Mlechhas. No Arya should be made a *dasa* (slave). Manu in *Smriti* states that a Sudra renders service to a twice-born (Brahmans, Kshatriyas and Vaishyas are considered to be twice-born as they wear sacred threads following the thread ceremony). A Sudra can be an agricultural labourer, a herdsman, a servant, or a craftsman.

Privileges of the Brahmans in the *Arthashastra*

Brahmans, who occupy a special position in the society, do not pay or contribute anything towards the common festivals, yet participate in them. They are invited for lunch or dinner during the festivals. They do not pay anything while passing military stations, or at ferries, or customs duties; cannot be forced to confess anything; but enjoy a privilege of occupying the residential areas in the north of the city or the village. The soldiers of a victorious king cannot seize the property of a Brahman who is a subject of the defeated king.

The Brahmans can reside in charitable institutions without making any payment. They do not appear as witness except in the case of transactions in their own community. In case of payment of fines, etc., they enjoy a privileged position in comparison to other castes. Thus, "if among the Brahmans, the Kshatriyas, the Vaishyas, the Sudras and the Chandals, etc., any of the lower castes abuses the habits of any of the higher castes, the fine imposed shall increase from three *panas* upwards (commencing from the lower caste). Similarly, if any of the higher castes abuses any of the lower castes, the fine imposed shall decrease by two *panas*. Hence, the fine levied upon Brahman is less than the fine levied on men belonging to other castes.

If a Kshatriya commits adultery with an unguarded Brahman woman, he gets the highest punishment; a Vaishya is deprived of his whole property and the Sudra is burnt alive for the same offence. But if a Brahman does the same, he is simply branded and banished from the state. He is not physically punished or tortured for his offences. The Royal Priest is not to lose any limb or his property even for his gravest crime.

In case of rape, the guilty Brahman is to be branded on the forehead and banished from the kingdom or exiled to the state mines. But if he makes an attempt to overthrow the king, forcibly enters into his inner apartments, instigates the forest tribes to revolt against him or causes disaffection in forts, he can be put to death by the king. Death should be caused by drowning or throwing for life into a dark chamber.

If a person unlawfully constructs a bridge, digs a well, constructs a temple, or sells others' property, or induces others to do so, he should be fined from 200 to 500 *panas*. But if such a bargain takes place in the presence of a learned Brahman, he should be awarded the highest punishment, that is, a fine of 500 to 1000 *panas* with bodily punishment.

Unlike other citizens, Brahmans enjoy the immunity of property from escheat. When new *Janapadas* are colonized, they are granted *brahmadeya* land for which they do not pay any land tax. But they cannot sell or mortgage them. They need not pay any toll for their personal consumption of salt, but they have to pay it if they take salt for sale. They can also take fruits and flowers from the lands of the king without any payment provided they are used for the worship of God. They can also take rice and barley from the same to perform Agrayana sacrifices.

Political Influence of the Brahmans

Brahmans occupy an important position in the state and society and enjoy great political influence. The two main Brahman dignitaries are the *acharya* and *purohita* (priest). Special suits are allotted to them in the royal palace. They can be asked to vacate the palace or removed if they conspire against the king. The king maintains a close and intimate relationship with them. It is only the ministers and the *acharyas* who prevent the prince from committing wrong or evil deeds. The king obeys the *purohita* as a student obeys the teacher, a son his father, or a servant his master. In case of recruitment of officials and the appointment of troops, the king takes the help of the *purohitas*. In the official hierarchy, the Royal Chaplain (*purohita*) as well as the sacrificial priest (*Ritvik*) and the Preceptor (*acharya*) occupy the first rank along with the Crown Prince, the Queen Mother, the Chief Queen, and the Minister.

The king appoints the Brahmans as his ambassadors.

Brahmans: Marriage, Inheritance and Duties

If a Brahman marries a Brahman woman, a Kshatriya woman, a Vaishya woman and a Sudra woman, then the child born of the Brahman wife secures maximum benefits in terms of property following his father's death. Of sons begotten by a Brahman in the four varnas, the son of a Brahman wife takes four shares, of a Kshatriya wife three shares, of a Vaishya wife two shares, and of a Sudra wife only one share. In case if only one son survives irrespective of his mother's varna, he inherits the entire property of his father.

The duties of a Brahman are: study, teaching, performance of sacrifices (*yajnas*), giving and receiving of gifts, etc. Teaching profession is mostly manned by the Brahmans. They also work as astrologers, *Purana*-reciters, story-tellers, spies, etc. Thus, the Brahmans are privileged and enjoy maximum benefits in Kautilya's state and society.

THE KING

Nature and Qualities

The king should be perfect in his actions, pragmatic and rational in his approach, sound in reason, well-versed in scriptures and canons of law, capable of taking right decisions at right moment, free from all blemishes and vices like anger, lust, greed, vanity, arrogance, and haughtiness. In other words, he should be an embodiment of virtues and have perfect control over his senses. Experts and specialists should help him in acquiring perfect knowledge which promotes his virtues like love, fellow-feeling, kindness, altruism, humility, sacrifice, devotion, dedication, etc. and never allows him to degenerate or become acquisitive and possessive. His hard work and sincerity make him a successful king and his developmental activities and welfare measures make him popular. He should not confiscate the property of his subjects without authorized by law; humiliate their women folk under any circumstances; resort to any wanton violence and adopt means like falsehood, treachery, deceitfulness to achieve his goal or lead an irreligious, immoral and ostentatious life.

The king should lead his life in such a way that he attains four goals of his life: 'Dharma' (devotee of God), 'Artha' (acquiring and possessing property),

'Kama' (fulfilment of desires) and 'Moksha' (attaining salvation). He should not give undue importance to any one of them and do his best to maintain a balance among these four while attaining them. Kautilya has, however, observed that Artha (finance) helps one in attaining other goals and, therefore, it is more important than others.

Duties of the King

The king is a tremendous source of inspiration to his ministers and they imbibe all their qualities as it helps them in giving good and effective governance. But his deviation from the norms may put him into great danger. His own ministers might seize the opportunity to their best advantage and misguide him. They might depose or kill him. Therefore, he must take necessary steps to protect his life.

The king, according to Kautilya, should

- get up early in morning, read scriptures and think about day's programmes;
- analyse defence, revenue and expenditure of the state;
- listen to the grievances of the people and take steps to redress them;
- receive taxes, duties, revenues and assign duties to his employees and servants;
- discuss administrative matters with his ministers; secret matters with spies and collect secret information from them; matters relating to the security of the state and warfare with the chief of the army;
- take bath, take lunch, and read scriptures; go for a stroll or relaxation; for prayer as the sun sets; for dinner followed by reading scriptures including the Vedas;
- inquire into the safety and welfare of soldiers and animals like horses and elephants;
- meet the priests, doctors, cooks and astrologers and discuss with them about scriptures, health, food and the influence of stars on him as well as on his kingdom;
- worship cow, calf and bull and then enter into his court.
- attend and enjoy music and dance programmes and then go to bed.

The above programme should be strictly followed by the king. However, there can be some changes if the situation demands so or in case there is any emergency. But he should not forget that he is solely responsible for the governance of his kingdom. Upon him, depends an effective administration. He should grant interviews to many people. Otherwise, they would be disappointed and frustrated and this might force them to support an enemy king.

Soon after the completion of his official work, the king should visit temples, saints, Brahmans, poor and downtrodden, centres of learning, stables and sheds, etc; try to solve the problems of minors, old and aged ones, patients, orphans, poor and helpless women; not ignore or neglect any work, however small and insignificant it may be; go along with the chief priest and learned ones to the places where *yajna*s are performed, salute the trainees (would-be saints), and take measures to solve their problems; discuss with saints and scholars of witchcraft the matters relating to the activities of the magicians and scientists; and not displease them as they may prove to be harmful and dangerous to the kingdom. Hence, he should protect and promote their interests.

The king should improve the conditions of his subjects, identify with them, share their sorrows and pleasures, treat them equally, help the poor, behave properly with his friends, punish the enemies, encourage *yagnas* and *tapas*, govern the country in accordance with law and scriptures, give employment to right persons, always consider himself to be the servant of the people, feel that people's progress and development are more important than that of his. If he performs his duties with such kind of feelings, he attains his goals and becomes a successful king in future. Otherwise, he suffers for his misdeeds.

COUNCIL OF MINISTERS

Why Ministers?

The king, however intelligent and capable he might be, cannot deliver his goods without the support of some trusted ministers as governance of the kingdom is not an easy job. Hence he has to depend upon dependable, reliable and trustworthy ministers and accept their sound advice.

Qualification of Ministers

Those who are good, honest, sincere, firm, pure, efficient, intelligent, truthful, loyal, wise, well-trained in arts should be appointed as ministers. They must be men of dignity, character, foresight and integrity. Free from vices, they must keep themselves away from such qualities that excite hatred and enmity

Appointment of Ministers

Kautilya's *Arthashastra* describes the methods of appointment of ministers by the king in a chapter entitled "Ascertaining by Temptations, Purity or Impurity in the Character of a Minister". With the assistance of the Prime Minister and the High Priest, the king should examine the character of the ministers by offering them temptations. Of these tried ministers, those whose character has been tested under religious allurements shall be employed in Civil and Criminal Courts; those tested under monetary allurements be employed as revenue collectors and chamberlains; those tried under love allurements be appointed as superintendents of the pleasure grounds, both external and internal; those tested by allurements under fear be appointed to immediate service; and those whose character has been tested under all kinds of allurements shall be employed as Prime Ministers, while those who are proved impure under one or all of these allurements be appointed in mines, timber and elephant forests, and as manufacturers.

Religious Allurement

The king after having a secret and confidential discussion with the priest appoints him to teach the Veda to an out-caste person or to perform a sacrificial performance (apparently) undertaken by an out-caste person. The priest pretends to be unhappy with the king's order and refuses to oblige him. As per the secret discussion, the king dismisses him. Then the dismissed priest, shall, with the help of spies under the guise of classmates, instigate each minister, one after another, saying on oath that as this king is unrighteous, he should be replaced by another king who is righteous, or who belongs to the king's family, or who is kept imprisoned, or who is a neighbouring king of his family and of self-sufficiency, or by a wilt chief, or an upstart. All of them agree with this proposal; what he thinks about it? If any one or all ministers refuse to agree with it, he or they shall be considered pure. This is religious allurement.

Monetary Allurement

The king has a secret discussion with the army commander. After this, the king dismisses him from service under the false pretext that he received condemnable things. Through the spies under the guise of classmates, the commander incites each minister to murder the king so that he can get immense wealth. Each minister is being asked, "all of us like this proposal; what do thou think?" If they refuse to agree, they are to be considered pure. This is monetary allurement.

Love Allurement

A woman-spy, a highly esteemed lady in the king's harem, may allure, under the guise of an ascetic, each minister one after another, saying, "the queen is enamoured of you and has made arrangements for your entry into her chamber; besides this, you are also likely to get much wealth." If they reject the proposal, they are pure. This is love allurement.

Allurement under Fear

With an intention of sailing on a commercial vessel, a minister (being persuaded earlier by the king) may induce all other ministers to follow him. Apprehending danger, the king may arrest them all. A spy under the guise of a fraudulent disciple, pretending to have suffered imprisonment, may incite each of the ministers thus deprived of wealth and rank, saying "the king has taken a wrong decision; well, we will murder him, and put some one else in his place. We all like this; what do you think?" If they do not agree, they are pure. That is allurement under fear.

Prime Minister to be Tested

The king tests the knowledge, intellect and wisdom of the Prime Minister while the latter participates in the discussion of the *Sastras* and makes a brilliant exposition of them. He further tests the Prime Minister's purity, influence, endurance, capacity and patience at the time of crisis. He tests the Prime Minister's loyalty towards him and his kingdom when he comes in close contact with the Prime Minister. With the help of his friends and relatives, he should test the Prime Minister's health, wealth, knowledge, wisdom, patience, balance of mind and depth of ideas.

THE BUSINESS OF COUNCIL MEETING

King's Secret Meeting with Ministers

Since the ministers are learned, virtuous and pure, the king should take them into confidence, discuss with them all important matters, accept their sound advice, consult with them secretly, if necessary, without the knowledge of any one. He should not allow even the birds to be present in such places as these birds are responsible for the disclosure of some secret information. The place, where secret discussion is being held, should, therefore, be closely guarded, secluded and solitary. No one can attend the meeting without the prior permission of the king. He who forcibly enters into such places should be banished from the kingdom or fined and given death punishment. Sometimes gestures, expressions, etc. are sufficiently responsible for the disclosure of secret information. Therefore, the king, the ministers and the employees should be very very careful about their expressions and gestures and should control their external behaviour in such a manner that no one can study their mind to know about the nature of king's secret consultation.

Vicious Character People Debarred

Those who are addicted, lustful, pervert, greedy, or prone to temptations might easily reveal the secret information to others. The king should, therefore, debar them. He should not disclose the measures that enabled and ensured his victory in the war. However, those who are to execute his orders might study the king's mind as they are intelligent and efficient. If they cannot, let them remain in dark until the end.

Decision Not to be Delayed

The king should discuss with a few, but not all superintendents when there is an emergency. If he consults with all, he cannot take any quick decision and the situation might aggravate and slip out of his control. A delayed decision is no decision as it does not yield any result. The king should avoid such a situation and take a final decision on all issues. Since he is capable and efficient, he can take any decision by himself. But, however good and intelligent he may be, collective decision is always more sound and fruitful.

Consultation with Three–Four Ministers

The king should not consult with one minister as the latter may be tempted to disclose the king's decision. If he consults with two ministers, he should respect their advices — whether good or bad. If both the ministers get united, they may deceive him. He may, therefore, be in danger if he consults with two ministers. Hence, it is always safe and better to discuss with three or four ministers. It will certainly be helpful to him in delivering a good administration. If he consults with more than four ministers, he does so at his own risk as the matter cannot be kept secret.

The king should avoid any lengthy discussion with his enemies and their relatives.

Strength of the Ministry

Scholars do not agree as to what should be the strength of the ministry. To Manu, the ideal strength is twelve, to Brihaspati, it is sixteen, and to Sukra it is twenty. Kautilya has, however, not fixed the number. To him, it should be an ideal one and it may differ from time to time.

Duties of the Ministers

Ministers are supposed to study various means that protect the interests of the king; take-up unsuccessful projects and complete them; complete all the pending projects; renovate the old buildings, white-wash them and appreciate those who are involved in these works, etc.

The king should discuss personally with those ministers who are placed in the headquarters and contact through letters with those who are away from the capital. When his life is in danger, he should summon the ministers, seek their advice and be guided by the majority opinion. But he should not ignore the minority view if it is right and correct. He should prevent his enemies from knowing about his secret missions and would be quite successful as a ruler if he collects their names through the spies. As the tortoise hides itself within the outer crest, so also the king should protect himself from the enemies and never give a chance to them to endanger his life.

THEORY OF PUBLIC ADMINISTRATION

The king is absolute, all-powerful and enjoys and exercises executive, administrative and decision-making powers of the state. Though the administrative mechanism is quite large and complex, it should not be identified with the modern civil service or bureaucracy. Nor the administration has anything like delegated legislation and administrative adjudication. Because all the *adhyakshas* are placed under the absolute control of the king.

Concept of Monarchy

Kautilya's concept of monarchy seems to be controversial. Did he think of it in terms of pan-Indian imperial political system? Or did he visualize it as small territorial entity? Scholars differ on this issue. But a careful analysis of his administrative structure reveals that he supported the latter argument. He mentioned about eighteen *Tirthas* occupying highest dignitary posts and offices. Such a small number of high officials could not run the administration of a vast empire efficiently nor they could govern a big imperial political unit effectively. It is also evident from the role assigned to the *samaharta* as he was placed over four *Sthanikas*, each of whom, in turn, was placed over four or five *Gopas*. From this, it appears that the *Samaharta* was placed in charge of only two to three hundred villages. And this is equivalent to a modern subdivision in area. Even if it extended the territorial jurisdiction of the *Samaharta*, it must be concluded that he must not have been in charge of an area bigger than a modern district. Hence it may be argued that Kautilya never stood for an imperial political unit.

Officers

Each department of the kingdom was headed by a director or head and under him were placed five officers:

1. Clerk
2. Inspector of coins
3. Accountant
4. Incharge of the balance, and
5. Supervisor.

There were thirty directors and one hundred and fifty clerical and supervisory staff. There were, thus, in total not more than two hundred officials. This also indicates that Kautilya thought in terms of a small kingdom.

Rural Administration

The rural administration covered five constituents:

1. Village
2. *Sthaniya*

3. *Dronamukha*
4. *Kharvatika*, and
5. *Samgrahana*.

The village occupied an important place in the ancient Indian economy and political organization. Administration of five to ten villages was placed under the control of *Gopa* who was responsible to *Sthanika*. One *Samaharta* controlled four *Sthanikas*. *Sthanika* and *Gopa* were also the designations of officers who looked after the urban administration. Both of them worked under the Nagaraka. Kautilya also mentioned about *gramabhrittaka*, *gramakuta*, *gramika* and *gramasvamin*. *Gramavriddhas* were the elderly persons who were in charge of properties of temples and of minors. Placing of so many persons in charge of village administration gives ample evidence that the village had an important place in the Indian administrative system. These officials were not elected by the villagers as all of them were appointed by the king. Officials did not represent the popular will but were the representatives of the king.

Urban Administration

In urban administration, there is mention of the *Pauravyavaharika* who might be the same as *Nagaraka*. *Dharamsthas* or civil judges were the dispensers of justice. There was a separate judicial organization but not an integrated system of judicial administration.

Absence of Provincial Governors

Absence of posts like provincial governors gives a clear indication that Kautilya's kingdom was small in size and he never thought in terms of a pan-Indian political system.

Responsible Administration

No doubt, the king was absolute and all-powerful, but at the same time, he was not allowed to be arbitrary and whimsical because the administration was to be carried on in accordance with canons, customs and conventions of *Dharma*, *Vyavahara* and *Samstha*. There was, therefore, no scope for irresponsible administration. Royal orders or *Rajasasanas* could not go against ethics.

Welfare Administration

As the administration was people-oriented, it was always geared to promote their well-being. Steps were taken to protect the interests of the afflicted and suppressed sections of the society. When natural calamities like flood, fire, drought, epidemic, etc. befell the people, relief measures were immediately rushed to the inhabitants.

ABSENCE OF PRESSURE GROUPS

The *Arthashastra* is silent about rigorous departmentalization, based on hierarchy and span of control, and vertical coordination, nor has it mentioned about anything like industrial and commercial corporations acting as interest and pressure groups.

THE INSTITUTION OF SPIES

Kautilya laid much emphasis upon the institution of spies as spies played a vital role in the state administration. They collected secret information and tested the purity and character of the ministers who run the state administration in accordance with law, norms and customs.

Appointment of Spies

The king appointed on the advice of the ministers spies who could be classified under nine heads which were as follows:

1. **Sastri:** Born in a royal family or closely related to it, brought up by the king's patronage, well-read and highly spiritual, and thorough in scriptures, he acquired mastery in various branches of knowledge including *Kamashastra*, *Dharmashastra*, music, dance, palmistry, astrology, witchcraft, sorcery, magic, hypnotism, grammar, etc. He understood the language of birds and by studying and analyzing it he predicted good and bad for the state and its people.
2. **Tikshna:** Courageous, brave and daredevils, they fought against the wild animals like tigers, lions, snakes, elephants, etc. This they did at the cost of their own lives and for the sake of money.
3. **Rasada:** Cruel and lazy, they had no affection for their family members and friends. Without any hesitation and with least compunction, they used to kill many by poisoning them.
4. **Bhikshyuki or Paribrajika:** The poor, old and intelligent Brahmin widows leading the life of a mendicant, were appointed to look after the comforts of high officials (of the state) like *Mahamatras*. Having free access to their houses, they also commanded respect from the queens.
5. **Kapatika:** People, who were middle-aged, unmarried, poor and always interested in finding faults with others were appointed as *Kapatika* spies.

Under the guise of fraudulent disciples, they kept a vigilant eye on the misdeeds and unlawful activities of the 'amatyas' and reported the same to the king.

6. **Udasthita:** Those disciples, who spent sometime in the 'Ashramas' as 'Sanyasins' but left the same for some reasons, were appointed as *Udasthita* spies. Under the guise of pure and intelligent mendicants or sanyasins, they set up their 'Ashramas' or Centres at different places, particularly centres of trade, agriculture and animal husbandry, with the help and support of the king. They asked and encouraged their disciples to go for cultivation and provided them a very comfortable life. Once the disciples decided to stay in the 'Ashramas' permanently because of good food and comfortable stay, some of them were given proper training in diplomacy and appointed as spies to collect secretly information about the enemies of the king. They visited under the guise of saints to enemy kingdoms to collect information on various aspects.
7. **Gruhapatika Byanjana:** A farmer or an agriculturist, who was intelligent but had given up his traditional occupation was appointed as *Gruhapatika* spy. Under the guise of a farmer, he spent his time with farmers and agricultural workers. Taking some of them into confidence, he engaged them in espionage activities. Whatever information he collected from them, he sent the same to the king.
8. **Baidehaka Byanjana:** An intelligent but poor merchant, who was no more in his business because of his poor financial condition, was appointed as a *Baidehaka* spy. With the help of his disciples, he influenced the *Vaisyas* (merchants and traders) to render their unconditional support to the king.
9. **Tapas Byanjana:** A *Tapas Byanjana* spy appeared outwardly to be a Buddhist monk or a mendicant, or a *sanyasin*. With long hair or no hair on his head he visited different places along with his disciples, pretended to live on fruits and milk but could be a non-vegetarian or take any type of food of his choice. By doing so, he misguided the poor and innocent people as they considered him to be a real saint. His disciples, particularly those engaged in trade and commerce, worshipped him and presented him with costly gifts or spread a rumour among the people that they had gained much wealth because of his blessings. They also propagated that he was a perfect *yogi* having endowed with supernatural powers that enabled him to do and undo anything that he liked. There was nothing that could not be achieved with his blessings. They also spread the information that he could predict one's future and fortunes particularly about acquisition of wealth. When the people met him and sought his blessings for wealth, he, on the basis of their gestures, behaviour, mode and manner of questioning, movement of their eyes,

and information collected earlier by his disciples about them, predicted their future including their financial gains, foreign visit or visit to distant places, loss of property as a result of theft, robbery and fire, annihilation of their enemies, etc. He made it a point that some of his predictions came true. For this purpose, he took the help of some who indulged in such activities as would cause theft, robbery, fire, etc.

Having come to know that the king had really done some injustice to some people, the ministers should provide them adequate compensation to enlist their support and cooperation to the king. No more they would hate the king. No more they would treat him as their enemy. The ministers with a view to translate some of the predictions made by the spies, should provide financial assistance to deserving persons to start their business or give them appointment in different services. On being informed by the spies that some people were really hostile to the king without any genuine reason, and had nurtured grudge against him, they were secretly punished and his enemies were annihilated and eliminated, or banished from the country.

The spies must have a thorough knowledge about the ministers, their activities and attitudes towards the king.

Spies secretly collected information on the activities of ministers, prime minister, priests, commander-in-chief (chief of the army), prince(s), officials in charge of the harem, *samaharta* (collector of revenue), *sannidhata* (storekeeper), mining officers and other important persons working in different offices. All these officials worshipped Gods or Goddesses like Ram, Krishna, Siva, Durga, Ganesh, etc. Spies under the guise of the devotees met them to collect information secretly. For example, if an official worshipped Lord Siva, then the spy also pretended himself to be a great devotee of that lord. This certainly helped him in establishing a good rapport with the officer and made his task easier.

People, who were deaf, dumb, blind and deformed, or who were the dancers, singers, performers of sport events on the streets, or eunuchs, or ladies who could deceive others without any hesitation, could be appointed as spies.

TRADITIONS OF *ARTHASHASTRA* AND *DHARMASHASTRA*

Every individual, as per the ancient Aryan culture and the classical texts like Shastras and Puranas, should seek to achieve four goals in his life — *Dharma, Artha, Kama* and *Moksha*. Accordingly, we have *Dharmashastra, Arthashastra* and *Kamashastra. Mokshashastra* can be comprehended in various schools of Indian philosophy which teach how to achieve salvation and emancipation of the soul. While the *Arthashastra* discusses political aspects, the *Dharmashastra* is concerned with them partly. There are certain basic differences between them: while the *Arthashastra* lays emphasis on *Artha* in the pursuit of temporal objectives, the *Dharmashastra* gives much importance to the aspect of Dharma. Kautilya, the author of *Arthashastra*, was secular and materialist while Manu,

Narada, Vishnu and Yajnavalkya—the exponents of the *Dharmashastra*— were conservative and traditional in their approach. Julius Jolly, for example, has observed that the *Dharmashastra* is opposed to any kind of divorce, while the *Arthashastra* permits it in case of a conflict or misunderstanding between the husband and the wife. But Kautilya did not allow it in four forms of Dharma marriages—Brahma, Prajapatya, Arsha and Daiva—solemnized with the consent of the fathers (of both the bride and groom). It was however, allowed in other forms of marriages—Rakshasa, Gandharva, Paisacha and Asura. In Rakshasa marriage, a man marries a woman by applying force and threatening her of dire consequences if she does not agree to it. In such cases, marriage takes place without the consent of the woman. When a man and a woman get attracted towards one another, fall in love and marry, it is the Gandharva marriage. In Paisacha marriage, a man marries a woman after kidnapping her while she is asleep and in Asura marriage, the father gives her daughter in marriage to a person out of greed or poverty, i.e. expecting (or demanding) property from the groom to meet his household expenses or purchase gold for the bride.

Kautilya was a positivist. To him, a legal dispute could be settled with the help of Dharma, Vyavahara, Charitra and Rajasasana. Here, the latter supersedes the former. Vyavahara was superior to Dharma, Charitra to Vyavahara and Rajasasana to Charitra. Recognizing the overall superiority of Rajasasana, Kautilya opined that the positive, determinate commands and ordinances issued or decreed by the king were deemed to be superior to the sacred laws and customs.

If there was a conflict between moral laws and logic, the latter enjoyed its supremacy over the former and be treated as more authoritative than the Sastra since the texts of Sastra were sometimes lost. Logic superseded the Sastras or the scholastic texts.

A rationalist, he was against the worship of planets and stars as favoured by the *Dharmashastras*. He ridiculed and condemned it. One's success depended upon economic ends. However, he did not oppose the use of magical practices as found in the Atharvaveda, and the worship of several deities like Varuna. He had a strong belief in the tradition and theology and was not a materialist, atheist or a scientific agnostic.

To the existing four Vedas — Rig, Sama, Yajur and Atharva — he added another one called Itihasa Veda. He advised the prince to listen to it in the latter part of the day. It included Purana (mythology), Itivrittam (descriptive stories), Akhyayika (anecdotes), Udaharana (illustrative examples), *Dharmashastra* and *Arthashastra*. Though the last two differed from one another, they were deemed to be the parts of the larger discipline called Itihasa. Kautilya showed his radicalism by calling Itihasa Veda to be a part of the Vedas.

Both *Arthashastra* and *Dharmashastra*, said to be the branches of the Itihasa Veda and deemed to be the parts of the same broad arena of knowledge, considered Swadharma as an important factor in the maintenance of systemic equilibrium and harmony in the social and political spheres.

In case there was any conflict between Samstha (institutional practices and regularized pattern of behaviour) and *Dharmashastra*, or between Sastra and customary evidences (Vyavaharakam), the controversy was to be settled by reference to the authority of Dharma. The importance of Dharma, and, by implication, also of *Dharmashastra* was partially recognized by Kautilya.

A writer on *Dharmashastra* devotes only one chapter or a section in his work to discuss the basic political problems and issues. Problems of polity, inter-state relations and diplomacy, warfare, etc. are the subject matters of the *Arthashastra*, but not of the *Dharmashastra*.

KAUTILYA'S *ARTHASHASTRA* AND PLATO'S REPUBLIC

Kautilya, a realist, a pragmatist, classified knowledge under four categories: "Anvikshiki" (dialectical logic and philosophy), "Trayi", "Varta" and "Dandaniti". Anvikshiki is eternal, the most important branch of knowledge and the protector of all Dharmas; it investigates the foundations and limitations of other three branches of knowledge, makes an inquiry into the factors responsible for national calamity and temporal prosperity, and seeks to accomplish excellence in the correct use of linguistic propositions and statements. A pertinent question arises here as to how many years one should take to study this supreme knowledge? Kautilya had no answer to it.

Plato, on the other hand, suggested that when a prospective philosopher-king attained the age of thirty, he should read dialectical philosophy for five years. This knowledge would help him in discriminating real from unreal, eternal from transitory, permanent from temporary. Kautilya said that the Prince should read Anvikshiki under the guidance of experts. The studentship of the Prince would end at the age of sixteen. This was not only too short a period, but also at this tender age it would be difficult on one's part to comprehend the Anvikshiki. It may, therefore, be argued that it is not as serious as Plato's dialectical philosophy which the prospective philosopher-king would read at a later stage. Plato said that it would be easier for one to understand dialectic if he read arithmetic, solid geometry, astronomy, etc. at least for ten years. But Kautilya did not prescribe any such background knowledge to understand Anvikshiki. He, however, prescribed 'Jyotisha' (Astrology), 'Samkhya', 'Atharvaveda', 'Trayi', 'Vedangas', etc. necessary for understanding dialectic. But their study would not be as serious as the study of higher mathematics and science.

Kautilya, exponent of traditionalism and conformity, stood for *swadharma* and believed that the world would prosper if it was protected by Trayi. On the other hand, Plato, being far more rational and critical in his approach to Hellenic Theology, said that portion of theology should be taught to the students which would make them brave, strong and noble. Nothing unseemly and unbecoming should be taught to them regarding the character of the gods. He did not even hesitate to criticize the writings of venerated Greek authors like Homer and

Hesoid. But Kautilya never prescribed a critical and rational study of the Veda and Theology.

While Kautilya's social order is based on four varnas 'Brahman', 'Kshatriya', 'Vaisya' and 'Sudra' and four Ashramas 'Brahmacharya', 'Grahastya', 'Vanaprastha' and 'Sanyasa', Plato's social order rests on a threefold hierarchy, i.e. Philosophers, Defenders and Producers, performing different functions in the society. Governance of the country and its defence are two different functions to be carried by two different categories of people. But in Kautilya's *Arthashastra* these two functions are combined in the hands of the Kshatriyas. Brahmans can at best be priests and advisors to the rulers. But they themselves cannot be the rulers. The king appoints a Brahman as a priest who is well-versed in the Vedas and Vedangas and who protects the people and the state from the natural calamities. Needless to say, the purohita is not a ruler. The king follows the priest or purohita as a student or disciple follows his teacher, or a son follows his father, or a slave follows his master.

Plato made his ruler a man of supreme knowledge. A thorough knowledge and understanding of dialectical philosophy is a stepping stone to rulership. The king must have knowledge of philosophy or a philosopher must be the king. In this regard, Kautilya was diametrically opposite to Plato. To him, the king need not be the man of knowledge. Kautilya did not give that much importance to philosophy as Plato assigned the same to philosophy.

To Kautilya, the social structure comprises, as said above, of four varnas and four ashramas. He is vary rigid and orthodox in this regard. But Plato is more democratic. There could be "transposition of ranks between the children of the guardians, of the auxiliaries and of the agriculturists." In other words, there could be circulation of elites. In ancient India, individuals belonging to lower order became Brahmans and Kshatriyas. But neither the *Arthashastra* nor the *Dharmashastra* records any theory of such social elevation.

Vasistha is said to be born in low caste. Vyasa's mother Satyabati belonged to a low caste. Nobody knows who was the father of Satyakama Jabala. Vidura was the son of a maid servant. Still, he could become a great saint. In spite of all these examples, authors of ancient Indian law and politics were not in favour of any democratic theory relating to the transposition of social ranks under the authority of the state.

While Kautilya's *Arthashastra* discusses four ashramas, Plato's Republic is absolutely silent over these four stages of life. However, he has advised the Philosopher-king to retire at the age of fifty. He should not, then, directly participate in the process of the government or in any political activities of the state. In other words, he should lead the Indian Vanaprastha life.

Plato, a philosopher of high order and famous for his profoundity, explains key concepts of metaphysics and political philosophy. His work helps one to understand the intricacies of the problems of philosophy and society. Kautilya's *Arthashastra*, primarily concerned with practical affairs and administrative organization and management, hardly discusses the profounder aspects of philosophy.

KAUTILYA AND ARISTOTLE

Politics has its dimensions: realistic, functional and instrumental. These are elaborately discussed in the writings of Aristotle and Kautilya. Both discussed the sociology and economics of slavery and property. Like Aristotle, Kautilya also supported the institution of slavery. It appears from his writings that any one from any Varna can be made a slave. But at the same time, he prescribed punishments for the practice of slavery. He was more liberal than Aristotle. To him, a slave can become an Arya. Aristotle defended slavery on psychological grounds. But this is not the case with Kautilya.

Aristotle denounced and condemned the accumulation of wealth. But Kautilya encouraged it as it was the foundation of Kama and Dharma.

Both of them have made significant contributions to Political Science. While Aristotle is universally acclaimed as the Father of Political Science, Kautilya is very rightly considered as the Father of Indian Polity. Both stood for an ideal state which should ensure a good life, justice and happiness to its citizens.

Aristotle and Kautilya differ from one another in several respects. Aristotle's *Politics* is not a complete work. It is inconsistent and full of repetitions. But *Arthashastra* is more well organized. Kautilya, however, did not give any detailed study of the constitution of any country as Aristotle did in his "The Constitution of Athens". Aristotle, unlike Kautilya, gave a definite concept of the origin of the state. Kautilya was more interested in statecraft and how to make it strong and vigorous.

Aristotle talked about an ideal state. Kautilya evinced a keen interest in actual state. Aristotle classified the forms of government and state. Kautilya was more committed to ideals of kingship but never discussed kinds of kingship.

Unlike Aristotle, Kautilya did not define the concept of law. To Aristotle, law was reason untainted by 'desire'. Kautilya was more occupied with a penal code. His legal exposition stressed on four categories of law that settled a dispute.

KAUTILYA AND MACHIAVELLI

Introduction

Kautilya's *Arthashastra* is said to be the first and last significant work in ancient Indian Political Science. He lived in an age which saw least contributions to ancient Indian Political Science. There was not much emphasis on political theorizing. Nor was there any competition to do so. Social scientists like Vyasa, Manu, Yajnavalkya and Vatsyayana made immense contributions to the field of non-political science. Scholars like G.B. Bottazi and M. Winternitz made a comparative study of Kautilya and Machiavelli as, to them, one could be compared to another. But rejecting this view, V.R. Dikshitara and Kalidas Nag asserted that Kautilya was not akin to Machiavelli. Both were men of knowledge, experience and intuition. And this helped them to make a deep and penetrating study of contemporary political affairs of their respective countries.

Methodology

Both Kautilya and Machiavelli adopted the method of observation to explain a phenomenon. While the latter made a lot of references to ancient Roman history and drew political lessons from it, Kautilya did not make in this regard any exhaustive reference to ancient Indian history. In a small chapter, he explained how sensuous kings perished because of their passions and how upright and morally strong kings flourished because of their control over the senses. To corroborate his statements, he hardly depended on history. He was not a historicist.

Sociology of Religion

While Machiavelli acknowledged the role of fortune or chance in the making of history, Kautilya laid emphasis on 'Karma' (deeds). To Machiavelli, religion provided a cohesive force and solidarity, unity and strength, discipline and harmony, and made the people law-abiding. At the same time, he lamented that religion was the opium of the people as it made them meek and mild, taught them to suffer and tolerate injustice and oppression. Religion indirectly helped the wicked rulers to perpetrate their tyranny upon the poor, innocent and God-fearing people.

Kautilya advised the king to follow the Veda. To him, religion was not the opium but brought prosperity and strengthened the base of social structure.

The Techniques and Foundations of Political Power

Both Kautilya and Machiavelli were concerned with acquisition, retention and perpetuation of political power. The latter provided an insight into the deplorable conditions prevailing in Italy during his times and advocated for its unification. Explaining the intellectual qualities of the king, Kautilya sought for the expansion of the empire. But while advocating for *mandala*-politics, he was a regionalist rather than a nationalist.

Machiavelli pinned high hopes in his hero: Cesare Borgia (1476–1507), the illegitimate son of the Pope Alexander VI. A champion of absolutism, the king should combine in him a lion and a fox: the fearlessness of the lion and the clever dexterity of the fox and he should adopt deceit and hypocrisy as instruments of success. Creator of a strong national army, he could suppress the religion for the sake of perpetuation of power. An imperialist, hegemonist and expansionist, he advised the prince to command awe and reverence. His subjects should not hate him and this could be possible only when they liked him and feared him. He should, at least, appear to be virtuous though devoid of any character. He would dig his own grave if he humiliated his women subjects. He should not disturb the existing social order, customs and practices.

Both Kautilya and Machiavelli advised the ruler to be merciless, cruel and unscrupulous while suppressing internal disruptions and external aggressions. The former provided different kinds of sanctions which were coercive in nature and punishments prescribed by him were stringent and cruel. But Machiavelli, while elaborating the theme of the art of war, did not mention cruel technics like blinding through the use of poisonous powders for attaining political goal. Kautilya surpassed Machiavelli and left him far behind while sanctioning several barbarous and cruel measures for attaining success. No ethical code supports Kautilya's methods for winning success. For the sake of the country's security, all kinds of measures including violence and fraud were welcome and they could not be considered as reprehensible. This is what both Kautilya and Machiavelli advocated. To them, end justified the means.

In case of Machiavelli, there is a dichotomy between means and end. He said that the end of the state justified the means adopted for its security. He, therefore, deliberately stated that at times cruelty might be preferred to clemency and faith might be kept only when it was not disadvantageous. He was, thus, aware of the dichotomy. It seems that Kautilya was unaware of an incompatibility that existed between the methods he sanctioned for political success and the code of compassionate ethics. This unawareness is "indefensible" as he himself noted six qualitative attributes: non-violence, truth, purity, freedom from spite, non-cruelty and forgiveness which should influence the behaviour of all men. It is this callousness which brought a bad name to Kautilya.

Coercive sanctions constitute a vital element in the game of power politics. Kautilya argued that severe punishment inflicted upon the subjects would breed contempt that might culminate in repulsion, revulsion and revolution against the king. But if it was mild the ruler lost his credibility, ceased to enjoy the trust and confidence of the people and became an object of hatred and derision. Kautilya, therefore, said that punishment should be neither too severe nor too mild. It should be in proportion to the crime. Machiavelli, unlike Kautilya, seems to have advocated for severe and harsh sanctions. But it should be remembered that on this issue he has not adopted a clear stand.

Human Nature

Both Kautilya and Machiavelli were quite pessimistic in their approach to human nature. It seems that the former treated men with contempt as they were unreliable and untrustworthy. Hence they should not be taken into confidence. He, however, made "no categorical statement regarding the corruptibility of human nature in general." Machiavelli, on the other hand, categorically said that people were ungrateful, fickle, deceitful, avaricious, vicious, evil, mean, corrupt and unreliable. He, therefore, suggested that there should be strong political force to restrain the deviant behaviour of the people. Force and fraud were welcome measures as they checked their psychological aberrations. He upheld a more pervert conception of human nature than Kautilya. He considered men to be greedy, selfish and cruel. They understood only the language of force. Kautilya nowhere made a generalized statement about the weakness or perversity, or selfishness of man.

Kautilya, not Machiavelli, recognized the importance of virtue as a factor in politics. An exponent of imperialistic power politics, he laid emphasis on control of senses and passions. But his views on personal morality of the king rest on the maxims and precepts of the idealistic, vedantic and Buddhistic schools.

Administration and Management

Machiavelli and Kautilya differ from one another in respect of the institution of monarchy. Theoretically, both of them stood for an absolute and centralized monarchy. But Kautilya, unlike Machiavelli, advocated that the king should be guided by the ministers. There should be a council of ministers to advise the king on the governance of the kingdom. But to Machiavelli, the king never functioned within any theological framework as he was not subject to any divine laws. But the Kautilyan king was, to some extent, to abide by these laws as well as the Vedic scriptures.

Machiavelli's main concern was the unification of Italy, while Kautilya was more concerned with administration, diplomacy and law. The former discussed the organization of a princely polity. However, he was silent how it was to be managed and how its policies decided by the prince were to be implemented. Kautilya described in detail the role and functions of various officials heading various departments. This showed that he had in his mind a highly developed civil service with quite a large number of officials. Machiavelli did not, however, discuss the role of the civil service.

Both Machiavelli and Kautilya had warned the ruler not to extort money from his subjects, as by doing so, they would not only incur their displeasure but also provoke them to revolt against him. Machiavelli said that an individual might easily forget the murder of his father but not the confiscation of his property. Both of them advised the ruler to adopt a moderate financial policy.

AN ESTIMATE

A product of the ancient Hindu society, Kautilya cannot be considered as a modern writer. Neither he was a scientific rationalist nor did he have any knowledge of modern science. He could not make himself free from the influence of the Veda and other scriptures as he recognized their importance.

A strong supporter of the Varnashrama, he failed to think of all-India nationalism based on social integration. Interested in the preservation of the *Shastras* (military weapons), *Sastras* (scriptures), he stood for a small kingdom. He did not have any interest in the people of Aryavarta. His only burning desire was to acquire and retain political power. The old social order should rest on priest-sanctioned legitimacy. Concerned with "orthodoxy, conformist legitimacy and stability", he did not discuss natural rights or the problems of political, economic and moral individualism. A theoretical discussion of the fundamental problems of politics and ethics, nature of the state, political obligation, legitimacy, etc. were hardly the subjects of the *Arthashastra*.

A profound scholar of Sanskrit and famous for his erudition in Sanskrit lexicons, Kautilya was deeply concerned with the organizational details of a small kingdom. A very popular name in the domain of Indian ancient political thought, his work has been quite significant as he highly appreciated the role of the 'past' in political science. It was the ruler who decided what to be spent on whom, how and when. It was he who allocated resources and values. In other words, values and resources were authoritatively allocated. A political actor wields his power and influence as well as manipulates the will of others through his charisma, popularity, strong determination, iron-will and self-confidence.

POINTS TO REMEMBER

- Kautilya, to some, is otherwise known as Chanakya or Vishnu Gupta. But others have rejected this view. Kautilya's 'Gotra' name was Vishnu Gupta, Kautilya and Chanakya were two different persons. Lot of controversy over the date of publication of *Arthashastra* by Kautilya.
- *Arthashastra* was published in fourth century B.C., fourth century A.D., in the early centuries of this era.
- King–Prince relationship: Prince to be well-trained by the king and trainers. He should be virtuous. His prenatal care to be taken.
- Prince: he should be virtuous, well-trained. If he is not so, he can be imprisoned or poisoned, or banished from the kingdom. In certain cases, the king comes to his rescue.
- The prince performs different jobs when his relationship with his father (the king) gets strained.
- Immigrants occupy the Janapadas for settlement. They are normally Sudra cultivators. Each and every village has a boundary wall for its protection. Certain lands are gifted to certain categories of people.
- Agriculture needs to be encouraged. Preferred lands were taxed. Unprepared lands cultivated by the tenants are not to be snatched. Tenants neglecting lands are to be punished.

- Lands to be irrigated. Industries to be encouraged, villagers to produce maximum output. People are to be punished for various reasons. No entertainment. Disposal of uncultivated lands; pastures to be made, a haunting forest to be created. Extraordinary measures to improve the financial position of the kingdoms.
- The king imposes taxes on certain items and other items are not taxed by him.
- Benevolences from dealers and demands on animal breeders.
- To improve the revenue position of the state, the king may ask for donations and, in return, be given presentations to the donors. No dubious means to augment the revenue. Kautilya was an advocate of capitalism. Agriculture to be improved.
- State rears domestic animals. Construction of stables. Superintendents to look after them.
- State's monopoly over the mines. Mining officials are appointed to look after them. Appointment of Superintendents to look after branches of the mining industry. State's important role in regulatory trade and industry.
- Appointment of Superintendent of Commerce, Superintendent of Weights and Measures, Superintendent of Ship, Superintendent of Liquor, Superintendent of Fabrics, Superintendent of Customs, and Superintendent of Coins. *Rupadarsaka* examines the coins.
- The state is to maintain Varnashrama dharma. It is divinely created. The king cannot change it. He has to maintain it, preserve it. It is found in *Dharmashastras* but it has been explained by *Smritis*.
- Privileges of the Brahmans: do not pay taxes, attend festivals and take food there. Good accommodation is provided to them.
- In certain cases, a Brahman can be given death punishment. No salt tax to be paid by him. Takes fruits and flowers from the king's land without any payment.
- Brahman enjoys great political influence. Acharya and Purohita — the main dignitaries. Provided with special suits in the palace. He can marry a girl belonging to any Varna. His duties: teaching, study, receiving gifts, etc.
- Nature and qualities of the king: virtuous, not to confiscate others' property or to humiliate others' wives. To attain four goals in his life.
- Duties of the king.
- Council of Ministers: the king depends upon reliable ministers for effective governance. Good, efficient, honest people should be the ministers.
- Selection of ministers through temptations or allurements: religious, monetary, love and fear.

- The Prime Minister, like other ministers, is put to task. The king holds secret meetings with ministers.
- Men of wicked character should be debarred from attending the meetings.
- The king should discuss with three to four ministers, but not less than that or not more than that. Strength of the ministry to be an ideal one.
- He should consult with them when his life is in danger. He should protect himself from the enemy.
- Kautilya's concept of monarchy remains controversial. Is it a small territory or pan-Indian Imperial political system? It seems he sticks to the former view.
- The rural and urban administration: their organization. Separate, but not integrated, judicial organization.
- Provinces did not have governors. Kingdom was small in size. Responsible administration. People-oriented administration. Absence of corporations and pressure groups.
- Importance of spies in the administrations. King appoints them on the advice of his ministers.
- Nine types of spies: (i) Sastri; (ii) Tikshna, (iii) Rasada, (iv) Paribrajika, (v) Kapatika, (vi) Udasthita, (vii) Gruhapatika Byanjana, (viii) Baidehika Byanjana, (ix) Tapas Byanjana.
- Spies collected information secretly on various officers and offices. Every individual's four goals in his life: (i) Dharma, (ii) Artha, (iii) Kama, and (iv) Moksha (salvation).
- *Arthashastra's* emphasis on 'Artha' (wealth) and *Dharmashastra's* emphasis on 'Dharma'. The former is secular and traditional, while the latter is conservative and traditional. Kautilya allowed divorce in restricted cases, while *Dharmashastra* refused it totally. Kautilya — a positivist. No worships of planets and stars. To him there were five Vedas.
- Importance of Swadharma and of the *Dharmashastra* was recognized by Kautilya.
- Kautilya's classification of knowledge under four categories.
- He stood for Swadharma.
- His social order is based on four Varnas and four Ashramas.
- Plato: Hellenic theology to be taught to the students. He criticized Homer and Hesoid.
- His social order rests on a threefold hierarchy.
- His ruler: a man of supreme knowledge. King be a man of philosophy or a philosopher be the king. Kautilya's less importance to philosophy.
- Persons belonging to low social order became Brahmans and Kshatriyas. Plato — silent over four ashramas.

- Dimensions of politics: realistic, functional and instrumental.
- Both Aristotle and Kautilya supported slavery. In this regard, Kautilya was more liberal than Aristotle. A slave can become an Arya. Unlike Kautilya, Aristotle denounced accumulation of wealth. They had common view points: association with royal families, an ideal state, etc. They also differed from one another.
- Both Kautilya and Machiavelli could be made comparable. They agreed and disagreed on various points.
- Machiavelli was both moral and amoral. Kautilya was moral as he gave much importance to religion.
- Prince's lion and fox policy. Hypocrisy and deceit were instruments of his success.
- He subordinated religion to politics. He was to command awe and reverence.
- To Kautilya and Machiavelli, the king should be cruel and merciless. Kautilya prescribed harsh punishments for violation of laws and norms. The king could adopt means for getting success. Punishments should not be too severe, nor too mild. But to Machiavelli, they must be harsh and severe.
- About human nature, both were pessimists. Men — not to be trusted as they were unreliable.
- Both stood for an absolute state. To Kautilya, king must be guided by his ministers and the customs, norms, ethics, etc. He had a highly developed civil service in his mind. Machiavelli was silent on it. Both of them advised the king not to extort money from the subjects.

3

Raja Ram Mohan Roy (1772–1833)

INTRODUCTION

An intensely admired and beloved leader dedicated to the service of mankind, a great multifaceted personality, the Father of Renaissance of Modern India, a profound religious scholar, a mighty social reformer, a champion of regeneration and upliftment of India, Raja Ram Mohan Roy inaugurated the Modern Age in India and stood for the introduction of new ideas and ideals in order to raise the country to the height of civilization. He, therefore, strongly advocated for the cause of social, religious, political, administrative and economic reforms. A great force to be reckoned with during the early part of the nineteenth century, he exerted a tremendous influence on social, religious and political thinking of people. "In social usage, in politics, in the realm of religion, the country had entered the zone of uncreative habit, of decadent tradition and ceased to exercise the humanity". In this dark gloom of India's degeneration, he rose up as a luminous star on the horizon of India's history. A champion of intellectual and social emancipation, he was perhaps the only one in his time in the whole world of fellow-beings to realize completely the significance of the Modern Age. A contemporary of Hegel, he had a quest for the Truth and evinced a keen interest in the study of Lamaist Buddhism of Tibet.

EARLY LIFE

Born on 23 May 1772 in an orthodox Brahmin family to Tarini Devi and Ramakanta Roy of Radhanagar, then a part of the district of Burdwan and later a part of the Arambagh sub-division in the district of Hooghly, West Bengal, he was greatly influenced by his mother spiritually. An orthodox and a great intellect, she was not an ordinary woman. Firm and intelligent, she was an ideal wife, a dedicated mother. Strict and stern and yet affectionate and sympathetic, on larger issues, her sense of duty prevailed over her internal affection.

EDUCATION

Ramakanta Roy had three children: two sons and one daughter. Raja Ram Mohan was the second son and Jag Mohan was the eldest one. Ramakanta was highly ambitious about his sons' education. During his time, a child was supposed to know three languages: his mother tongue; Sanskrit, the language of the scriptures; and the Persian, the language of the courts and administration. A maulavi was appointed to teach the Persian language to Ram Mohan. The latter was so much attracted towards the Persian literature particularly the poetry, that he made tremendous progress in this field. Therefore, at the age of twelve he was sent to Persia for higher studies.

HIS STAY IN PATNA

He went to Patna to learn Arabic. As he was a brilliant student, he grasped the fundamentals at a very early age. His study of Koran and acquaintance with the philosophy of Islam changed his religious outlook. Admiring and appreciating the works of Mutazilas and Muwahudins, he became a staunch believer in one God. The Hindu worship of too many idols and images was not in tune with the principles of monotheism. Study of Arabic greatly changed his thoughts. He studied Euclid and Aristotle in this language.

HIS STAY IN BANARAS

At the age of sixteen, he became a master in the Arabic and Persian languages. After his return from Patna, where he stayed for three years, he was sent to Banaras to learn Sanskrit. There he not only came in contact with great Rishis of India but also read the Vedas and learned treatises in Sanskrit. Comparing the Hinduism with Islam, he reached at a conclusion that everywhere man was trying to attain the One. With the help of Sanskrit, Arabic and Persian literatures and languages he made a grand synthesis of different cultures. With this, started the Renaissance of Modern India.

VIEWS ON RELIGION

He held pleasant, prolonged and fruitful discussions with his father, a devout and orthodox. Unlike his father, he was logical and heterodox. Therefore, he differed from his father on fundamental issues. The monotheism of Muhammedan theology and the Brahma knowledge of the Hindu sacred books changed his mind. He opposed the idol worship and criticized the superstitions. He felt that spiritual purity had been polluted by the superstitions and blind beliefs. His parents were, therefore, unhappy with him. He married again following his first wife's death. And within another year, he married again. He lived with two wives, though he resented polygamy from his youth.

HIS STAY IN TIBET

At the age of sixteen, he wrote an essay on idolatry and superstitions prevailing in the then Hindu society. His action deeply hurt the sentiments of his parents and the rift between him and his father widened. This forced him to leave his home for Tibet, where he came in contact with the Lamas. By strongly criticizing their religious conduct and rituals, he not only incurred their displeasure and wrath but also put his life in danger. Attempts were made to kill him. But some kind-hearted ladies came to his rescue by providing him timely help and protection. This kindness had such a deep impact on him that later he became one of the staunch supporters of women and their cause. He returned back to his home after staying for about three years in Tibet with a vast treasure of experience. But he could not stay with his parents for a long time as he left for Banaras.

LEFT FOR BANARAS

In Banaras, he did a part-time job and studied the Hindu scriptures. He was deeply impressed by the teachings of the learned scholars. The intensive study of the scriptures including the Upanishads cleared his doubts and confirmed his belief in the oneness of God.

LEFT FOR CALCUTTA

As his beliefs and ideas were not compatible with those of his father, he again left his home and gave up his claim to a share in the family estate. He was convinced that by remaining with his parents he could not develop his own ideas. He left for Calcutta and settled there as a financier to traders and officials of the East India Company. This gave him an opportunity to pick up English.

IN MURSHIDABAD

After his father's demise in 1803, he left Calcutta for Murshidabad as he got a government job there. There he wrote in Persian language with a preface in Arabic a treatise, his first literary work entitled *Tuhfat-ul-Muwahhidin* (A Gift of

Monotheists) and published in 1804, wherein he strongly protested against the idol worship found in many religions. It was a strong reaction against religious hypocrisy and social abuses.

He laid emphasis on a comparative study of religions and drew attention to the achievement of monotheism throughout the world. He believed that every human being had an innate faculty and if he inquired impartially into the nature of the principles of religious doctrines, primary or secondary, laid down by different nations, there was a strong hope that he would be able to distinguish the truth from untruth and the true proposition from the fallacious one; no more biased against any religion; no more averse to any religion; not subject to the useless bondage or restraints of religion; and would turn to the One Being who created this wonderful universe, and would pay attention to the good of the society.

In 1822, he published "Modern Encroachments on the Ancient Rights of Female According to the Hindu Law of Inheritance". In this work, he strongly argued that the Hindu women should have a right to inherit the property of their parents and husbands. In Vajrasuchi, a Sanskrit work published in 1827, he condemned the prevailing caste system.

BRAHMO SAMAJ

As Roy was closely associated with the unitary mission in Calcutta, he built a Unitarian Church in Calcutta. In 1822, he founded the Anglo-Hindu School under the auspices of the Unitarian Association, which was later known as Hare's School. The British Government wanted to establish Sanskrit schools with Pandits as teachers to impart education. Such a decision was strongly opposed by Roy. His Indian friends suggested that he should organize an association of Indians where they could worship the one God in their own way and in their own mother tongue. This resulted in the foundation of the Brahmo Samaj in 1828. This name literally means 'a society for the followers of Brahmans'.

The purpose of the Samaj was 'the worship and adoration of the eternal Unsearchable and Immutable Being who is the Author and Preserver of the Universe'. Since Roy believed that every religion believed in existence of the Supreme Being as the creator and preserver of the universe along with a moral code necessary for social peace and happiness, the Samaj was widely acclaimed by the people. It was directly or indirectly responsible for giving rise to a great movement called Indian Renaissance or new awakening, which stood for a national reorganization of society and rediscovery of the ancient Indian heritage.

Roy struggled hard throughout his life to erect this Samaj as a tower of victory. He put all his labour and efforts for propagating the Brahmo Dharma; spent all his money; sacrificed his entire property; and worked very hard to achieve success in this direction. As a result, he got heavily involved in debts. His house was sold by auction. He ignored all his troubles that he faced while introducing a new religion.

SOCIAL REFORMS

Practice of Sati

Practice of Sati in India during the eighteenth and early nineteenth centuries was an outrageous social evil. Hindu woman was burnt on the funeral pyre of her husband. Her sacrifice was considered as an act of deep love and attachment for her deceased husband.

An age-old phenomenon, the practice of Sati afflicted more or less every society at different points of time. The widow sacrifice prevailed from Scandinavia to the South Sea Islands. In India, during the fifteenth century, a large number of women became the victims of this practice. Earlier in Egypt, the practice of Sati also existed in a different form. Instead of being burnt, the women were buried along with their deceased husbands.

The Moghul emperors including Akbar and Jahangir took steps to suppress this evil. But they failed. Deeply rooted in a society and in its socio-religious life, its abolition was not only difficult but also next to impossible. It was believed that a woman when burnt alive on the funeral pyre of her husband went to heaven. The Smrities were cited as authority in this regard. The saints and rishis like Angira, Harit and Vishnu had sanctioned the Sati practice. They argued that the woman who, on the death of her husband, ascends the burning pile with him was exalted to heaven, as equal to Arundhati. She followed her husband to another world, dwelled in a region of joy for many many years.

Attempts were made earlier by some rulers to suppress the evil. Peshwa Baji Rao was one of them, who abolished it in his kingdom as it had become extremely unpopular because of its inhumanity. But still then the practice continued in many places. The British Government was also afraid to abolish this practice.

Roy opposed this evil practice which was most barbarous and inhuman. It was a cruel custom based on an irrational philosophy. His sound argument was considered to be an onslaught on Hinduism. Describing the practice of Sati as heinous, he treated it as murder as the widow was forced to commit it. He, therefore, requested the government to stop this practice. He was opposed by the fundamentalists who argued that the custom was bound up with the religion of the Hindus and any kind of interference would offend the religious sentiments of the people. He paid a heavy price for his progressive policies as he was humiliated and ridiculed by orthodox members of the society.

Taking up the challenge, he argued that though the practice of Sati was sanctioned by some authorities, a better course of life other than self-immolation was also prescribed by some other authorities of equal, if not more, eminence. Since he was well-versed with the scriptures and a scholar of eminence, he published in 1818, 1819 and 1820 a few books in Bengali, which were later translated into Sanskrit in 1820, in dialogue form to clear up the mystery of the age-old experience. He firmly believed that the Sati practice could be abolished only with the help of the scriptures. With a view to convince the people, he quoted Manu, the greatest, the most famous lawgiver. The latter said:

> Let her emaciate her body, by living voluntarily on pure flowers, roots and fruits, but let her not, when her Lord is deceased, even pronounce the name of another man. Let her continue till death forgiving all injuries, performing harsh duties, avoiding every seasonal pleasure and cheerfully practising the incomparable rules of virtue which have been followed by such women as were devoted to only one husband.

He strongly argued that the opinion given by Angira and Harit on the practice of Sati was contrary to that of Manu and Yajnavalkya. The latter in their respective codes observed that the widows should perform the duties of ascetics only.

Those who favoured widow-burning were of the view that leading the life of an ascetic was merely an alternative. But Roy firmly opposed this view. To substantiate his arguments, he cited *Kathopanishad*, *Bhagvad Geeta* and *Mandukopanishad*.

He strongly argued that forcible cremation was against the spirit of scriptures. The practice of forcibly tying down women to the pyre and burning them to death was inconsistent with the scriptures, and, therefore, highly sinful. It was of no consequence to affirm that this was customary in any particular country. Even it were universally practised, it would still be criminal. The practice that might be followed in matters where no particular rules were prescribed in the scriptures was not to be justified by the practice of a few.

Respect for Women

Roy had a tremendous respect for women. He ridiculed those who believed that women by nature were inferior to men mentally, without resolution, unworthy of trust, subject to passion and void of virtuous knowledge. He argued that women were inferior to men in physical strength and energy. It is because of this, they were exploited by men and deprived of their dues. He considered women to be as competent as men.

Strongly criticizing the social conditions in which women lived, he was strongly opposed to polygamy.

It is because of his crusade against the practice of Sati and criticism against the Pandits for their misinterpretation of the scriptures, he not only incurred the wrath and displeasure, as said above, of the fundamentalists but also was debarred from his caste. The Indian Press strongly criticized him for his views on Sati. The Samachar Chandrika observed that he no doubt was born in a Hindu family, but how could he represent all or majority of the Hindus. Without paying any heed to all these baseless criticisms, he tried to abolish the evil. His mission was fulfilled when the British Government passed a resolution against this heinous crime. He was also present in England when the Privy Council took up this issue in 1832. On hearing arguments from both sides, the Council approved the Government's decision to suppress the Sati.

Roy's name, along with Lord William Bentick's, will go down the annals of Indian history for his ceaseless efforts in preventing as well as eliminating, if not completely, this deadly evil practice from the Indian society.

When the 1829 legislation brought an end to the practice of Sati, Bentick observed:

> The first and primary objective of my heart is the benefit of the Hindus. I know of nothing so important to the improvement of their future condition as the establishment of a purer morality, whatever their belief, and a more just conception of the will of God. The first step to this better understanding will be dissociation of religious belief and practice from blood and murder.

When Roy was tirelessly working for the abolition of Sati, the Dharma Sabha opposed him vehemently. Surprisingly, Horace Heyman Wilson, a renowned orientalist, came to the conclusion that the abolition of Sati would be considered an act of interference with the Hindu religion. Roy proved that it was not so. Francis Bathie, an attorney of the Supreme Court of Calcutta, was employed by the Dharma Sabha to present the petition of the orthodox Hindus to Parliament soliciting permission to burn the widows alive. Bathie in the course of his speech in Calcutta said:

> I am now proceeding to England on your behalf, and to fulfil your wishes will spare no labour either of body or mind or speech. I go to witness that there shall be no negligence on my part.

But in spite of all his efforts, Sati was abolished due to his (Roy's) heroic efforts.

Women's Right to Property Denied

Women were not only forced to become Sati, but also debarred from inheriting any property from their parents or husbands under the then existing Hindu law. They were forcibly deprived of the means of sustenance, they became a liability for those on whom they depended. Therefore, their physical extermination had its financial advantages. This was the naked, bitter and gruesome truth that lay beneath the killing of the widows in the name of religion.

Protesting against the practice of denying the right to property to women, Roy wrote, as said above, a pamphlet entitled "Modern Encroachment on the Ancient Rights of Hindu Females According to the Hindu Law of Inheritance" in 1822. It said that it was an unjust practice to deprive the women from enjoying property as a matter of right. It was the result of deliberate distortion of traditional Hindu law.

Kulinism and Polygamy

Kulinism and polygamy were other evils that existed in the contemporary society. Kulin Brahmins were placed on the highest pedestal of the caste structure as they were treated with utmost respect. A girl married to a Kulin Brahmin was considered to be very lucky. "Caste" was the only factor that was taken into consideration for solemnizing any marriage. Physical ability, height, age, education, wealth, etc. were secondary and caste was the primary factor.

Therefore, the Kulins, highest in the hierarchy of castes, were much sought after. As a result, they exploited their position to their own advantage. They married as many wives as possible, invariably for monetary consideration. In some cases, the age gap between the husband and wife ranged from 30 to 70 years.

Ram Mohan Roy was deadly opposed to this Kulinism and its concomitant, polygamy. Through Press as well as in various platforms he articulated his views on this problem. He argued that anyone who wanted to go for a second marriage or more than that during the life time of his first wife, should be allowed to do so only on proving before competent legal authority that the conditions under which polygamy was permitted by the Hindu Shastras were fulfilled.

Roy also strongly criticized the caste structure in the Indian society as it was not only a divisive and destructive force but also had a deleterious effect on the political life in India. The distinction of castes with innumerable divisions and subdivisions among them had entirely deprived them of patriotic feeling.

He encouraged inter-caste marriage and at the same time he did not want to become too violent to break a Hindu tradition. He simply argued that the Hindus should consider Saiva marriages just as valid as Vaidik marriages. In the Saiva marriage, there is no discrimination of age and caste, or race.

Nationalism

A staunch nationalist, Roy loved everything that was Indian and did his best to promote the country's progress and prosperity. Right type of education, national in character and austere in make-up, should be imparted. Emphasizing nation's rights and privileges, he suggested that steps should be taken to remove socio-economic backwardness from the country.

Since the Indian society was multilingual and multi-religious, people professing different religions should co-exist together with perfect harmony. Political stability, social advancement and economic progress could be achieved in a society only when it was free from social evils like polygamy, caste system, child marriage, Sati system, etc. To achieve his goal, he struggled very hard. As a true nationalist, he did not desist from adopting any means to achieve his goal. He believed that customs, traditions and usages responsible for the schism or division among the people should be scrapped and a new social morality based on social justice and economic equality evolved. To him, the purpose of religion and politics should be to establish a welfare society.

Supported the English Education

Opposed to all kinds of social injustice, he felt that people should be given education on the British model as this could help them in rebuilding a modern society for India. A master of many languages, he felt the importance of the English language as it was not only relevant but also the need of the day. Impressed by Western art, culture, etc., he laid emphasis on science-oriented education. Therefore, he always supported education undertaken by the missionaries.

Economic Development

As a nationalist, he took up the question of economic development as at that time the economic condition of the people was highly deplorable.

He believed that with the help of Western technology and financial assistance, India could be in a position to improve her economic conditions. But he was deeply distressed when he found that India was exploited by the British regime. He, therefore, laid stress on a self-governing India and the latter must allow the Europeans to stay in India as their presence itself would bring all-round development to India.

He always argued that Indian culture and civilization are always superior to that of the west. In London, he gave a suggestion that natives should be appointed as collectors and judicial officers. One of the first Indians to dream about India's independence, his dream, however, was realized one hundred and fourteen years after his death.

He had a tremendous faith in the people. He felt that they should be educated so that they could grow with a new vision, a new thinking and a new attitude. As a true patriot he strived for all-round development of the country — educational, social, political, economic, administrative, etc.

Internationalism

A staunch believer in the freedom of the human race, he considered the whole world to be one large single family and all nations its members. He felt that the economic conditions of the downtrodden living in different countries of the world should be improved. A man of very broad and clear ideas, he was a true internationalist.

He keenly felt the need of an instrument that would ensure and guarantee peace in the world. As an individual needs the help of his neighbour to resolve his family or domestic problems, so also a nation at the time of crisis should seek the help of other nations. He wanted that people belonging to different races, speaking different languages and professing different religions should live together so that peace and happiness would be established. He believed that religion could bring peace to mankind. An advocate of peace, he suggested that a central organization or a Congress of all nations should be formed so that it could amicably resolve all crises that confronted the nations. He, thus, in his own limited way, conceived an idea of a League of Nations or United Nations. To him, all the disputes affecting different nations should be settled by an international organization. The end of the First World War and the Second World War witnessed the formation of the League of Nations and the United Nations respectively. This shows how progressive were his political ideas and how prophetic he was. He was the first man of the eighteenth century who was in true sense of the term 'an internationalist'. He strongly believed that not isolation but interdependence and interaction among the individuals and the nations would enrich the culture and strengthen as well as ensure a civilization of high order.

It is because of his love for internationalism and freedom, he supported the British Reform Bill. Probably the same spirit motivated him to support the people involved in struggle for their independence. He supported the people of South America who fought against their colonial master Spain and the people of Greece who wanted to throw off the Turkish yoke. He strongly criticized and condemned the British occupation of the Ireland. All this shows how deeply he was involved in international politics. He was interested not only in the all-round development of his country but also of the whole world.

Liberty and Freedom

Like Montesquieu, Voltaire and Rousseau, he was also a champion of liberty and freedom, a priceless possession of human being. His love for liberty and freedom was the basis of all his social, political and religious activities. Forcefully arguing that personal freedom was indispensable, he strongly championed the cause of struggle for freedom and democratic rights. It was this spirit which made him to host a dinner when the Spanish colonies of South America were liberated from Spain and when King Ferdinand VII of Spain was compelled to grant a constitution in 1821. He was very happy when he came to know about the introduction of constitutional government in Portugal. He also supported the Greeks in their struggle for independence against their colonial master. He was deeply hurt when autocracy was restored in Naples (Italy) after an abortive rising.

He fully supported the Reform Bill agitation in England. To him, the struggle between reformers and anti-reformers was nothing but a struggle between liberty and tyranny throughout the world; between justice and injustice; and between right and wrong. He said that liberal principles had been steadily entering into the domain of politics and religion.

He was the first Indian to emphasize that India must cultivate a rational outlook so that it could grow into a nation. He said that a nation might not have one religion but it must have one State with common economic and social objectives seeking welfare of all its citizens; it must have political freedom to pursue its objective in any manner its people considered most suitable, and without any interference from any quarter.

As the socio-economic conditions of the poor peasants were miserable, he strongly criticized the prevailing economic settlement of the British Government. The farmers and cultivators were at the mercy of the landlords, Zamindars and the

Government officials. He vehemently protested against the monopoly of the salt trade by the East India Company. First to deliver the message of political freedom to India, he did his best to create 'self-consciousness' and 'self-confidence' in his countrymen through his multifarious activities — social, economic, educational, judicial, etc.

He strongly criticized all administrative measures which were detrimental to the national interest, protested against certain invidious features of the 1827 Jury Act, and opposed the 1828 Press Ordinance and Regulation giving arbitrary powers to revenue officers. These were the first collective political actions in the modern sense. He also opposed the Jury Bill of 1828, not because it discriminated against Indians but it introduced the pernicious element of 'religious distinction in the judicial system of the country.'

The aforesaid facts reveal his modern outlook. A lover of freedom, he was never parochial in his outlook. In the spiritual world, he was the prophet of universal religion and in the realm of politics, he wanted to see that the principle of liberalism triumphed in every nook and corner of the world. He believed that India could achieve her independence when other nations became free and independent. He hoped that all the colonies would become independent nations in future.

He wanted to see India independent and free. But, at the same time, he felt that the British should be allowed to rule India for sometime as the Indians were too immature to secure freedom. He saw that there was no unity among them as they were divided on the basis of caste, religion, language, region, etc. He said that conquest was very rarely an evil when conquerors were more civilized than the people conquered, because they brought to them the advantages of civilization. Many years of English domination would be necessary before India would be able to resume the political independence without lapsing much.

A crusader against blind beliefs and superstitions, he wanted his people to be self-confident but not diffident and admired Great Britain which guaranteed civil and political liberties to its people and promoted freedom, social happiness and rationalism.

Freedom of Press

Press plays a vital role in a society as it creates, influences and shapes public opinion and provides information to people on various aspects. And without information, there would be a communication gap which might prove disastrous to a society. It acts as a deterrent to the arbitrary rule and *mala fide* functioning of the government. Because of its role and importance, it has been rightly described by Edmund Burke, Carlyle and others as the Fourth Estate.

The British Government in India did not tolerate the role of the Press during the freedom struggle. Therefore, it was taken to task on flimsy grounds. Like Milton, Roy argued that Press was as beneficial to the governed as to the government. Excellence in government and greatest virtue and enlightenment in the society could be secured only when the Press is free.

When he came to Calcutta in 1815, he was deeply distressed to see the conditions in which the Press functioned and took interest to improve them. The freedom of Press was curtailed during the British regime in India. In 1791 and 1799, censorship was imposed on the Press published from Bombay, Madras and Bengal respectively. Lord Hastings, however, abolished it in Bengal. Editors, publishers, printers, etc., who did not obey the authorities were arrested, imprisoned, fined and even deported. The following conditions were laid down for publications of the newspapers:

1. Every printer of a newspaper was required to print his name at the bottom of the paper.
2. The editors and proprietors of the newspapers were asked to inform the Secretary to the Government about their names as well as the places from where the newspapers were published.
3. No paper was to be published on Sunday.
4. No newspaper was to be published at all unless the materials to be published were inspected by authorized persons.
5. The penalty for offending against any of the above regulations to be immediate embarkation for Europe.

In spite of all these repressive measures, the Press in Bengal could not be completely controlled and regulated by the authorities. The *Bengal Gazette* (1780), a weekly, published a lot of articles written by Raja Ram Mohan Roy on the practice of Sati. In 1821, he himself published and edited a weekly called the *Sambad Kaumudi*, highlighting many important and current topics of the society. He also started a Persian paper, *Mirut-ul-Akhbar* in 1822 for the benefit of those who did not know either English or Bengali. Along with J.S. Buckingham, who started the *Calcutta Journal* in 1818, he exposed the misdeeds, highhandedness, nepotism and oppression of the company officials. As a result, Buckingham was deported.

John Bull, an official of the Company Government, continuously provoked the officials against Roy and his publications. John Adam also did not like Roy's views on freedom of the Press. He, therefore, issued in March 1823 an ordinance under which no newspaper or periodical could be published without having obtained licence from the Governor-General-in-Council signed by the Chief Secretary. The application for licence should mention the name (or names) of the printer and publisher, of the proprietors, their places of residence, the location of the Press, and the titles of the newspapers, magazines, pamphlets, books, etc.

The ordinance issued in 1823 became a must or a necessity when Roy published in his Persian paper, *Mirut-ul-Akhbar*, an obituary on Dr. Middleton. He made some laudatory remarks on his learning, and concluded the obituary by stating that the Bishop, having been now relieved from the cares and anxieties of this world, had 'tumbled on the shoulders of the mercy of God the Father, God the Sun, God the Holy Ghosts'. It was considered to be highly offensive to the sentiments of the

Christians. The second event was the subject of the appointment of Reverend Dr. Bryce as a clerk in the East India Company. These two events made Adam very angry which resulted in the seizure of the documents prepared by Roy. Adam, therefore, immediately promulgated an ordinance to curb such type of writing.

On 17 March 1823, Roy along with Dwarakanath Tagore, Harachandra Ghosh, Gauri Charan Banerjee, Prasanta Kumar Tagore and Chandra Kumar Tagore made a petition to the Supreme Court objecting the ordinance. Its consequences would be disastrous as it would suppress the political aspirations of the people. The petition drafted by him was described by Miss Collet as the Areopagitica of Indian History. It formed "a noble landmark in the progress of English culture in the East". With the submission of the petition ushered in a new era of political awakening. He sent a message in clear cut terms on the future political rights as well as the Constitution that the Indians would like to have for themselves.

The petition criticized the invasion of civil rights of the people by the local executive which suddenly assumed the power of legislation and abolished legal privileges of long standing, without the least pretence that they had ever abused them. Roy very forcefully argued that whatever civil, political and religious rights were enjoyed by the people of Great Britain, should also be enjoyed by the Indians. When India was ruled by the Muslisms, the natives enjoyed every political privilege in common with Musalmaans, as they were eligible to hold the highest office in the State, command the armies, govern the provinces and act as advisors to the king or the prince. They were not discriminated on the ground of religion or place of birth.

But the British regime in India deliberately and mischievously discriminated against the Indians by introducing certain measures highly detrimental to their interests. He discussed point by point all the objections against the grant of full liberty to the Press and made a fervent plea to the king not to ignore the demands of the natives.

Roy never argued for the absolute liberty of the Press. He anticipated many of the arguments of John Stuart Mill on behalf of liberty in his appeals for protection of Press freedom. He always emphasized that a free Press has never yet caused a revolution in any part of the world. He believed that it was only a despotic government that always wanted to suppress a free flow of knowledge and information as it considered the spread of knowledge dangerous to the existence of all kinds of authorities.

When his petition was rejected by the Supreme Court, he made an appeal to the King in Council, which reflected the governmental mechanism of the day. It said that men in power were always hostile to the freedom of the Press, which was a disagreeable check upon their conduct. They had made an attempt to make the world imagine that the Press might, in some possible contingency, afford to work against the government. A free Press had never caused, as said above, a revolution in any part of the world. Because men could easily represent their grievances against the local authorities to the supreme government and get them redressed. Thus, the grounds of discontent that excited revolutions were removed. But where no freedom of the Press existed, grievances continued to exist. Innumerable revolutions have taken place in all parts of the globe. When they are prevented by the armed force of the government, the people get ready for insurrection.

Bold, fearless and courageous, he said that the publication of truth, the natural expression of men's sentiments, through the medium of the Press, does not pose any problem to the State. Hence, there should not be any restrictions from the government.

VISIT TO ENGLAND

On 15 November 1830, Roy left for England and reached there on 8 April 1831. By this time he was a very well-known figure in England. In 1816, his first English work 'An Abridgement of the Vedanta' was published. It was well reviewed at length by the *Monthly Repository of Theology and General Literature* of England. Therefore, when he reached Liverpool, almost all the celebrities of the town met him.

Roy visited England because he wanted to submit a memorandum to the King of Great Britain on behalf of Akbar the Second, the then Emperor of Delhi; to present a memorial to the House of Commons for the abolition of Sati; and to be present in England during the approaching discussion in the House of Commons on the renewal of the East India Company's Charter.

Soon after reaching England, he submitted the memorandum on the claims of the Emperor of Delhi not only to the Court of Directors of the East India Company but also to a number of influential persons of London. Though the claim of the Emperor was not fully met, it was partially granted when on 13 February 1833 the Court of Directors sanctioned an increment in the annual stipend of the Emperor of Delhi by three lakh rupees. Roy was introduced by the Duke of Cumberland, the brother of the King of England, to the House of Lords. The Directors of the East India Company entertained him on 6 July 1831 at a dinner in the city of London tavern. He was assigned a seat at the coronation of William IV among the ambassadors of the crowned heads of Europe. Roy also met Jeremy Bentham and Robert Owen.

On 7 September 1831, he met the king William IV who later invited him to a banquet on the opening of the London Bridge. He was highly admired, appreciated and accepted as a member of the highest circles of English society. Quite a number of receptions were held in his honour in London where men of eminence like Jeremy Bentham were present.

LAST DAYS

Financial difficulties and physical strain because of overwork adversely affected his health. On the advice of his friends, he left London for Bristol in September 1833 for a change. However, his health condition deteriorated and he died on 21 September 1833.

AN ESTIMATE

Rabindranath Tagore made a remarkable observation on the impact of Raja Ram Mohan Roy on the modern age in India:

> It takes time to understand and appreciate any rare personality who comes at an age when his country has lost itself and contradicts its own majesty. His voice sounds painfully discordant only because the people have allowed the strings of their own instrument to slacken, and fail to make them harmonise with the music of truth which once originated in the sublime height of their nature.

A remarkable figure with vision and foresight; a dedicated spirit with deep love towards the mankind and God; bold, courageous, sincere, honest and fearless to preach his convictions; an earliest feminist in modern India and keen to see the emancipation of women from their bondage; a social reformer to the core; an exponent of the press freedom; he was hailed by the Swiss economist, Sismondi, for his views on morality and religion.

Symbolizing the spirit of new India; fighting against ignorance, superstition, social and cultural decadence in Eastern India; arguing for a deeper unity through the synthesis of monotheism and social reform; typifying the spirit of religious accommodation and cultural assimilation and standing for inner unity, he had been considered as one of the architects of modern India. A great scholar of comparative religions, a prophet of universalism, founder of Bengali prose and journalism, an ardent champion of liberty, he was, thus, one of the leaders in the evolution of modern India.

A great champion of freedom, a lover of humanity, Roy pleaded for religious and social reforms. Providing a rational basis for religion, he condemned all irrationalities found in Hinduism. He did his best for the revival of Hinduism. He had a broad vision and instead of confining himself to the religious problems of India, he synthesized various religions and civilizations to bring to an end chaos and confusions prevailing all over the world. He did his best to bring a harmony between materialism of the West and transcendentalism of the East.

A great modern Indian thinker, he stood for human emancipation. In a world beset with problems and torn by conflicts, he set a lofty example of cosmopolitan thinking and humanitarian endeavour. Whatever he did, whatever he felt, whatever he said, whatever he achieved — all these were directed to improve the human race. He recognized individualism, nationalism and internationalism and their respective claims. A cosmopolite, a rationalist, his outlook on human civilization was universal. He was, by pre-emption, a citizen of the world, an embodiment of the noblest form of human culture and civilization. He had a vision of a League of Nations, whose sole aim should be preservation of human values.

A great soul devoted and dedicated to the cause of the humanity, a towering personality untainted by selfishness, a pioneer of the world movement towards mutual understanding between the East and the West, he strongly believed the adage: "service to mankind is service to God".

Sophie Dobson Collat, the English biographer of Roy made a brilliant estimate of the life and contributions of Roy in the following:

> Ram Mohan stands in history as the living bridge over which India marched from her unmeasured past to her incalculable future. He was the arch which spanned the gulf that yawned between ancient caste and modern humanity, between superstition and science, between despotism and democracy, between immobile custom and a conservative progress, between... Polytheism and ... Theism. He was the mediator of the people harmonizing in his person, often, by means of his own solitary sufferings, the conflicting tendencies of immemorial tradition and of inevitable enlightenment...
>
> Roy embodied the new spirit which arose from the compulsory mixture of races, faiths and civilizations. He embodied its freedom of inquiry, its thirst for science, its large human sympathy, its pure and gifted ethics, along with its reverent but not uncritical regard for the past, and prudent disinclination towards revolt.
>
> He was a genuine outgrowth of the old Hindu society in a soil watered by new influences, and in an atmosphere charged with unwanted forcing power, but still a true scion of the old stock. He was no merely occidentalized oriental, no Hindu polished into the doubtful semblance of a European. He was just a spiritual Eurasian.
>
> If one followed the right line of his development one would find that he led the way from the orientalism of the past, not to, but through Western culture, towards a civilization which was neither western nor Eastern, but something vastly larger and nobler than both.
>
> Ram Mohan Roy, thus, presents a most instructive and inspiring study for the New India of which he was the type and pioneer. There can be little doubt that whatever future the destinies have in store for India, that future will be largely mapped by the life and work of Ram Mohan Roy. And not the future of India alone.

SIGNIFICANT DATES AND EVENTS IN THE LIFE OF RAJA RAM MOHAN ROY

1772	Born on 22 May at Radhanagar.
1809	Appointed Dewan under John Digby, Collector at Rangpur.
1815	Took up residence in Calcutta, Founded Atmiya Sabba. Published *Vedanta Grantha* in Bengali.
1816	Wrote *Abridgement of the Vedanta* or *Vedanta Sar*, published in Bengali, Hindustani and English. Translated *Kena* and *Isha Upanishads* in Bengali and English.
1817	Hindu College was established. Translated *Mandukya Upanishad* and *Katha Upanishad* in Bengali.
1818	Published his first tract on Sati.
1820	Published *The Precepts of Jesus*.
1821	Started *Sambad Kaumudi*.
1822	Started *Mirat-ul-Akhbar*. Started Anglo-Hindu School. Published *Brief Remarks on Ancient Female Rights*.

1823	Submitted a memorial to Supreme Court against Press Ordinance. *Mirat-ul-Akhbar* ceased publications. Letter to Amherst pleading for promotion of a more liberal and enlightened system of instruction.
1824	Elected member of Soviete Asiatique, Paris.
1826	Founded Vedanta College.
1828	Established Brahmo Samaj. Advocated Trial by Jury.
1830	Sailed for England in November.
1831	Arrived in England in April, met Jeremy Bentham in London, presented to King William IV, wrote to Talleyrand advocating abolition of passport system and the establishment of a supra-national organization.
1832	Vigorously supported the Reform Bill which was passed. Visited Paris and had audience with King Louis Philippe of France.
1833	Left London for Stapleton Hill near Bristol. Died on 27 September.

POINTS TO REMEMBER

- A towering personality, Raja Ram Mohan Roy inaugurated the modern age. A great reformer, a champion of social and intellectual emancipation.
- Born in 1772 in an orthodox family in West Bengal. In his childhood, he had a strong liking for Persian literature. Went to Persia when he was twelve-year-old.
- His study of Persian language changed his outlook. Went to Banaras to learn Sanskrit. Compared Hinduism with Islam. Everywhere man is trying to attain the One. Father of Indian Renaissance.
- He was logical and heterodox, while his father was a devout and orthodox. Bitter relationship between father and son. His belief in one God. He criticized idol worship and superstitions. Went to Tibet. Criticized the Lamas for their spiritual conduct. His life was in danger.
- He was saved by women. From Tibet, he returned to his home. He then left for Banaras. He left Banaras for Calcutta. Settled there as a financier to the officials of the East India Company. From Calcutta, he went to Murshidabad where he got a job. His emphasis was on comparative study of religions. He drew the attention to the achievement of monotheism.
- Women should inherit their parents' and husbands' property. He condemned the caste system. Established Brahmo Samaj in 1828. It gave rise to Renaissance. His mission cost his property.
- Sati — an outrageous social evil. Steps were taken by different rulers to suppress it. Roy wanted to abolish this evil with the help of scriptures.
- Sati was allowed by Angira, Harit, Vishnu and others, while it was opposed by Manu, Yajnavalkya and others. Burning women to death was against the scriptures.

- Roy was a strong supporter of women. To him, women are not inferior to men. They are as competent as men. They are inferior to men physically. He was strongly criticized by his critics.
- He succeeded in abolishing Sati. In this regard, he was opposed by Dharma Sabha and H.H. Wilson.
- Kulinism and polygamy were other social evils. Kulin Brahmins were considered to be the 'best' and 'highest' among all the castes. A girl marrying a Kulin Brahmin was considered very lucky.
- There was a wide gap in age between a Kulin Brahmin and his wife. Roy strongly opposed such marriages. He also condemned the existing caste structure in India. He encouraged inter-caste marriages.
- He favoured and preferred 'Saiva marriage' to 'Vaidik marriage'. He loved everything that was Indian. Right type of education. It should be national in character, on British model and science-oriented.
- To him, the purpose of politics and of religion is to establish a welfare society. He favoured science-oriented education. His stress on economic development and on self-governing India.
- To him, Indian culture is superior to Western culture. Natives were to be appointed as collectors and judicial officers. He was for all-round development of the country. He was an internationalist.
- There should be communal harmony. He opposed colonialism. Favoured internationalism. An international organization be set up to solve problems faced by different countries.
- A champion of liberty and freedom. Supported the struggle for freedom and democratic rights. Happy when Spanish colonies in South America were liberated by Spain. Encouraged the fight against the colonial masters. Supported the Reform Bill.
- Socio-economic conditions of the peasants were quite miserable. Criticized the existing economic settlement and the monopoly of the salt trade. Opposed administrative measures.
- He was never parochial; always modern in his approach. India was not matured to be free and independent. Praised Great Britain.
- Press freedom was opposed by the British Government. He was distressed to see the conditions in which press functioned.
- In 1821, Roy published a weekly called the *Sambad Kaumudi* and in 1822, a Persian paper, *Mirut-ul-Akhbar*.
- 1823 Ordinance — no publication without licence.
- During the Muslim rule, there was no discrimination between the Hindus and Muslims. But the British administration not only discriminated against the Indians but also harassed them.

- Roy was against the absolute freedom of press. He anticipated John Stuart Mill. Free Press never caused any revolution.
- He visited England in 1830 to achieve his goals. Publication of his first English work "An Abridgement of the Vedanta" made him extremely popular in England.
- The annual stipend of the Delhi Emperor was raised by three lakh rupees. Roy was introduced to House of Lords.
- A remarkable figure, a man of vision, a man with foresight, dedicated and devoted, a feminist, a reformer who fought against social evils and stood for assimilation of culture, an architect of modern India, a great scholar of comparative religions, an ardent champion of liberty, a lover of humanity, Roy exposed superstitions found in Hinduism. He revived it. A cosmopolite, his outlook on human civilization was universal.
- He had a vision of League of Nations.

4

Swami Dayanand Saraswati (1824–1883)

INTRODUCTION

A profound Vedic scholar, a radical social reformer, a powerful agent of change, a great champion of equality and justice, a great path-maker in modern India, Swami Dayananda Saraswati was a prophet of peace; a savior of mankind; the strength of the weak, exploited and marginalized; a friend of the orphan and a sympathizer of the widow. With him ushered in a new era, an era of renaissance. Influencing Indian nationalism to a considerable extent, he was a great emancipator of mankind, a great supporter of the people. A born fighter against injustice, ignorance and superstitions; an arch-rebel, who refused to yield to the authoritarian traditional dictates of his father, a Saivite (a great devotee of Lord Shiva), in the realm of religious conscience, he felt it below his dignity to dance to the tunes of orthodox Hindu leaders whom he hated from the core of his heart. His only mission in his life was to seek after the Truth in thought, speech and deed. He vehemently opposed, denounced and renounced the Untruth. He stood for the sanctity and supremacy of the individual. Greatly responsible for the great upsurge in the Hindu community and in the country, he was pure in his thought, deed and action, and led an unblemished life. A yogi, an ardent prophet of reconstruction and national organization, he surrendered himself at the feet of the God, knowing it pretty well that total surrender would give him Salvation by unchaining all kinds of bondages. His physical strength, mental prowess, his brillinance, his mastery in the fields of grammar, philosophy, religion, and Hindu literature made him immortal. He could be made comparable with most outstanding personalities like Sri Sri Shankaracharya, Sri Ramanuja, and Sri Sayanacharya. An ethical idealist, an ascetic, a puritan, he carved out a niche for himself in the hearts of millions of the people who were inspired and encouraged by his powerful arguments.

EARLY LIFE

Swami Dayanand, a Vedic scholar, a dialectician and a social reformer, was born at Morvi in Kathiawar (Gujarat) in a Samvedi Brahmin family in 1824. His father, Karsanji Lalji Tiwari, highly religious and orthodox, and his mother with a tender humanitarian outlook left a deep imprint on his life. They made him a true devotee of the existing religion. When he was only thirteen-year-old, he had a very strange but unique experience on the day of Sivaratri. He saw mice moving over the idol of Lord Siva. With a view to clarify his doubt about idol worship, he enquired about it from his father who told him that the idol symbolized Lord Siva but not the God Himself. This was a turning point in his life. He developed an urge to inquire into the Truth. Like the Buddha, he was terribly shaken by the phenomenon of death. Three ideas, which he had developed in him, shaped his personality and philosophy of religion: disrespect for idol worship; detachment from the world; and disbelief in ritual ceremonies.

At the age of twenty-one, he fled from his home in May 1846 as he was least interested in leading a family (married) life. He always considered it a bondage that suffocated and stifled one's life, degenerated and destroyed one's personality. Quest for Truth and Knowledge, search after Light and Immortality became his sole motive in his life. He wandered from place to place during 1845–1860 to achieve his goal. In 1860, he became a disciple of Swami Virajananda Saraswati (1778–1868) of Mathura and studied under his able guidance and supervision Panini and Patanjali.

Sitting at the lotus feet of his Guru, he learnt many things. He made a promise to his Guru that he would spread the message of the Veda to the mankind. It was his "Guru-Dakshina". His ardent love for his Guru, his continuous and ceaseless quest for the Truth made him a real Mahatma, a sage and a prophet.

TO RE-ESTABLISH THE VEDIC RELIGION

The message of Swami Dayanand was that the Vedic culture

1. was universal in its approach and outlook;
2. did not oppose any religion;
3. wanted to satisfy the spiritual urge of every human being;
4. catered to their spiritual beings;
5. was a way of life;
6. ensured to each and everyone material and spiritual goods so that they could lead a life of bliss and happiness; and
7. the Vedic civilization was ideal, pure and eternal.

The Swami promised that the Veda would be helpful in promoting world's good, in maintaining peace on earth and in bringing happiness to every home.

With the Veda a new era — era of the Golden Age, the age of which the poets have sung, the philosophers have dreamt and to which the prophets have pointed— would emerge.

To him, the Vedas were the ultimate source of all religions. All the religious texts of all the religions were their products. They were the storehouse of Supreme Knowledge. Once it is recognized, all the conflicting interpretations of religion could be resolved. The whole mankind should accept their importance and understand their spirit and essence. He felt very sad as the Vedas were misinterpreted. He condemned the false and distorted representation of ancient views of Indian life.

He made the Vedas the basis of humanism. He had a great conviction that their study and understanding would certainly resolve both national and international crises.

With a socio-religious mission in his life, he highlighted the spiritual aspect of the man, the importance of religion in the life of man. Urging that no one should accept religion blindly, he said that one should enquire into its truth, must find out how far it is rational; must not be guided by false interpretations of religion. To him, the life as explained in the Veda was the most comprehensive religion. During the Vedic period, observance and performance of religion was considered to be the highest duty. An individual would get maximum happiness if he strictly followed the religion.

To Swami Dayanand, religion consisted of justice, truth and benevolence. He was the first modern Indian to strongly condemn the Brahmin priests for their hypocrisy, for misguiding the society. Any prescription that went against the Veda was deception and fraud on Hinduism.

Dayanand said that religion revolved around God, Man and the Nature. Explaining them, he wrote a comprehensive and elaborate commentary on the Vedas. He criticized idol worship as God did not have any shape or image, or form. Relying on the Yajur Veda, he proved that idol worship was anti-Vedic. God should be contemplated as the Creator and Sustainer of everything, the source of every object both living and non-living; as the Lord, the Master, the eternal and all-pervading. It is this knowledge that gives one true happiness and prayer to him promotes one's virtues like simplicity, humility, brevity and divinity.

As far as idol worship was concerned, he strongly argued that God could not be worshipped either through His creations, i.e. Earth, Water, Fire, Air and other things, or as an idol. Idol-worshippers wandered from temple to temple and place to place in an illusory expectation (to find God) and suffered afflictions by losing their religion, their worldly prosperity, their love of benevolence, besides falling victim to the mischief of thieves and cheats.

Some allege that the Vedas stand for polytheism, for worshipping of the elements, etc. To Dayanand, all these charges were false and unjust. No doubt, words (or elements) like Surya, Agni, Varuna, Indra, Mitra were found in the Vedas. He said all these Vedic terms must be interpreted in their derivative sense.

In his book *Satyartha Prakash*, he gave the derivating meanings of various terms mentioned above. He argued that since these terms signified the one Almighty God, the questions of polytheism did not arise. The Rig Veda categorically said God was one although the wise called it by many names. The learned and the wise described one existing God in many forms of expressions. The Yajur Veda distinguishes God from the elements of nature. With his arguments, he reinstated and re-established the monotheism of the Vedic religion in place of distorted Hindu belief in the multiplicity of Gods and Goddesses.

The word 'Devata' is very often misinterpreted as God. He explained its true meaning. Derived from the word 'div' or 'deva' which means 'to shine' or a 'bright thing', it was applied to the Sun, the Moon, and other forces of nature. Swami Dayanand brought a significant change by providing that the Vedic religion was not polytheism and the Vedas taught pure and perfect monotheism. Man got maximum happiness when he believed God and his existence.

MAN AS A SPIRITUAL BEING

It is believed that man is created after the image of God. But Dayanand did not believe it. To him, the statement 'I am God' is found not in the Vedas but in the Brahmanas. Man is never God but he lives in God. Like God and matter, human soul is eternal and permanent. Rejecting Darwin's theory of evolution as absurd, he argued that man never evolved from ape or monkey and the latter could not produce human beings.

He believed that human life should be properly regulated and disciplined. In his book *Panch Maha Yajna Vidhi*, he said that this could be possible if he performed five duties: promising the Lord not to commit any harm to others; burning the odoriferous substances, sewing, giving food and paying respect to elders, teachers and useful members of the society; parting with a part of the meal for the needy to bring rich near the poor; and lastly welcoming the guests.

Besides these duties, one has to perform and observe certain *samskaras* at different stages of life in order to discipline his conduct. Four ashramas as mentioned in the Vedas were supported by Dayanand. These were: Brahmacharya, Grihastha, Vanaprastha and Sanyasa. In the first stage, one takes recourse to learning and keeps himself away from all the sensuous objects which normally deprave and pollute him. All these shape one's personality. It is the preparatory stage which teaches him how to lead a happy and peaceful life. He observes celibacy in this stgage. When one becomes twenty-five-year-old, he enters into his second stage, i.e. the 'Grihastya'. He gets married, begets children, fulfils his worldly commitments with all sincerity and seriousness. He is guided by the values which he learnt and inherited from his teachers in his first stage. At the age of 50, he enters into the third stage, i.e. Vanaprastha. He gives up all his worldly objects and goes to the forests to lead an isolated life as it helps him in meditating on God. He devotes all his time to God only. He survives only on fruits and water. The last stage, i.e. the Sanyasa teaches one to think and work for the good of others regardless of all considerations. Through the Varnashrama dharma one would attain supreme happiness in his life. He repudiated all sorts of meaningless ceremonies observed or performed in the name of Hinduism. To him, perfection of life in this world was more important than attaining salvation or moksha after death.

MATTER AND WORLDLY LIFE

To Dayanand, like God and man, matter is also real. Though a saint or sanyasin, he never opposed the enjoyment of worldly life. He vehemently condemned all kinds of hypocrisy found in Hinduism. The Brahmins and priests gave importance to the 'other world' where man goes after his death. By doing so they presented a false picture of Hinduism and did a great blunder to the Hindu society. He observed that Vedas nowhere denounced the worldly life. Rather they asserted its importance. Man is a social animal as he interacts with other members. He is supposed to lead a good, virtuous and qualitative hie. He should, therefore, cultivate virtues like love, kindness, sympathy and sacrifice, and be helpful and benevolent.

RELIGION: STRENGTH AND WEAKNESS

Like Raja Ram Mohan Roy, Dayanand exposed the flaws and weaknesses of every religion. Emphasizing the truth, he discovered the common element in all religions of the world. Criticizing falsehood, dogma and artificiality in the observance of religion and led by humanitarian considerations, he fervently prayed God to inspire the people to evolve a great religion on the earth. His aim was to elevate the human race and encourage all to separate truth from falsehood. He was not against any religion.

Had he been biased he would have championed any one of the religions prevailing in India. But he did not do this. On the contrary, he did not approve of what was objectionable and false in the institutions of India, or any other country, nor did he reject what was good and in harmony with the dictates of true religion, nor had he any desire to do so, since a contrary conduct was wholly unworthy of man.

A lover of peace and harmony, a tolerant of all religions and least dogmatic, he recognized the element of good in all religions and exposed their errors fearlessly. In *Satyartha Prakash*, he wrote that whatever he wrote in favour of true religion and against false religions was written to enlighten all. He placed before the public his opinion on four great religions (Jainism, Buddhism, Christianity and Islam) according to his understanding and knowledge after a thorough study of books on which they were based.

To Dayanand, religion always aimed at improving the conditions of man and approving what was good and beneficial to him. Men of different religions should accept the universal truth and reject all those on which they differed. By doing so, they could promote the universal brotherhood. He established contact with leaders of other religions and strived to evolve a common approach. But he failed. He made an appeal to God to sow in the minds of the people the seed of pure religion, so that false religions would disappear and wise men give up their hostilities and increase happiness.

Strongly criticizing Hinduism in existing form; forcefully arguing that the sects of Hinduism like Vaishnavism, Saivism, Sakatas, etc. challenged the Vedic monotheism; expressing unhappiness with Brahma Samaj, Prarthana Samaj and other sects; firmly believing that with sectarianism, the Hinduism degenerated and became corrupt and pervert as these sects created discord, introduced meaningless rituals and ceremonies just to cater to the needs of vested interests of the Brahmins and priests. Dayanand argued that the most rational scheme of life as designed in the Veda was reduced to a few dogmas and superstitions. Doing best to remove ignorance from the minds of the Hindus, he considered the construction of temples as wastage of money; poor must be served but the dead matter should not be worshipped.

Dayanand's aim was to revive the Hinduism, which consisted of certain universal and eternal doctrines belonging to all countries and all men. It could promote unity among different people of different faiths. He argued that the Vedas constituted the foundation of all religions. They were not the books of any particular sect or people but the sacred scriptures of the entire human race.

A true representative of the ancient human sages, his mission was universal. Striving to emancipate the Hindus from degradation and ignorance, he never considered that the river Ganges could be a source of salvation. An embodiment of truth, tolerance, courage and conviction, he tolerated all criticisms levelled against him. He bravely fought against the dogmas single-handedly and that is why he is considered to be the first and greatest reformer of the Hinduism.

SOCIAL RECONSTRUCTION

Dayanand strongly believed that revival of Vedic culture and civilization would help in reconstruction of the society on the basis of humanism. Therefore, he prescribed the following principles to make the world a happier one: a caste system based on action, Varnashram Dharma to be strictly followed by every one, right education and effective governing machinery of the society. The existing caste system, hereditary in nature, was, to him, one of the ugliest features found in the Hindu society and he attributed this to the degradation and the degeneration of the Hindus and the Hindu society. Such a society was never advocated by the Vedas. The Vedic classification of human society into four castes was totally different from the present caste structure. The proliferation of castes with their off-shoots has posed a serious threat to the present society as it is mainly responsible for social disorder leading to clash and conflict, distrust and suspicion, hatred and animosity.

Deadly opposed to the caste system based on birth, he suggested that it should rest on merit, personal qualification, division of labour and mutual cooperation. The Vedic division of the society made the Aryan society stable, strong, united, progressive, and advanced. It aimed at the distribution of duties and rights in order to effect the adjustment between the individuals and the society.

Dayanand said that all men were equal in the eyes of Lord and it was ridiculous to say that some one belonged to a high caste or a low caste. A lover of mankind, he treated all equally irrespective of their castes and religions.

UNTOUCHABILITY

Strongly criticizing untouchability, Dayanand argued that the *Sudras* had every right to mix freely with others, participate in all socio-religious and cultural functions, and read the sacred texts like the Vedas. In support of his views against untouchability, he quoted references from the Yajur Veda and the Atharva Veda. The Hindu society could not prosper unless untouchability was thoroughly given up. Since the Vedic times down the advent of the Muhammadan invasion, there was no such class of people as *bhangis* for removing the night soil. He forcefully argued in favour of the Sudras for their rightful place in the society. Inspired by Dayanand, his disciple Swami Shradhanand and others organized the 'Dalitoddhar' (uplift of the depressed classes) and Achut-Shuddhi (reform of the untouchables) movements. Dayanand and his disciples inspired Gandhi to launch the Harijan movement.

STATUS OF WOMEN

Swami Dayanand was very much against the discriminatory treatment of woman in Hindu society. Condemning the evils like *purda*, child marriage and illiteracy among women, he said that they were mainly responsible for women's plight and sufferings. Expressing anguish over their secondary status in the society, he wanted to restore their rightful place and position of which they were deprived. Opposing the child marriage, he fixed the marriage age of girls at sixteen. The efforts of Swamiji and other social reformers later on resulted in the enactment of the Sharada Act which fixed the marriage age of boys and girls.

Dayanand was in favour of inter-caste marriage. He was fully convinced that society could not prosper without the development of women folk who constituted fifty percent of the population. They could no more be ignored and neglected as the society had already paid a heavy price for it.

IDEAL GOVERNMENT

In *Satyartha Prakash*, Swami Dayanand said that an ideal government could be possible if people elected most learned men as members of the educational assembly, most devout men as members of the religious assembly, and men of most praiseworthy character as members of the legislative assembly and let the great (man) among them, virtuous, highly accomplished, and who possessed most excellent qualities be made the Head or President of the political assembly.

Keen to improve the conditions of mankind, he said that the then Government was a constituent of fools and foreigners. Therefore, they failed to deliver the goods.

SWARAJ

Dayanand firmly believed that unless India was politically awakened, morally elevated and socially upgraded, the cry of Swaraj would not have much impact upon the freedom struggle. Reminding the Indians of their ancient past, glory, heritage, culture and values, he asked them to love their country but not to hate the enemies and foreigners.

ARYA SAMAJ

Dayanand did his best to revive the ancient Indian religious and cultural values. Though he could not succeed fully, he kept the movement alive by founding the Arya Samaj on 7 April 1875. Through it he wanted to bring the whole mankind under one umbrella. He prayed God to bless India so that it could have peace and love.

The Arya Samaj was set up to propagate lofty ideals of the Vedas, introduce radical reforms in society and make efforts to promote the good of the mankind. Its leaders all along tried to strictly follow the footprints of Swami Dayanand. It would be absolutely wrong to consider it as the communalistic church. From the cultural point of view, it was as good as the Hinduism. They differed from one another only in their attitude. Dayanand's aim was to purify the Hinduism, purge it of foreign and diseased matter and make it a cosmopolitan religion. If the existing Hinduism could be made identical with original Vedism, it would be the finest and fittest religion for the whole world, and all the nations would heartily accept it.

The Arya Samaj was accused and is still accused of being an anti-Islamic and anti-Christian movement because of its Vedic affiliation. But it should be remembered that whatever the Vedas have said are of universal application. There is no reference to any community or religion. Therefore, whatever charges are levelled against the Arya Samaj are illogical and irrational. The Vedic Dharma is a creed, a complete system of thought, a perfect and rational code for the guidance of the humanity in every sphere of human activity, a polity as well as a science of living, and a definite point of view.

But, unfortunately, the Arya Samaj is misunderstood and its policy misinterpreted. Its creed is universal, its teachings are for the mankind and in no sense it is a Hindu movement. Swami Dayanand had tremendous faith in the Vedic religion which is distinguished from other religions in one most important point, viz., that it is a system of training rather than a creed or faith as other religions are.

Aimed at purging the society of evils such as illiteracy, child marriage, impurity, polygamy, the Samaj set up quite a large number of schools and colleges throughout the length and breadth of the country to spread right education. Certainly, it was a splendid job done to the Hindu community propagating the spirit of nationalism among the Indians by creating a feeling of oneness in them and supporting the Truth and denouncing everything that is False, it tried to unite all the people irrespective of their caste, creed, race, sex or community.

AN ESTIMATE

Dayanand, one of the greatest preachers of India, wanted to see that every man remained happy, good and noble. A social reformer, a revivalist of brahmacharya (celibacy), an educationist, a patriot, he was the saviour of mankind, a prophet of peace, love and truth and an eminent teacher of the humanity.

Science and technology have enslaved the man; reduced him to a machine and in due course of time he has lost his individuality. His life has become more comfortable. But he has no peace of mind. He lives in a society characterized by hatred, animosity, ill-feeling, clash, competition, confrontation and perversion. Dayanand wanted to give him a respite, a relief. He was born with a mission to serve the mankind. And in doing so, he sacrificed everything including his life. It was for speaking the Truth, like Socrates, he was poisoned to death. He rebuked his disciple, the king of Jodhpur for his association with a prostitute. The latter could not digest it as he felt terribly offended. Overtaken by anger and vengeance, he took revenge by poisoning the Swami to death through his cook on 30 October 1883. In the words of Tarachand:

> In Rishi Dayanand died the prophet of peace, the saviour of mankind; the very heart of the land that is the centre of human hopes; the advocate of rightful religion, the supporter of the weak, the helper of the cow, the friend of the orphan and the sympathiser of the widow.

Dayanand passionately loved truth and condemned falsehood; dedicated his life to the service of mankind and wanted to save all men, irrespective of religion and nationality, creed and colour, sex and race. An embodiment of supreme virtues, an incarnation of mercy and love, he was very rightly compared with the Jesus and the Buddha. He was one of the greatest benefactors of humanity: the true Redeemer and Deliverer, the Regenerator of mankind.

POINTS TO REMEMBER

- Dayanand was born in 1824 at Morvi in an orthodox family. He was influenced by his parents. His three ideas — no idol worship, detachment from the world and disbelief in ritual ceremonies.
- In 1845, he left his home to become a sanyasi. Marriage, to him, was a bondage. His sole motive was the quest for truth and knowledge, search after light and immortality. He became a disciple of Virajananda Saraswati of Mathura. His motive was to re-establish the Vedic religion.
- Veda is the source of all religions; the storehouse of supreme knowledge; it could resolve any crisis. His emphasis on spiritual aspect of human life and on religion. Happiness lies in being religious and spiritual. Condemned those Brahmins who were hypocrites. Nothing should go against Veda. Against idol worship. God does not have any shape. Idol worship was anti-Vedic. God—the Creator, the Sustainer and the Destroyer of everything. He is the Lord, the Master, the Eternal. He was against polytheism and the worship of the elements.
- He re-established the monotheism of the Vedic religion. To him, man is a spiritual being. Man is not created after the image of God. Man is never God but he lives in God.
- Criticized Darwin's Theory of Evolution. Five-fold duties. Observing certain samskaras at different stages of life, supported the Varnashrama Dharma.
- Attainment of salvation is less important than perfection of life in this world. He repudiated all ceremonies as meaningless. He didn't believe in the 'other world'. He was not opposed to material pleasure.
- He was in favour of a 'great religion'. To him, the human race was to be elevated. Religion, to him, to improve the human race.
- He was against the sects like Vaishnavism, Saivism, Saktas, etc. as they challenged monotheism. Unhappy with Brahma Samaj. Sects spoiled the sanctity of religion. Hinduism, like any other religion, was full of superstitions. Sectarianism was a threat to Hinduism. Construction of temples was a wastage of money. Better to serve the poor than to worship the dead matter.
- He wanted to revive Hinduism. Veda: the most sacred scripture of the entire human race. Strived to emancipate the Hindus from degradation. Principles for better world: caste system based on action, right education, Varnashrama Dharma to be strictly followed by every one; effective governing machinery of the society
- Present division of the society is highly unethical as it has raised it. All men are equal in the eyes of the God. He was against untouchability. Sudras are as good as others. They must be allowed to participate in all socio-cultural functions.

- He was for the upliftment of the *Dalits*. He fought for women, for their status and position. He was against child marriage and in favour of inter-caste marriage.
- Ideal government could be possible when good people were elected. Let the people with virtues rule. There should be socio-economic and political emancipation of the people.
- He established the Arya Samaj in 1875. Its objectives were ideal, to propagate lofty ideals of the Vedas. The Arya Samaj was criticized as anti-Christian and anti-Islamic. Veda — it does not refer to any particular religion.
- The Samaj set up schools and colleges to propagate right education. It tried to unite all the people.
- A reformer, a preacher, a noble soul dedicated and devoted to the cause of mankind, he did his best to reform the Indian society in the light of the teachings of the Vedas. Supported the Truth.

5

Swami Vivekananda (1863–1902)

INTRODUCTION

Swami Vivekananda, a brilliant philosopher, a subtle metaphysician, an ardent patriot, a zealous reformer, a realized and illumined soul, a seer, an outstanding personality and a saint of high order gifted with supreme knowledge, did not, as has been stated, seem to belong to this world. It is said that he belonged to the "Satya Loka" where only seven saints of high order live and they are always in meditation. Once a portion of this Satya Loka melted and soon there emerged a small boy with a radiant glow and sweet smile on his face. He approached one of the saints and asked him to follow him. That boy, it is said, was Sri Ramakrishna Paramahamsa, the Master, an "avatar" of God. And that saint was Swami Vivekananda. He was born with a mission, i.e. to make the people spiritually oriented. Once Paramahamsa said about this young disciple:

> He is not a pond, he is a reservoir. He is not a pitcher or a jug, he is a veritable barrel. He is not a minnow or sardine, he is a huge red-eyed carp. He is not an ordinary sixteen-petalled lotus, he is a glorious lotus with a thousand petals.

On another occasion, the Master also said:

> He is not a twig floating in a river — a twig that sinks even if a bird alights upon it. Rather he is a great tree-trunk carrying men, beasts and merchandise upon its chest.

Gifted with strength, vigour and endurance, Swami Vivekananda possessed a strong, powerful and formidable personality. With large, shinning and penetrating eyes, a broad forehead, he was gifted with tremendous self-confidence. He had an intense desire to renounce everything in this world as he was a seeker after the

Truth; to roam like a wandering unknown pilgrim; take shelter under a tree and meditate alone in a lonely cave in the Himalayas. In 1895, he said:

> I long, Oh, I long for my rags, my shaven head, my sleep under the trees, and my food from begging.

A prophet of modern India, he did his best to awake the nation from its deep slumber and mental stupor so that it could rise and stand on its feet and march freely. Symbolizing courage and fearlessness, he wanted the people to be divine-oriented, to march on the spiritual path to realize God, which is the only goal in one's life. He told them not to forget the glory of human nature!

Influenced by the scientific as well as political thought of Europe, particularly ideas like democracy and liberalism and impressed by the writings of J.S. Mill, J.J. Rousseau, Montesquieu, Voltaire, Immanuel Kant, W.G.F. Hegel and others, he had correspondence with Herbert Spencer, though he criticized some of his ideas. Not only he had a great fancy in the Western thought but also a keen interest in Hindu scriptures.

His constant and continuous studies on philosophies and scriptures and his tremendous faith in reason made him an agnostic and a sceptic. But a dramatic change took place in his life when he came in contact with his Master Sri Ramakrishna Paramahamsa in November 1881. It was a turning point in his life. His staunch faith in logic slowly and gradually gave way to the importance of self-realization in one's life. He was constantly guided and goaded by his Master while he was moving step by step into his spiritual realm. Being in 'Samadhi' for hours together and getting lost in one's own self and enjoying the taste of ecstasy—all these brought a tremendous spiritual transformation in his life. He was transformed from 'Naren' to 'Vivekananda', from 'ordinary' to 'extraordinary'.

EARLY LIFE

Born on 12 January 1863 in an aristocratic Kshatriya family of Calcutta, Vivekananda's real name was Narendranath Dutta, popularly known as Naren. His father Vishwanath Dutta, his grandfather Durgacharan Dutta and his great grandfather Rommohan Dutta were all lawyers. Like him, his grandfather had also renounced the world quite at an early age of his life.

His father, Viswanath Dutta, was the son of a Sanyasin as well as the father of a Sanyasin. A Sanyasin in spirit and outlook, a man of learning, a great scholar in his time, particularly in the field of law, he was distinguished from others by his lifestyle as well as his hospitality. Immensely proud of his father, Vivekananda was terribly shocked at his father's sudden and unexpected demise as it was a great loss to him and his family. His mother, Bhubaneswari, was gifted with uncommon intellect and extraordinary memory power. He also claimed that he owed his intellectual life to his mother.

After a course of Vernacular instruction, partly at school and partly at home, Naren joined the Metropolitan Institute, Calcutta, at the tender age of seven. In 1879, he passed his entrance examination. He was not so serious in his studies. But with a tremendous memory power, he always stood first or secured very good marks in all examinations that he appeared. Not only he was excellent in his studies but also excelled in everything including music, art and games. He endeared himself to one and all. He took great fancy in cricket, rowing, fencing and acting in dramas.

His father had a tremendous influence on him. His interaction and conversation with him opened a new chapter in his intellectual life. It developed his logic and broadened his outlook.

In 1879, Naren joined the General Assembly's Institute, one of the oldest colleges in Bengal. He graduated in 1884. In 1886, he could have secured a degree in Law. But he was destined to be something else. He renounced the world and became a monk.

During his college days, he came in close contact with Sri Ramakrishna Paramahamsa and spent most of his time with him. Endowed with both worldly and unworldly qualities, he excelled both in science and music. Most of his friends were materialists in their approach and outlook, but he was least influenced by them. This showed his innate strength of his character. Though born and brought up in a rich family and was surrounded by purely worldly-minded people, neither matter nor the environment could attract him to worldly life or divert his attention from the spiritual path. It is significant to note that before entering into the portals of the spiritual world, he practised rigorously two spiritual courses, namely, asceticism and Brahmacharya (celibacy). He controlled his diet and sleep. He often slept on bare-ground. He did not want to marry as this would have certainly hampered his spiritual life. However, he yielded to the demands of his parents and agreed to lead a married life.

But he had come to this world with a different purpose. Something unexpected happened in his life that changed his course of history. After the sudden death of his father, he gave up the idea of marriage. No doubt, his father's demise shocked his family members as they became paupers. However, at the same time, it was a blessing in disguise for him. He was supposed to give up everything, renounce this material world and move on the spiritual path to attain salvation. He was not supposed to follow a semi-worldly and semi-patriotic or semi-religious life. His goal in his life was not family, money, prestige, position, status. He was not supposed to lead a life of patriotic spirit or religious fervour. Everything was to go before the call of the Divine?

Aware of his power and potentialities, Naren wanted to join politics as it would be a gateway to all worldly pleasures and achievements including power, position and status. At that time the young people were under the influence of Gandhi, B.G. Tilak, W.C. Banarjee, Keshab Chandra Sen and others to whom they adored. The young Naren was attracted by them and their position in public life. But after coming in close contact with Sri Ramakrishna Paramahamsa, he gave up, as said above, all his worldly desires. He was attracted more and more towards the spiritual life, and to achieve his goal he had to give up everything.

After his father's death, Naren frantically searched after a job. Starving and barefooted, braving the scorching sun and often accompanied by one or two friends he moved from pillar to post. Fortune did not favour him. Disappointed and frustrated, he came to realize that selfless love, sympathy and help were rare commodities in this world. Poor, weak and destitute were born to suffer. No one would come to their rescue by giving them solace and consolation.

He did his best to improve the financial position of his family. Eager to renounce the world and become a monk, he was at the same time, determined to stand by his family until some arrangements were made for its maintenance. After serving as a school teacher and working for sometime in an attorney's office, he gave up everything and renounced the world when his family prospects improved.

THE GODWARD QUEST

Naren searched after three quests: the Truth, the Beauty and the Bliss, and this ultimately led him to the final quest, the quest for the Infinite. The first led him to the "confines of the Infinite, the second to sublime ethical heights, and the last to renounce everything". Each of these quests suggests in a way the quest for the Infinite. The knowledge that one acquires and the perception that he develops through the senses are not real and eternal as they are illusory and transitory. The quest for the Truth prepares the mind to have that perception and knowledge which is independent both of the senses and of the mind. Every beauty born of matter is contemptible. Therefore, the quest for the Beauty proves this and longs for that higher beauty of the spirit. This can be possible only when the mind is pure and free from all the vices. A vicious and pervert mind can never enjoy real beauty; it enjoys that which is ephemeral. It is a known fact that both good and evil are the two sides of the same coin. The quest for the Bliss helps one to find a heaven where he could live in a state of perfect happiness, without having any attachment to anyone. The quest of the Truth helped the scientists and philosophers like Huxley and Spencer to reach the Infinite; of the Beautiful made Shelley and Wordsworth to reach the same destination and of the God-led reformers like Buddha to an appreciation of the Infinite. In case of Naren, his triple quest of the Truth, the Beautiful and the Bliss helped him in achieving his goal. He first met his Master Sri Ramakrishna Paramahamsa in 1880 and in 1886, when he was barely twenty-three years old in age, he attained the Nirvikalpa Samadhi.

Sri Ramakrishna referred to two classes of persons: the Mukta or the liberated and the Nitya Siddha or ever-free. To him, Naren belonged to the latter category who never wanted liberation because they were never caught in the net of Maya and who lived in the world to serve others by teaching them the Truth.

REALIZATION

The career of Swami Vivekananda stretched over three distinct phases: first, his first meet with his Master in November 1880 and later with Mahasamadhi in August 1886; second, establishment of monastery covering a period of full seven years to the meet of the Parliament of Religions at Chicago; and third, his involvement in various social activities from 1893 to 1902. The first was a period of inspiration, the second of experience and the third and last of work —national and international.

The first-three meetings of Vivekananda with his Master did not have any significance. But, for his Master, the very first meeting with him at Dakshineswar was "a lightning flash of memory and recognition". "My boy, my boy, at last you have come. Why did you not come early?" These were the words that greeted Naren when he finished his song. As his Master's behaviour was quite strange, he felt embarrassed and not impressed when he was taken alone into a private room and fed by the Master with love, care and tenderness. The latter told him, "You are the ancient sage Nara — the incarnation of Narayan — born to remove the misery of mankind."

In his second meeting with his Master, something extraordinary happened to Naren. The Master asked him: "My boy, do you see a light, a Jyoti, when you close your eyes at bed time?" Agreeing with him, he narrated his daily experience. He was highly impressed with his Master's question, since he had never revealed his experience to anyone. He did not also consider it important as he thought that every one might have the same or similar experience. Now for the first time he learnt that it was a rare and peculiar phenomenon and wondered how the Master could know about it. He was very much convinced that the latter was not a lunatic, but possessed wonderful insight into men and things.

While he was lost in his own thought, the Master came to him, muttered something and touched him. It produced a strange feeling in him. He felt as if the whole universe including himself and all the persons and things in the room were whirling and whirling as if being shattered to pieces and then merging he did not know where. He was scared and cried out "what are you doing to me? I have parents at home". The Master laughed and said "All right, no more of it now" and removed his hand from his (Naren's) chest. Immediately Naren came to his normal senses and saw everything just as it was before. This little incident was the turning point in his career.

When he visited his Master on another occasion, the latter in a trance touched his body and immediately he lost all his bodily consciousness. While he was in this condition, the Master asked him several questions about his antecedents and whereabouts, his mission in this world and the duration of his mortal life.

Naren was happy because his Master had seen God, known Him, felt Him and could prove His existence. He was convinced about his spiritual powers. But, at the same time, he did not sacrifice his reason at the altar of faith; did not surrender his intellect to anyone, however exalted he might be, because he felt that the surrender of intellect meant the surrender of honour or the surrender of personality. In other words, he never blindly believed his Master. He won the heart of his Master who appreciated him for his bold, courageous and independent thinking.

His Master always told him, "Reason is weak; Faith is omnipotent." He took years before he could understand its spirit and meaning. Influenced by Bhrahmo Samaj, he did not like image-worship. It was because of his English education he lost his faith in God and demigods of Hindu mythology. Shocks, sorrows, starvation and sufferings forced him to take refuge in a Guru who had tremendous faith in image-worship and considered Ram and Krishna to be the highest incarnations of God.

How marvellous and splendid was the spiritual insight of the Master? At the very first sight of Naren, he knew that his man had come. Naren, an evolved soul but sceptical, was under the spell of western rationalism.

One evening when Naren was meditating in the garden house of Cassipore, he suddenly felt a dazzling light at the back of his head. It was not a light as one understands in the ordinary sense of the term, but the light of Knowledge and Eternal Bliss. He lost his bodily consciousness and his individuality. All his bodily functions stopped. He entered into the Nirvikalpa Samadhi. Words would be insufficient to describe such a thrilling experience. It was a moment of bliss, happiness and ecstasy. But, interestingly, he could not understand his new experience. He was taken aback. His friends, who were also meditating along with him, knew nothing about his experience. But they woke up from their stage when Naren cried "Oh Gopal Da where is my body? Where is my body?" They could assess the situation. Apprehensive and shocked, they shook his body furiously and ran to the Master, who was in the upstairs, to describe him the situation. He quietly asked them not to be anxious.

On becoming normal, he looked extremely happy and an inexpressible joy beamed on his face. He silently prostrated at the feet of his Master who blessed him and said: "Mother Kali was kind enough to shower Her grace and sympathy upon him. He could feel within himself the Supreme, the Divine, the highest Bliss. He would not have such kind of experience in future. Within less than six years since his first visit to his Master, he could reach his destination and accomplished his mission for which he was born". He was, then, only twenty-three-year-old. He was free to do Mother's work.

THE WANDERING MONK

Following the demise (Mahasamadhi) of his Master in 1866, Vivekananda went on a pilgrimage and visited many holy places. However, he stayed in the Belur Math for some time to serve the devotees. But he was destined to move in another direction and it was so powerful that he could not avoid. He developed a strong urge to lead the life of an itinerant monk. He thought that there must be something behind this desire. It might be the wish of God and of his Master that he should enlighten himself by coming in contact with the saints and seers living in different parts of the country. Besides, was it not necessary to say goodbye to even this last and golden tie and attachment? If every bond was to be dissolved, why not also dissolve this golden thread of monastery? Even this bond was also unreal. Thinking this, the Swami decided to leave Calcutta and wander about, visit holy places and practise austerities. Before leaving the monastery, he visited the Holy Mother (Kali) and sought Her blessings. She asked him to see his mother and seek her blessings. He replied, "Mother, you alone are my mother".

His desire was to go back to nature and practise the severest forms of austerities sitting on the lap of the Himalayas, and gain the highest knowledge. At Almora, Srinagar and Hrishikesha, he meditated for hours together, days together on the eternal truths. It had an adverse effect on his health. He suffered from a very malignant type of fever. And it was thought, he would die soon. Just at the critical moment, he was saved by a saint.

When he was struggling for life and remained apparently half-dead and unconscious, he had a vision which convinced him that instead of meditating upon God, he should serve the mankind as it was his mission in his life. He came out of the caves and mountains, reached the plains and worked for and amongst the people, moving from place to place to make himself familiar with the Hindu customs, culture, traditions and scriptures. He came in contact with many people and solved their spiritual problems. He spread the message of his Master. During the years of travel, he had a unique opportunity for study. He read a lot, came to know much about different sects of Hinduism. He saw poverty, degradation and misery. But he also saw that the heart of India was sound; that India had not lost her spiritual instinct; that even though the society was full of superstitions and blind beliefs as practised by the uneducated and the illiterate masses and notwithstanding the fact that most of the educated Indians were sceptic, it still retained spiritualism.

He visited the West and had his exposure to its culture, tradition and scientific outlook. He admired them. Their dynamism, social awareness, work culture, spirit of adventurism, concern for practical values — all these tremendously influenced him. But during his second journey in 1899, he was very much disillusioned with some of the Western values. Before he left for the West in 1899, he again had a whirlwind tour in India, spreading in its every nook and corner the message of resurgent Indian spirituality. The message helped a lot in restoring the self-confidence of the intelligentsia and stimulated them to study Indian philosophy and religion. In 1897, he founded the Ramakrishna Mission at Belur neat Calcutta. He had his last breath on 4 July 1902.

THE PARLIAMENT OF RELIGIONS

While he was moving from place to place as wandering monk, it was perhaps at Porbandar, he came to know that a Parliament of Religions would be held at Chicago in the US in 1893. He wanted to attend it as the representative of Hinduism. At the same time, he wanted that his Master should ask him to attend the Conference. Otherwise, he would not like to attend the same. His desire was fulfilled when his Master appeared before him in his dream, walked from the seashore, right up to and into the waters of the sea and asked the Swami to follow Him. He was convinced that his Master was guiding him with his invisible hands. He left the country on 31 May 1893.

The Swami reached Chicago in July 1893 and when he reached at the Information Bureau of the Parliament of Religions and said that he would represent Hinduism, he was asked to produce his credentials. But he could not as he did not feel their necessity. He was also not aware of such formality. He was disappointed not because the Parliament was everything, not that he could not start his work in some other way, but representation and success at the session of the Parliament might have served his purpose. Besides, he was running shortage of funds and left with no other means to live in a new country. He could not live on begging as it was prohibited. His difficulties were compounded when he came to know that the Parliament was postponed to September 1893. In such a situation, he had to ask money from India. Soon all his difficulties came to an end as his immediate requirements were fulfilled. His fooding and accommodation problems were solved at least up to the end of the session of Parliament and he was admitted to that session as a representative of Hinduism. Since Boston was both a cheaper and more learned city than Chicago, he stayed there for some time.

While travelling to Boston he met an old lady, who invited him to stay with her as he did not know where to stay in Boston. He readily accepted it and felt it to be a God-send. Here he met Dr. Wright of the Harvard University and Dr. Barrows. It was through their help the technical difficulty was solved and he was allowed to attend the Parliament.

The Parliament of Religions, like the League of Nations or the United Nations, was a grand conception. Men of knowledge and wisdom belonging to different faiths should meet in a friendly atmosphere to discuss on what was best and permanent in every faith. It was an achievement, novel and unique in the history of the world. On such occasions, the essentials of religions are discovered, fanaticism gives way to a spirit of broad-mindedness and meanness to friendliness. Superstitions and blind beliefs are exposed and discarded. Contradictions were resolved. All aggressive spirit is replaced by mutual recognition and esteem. The whole atmosphere becomes vibrant as it produces catholicity, toleration, and mutual appreciation. But, unfortunately, the Parliament failed to produce any substantial results for the very simple reason that no such results were intended to be accomplished as the delegates were not really serious. However, there emerged an idea of a universal religion, a glorious contribution of the Parliament to the sum-total of the religious aspirations of the mankind. Leaders of different religions are expected to create good-will and promote harmony among contending sects and faiths and this they can do by frankly recognizing their diversities. By doing so, they would be blessing the mankind. It was not sure whether such an ideal could be realized through the Parliament of Religions. But it was with this spirit the Swami valued the work of the Parliament of Religions. To him, a Christian was not to become a Hindu or Buddhist, nor a Hindu or a Buddhist should become a Christian. But each must assimilate the spirit of the others and yet retain or preserve his individuality and grow.

In the Parliament, Mazoomdar and Chakravarty spoke and then spoke the Swami. Since he never addressed the public before, he became nervous. His tongue nearly dried up. He prayed Goddess Saraswati and made a short speech. He addressed the Assembly as, 'sisters and brothers of America'. A deafening applause of two minutes followed and then he proceeded. When his speech was over, he felt exhausted with emotion. He spoke on religious toleration and its enemy, religious fanaticism. Described as the 'cyclonic monk from India, he was given a grand reception by the American public at the Parliament. His charming personality, his sterling character, his patriotism, his in-depth learning and his modern and scientific approach, and sophisticated outlook made him the man of the hour at the Parliament.

His grand vision, his brilliant exposition and his in-depth capacity to inquire into the innermost recesses of the human heart attracted the attention of the American public. He said:

> Is man a tiny boat in a tempest, raised one moment on the foamy crest of a billow and dashed down into a yawing chasm the next, rolling to and fro at the mercy of good and bad actions — a powerless, helpless wreck in an ever-raging, ever-rushing, uncompromising current of cause and effect; and little moth placed under the wheel of causation, which rolls on, crushing everything in its way and waits not for the widow's tears or the orphan's cry? The heart sinks at the idea. Yet this is the Law of Nature. Is there no hope? Is there no escape? Was the cry that went up from the bottom of the heart of despair? It reached the Throne of Mercy and words of hope and consolation came down and inspired a Vedic sage and he stood up before the world and in a trumpet voice proclaimed the glad tidings. Here ye children of bliss immortal, even ye that reside in higher spheres; I have found the Ancient one, who is beyond all darkness, all delusion; knowing Him alone You shall be saved from death over again'. Children of immortal bliss what a sweet, what a hopeful name! The Hindu refuses to call you sinners! Ye are the children of God, sharers of immortal bliss, holy and perfect beings. Come up, Oh lions, and shake of the delusion that you are sheep. You are souls immortal, spirits free, blessed and eternal.

OPPOSED TO ORTHODOXY AND EXCLUSIVENESS

Vivekananda was born with a mission to make the people spiritual and remind them of the importance of religion which constituted their real life and the country would disintegrate if they forgot it. If they ceased to be spiritual and became materialists by imitating the West, they would soon perish. The backbone of the nation would be broken, the foundation upon which the national edifice had been built would collapse and the result would be distressing.

He strongly criticized all kinds of orthodoxy in matters of religion as they were nothing but "Kitchen religion" and "don't touchism". Condemning the influence of the West on Indian value system, he said that that India was not only the mother of spiritualism but also spread it in the world throughout her long history. She contributed it long before the rising of the Persian Empire, during the Persian Empire and during the ascendancy of the English and she was going to fulfil the same destiny once more.

He condemned the social evils, social exclusiveness, rigid caste structure, untouchability, etc. found in the Indian social system and opposed the fatalism. People's too much emphasis on "fate" as the determining factor in influencing the course of history made them lazy and inactive, dull and docile, meek and mild. He was quite unhappy with such kind of attitude, as in due course of time social evils were, instead of being challenged, accepted as the essence of Hinduism and this was mainly responsible for the society's decline and degeneration. To him, it was not the fault of Hinduism but of the people, who misunderstood it, misinterpreted it and did not practise its basic principles.

He, therefore, asked his people to destroy the barrier of social exclusiveness and urged them to share with others what they possessed. As "give and take" was the fundamental principle of life, India could learn mechanism and scientific devices from the West and, in return, give it the spiritual message of the Hinduism.

HIS PHILOSOPHY OF NEO-VEDANTISM

The essence of Hinduism lies in the *Gita,* the *Upanishads* and the *Sutras*. The term 'Vedanta' covers various systems of thought expounded by Sankara, Ramanuja, Madhava, Chaitanya and others. It includes Advaita, Visisthadvaita and the dualist systems of thought. Vivekananda said that there was no incompatibility among these different systems of thought. The human mind began with dualism, rose to qualified dualism and ultimately reached the qualified monism or Advaita which proclaimed the highest truth: *Tat Twam Asi* (Thou Art That). To him, Vedanta made an attempt to find out the ultimate unity of things.

Tat Twam Asi means that man is not that what he appears to be, outwardly he appears to be the body, the mind and the intellect. But, indeed, he is neither the body, nor the mind nor the intellect. He is the Soul or Atman, which is not subject to decay. Neither water can submerge it, nor fire can burn it into ashes nor any sword can cut it into pieces. It is immortal, the only Truth, the Eternal, the Real. That is why it is a part of the Universal Soul. Since man is the Atman, he can not be bad, or a sinner as is believed to be so by some religions. Instead, he is divine, pure, simple, innocent, virtuous. He is the Chit-Anand, but not weak, sinful, evil. Hence Vivekananda urged upon the people to consider themselves as immortal souls but not as sinners. Since all of these were divine and part and parcel of that Universal Soul, all of them were one. This belief gave rise to concepts of equality of man and the unity of mankind. Since God was present in all beings, they should love one another and serve one another. Vedanta while preaching the message of universal love and service insisted upon qualities like sacrifice and renunciation. Vivekananda said that the essence of religion was love, service, sacrifice and renunciation and it inculcated into the minds of people virtues like courage, bravity, purity, truthfulness, etc. Material progress alone did not make a nation great and perfect. The strength of a nation lay in the character of the people. They should, therefore, be strong and great. Vedanta wanted to improve their quality by infusing in them the strength of character. That is why Vivekananda wanted to give to the West the message of the Vedanta in exchange for the means to improve the conditions of the poor people in India. He felt that India should guide the whole world spiritually. It should teach them, preach them. He was shocked to find that its people had forgotten their own religion, their past, their heritage, the basic purpose of their life partly because of their long subjection to foreign rule and partly due to their own ignorance and inertia. He said that religion or its essence had been assimilated in us, become a part of life. For good or evil, people had been under the grip of religion for thousands of years. It had permeated the atmosphere, entered their very blood, tinged with every drop in their veins, become one with their constitution and the very vitality of their lives. Therefore, it could not be given up. Without it, man behaves like an animal as his reason errs and conscience sleeps. It is one's best friend, philosopher and guide.

Vivekananda strongly believed that the message of religion would have the least impact on people if they remained backward and poor. They suffered from acute poverty, and cried not for religion but for food. It would be ridiculous as well as a futile exercise if hungry stomachs were taught metaphysics. An empty belly always rebelled, but hardly learnt anything. It would, therefore, be one's duty to feed these poor. Otherwise, they would be dying of starvation. They must be sufficiently fed so that they could have a future: of hope, assurance, expectations and growth.

SERVICE AND ECONOMIC ORGANIZATION

Vivekananda had an important mission to accomplish. That was the emancipation of the masses, upliftment of the poor, progress of the downtrodden. Rendering his service to the mankind, he firmly believed that application of scientific technologies borrowed from the West would improve the conditions of the Indians. As the people of the West were hard-working and sincere, the Indians should learn all these qualities from them. Initially, he was highly impressed by the material prosperity of the West. But gradually its dark side was revealed. He discovered "the love of lucre, the spirit of greed, and the ferocious struggle for supremacy which lay at its basis". In a letter to Sister Nivedita, he said, social life in the West was like a peal of laughter; but underneath it was wail. It ended in a sob. The fun and frivolity were all on the surface; really it was full of tragic intensity. But in India it was sad and gloomy on the surface, but underneath were carelessness and merriment.

He felt that what the people of the West needed most was solace, inspiration and proper guidance and they could get all these from the Vedanta. Lust for wealth made their life unhappy and miserable. They forgot that external comforts and luxury could not give them peace. Materialism could never give them permanent satisfaction. The man was the Atman and his chief aim was to realize the divinity latent in him. Self-realization should be the basic goal of human life.

DEFENCE OF HINDUISM

Vivekananda said that image worship alone would not help by any means, some one in attaining salvation. But, at the same time, he did not disregard or undermine its importance and usefulness. It prepared ground for a common man so that he could realize God. It was the preliminary or beginning stage in one's spiritual development. It was, therefore, not a sin to worship an image of God. It was as necessary for the realization of God "as infancy and childhood were for maturity and wisdom of old age". Idolatry could be a sin if childhood or youth was a sin. But he knew that the entry of certain undesirable things like mystery-mongering cult, the so-called Yogism magic, into the Indian society was responsible for its spiritual and social degradation and downfall. Dogmatism, to him, in any sphere of life stood as an obstacle which deterred progress. It stifled one's soul, suffocated one's mind, regimented one's thoughts and enslaved one's conscience. When it crept into one's mind, it becomes pervert and imbalanced. One's approach to religion, to him, should be rational.

Considering Hinduism as a "universal gospel of ethical humanism and spiritual idealism", he defended it by championing its cause. By doing so, he rendered a distinct and notable contribution to world religion. Hinduism suffered a lot at the hands of Christian missionaries who misinterpreted it and undermined it and tarnished its image. They could not succeed in annihilating it partly because of its comprehensiveness and because of its supreme knowledge enriched by 'Nyaya', 'Samkhya', 'Vedanta'. That was why it was a source of tremendous inspiration to the whole mankind. To him, obscure cults, ritualistic superstitions, orthodox dogmas and primitive ceremonialism did not constitute the Hinduism. But, unfortunately, the missionaries considered all these the essence of the Hinduism. Strongly criticizing them Vivekananda said that "it was a body of moral and spiritual injunctions and primordial supertemporal laws for the uplift of the humanity".

Mother of religions, Hinduism could be explained in the light of history and historical developments. No doubt the ancient Vedic religion influenced

Buddhism, which was possibly a very potent factor in giving birth to Christianity, the religion of Persia. During the sixth century B.C., the reformist ethical movement inspired by some aspects of the Western Asiatic religions (of Persia and India) began in Judea. The Jews came to learn them when they were under the control of Babylonia.

Vivekananda laid equal emphasis on every aspect of the Hinduism, beginning from the Vedas to the Vaisnavism. Unlike Swami Dayananda, he did not give more importance to the Samhitas of the Veda. He was, however, greatly impressed by the Jnanakanda of the *Upanishads*.

His restatement and reinterpretation of Hinduism could not be considered as a piece of mere literature. It was part of a crusade, accepting essentials and rejecting non-essentials; emphasizing the eternal truths preached and professed by the ancient Yogis and sages. Unhappy and distressed, he wanted spiritual regeneration as the country was mistakenly treating the non-essentials to be the essentials of religion.

Disgusted with the increase of sects, he wanted that their number should be reduced as it would bring down friction among them. Instead of indulging in clash, confrontation, they should be united to offer strength and sustenance to religion and the country. He knew that these sects were narrow, parochial and were not prepared to accommodate one another, tolerate one another. They suffered from terrible ego-clash, thereby caused a great injury to Hinduism. He was prepared to accommodate as many sects so that they could afford to live under the big sheltering banyan of the Vedas. It was very unfortunate that unhealthy sectarianism posed a great threat to Hinduism as it would cause social disintegration. All the sects should, therefore, respect and tolerate one another and work in union with others in the interests of the country and religion. These sects behaved as if they were different regiments in the army of Hinduism. They could achieve their goal if they remained loyal to the banner and the cause and should recognize the authority of the Vedas. He rightly attributed the downfall of India to the cause of non-observance of this elementary rule. When sectarianism was allowed to have its free-play, there was no end to the misfortune of India. Once it was buried, a new India would be born — recreated, reunited and rejuvenated.

Vivekananda brought reputation and glory, name and fame to India by his brilliant exposition of Hinduism through his writings and speeches. Every religious thinker restated the glorious aspects of the Vedas in the local language of the people of his times. This significant service was rendered by preachers and religious thinkers like Vyasa, Baudhayana, Sankara, Vidyaranya and many others in their own times. But compared to them, Vivekananda faced many difficulties as he appeared on the scene after centuries of intellectual lull and stagnation and India was invaded by other civilizations. As a result, the old, ancient and time-tested values were replaced and substituted by new ones. His job was more difficult as he had to restate the ancient metaphysical thought of India in the light of modern science and philosophy and in a language which an average student could understand. It would, however, be wrong to think that his work was merely a translation of something from Sanskrit to English. He gave a new interpretation, a new dimension, a new direction and a new shape to Hinduism.

He was unhappy when the people changed their religions and accepted Christianity or Islam, because it was unethical. It was the weakness of the Hindu social organization that enabled the foreigner(s) to make inroads into the religious citadel of the people. The situation could be changed if the material and spiritual conditions of the masses were changed. He was, thus, not only a seeker after the Truth but also a World Teacher.

RELIGION, INDIVIDUAL AND SOCIAL FREEDOM

An individual becomes religious only when he develops certain spiritual urges. Religion without spiritualism becomes a dry formality or a dull mechanized drilling, or a routine matter in life. True religion gives everyone proper guidance, makes his life perfect, rational and enlightened, and removes ignorance. Vivekananda attributed origin of religion to innate struggle of human mind to go beyond the limitations of human senses and not to worship of nature or of ancestors. It was neither a word nor a creed but it was realization. It was not hearing and accepting of something. It was being and becoming. To him, a good, virtuous and noble individual could realize God in his lifetime. This realization was open to everyone. One could be truly religious and spiritual if he renounced the material world. He did believe that it was only through knowledge that personal realization could be achieved. Service to mankind, particularly the poor, would help in achieving the goal. The Ramakrishna Mission was set up for this purpose.

One should fight for his own religion. It, however, did not mean that he would criticise other religions. If the Parliament of Religions gave anything to this world it was this: "Help and not fight", "assimilation and not destruction", and "harmony and peace and not dissension".

Freedom is a must for everyone — be he an individual or a beast. It helps him to grow, prosper and realize his best-self. A society can be free only when its people are free and perfect. Its strength and vitality depends on their freedom. It should, therefore, take necessary steps to ensure this. As it is simply a social agency, it should not suppress it. Since freedom is 'natural' to an individual, he should not be discriminated. All kinds of privileges that exist in the society should be abolished as they are, to Vivekananda, baneful and tyrannical. He strongly pleaded for social equality. Individual freedom should be discussed in the context of society as it is closely related to social freedom, which refers to growth-oriented social life based on individual freedom and equality. Society should spend more on the education of the poor than on the rich and intelligent. His concept of freedom is comprehensive and all-inclusive — social, material and spiritual. It stood for a synthesis of the individual and social freedom, material and spiritual freedom.

DEMOCRACY AS A WAY OF LIFE

Arguing that people's participation in the democratic process liberated them from social and economic bondages, Vivekananda strongly believed that in future there would be some form of government run by the "Sudras" and the future belonged to them. By democracy, he meant not representative democracy as is understood today. It was a man-making process; it stood for self-reliance and self-government, eliminating the dependence of the individual on Parliament and giving an opportunity to shoulder the responsibilities of the government. In other words, it made the individual ethical, social and spiritual. Once he became perfect, he must go for spiritual realization. Because it was the end of human life.

To Vivekananda, democracy was a form of government as well as a way of life. As a way of life, it envisaged equality, fellow-feeling and brotherhood among the people. Speaking on democracy as a form of government, he maintained that the cyclical rule of the caste system helped the process of social evolution. It provided the theory of forms of government, namely the Brahmin, the Kshatriya, the Vaisya and the Sudra. He argued that the forms of government were evolutionary, and not based on individual whims and fancies. During different regimes of different castes, society gained many things. He praised the Brahmin rule for making the society more spiritual, the Kshatriya rule for making it civilized and rational, and the Vaisya rule for forging international contacts.

Vivekananda very sadly commented that all these forms of caste rule in course of time became degenerated and estranged from the majority of the population who constituted the main source of power in all forms of caste rule. He observed that one day the Sudras would come to power and rule the society. Identifying their rise with democracy, he strongly advocated their cause. Democracy encouraged individual initiative and self-reliance in administering and conducting the affairs of the government. He opposed the party system which was thought to be very much essential for forming a government, since the Vedanta did not support it. To avert the evil effects of representative democracy and to strengthen it, he emphasized the man-making process through education, sacred and secular.

UNIVERSAL RELIGION AND INTERNATIONALISM

To Vivekananda, religion did not mean any kind of belief in any particular creed or faith. It assisted in spiritual realization. He believed that India being great and famous for its spiritualism showed light to the whole world and inspired the mankind. It did not mean the changing of manners and customs, but the idea of "oneness of all, the infinite, the idea of the impersonal, the wonderful idea of the eternal soul of man, of the unbroken continuity in the march of beings, and the infinity of the universe." This was the message of the Vedanta and it was because of this Vivekananda accepted its sound metaphysics and universality. He stood for what was called Universal Religion. To him, Hinduism was a Universal

Religion. He felt proud of belonging to it as it taught the world both tolerance and universal acceptance. Every religion consisted of three parts: its philosophy and ideals, its mythology, and its rituals. The last two varied from one religion to another, but there was an essential identity in regard to the first.

To Vivekananda, a seeker after the Truth, found answers to all his questions in the Vedanta as it consisted of eternal principles with strong foundations and which did not seek any support from any person or incarnations. The Hinduism alone could be considered as universal religion as it taught principles, not persons. Any religion built upon the authority of a person or a group of persons could not be universally accepted by all the races of mankind. The Vedanta created a spiritualized environment for the man; it kindled the fire of spiritualism in him; it set for him the foundations of a new world to live in, free from all kinds of creeds and dogmas. "The sanction of the Vedanta is the eternal nature of man, already existing, already attained". It served the whole mankind and created world brotherhood.

Vivekananda believed that like Vedanta, science also promoted unity and cooperation among the people and developed a feeling of brotherhood among them. If modern science proved anything again and again, it was this that the people living in this world were one — mentally, spiritually and physically. Expediting the process of universal unity, bringing the whole world together; causing the old lines of demarcation and differentiation disappear very rapidly, helping the people to interact with one another on a wider scale since inter-communication among them could be possible because of the scientific developments. both science, along with Vedanta taught that nations were not different from the universe. All individuals and nations were the constituent parts of the Universal Existence. Existence of different nations as a concept was not acceptable to either the Science or the Vedanta. Notwithstanding the existence of different regions, religions, languages, etc. there existed international unity and brotherhood.

A SOCIAL REFORMER

The Indian civilization, since the ages, has been afflicted by social evils. Vivekananda felt that social reform through religion could not be possible without bringing spiritual reform first. He said that he could not preach even religion to Americans without showing them its practical effect on social life; he could not do so in England without showing the wonderful political changes the Vedanta would bring; so in India, social reform had to be preached by showing how much it would improve the one thing that the nation wanted, its spirituality.

Emancipation of Women

In modern Hinduism which is largely Puranik, i.e. post-Buddhistic in origin, the status of women became somewhat inferior. But, certainly, the Aryan ideal of womanhood was distinctly higher. Vivekananda wanted that women should solve their own problems without seeking the help of others. They should not get married at a tender age. Proper training should be given to them so that they could learn about the importance of renunciation and this would certainly help them in practising virginity throughout their life. Along with this, they should be taught sciences and other things which would be of benefit not only to them but to others as well.

Caste Structure

He argued that caste had nothing to do with religion and it could very easily be destroyed without causing any harm to Hinduism. He said that beginning from Buddha down to Rammohan Roy, every one made the mistake of holding caste to be a religious institution and tried to pull down religion and caste together, and failed. In 1893, he wrote notwithstanding the loud claims of the priests, caste was simply a crystallized social institution which after doing its service filled the atmosphere of India with its stench and it could only be removed by giving back to the people their lost social individuality. Every man who was born here knew that he was a man. Every man born in India knew that he was a slave of the society. With the introduction of modern competition, caste was disappearing fast. No religion was necessary to kill it...

It is important to note that Swamiji wanted to strengthen, preserve and ameliorate caste system, but at the same time, did his best to remove its anomalies, inequities and extravagances. It was certainly a problem that haunted him as long as he was alive. Since he died at an early age, that problem was left in the same incomplete state.

AN ESTIMATE

A strong advocate of universal, secular and religious education, a champion of equal rights and equal opportunities for all, a reformer who wanted progress in every sphere of life, he stood for the assimilation of all that was good in Western civilization. Thinking that all the social institutions should adjust themselves to the changed economic and political environment, he insisted that social reforms should not be encouraged or brought about at the cost of Hinduism.

POINTS TO REMEMBER

- Vivekananda was born in 1863 in Calcutta. He came from "Satya Loka". Ramakrishna Paramahamsa was his Master. He was born with a mission—to make the people spiritually oriented.
- His interest was in Indian scriptures and Western philosophies. His mission was to awaken the nation from deep slumber.

- His grandfather was a monk.
- He was influenced by his father Viswanath Dutta and his mother Bhubaneswari.
- He passed his Entrance Examination in 1879 and then joined the General Assembly's Institute, one of the oldest colleges in Bengal. He graduated in 1884.
- He spent most of his time with Ramakrishna Paramahamsa.
- He rigorously practised asceticism and brahmacharya.
- Initially, he wanted to join politics so that he could have name and fame, status and position, wealth and power.
- The career of Naren stretched over three distinct phases. Ramakrishna Paramahama's joy knew no bounds when he first met him. Naren was, however, not impressed with his Master's behaviour. The moment was quite embarrassing. Naren was "Nara" born to remove miseries.
- Naren's second meet with his Master was significant. He was impressed by his Master's question: "do you see a light when you close your eyes?" Naren's opinion about his Master: he was not a lunatic, but a man of insight. In spite of his divine experience because of his Master's efforts and actions, Naren did not surrender reason at the altar of faith.
- His meditation in the garden house of Cassipore. His divine and unique experience in that stage. He felt divinity within himself. It was the moment of highest bliss. He wanted to become a wandering monk so that he could come in contact with saints and seers. His severe practice of austerities and his constant and prolonged meditation had an adverse effect on his health. He narrowly escaped from the jaws of death.
- His dream when he was half-dead and unconscious — that he should serve the mankind instead of wasting time on meditation. He visited the Western countries.
- Chicago Conference in 1893. He wanted that his Master should ask him to attend the same. He reached Chicago in July 1893. His difficulties at Chicago. Left for Boston. Met Dr. Wright and Dr. Barrows. Technical difficulties in attending the Parliament were removed.
- The atmosphere in the Parliament of Religions: nothing expected happened.
- In the Parliament, he spoke next to Mazoomdar and Chakravarty. Initially, he became nervous. His speech had a mesmerizing effect on the delegates and the American public. He won their hearts and soul. Overnight, he became their hero.
- To him, every one was a child of immortality. He was not a sinner. Indians should not be material-oriented, should not blindly follow the material-

world. His sole aim was to make the Indians God-oriented. The country would perish if they become materialists.

- He was against orthodoxy; condemned the influence of the West on Indians; criticized social evils and people's emphasis on 'fate'. Social evils became a part of Hinduism. To him, there was no fault with religion, it was with its interpreters.
- Barrier of social exclusiveness was to be destroyed. No incompatibility among different systems of thought. *Tat Twam Asi*. He is not body, nor the mind, nor the intellect. He is the Soul or Atman.
- Soul is immortal, eternal, the Real. It is a part of the Paramatman or the Universal Soul. He is Chit-Anand. The strength of a nation lies in the character of the people.
- People had forgotten their religion. Religion would have least impact on them if they are poor and backward. Poverty must be eradicated. His mission was to see people's emancipation.
- Indians should learn good qualities from the West. The growth and development in the West was superficial, but never substantial. Vedanta must be taught to the West. Self-realization be the end of life.
- Idol worship was not a sin. It was the beginning of one's spiritual development. Dogmatism was an impediment to one's real progress.
- Hinduism is the oldest religion, the mother of all religions including Christianity. Vivekananda's equal emphasis on every aspect of Hinduism, beginning from the Vedas to the Vaishnavism. Dayanand's more importance to the Samhitas of the Veda.
- He was against sectarianism. Growth of sects threatened the religion as well as the country. They should cooperate with one another and must take shelter under the Veda.
- He gave a new meaning, a new dimension, a new direction, a new purpose to Hinduism. He was against conversion of religion (from Hinduism to Christianity or Islam).
- Religion provides proper guidance to every one, a meaning and a purpose to every one's life. A divine, a pure, a noble soul could certainly realize God. Service to mankind helped one to achieve the goal.
- Freedom is essential to one's progress and prosperity. It is 'natural' to an individual. He was for social equality. More money should be spent on poor for their education.
- The future, to him, belonged to 'Sudras'. Democracy was a form of government as well as a way of life. At different times, different castes ruled. Caste rule becomes degenerated and estranged.
- One day, Sudras would rule the society. Democracy encouraged individual initiative and self-reliance. He opposed the party system. Religion: not a

blind belief, assisted self-realization. Hinduism was a universal religion. He praised it for its essence and qualities. He was proud of being a Hindu.

- Every religion consisted of three parts. Answers to all questions were provided in Vedanta. It contained eternal principles. Vedanta made one spiritual. Science promoted unity and cooperation among men.
- Both science and Vedanta taught that nations were not different from the universe. There existed international unity and brotherhood. He was a social reformer, a reformer trying to reform the society through religion. In post-Buddhistic period, the status of women became inferior.
- Women to solve their problems without depending on any one. Practising virginity throughout our life; not to marry at a tender age; they should learn science and other things.
- Caste and religion were two different things; caste structure could be removed without affecting Hinduism. Caste was not a religious institution. It was a crystallized social institution. He wanted to protect the caste structure in a different form.

6

Bal Gangadhar Tilak (1856–1920)

INTRODUCTION

An erudite scholar, a brilliant statesman, a great intellectual, Bal Gangadhar Tilak was an educator, a sincere and dedicated promoter and patron of education. An outspoken and outstanding journalist, he fought against economic injustice and passionately preached the cult of Swadeshi. A powerful and influential orator, a towering personality, he exerted a tremendous influence upon Indian politics and, in this regard, he surpassed all his contemporaries. His powerful assertion, "Swaraj is My Birthright", still reverberates in every nook and corner of the country. A man of dignity and self-respect, of indomitable spirit and courage, he was gifted with knowledge, intellect and statesmanship. Selfless and fearless, he was a committed soldier who fought boldly for his country's independence. A man of character and integrity, of iron will and strong determination, he was bold, steadfast and consistent in his approach to different problems that confronted the society.

Gifted with moral strength, he faced all ordeals and onslaughts, encountered all adverse conditions, handled all hostile situations with courage and conviction. Strongly believing that "it would be better to die in peace than to live in humiliation", he never bowed his head before nay one, however powerful he might be. He experienced several tragedies and bereavements, sorrows and sufferings, pain and anguish without losing his balance of mind. He stood like a rock never to be swept away by Nature's fury like super cyclone, tsunami, etc. Free from meanness and pettiness, arrogance and vanity, he was, however, defiant and aggressive. He never lost his equanimity even though he suffered form unjust, vindictive and savage sentences. Neither a cynic nor a pessimist, he did many things with amazing firmnes.

EARLY LIFE

Bal Gangadhar Tilak, a man of indomitable spirit with a clear vision, was born on 23 July 1856 at Ratnagiri in the state of Maharashtra. He was the only son and fourth child of Gangadhar Pant and Parvathibai. His mother, a kind-hearted and intensely religious lady, strongly believed that he was the hard-earned fruit of her extreme penance and strong devotion to the God Sun. She died in 1866. Named earlier as Balwantrao and later came to be known as Bal Gangadhar Tilak, he was reverently called Lokamanya Tilak or Tilak Bhagwan. His early childhood was quite distinguished in the sense that he had a very strong memory power and was quite stubborn and obdurate. His father gave him a good grounding in Sanskrit, Arithmetic and Marathi. He was taught to recite Sanskrit verses and given a pie for every verse he recited.

In 1861, he was admitted into a school. In 1866, he joined the Poona City School where he quarrelled with his teachers. He was more a rebel than a student. His father died in 1872, leaving behind for his son some money and resources. He was brought up by his uncle, a good and noble man. He married in 1871 to Tapibai.

Tilak took admission in the Deccan College in 1873. But he evinced a keen interest in physical exercises like swimming and gymnastics and neglected his studies. As a result, he failed his F.A. examination. But he had no regrets, no repentance. Rather he was proud of his physical attainments and in the hostel he indulged in athletic activities. During his college days, he felt happy by spending most of his time, next to physical exercises, in unending gossip and ridicule. He rarely attended his classes. Soon after the roll-call, he left the classroom. He did not feel guilty for it. As he was blunt and unusually outspoken, his fellow-students called him "Devil". Yet he was gentle in his manners and a man of strong character without any vices.

He began and completed his education at Poona. But for one term he left for Bombay and joined the Elphinstone College. Unimpressed with the teachings there, he came back to Poona where he graduated in 1876 in the first class. Next year he joined the M.A. course and failed in the examination. However, he got his LL.B. degree. Once again he appeared at the M.A. Examination, but again failed.

Like his father, Tilak was a great scholar in Sanskrit and Mathematics. With a strong background in ancient knowledge and mathematical training, he wrote *Orion: Studies in the Antiquity of the Vedas*. In his work, he strongly argued that the Rig Veda was composed in as early as 4500 B.C. This argument based on his astronomical calculations from the Sanskrit texts, made him extremely popular both in the East and in the West. In his second immortal work — *The Arctic Home of the Vedas* — based on astronomical and geological data, he argued that the Aryans were probably the original inhabitants of the far northern reaches of the Asiatic continent. This book is said to be one of the most original and authentic works in the Sanskrit literature. Basing on his notes and observations, the Vedic chronology was published after his death. His greatest work was the *Gita Rahasya*, a philosophical inquiry into the secret of the teaching of the Gita, the holiest book of the Aryadharma. He was, thus, one of the greatest scholars and philosophers of India. Though educated in English, in his heart of hearts he remained a humble student of India's greatness.

AN INDIAN JESUIT

Tilak entered into public life through education with a missionary zeal. His work reflected his character, personality, unbending and indomitable spirit, tenacity of purpose, strong determination and above all the fighter in him. It was in July or August 1879, he discussed the importance and practicability of establishing private schools on the model of missionary institutions, with his friends like G.G. Agarkar, B.A. Bhagwat, V.B. Karandikar. A new era began in the field of education when they decided to start a new school in 1880. But Bhagwat and Karandikar withdrew themselves from the scheme as they felt it would not give them any monetary benefit. Agarkar deferred joining the scheme for one year as he got a fellowship in the Deccan College. The New English school was set up with the efforts of Tilak and Vishnu Krishna Chiplunkar on 1 January 1880.

In Poona, the Christian missionaries had virtually controlled the education of children. Resenting it, self-respecting Indians felt the need of a national system of education. The New English School, in a way, was considered as a challenge to the mission schools. Its grand success encouraged Tilak and others to found the Deccan Education Society at Poona in 1880 and the Ferguson College in 1881.

A JOURNALIST

Before completion of one year of the New English School, which was self-supporting and extremely popular, Chiplunkar and Namjoshi suggested that two newspaper weeklies — one in Marathi and another in English — should be founded. Both of them had vast experience in the field of journalism. The former had already made a name as a fearless Editor of the *Nibandha-Mala*, and the latter also owned and edited a paper called the *Deccan Star*. Tilak was indifferent to the new proposal. But when it was strongly put forward by others, he agreed to cooperate. Namjoshi's *Star* was converted into *Marhatta* and it appeared on 2 January 1881, *Kesari*, the Marathi weekly, saw the light of the day on 4 January 1881.

The weeklies were jointly conducted by Tilak, Chiplunkar, Agarkar and Namjoshi. Since they began to take active interest in politics, in the very first year of their publication, they became "unfriendly to the Government". Tilak wrote mostly on religion, law and political issues.

DIFFERENCES OF OPINION

Tilak differed from his friends on the issue of social reform. Therefore, he dissociated himself from the Deccan Education Society and finally parted with his co-workers. It was finally decided at the end of 1890 that Tilak should purchase the *Kesari* and the *Marhatta* and dedicate himself to the cause of journalism while Agarkar and others would look after the Deccan Education Society. As an Editor, Tilak was a great success and unsurpassed. He made his dailies economically viable and politically influential. His sincerity, courage and conviction made him one of the greatest champions of the cause of the people. He fought against injustice, autocracy and arbitrariness. By awakening India, he became the Lion of Maharashtra, and by editing the *Kesari*, he became the most influential Indian newspaper Editor of his day. As an Editor, he fought three great battles: against the westernized social reformers, against the inert spirit of orthodoxy and against the British Raj. As a leader, he became a great leader of the new forces in the Indian National Congress and the Indian nation.

FIRST IMPRISONMENT

As Tilak was free, frank and fearless in his expressions, he was treated with contempt and suspicion by the Government. He incurred the latter's displeasure when he took keen interest in the affairs of the states of the Indian ruling princes and vigorously pleaded the cause of the rulers against the paramount power of the British crown. It was officially stated that the *Marhatta* frequently quoted paragraphs and articles of a violent and democratic nature from the *English Radical*.

It was alleged that in Kolhapur a minister, Rao Bahadur Madhav Rao Wasudev Barve, hatched out a conspiracy with the support of the British Government to poison the king. It was evident from his private letters to the British Resident. There was strong public protest against the minister when the *Gyanprakash* published them. Believing in the authenticity of the publication, *Kesari* and *Marhatta* also quoted these letters at some length and challenged Barve to fight it out in the court of law. The latter accepted the challenge and filed a suit. But when Tilak came to know about Barve's innocence, he burnt the letters and offered his apology to him. But since the case had proceeded too far in the court, Barve did not withdraw it. Tilak and Agarkar admitted their guilt. They were sentenced to simple imprisonment for four months and released from the jail on 26 October 1882.

FAITH IN INDIAN VALUES AND PHILOSOPHY

Opposed to Western values, Tilak was against their blind imitation. As he had strong faith in Indian philosophy and value system, he did not accept and appreciate, unlike many other Indian intellectuals, the Western philosophy. He, however, felt that the Indian social system should be drastically reformed. But instead of judging Indian social practices from the Western perspective, he interpreted them and looked for their reform in the light of Indian standard.

Tilak knew that change was inevitable as it would remake and regenerate India and reshape its future. A philosophy must guide it and inspire it. But a pertinent question comes to one's mind that whether this philosophy would be Indian or Western. He wrote: "It is difficult to see the way in darkness without light or in a thick jungle without a guide". Rejecting rationalism and scepticism of Western philosophy, he said: "Mere common sense without faith in religion is of no avail in searching for the truth". He believed that Indian philosophy would help and guide us in reawakening India and rekindling its spirit. His initial motive was not to rediscover or build up a theory of social and political action, but rather to find a satisfying personal philosophy of life. In his private life, he attempted to rediscover and reapply the Indian philosophy. And his achievements helped him in building-up a new theory of political action, obligation and ordering. He always believed that every human life had a moral purpose. He rejected any theory which did not believe in the existence of soul or in spiritual purpose of human life.

From this idea of spiritual rediscovery, Tilak, like Aurobindo Ghosh and others, developed a personal philosophy of life. It is based on the knowledge that the individual soul and the Supreme soul are one, and that the 'ultimate goal of the soul is liberation'. He distinguished between the 'real' and 'illusory' world; knew about the meaning of creation and the cosmic evolution towards liberation; and understood the basic purpose of life, i.e. to live in accord with dharma, and the integrating principle of the cosmic order. Once these principles were accepted, Western rationalism and scepticism, materialism and utilitarianism could hardly appeal. It was with this basic understanding he criticized the West whose so-called educated, literate and rational people did not hesitate to destroy these values.

Tilak was proud of India's past heritage, culture, religion, philosophy and values. India's history and civilization provided him a new insight for his theory of social and political action. He felt that there was no reason to feel ashamed of India's civilization when compared to the West. The westernized intellectuals, who were critical of Indian philosophy and value system and wanted to change them and remake India in an alien faith, were quite wrong. He, therefore, reminded them, "how can a man be proud of the greatness of his own nation if he feels no pride in his own religion?"

It was with this conviction, faith and inspiration, Tilak, along with his friends, began his battle for the creation of a new India not in the image of an alien system of values, but on the foundations of her own greatness. With the help of Indian philosophy of life, he constructed an Indian philosophy of social reforms and politics that was to become the political theory of the Indian Independence Movement.

A SOCIAL REFORMER

Tilak had a strong faith in the Sanatana Arya Dharma. But, at the same time, he was not an orthodox. He knew it very well that the Indian society was ridden with evils and this motivated some social reformers to get rid of them by adopting some measures. He was educated but did not join the reformers. It indicated that he was a strong defender of orthodoxy. The reformers not only considered him to be an orthodox but also a spokesman for backwardness. But this criticism was baseless and not true as he never opposed reforms. He believed that once the society was reformed and restructured, the society would be free from the evils. And for this, he had his own plans and proposals. But he did not like the grand schemes of the Westernized reformers as these were impractical measures. His reform was direct, as in the case of the famine relief programmes, the plague prevention works, etc. He was a practical but not an armchair reformer.

Reformers like Ranade, Gokhale, Bhandarkar, Byramji Malbari, Agarkar and others were in favour of adopting extreme measures to reform the society and remake India in the image of the West, or in the light of Western values they had acquired from the Western education. Tilak was against it as it would destroy the Indian values and religion. Taking a strong exception to their reform proposals and their way of thinking, he once wrote that a number of educated Indians accepted without any proper analysis the materialistic doctrines of the Westerners. As a result, India was passing through a pathetic situation as most of the Indians had become gross materialists.

He reminded them that the existing debacle and downfall was not because of Hindu religion itself but because Indians had ignored their religion and felt shy of it. Since the proposed reforms of Ranade and others were not acceptable to the people, the former wanted to implement them through administrative measures with the help of the state to bring social change.

He believed that reforms could be possible only when people wholeheartedly accepted them, eagerly responded to them, sincerely implemented them and made them their way of life. Reforms must grow from within and no amount of force or pressure would help in implementing them as long as people themselves did not want them. Reforms would have to be based upon their value system and not on the Western values. India should not blindly copy from some other civilization when she could confidently rely upon her past greatness. Unlike other reformers, he did not shun religion from social order.

Tilak wanted to reawaken India and shape her future in the light of her past glories. He believed that progress could be possible only with a self-governing people. Therefore, Swaraj or self-rule was the most essential prerequisite of real social, political, economic, cultural and spiritual progress. He thought in terms of the restoration of Swaraj. As said above, the social reformers criticized everything that was Indian, easily accepted the Western values, imitated them in the name of improvement, and relied upon the power of a foreign Government to bring about this improvement and change. To them, social reform must follow the political reform. Self-government is the moral government and it brings moral and social changes. Therefore, self-rule is necessary and should be restored to the Indians.

He felt that to bring about meaningful changes, it would not be enough to change simply the forms and practices of Indian society. Abusive social practices like "Sati", female infanticide, caste system, etc. were the direct products of the 'spirit of orthodoxy' which perverted the social order and never allowed any changes. This might be attributed to a thousand years of political instability, ignominious defeats, foreign domination, defensiveness and rigidity. The true spirit of the Indians should, therefore, be reawakened. Instead of criticizing social form as a great evil, he fought against the 'atrophied' spirit of orthodoxy and the westernized reforms. He said that orthodox opinions of the Pandits and others were one-sided. So was the case with the westernized reformers. The former were not aware of the new changes whereas the latter were ignorant of the traditions and traditional philosophy of Hinduism.

Over the years, the spirit of orthodoxy became perverted and its degrading, distressing and disgusting aspects were lethargy, indolence, exclusiveness and inaction. And this gave rise to defeatism, fatalism and casteism in all its worst manifestations. There was also loss of self-respect, courage and social harmony and cooperation. In other words, the dynamics of classical philosophy of life had been perverted into negation and passivity. This spirit was to Tilak, highly detrimental to India's progress and prosperity. To him, atrophied orthodoxy had no religious justification.

The *Bhagawat Gita* taught us to fight against injustice and oppression. No where it said that people should resign themselves to their fate and not take any action against the oppressor and the perpetrator of crimes. But people, unfortunately, started relying more and more on fate. They tolerated any kind of injustice believing that it was their destiny to suffer. What a change in our approach to life?

He believed that India could not be reawakened merely by removing philosophical controversies or disputations. This could be possible only when people would change their attitudes and approaches. Changes in the forms of institutions would not reawaken India. He made sincere attempts to reach the people and educate them through his writings in his newspapers and through festivals. His efforts in popularizing two festivals — one for Ganapati, the Hindu deity of learning and propitiousness, and the other to revive the memory and glory of Shivaji, the liberator of Maharashtra, and the restorer of Swaraj through his battle against the Moghul Empire. He inculcated in the minds of the people a new spirit by educating them through religion and history, associating them with gods and heroes, glorifying their past heritage and making them feel proud of it. He became the defender and the awakener of India's philosophy of life.

MESSAGE OF ACTION AND UNITY

Inspired and encouraged by the *Bhagawat Gita*, Tilak said that the people should be action-oriented. Indolence, laziness and lethargy should not be their way of life. They must work, work for the betterment and welfare of the society, for its moral progress and reawakening. At the same time, they should not expect any reward for their work or service. He reminded them that India had not achieved its greatness through negativism and indolence, but rather through a dynamic willingness to meet the problems of the day and solve them with courage and confidence. He said that God helped those who helped themselves. No one should expect that God would protect one who sat with folded arms and shifted his burden to others. One must be doing all that he could to lift himself up and then only should rely on the Almighty to help him.

To Tilak, the unity of India was the Bharat-Dharma, which was spiritually-based and spiritually-dedicated way of life. But, unfortunately, this along with heritage and common cause had been ruined by the spirit of orthodoxy, which had divided the people on the basis of caste. The result was the compartmentalization of the society. The Varnashrama-Dharma stood for harmony, cooperation and unity and Tilak wanted to reawaken this spirit through religious education. He wrote: "It is possible to unite the followers of Hinduism by the revival and growth of the Hindu religion", for "the Hindu religion does not lie in caste, eating and drinking".

As said earlier, he wanted to unite the people through the Gajapati and Shivaji festivals. When they recognized one common deity, one common historical tradition, one common past heritage, they would develop, undoubtedly, a moral power, a moral strength to overcome all social evils like disunity and divisiveness and to reconstruct a social order that would bring good to one and all and make them happy and prosperous. He hoped that they should be united, united among themselves, united with their traditions, united to face the future by the common ideals they held. This united effort would certainly help them to remove the social evils. He believed that the spirit of national revival, the restoration of national self-respect, an essential pre-requisite for self-rule (Swaraj), depended upon the restoration of national unity and mutual respect.

PUBLIC OFFICE AND POLITICAL CAREER

A social reformer and a political activist, he did not make any compromise with principles and values. Therefore, he left the Deccan Education Society in 1889 and joined the Indian National Congress with an intention that it would help him in achieving his goal: national unity and political reforms. In 1892, he became the Secretary of the Bombay Provincial Conference. Actively participating in public affairs, he held various offices: a Fellow of Bombay University (elected in 1894), a post in Poona Municipality (1895) and a Member of the Bombay Legislative Council (elected in 1895 and in 1897). Describing the powers of the Council and the manner in which it worked as "huge joke", he never sought after any public office. But when he held the same, he believed that it would be an instrument to achieve his desired goal — reawakening India. He fully realized that it would be a disgrace to hold any office under an alien rule. Dissatisfied and disillusioned with the programmes and principles of the Moderate-dominated Congress which never realized the problems of the people, he left the organization. Denouncing the indifferent attitude and hostile policies of the Government, he said that for the last twelve years they had been shouting hoarse, expecting that the Government would hear them. But their shouting did not have any effect on the Government which never believed them. The time had come to put forth the grievances before them (the Government) through strong "constitutional means". He urged that the best political education should be given to the ignorant villagers. They must be taught about their rights and made aware how to fight their issues constitutionally. Then only would the Government realize that to despise the Congress was to despise the Indian Nation. Then only would the efforts of its leaders be crowned with success. It would not be easy job. It would rather be a Herculean task which could be accomplished only with the involvement of a large number of people who should serve the country with a purpose and be prepared to undergo any amount of self-sacrifice to realize the goal, i.e. the liberation of the country and awakening India.

Tilak wanted to make the people politically educated. Through *Kesari*, he made them conscious of their legal rights and urged them to protest against government's attitude and inaction. He sent volunteers to affected areas to collect information on damages and destructions caused by the famine. He then prepared a report and forwarded the same to the Government for necessary action. He printed and distributed a leaflet explaining the provisions of the Famine Relief Code among the people and urged them to draw the attention of the Government to their plight. His sincere efforts yielded the desired result: arousal of the people against the administration. The situation in Poona further deteriorated and worsened following the outbreak of plague which took a heavy toll of human lives. Panicked, the people and the so-called intelligent social reformers fled Poona. But Tilak did not. Instead, he extended his full cooperation to the administration in handling the plague situation. He set up hospitals and opened a free kitchen for the victims. His selfless service made him extremely popular and earned for him the title "Lokamanya". He was considered as one of the greatest social reformers.

The Anglo-Indian Press and the British administration considered him as a rising star on the political horizon of the Indian sky as well as an emerging leader of a new spirit in India. Some were scared of him, some feared him, some were jealous of him, some also hated him. Following the incidents of famine and plague in Poona, Rand, a British official was assassinated on 22 June 1896 by Chafekar brothers as a revenge for the repression of the people unleashed by him during the plague. Tilak was neither involved nor aware of it. But some held him responsible for this incident. Nevertheless, he was convicted in 1897 and sentenced to two years imprisonment for publishing in his paper his speeches delivered during the Shivaji festival, observing that Shivaji was a great patriot and he did not commit any sin by killing Afzul Khan, a Mughal Army

Commander, who wanted to kill him through conspiracy. This was not to be his last imprisonment. He was hounded, persecuted by the British authorities as they saw in him the greatest challenge to their regime.

SWARAJ

A man of strong will power, Tilak was prepared to sacrifice anything and everything to reawaken India. Therefore, he could not be suppressed by the Government. Persecution and threats to his life could not deter and discourage him from pursuing his goal. To him, self-rule must precede social reform. Strongly criticizing the policies of the moderates of the Congress, he put forward a positive programme centring around the concept of Swaraj or self-rule for India. As early as in 1895, he preached the necessity of Swaraj. He reminded the people that Shivaji liberated Maharashtra, established Swaraj and then introduced social and political reforms. He said that self-rule would be the only enduring basis for national unity and national self-respect. His views on Swaraj were consistent with his personal, social and political philosophy. Appreciating Tilak's Swaraj or self-rule, Aurobindo Ghosh said that Indian politics could be infused with Indian religious fervour and spirituality as this could be a great and powerful factor in awakening India. Others — writers, thinkers, spiritual leaders — had seen this truth. Tilak was the first to bring it into the actual field of practical politics.

By advocating Swaraj, Tilak became the mouthpiece of India's will to be free. In his speeches, he urged the people to work for Swaraj and was ready for suffering. That was the subject of his speech at the Shivaji celebrations also. He said that since the people were interested in Swaraj, they should celebrate the Shivaji festival. If Shivaji was able to establish Swaraj centuries ago, they too might expect to achieve it some day. Swaraj belonged to them by birthright. He further said that the Moderates could be compared to Shivaji's father Sahaji, who always used to advise his son not to take up arms against the mighty Mohammedan monarchies of the Deccan. But Shivaji gave a new turn to events. People being the masters of their fortunes could govern themselves if they only decided to do so. Swaraj was not far off from them. It would come to them the moment they learnt to stand on their own strength. At every meeting, at every function that he attended, he gave this slogan: "Swaraj is my birthright; I will have it".

Tilak thought of a federal type of political structure under Swaraj. Influenced by the American Constitution, he hoped that India should go for such type of Constitution. Although in his speeches and writings, he repeatedly said that Swaraj did not mean the end of the British rule in India, in his heart or hearts he wanted complete independence. He once said that there was no such thing like partial Swaraj. Self-rule under Dharmarajya either existed fully or did not exist at all. Partial Swaraj was contradiction in terms. Through Swaraj alone could the mission of India be fulfilled.

NON-VIOLENT PASSIVE RESISTANCE

Tilak wanted to implement his programme through non-violent passive resistance. His critics considered him to be a revolutionary both in words and deeds, and responsible for many political crimes including murders. But this was not true. No doubt, he supported Shivaji for killing Afzul Khan, appreciated the fighting spirit of Chafekar brothers in assassinating Rand and praised the patriotic spirit of the Bengal revolutionaries, but as a moralist he strongly believed that politics should not be separated from ethics. He put the highest emphasis on noble, good and purified intentions. He never preached political murder, nor should this be used as a means. Though a realist and pragmatist, he never supported the views of Machiavelli and Trietschke — who always argued that end justified means and any means, whether fair or foul, could be adopted to achieve the goal. To him, Swaraj could be attained through democratic means and non-violent passive resistance. Boycott and Swadeshi were, in effect, precursors of the later non-cooperation as well as non-violent civil disobedience movements. Having faith in democratic and constitutional means and methods, he adopted a practical programme to achieve his goal and believed that action must be straight and passive as well. Criticizing violence as a means to an end, he said that the fight was going to be constitutional and legal.

AN EXTREMIST

A man of action, Tilak had only one mission to accomplish, i.e. India should be free. He changed the image of politics by making it more practical and was prepared to sacrifice anything to achieve his goal, while the Moderates were not. He said that extremism was the natural growth of politics, and it was wrong to call it extremism.

Tilak did his best to make the people confident and assertive. With a clear vision of India's future and certain objectives to achieve, he worked very hard to give them a concrete reality. By doing so, he proved his political maturity and acumen. He felt that politics would drift away from ground reality, lose its base, and become dull and dry unless it became mass-based and mass-oriented. It was criticized by many that the Congress did not represent the people. But Tilak proved that it was false and baseless. He identified himself with the masses. As he departed from the conventional politics of the day, he was not appreciated by the Congress leaders who called him an extremist.

The Government's anti-people measures like racial discrimination policy, imposition of taxes and ruthless collection of land revenue were severely criticized by intellectuals. The Congress did not do anything to help the people. They were disappointed as they expected such practical help from their leaders as Tilak rendered during 1896–1897 famine. That kind of politics was dubbed as extremist by the Congress leaders. If that was extremism, the people very much welcomed it.

Even the progressive politicians in England were not happy with the Moderates of the Congress. In a letter to Dadabhai Naoroji, the socialist leader, Hyndman said that he would not help feeling contempt for the Indians in UK and in India who, instead of seriously taking up their own cause in a serious way, passed such a silly resolution of congratulating the Queen as was passed earlier at the Indian National Congress. Hyndman posed a question: Congratulations for what? For having ruined India for two or three generations? It was painful and a great pity. Intellectuals and distinguished citizens of Britain asked him to show them the evidence of discontent. Did the Indians cry for justice? Did they ever protest? Did they draw the attention of others to their plight? If they were so poor and oppressed, as had been claimed by him (Hyndman) let them articulate their grievances so that the people of Britain could hear them a little more of it than they had heard before.

As the people were exploited by the British regime, they often challenged the authority of those exploiters. But they could not succeed as they were docile and weak, devoid of courage to fight against injustice perpetrated upon them. There was little contact between them and the Congress. To arouse them even for constitutional agitation was considered by the authorities as sedition, and leaders were not prepared to take the risk. The British, who were very much conscious of their rights and prepared to fight at any cost against injustice and oppression, could not believe that there was oppression in India, for those who were opposed did not raise a voice of protest.

It was, therefore, felt that there should be an extremist party which should mobilize the manpower of the country for its political emancipation through agitation as followed and practised in Great Britain. Tilak's courage was admired by many and he was hailed as the future leader of India. A demarcated and divided line between the two schools became visible, a new party came into existence and Tilak became its undisputed leader.

THREE-FOLD PROGRAMME FOR POLITICAL ACTION

Tilak and the Nationalists strongly believed that unless people were made politically conscious, India could not achieve its freedom. Along with the Nationalists, he therefore, prepared a three-fold programme for effective and practical political action. It was: boycott, swadeshi and national education. Earlier, it was designed and intended to be used in Bengal as an effective means to teach a lesson to the British rulers and bring them to their senses over the issue of Bengal partition. But later it was decided that the entire nation could follow these principles so as to put tremendous pressure on the British Government.

The people were persuaded to boycott the British manufactured goods so that the British economy and its business interests both in India and abroad would be ruined. But soon Tilak realized that the whole British administration used to rest on the willing, or at least unthinking, consent and cooperation of the Indians. As early as in 1902, while addressing in Poona, he said that every Indian was a part of the British administration in India. The people themselves were responsible for the smooth functioning of the British administration. Though downtrodden and neglected, poor and backward, illiterate and uneducated, deprieved and neglected, they must be conscious of their power to paralyze the administration if they so desired. It was they who managed the rail-road and the telegraph, it was they who made settlements and collected revenues, it was, in fact, they who did everything for the administration though in a subordinate capacity. They must divert their energy towards the liberation of the nation, concentrate their attention for its freedom.

Tilak observed that Great Britain was free to rule India and its people did not have either power or inclination to fight against it. But they had every right to take steps to prevent the drain of millions of rupees from the country.

Boycott was no more confined to economic sphere. In due course of time, it acquired a political dimension. From economic sphere, it moved into the arena of politics. It moved from Bengal to the rest of the country. Boycott as a political weapon, was the first principle of the programme of Tilak and the nationalist leaders.

Swadeshi initially began as a primary economic counterpart to the programme of economic boycott. Swadeshi meant self-help, use of Indian-made goods rather than go for the goods manufactured at Birmingham and Manchester. European clothes were lit fire and reduced to ashes. People turned to local Indian production of Swadeshi goods. Swadeshi Movement expedited the process of industrial development in India. Local production was encouraged to meet the local demands. But like boycott, Swadeshi also meant something more than simple economic self-sufficiency. If self-help could be possible in economic sphere, why not the same in other spheres of life. In 1906, Tilak said that if people did not want to be white men's slaves, they should make the Swadeshi Movement more vigorous. It was the only effective method for achieving their goal. The object of the movement was to bring to an end a system which treated the Indians like slaves and force it to give them all the rights of British citizenship.

Throughout in 1906, Tilak remained extremely busy. He visited various places taking the message of Swadeshi and Self-Government to every home. The Swadeshi Movement quickly became a movement of national regeneration. Swadeshi makes one feel proud of his/her country. He loves his mother country very much and is prepared to sacrifice anything for its safety, security, unity and integrity. It was an economic, political and spiritual weapon. Swadeshi was *Bande Mataram* in action.

Tilak strongly believed that the Western education started by Lord Macaulay posed a great challenge to India's culture, tradition and civilization and created a barrier between the youths and their glorious heritage. As a result, they were not Indians in true sense of the term. Criticizing such type of education Tilak and his friends advocated for the establishment of schools and colleges throughout the country so that inexpensive and wholesome education could be provided to the young people and this would make them self-reliant. National education became an integral part of the Nationalist programme for India of the twentieth century. Western education prevented the students from knowing the true condition of their country, and did not help them in adopting or choosing a right vocation in their life. He said that reading and writing alone did not constitute education. Right education would throw light on the past events, incidents and the experience of our ancestors, and it would enable the people to become true citizens and earn their bread by right means.

The second aspect of National Education was religious education. Inspired by the religious scriptures and ancient heroes, Tilak expressed his shock and surprise as the education imparted in India did not cover the lessons on patriotism. Therefore, setting-up of national schools and colleges would go a long way in fulfilling the needs of the Indians. The medium of instruction in these national schools and colleges should be the mother tongue, and English should take the second position in this regard. He said that one who spoke and wrote good English was considered to be educated. But a mere knowledge of the language was no true education. Such a compulsion for the study of foreign language did not exist anywhere except in India. People spent twenty or twenty-five years for the education which they could easily obtain in seven or eight years if they got it through the medium of our vernaculars. They could help learning English, but there was no reason why its study should be made compulsory. Under the Mohammedan rule, the people were required to learn Persian, but not compelled to study it.

THE END

In July 1920, he suffered from malaria. Soon he recovered from it. But after some time he fell ill, as he suffered from pneumonia. His right lung was affected. His condition began to deteriorate and in the early hours of 1 August 1920 doctors declared him dead and he was no more. It was one of saddest moments for his sons, daughters and grandchildren and a large number of friends and admirers. The night was dark and drizzling. The whole city of Bombay was in deep slumber, completely oblivious of the fact that one of the greatest luminous stars disappeared, never to appear again, never to shine again, never to guide again, never to inspire again. His death was universally condoled. More than two lakh people joined his funeral procession, about a mile and a half long. When his mortal remains were consigned to flames, thousands of emotion-chocked voices were raised: "Tilak is immortal". "Tilak is immortal". "He is always with them". "He is always with them."

AN ESTIMATE

The generation that moulded the twentieth century India was born in the middle of the nineteenth century. The oldest was Bal Gangadhar Tilak, an extremist.

Along with others, he stood for Swaraj, Swadharma, Dharmatattwa, i.e. national rule, national religion, national identity. This version of patriotism found its first powerful exponents in the Extremist wing of the Congress. Other proponents, among others, were Lala Lajpat Rai of Punjab, Bipin Chandra Pal of Bengal.

In complexion, he was not fair. But he had an Aryan (sharp) nose and a pair of remarkable and brilliant eyes. The dark red turban that he put on his head made his appearance quite attractive, admirable and assuming. Gifted with a husky voice, he could not raise it to a very high pitch. But he spoke very impressively and assertively. His speeches were lucid and straightforward, having mesmerizing effect on the audience. They were spell bound when they listened to him with rapt attention.

His critics never believed that he was in favour of introducing social reforms in the evil-ridden Indian society. Said to be conservative, he was never considered to be progressive in his outlook. But they were taken aback when he said in 1907 that the Hindu religion never allowed or sanctioned caste system in India. The Hindu scriptures never supported the gradation of castes and no caste can claim its superiority over another. The prevailing social evils including caste system would ruin India if not checked in time.

Simple and frugal in his habits, Tilak fought against injustice, battled with his political rivals and always had a confrontation with the Government and authorities. Notwithstanding all these adverse conditions, he was calm, quiet and serene. He never lost peace of his mind. Hardly was he ever disturbed and perturbed, frustrated or disappointed when he was in difficulties. Rather he maintained his cheerfulness and always proved to be a source of inspiration to others. Deep anxieties and dismal failures never shocked him, disturbed his composure, deterred him from pursuing his desired goals.

Tilak was a great scholar in Sanskrit. He requested his friends to speak and write in Sanskrit. A versatile genius, a great journalist, he acknowledged Sisir Kumar Ghose, the founder Editor of the *Amrit Bazar Patrika* as his master in the field of journalism. Sitting at his feet, he learnt many lessons from him and treated him as his father.

An apostle of Hindu–Muslim unity, a friend of Muslims, a constitutional-agitator, he was a terror for the British Government. The latter was so scared of him for his involvement in violent activities, even the Rowlatt Committee, which was appointed to suggest measures to deal with political "crimes", cast unwarranted aspersions on him. Since he fought against injustice, he served a notice on the Government and asked it to withdraw the allegation and express regret for it.

Tilak was a man of principles and he lived up to it. What he professed, he practised it with all earnestness and sincerity. He believed that no one should possess anything more than what he required. Whatever excess he had, he shared the same with the poor and needy.

A great, indisputable and courageous leader, he was unparallel in the history of India as far as his personality was concerned. Giving a new dimension, a new image to politics, he made it more practical and more action-oriented. His reformation was highly appreciated and acclaimed. He struggled hard to ennoble, elevate and purify public life. Symbolizing self-sacrifice, he was a "Karma Yogi". Work was worship for him. Hard work, to him, was a passport to Heaven. He had a tremendous faith in his own self, in his leadership, in his capacity to deliver goods.

POINTS TO REMEMBER

- Tilak was born in 1856 to Gangadhar Pant and Parvathibai. Mother died in 1866 and father in 1872. He was interested more in sports other than in studies. He had a strong memory power. Early studies in Poona. Admitted into Deccan College in 1873.
- He was failed in F.A. Examination. Blunt and outspoken, he spent his time in unnecessary gossips. Gentle in manners. Strong character without vices. Passed B.A. in first class. Failed in M.A. Passed LL.B. A great Sanskrit and Mathematics scholar. His argument: Rig Veda was composed in 4500 B.C.
- His works on Vedas and Gita made him extremely popular. His efforts to establish private schools on the model of missionary institutions. Set up a new school in 1880.
- His school challenged the mission schools. Encouraged, he along with others set up the Deccan Education Society in 1880 at Poona and Fergusson College in 1881. He and his friends set up two newspapers: *Marhatta* and *Kesari* in January 1881.
- Differences with his friends. Purchased *Marhatta* and *Kesari*. A great and brave journalist. Left the Deccan Education Society. Lion of Maharashtra. Disliked by the Government because of his support to the ruling princes.
- Published news items from the *English Radical*. Allegation that Barve, a minister of Kolhapur, hatched out a conspiracy to poison the king. Barve's letters to the British resident. *Gyanprakash* published them. *Kesari* and *Marhatta* also quoted them. Matter was referred to court. Letters were found to be false. Tilak's apology to Barve. Tilak and his friend proved to be guilty. Sentenced to imprisonment for four months.
- He had tremendous faith in Indian philosophy. Not to imitate blindly the value system of the West. To reform the Indian value system not from the Western perspective, but in the light of the Indian standard. To Tilak, change was a must. His philosophy of life. He rejected Western philosophy.
- He wanted to create a new India in the light of its own values.

- He was not an orthodox, he was a strong supporter of Sanatan Dharma, a practical reformer. Ranade, Gokhale and others favoured extreme measures to reform the society. They were under the influence of Western values. But Tilak was not.
- Reforms possible only when people accept them, only when they are based on Indian values but not on those of the West.
- Self-rule only promotes progress and prosperity. It brings change. Social reformers adopted Western values, undermined Indian value system. To him, there should be a middle path between "too much orthodoxy" and "too much westernized".
- India could be reawakened when people changed their approaches and attitudes. Tilak wanted to bring out changes through writings and revival of festivals.
- He wanted to educate the people through religion and history. He was the defender and awakener of India's philosophy of life.
- He was against compartmentalization of society. Caste system must be abolished. Common history, common tradition, common festivals would promote unity. Did not compromise with principles and values.
- He joined the Congress in 1892. Held various political offices. Never wanted to occupy any office. Opposed the politics of the moderates in the Congress. Dissatisfied, he left the Congress. He criticized the Congress. To educate the innocent and ignorant villagers.
- He made the people politically conscious, conscious of their rights and duties, asked them to challenge government's indifferent attitude and inaction, Sent volunteers to famine affected areas. His efforts to arouse the people to fight against government's inaction. Poona plague. His service to the victims.
- Assassination of Rand in 1896 following the plague. Tilak was innocent, even then sent to jail. Self-rule must precede social reform.
- His criticism against the moderates. Highlighted the achievements of Shivaji. Swaraj was their birth right.
- He always said: "Swaraj is my birth right". Followed non-violent passive resistance to achieve his goal. Criticized as a revolutionary.
- He was not a Machiavellian. Faith in democratic means. Not in favour of violence. India should be free, it was his only mission in life.
- Politics to be mass-oriented, mass-based. Otherwise, it would be dull. Government's anti-people measures. No relief from the Congress. People were disappointed.
- Hyndman's comments and observations: The Indians should raise their voice to protest so that Britain would know about their oppression. He was unhappy as the Indians were dull and docile.

- Tilak's efforts to arouse the Indians against the British regime. Emergence of extremists with Tilak as its leader. Tilak's new proposal: boycott, swadeshi and national education.
    - Lord Macaulay's education created a barrier between the youth and their heritage. Unhappy, Tilak and his friends set up schools and colleges to provide inexpensive and wholesome education.
    - Setting-up of national schools and colleges. Medium of education — mother tongue. English to enjoy the secondary status. Study in English not to be compulsory.
    - In July 1920, he suffered from malaria. Soon he recovered. Again fell ill, as he suffered from pneumonia. Died on 1 August 1920.

7

Gopal Krishna Gokhale (1866–1915)

INTRODUCTION

A noble soul, a great statesman, a man of gifted talents and virtues, Gopal Krishna Gokhale passionately devoted himself to the cause of the people. Evincing a keen interest in the field of journalism, he edited the journal of the *Sarvajanika Sabha*, and the *Sudharak* for four years. In 1914, he was honoured when the title of Knight Commander of the Indian Empire was conferred on him. But he refused to accept this. By doing so, he made the country proud of him. What a sacrifice! Unparallel in the history of any country. A profound scholar of History and Economics and one of the great architects of India's freedom, he read a lot on British classical economics and the writings of Edmund Burke, particularly his *Reflections on the Revolution in France*. In 1902, he became a Member of the Indian Legislative Council and continued to be so until his death in Poona on 19 February 1915. Mahadev Govind Ranade was his political mentor, and from 1887 to 1901, he was also his guiding spirit. Like Ranade, Pherozshah Mehta also exerted a tremendous influence on him.

Justice Ranade founded the Sarvajanik Sabha in Poona much before the Indian National Congress, which was set up in 1885. Unlike other similar organizations, it was more vocal, articulate and effective. G.V. Joshi and Gokhale, Ranade's closest disciples, started a political quarterly to make the people educated and conscious of their rights and duties. They criticized the Government whenever necessary. In case of any natural calamity, they sent workers to the spot to conduct inquiries and prepare the reports. Gokhale served the Sabha with devotion and selfless interest for a decade under the guidance of Ranade without any desire to come to the limelight.

Gokhale, along with Ranade, a brilliant political economist and historian, and a towering personality highly acclaimed for his religious fervour and prophetic vision, brought a change in Indian politics by 'spiritualizing' it and by insisting that one's motive and action should be pure and not biased. Intending to bring political and social regeneration of India through peaceful means, he was fully convinced that any violent or revolutionary action, even if successful in realizing this goal, would retard the process and take things backward. As he was free, frank and fearless, he incurred the displeasure of many who hated him like anything. Very rightly, his biographer stated: "The followers of Mazzini hated Cavour even more than they hated the Austrians; and it is, perhaps, true that some Indian politicians hated Gokhale worse than they hated the British".

His only mission in his life was to serve the people. To him, it was one's dedication to a noble cause that gave him joy, peace and happiness. Men of vision like him created a turbulence or an agitation in society. Lord Rosebery once said that men of vision lived on a mount senai of their own, and when they came down to the earth, they came with the decrees and terrors of the Almighty Himself. Gokhale belonged to this class. People admired him for his lifestyle, his way of thinking, his approach to life and his vision. There were very few at that time anywhere in India who could be made comparable with him. His influence on successive generations was tremendous, powerful and lasting.

EARLY LIFE

Gokhale was born on 9 May 1866 in Kotluk, a small village in the Ratnagiri district under the Bombay Presidency. His mother Satyabhama also belonged to this village. Tamhanmala was the native village of his father Krishnarao Gokhale, who owned a small house in his village and worked as a rent collector. He had one brother and four sisters. In 1876, Gopal Krishna and his elder brother Govind went to Kolhapur for admission in the High School. As students, they were intelligent, industrious and responsible. In 1879, Krishnarao expired. Helpless and orphaned, they were forced to look after themselves. Govind gave up his studies, returned to his village, Kayal, to take up a job for which he was paid fifteen rupees as salary per month. At a tender age of eighteen, he shouldered the responsibility of his family consisting of his wife, mother, brother and four sisters. Gopal, who was only thirteen-year-old at the time of his father's death, realized the harsh realities that his family confronted and decided to give up his studies to take up a job to share the burden of Govind. But Govind rejected his proposal and asked him to continue his studies and sent him seven rupees per month to complete his studies. From the very childhood, Gopal faced innumerable difficulties and formidable challenges, leading a hard and frugal existence, cooking his own food, and reading under a street lamp to save kerosene.

His success in the matriculation examination from the Bombay University in 1881 did not give him much pleasure or happiness as he wanted to discontinue his studies because of economic difficulties. But he gave up this idea following Govind's persuasion to take up his higher studies. He was admitted into Raja Ram College at Kolhapur in 1881 and then went to Poona to study in the Deccan College. Later he joined the Elphinstone College in Bombay as a student of final year of the degree course. As a student, he was highly ambitious, competitive, and gifted with good memory power. He married quite at an early age of fifteen. His first wife, Savitribai, suffered from leprosy and never lived with him. In 1887, with the consent of his first wife he married Radhabai. But he was very kind enough towards Savitri who died a few years later. He was blessed with two daughters: Kashibai (1893) and Godavari (1896). On 13 October 1900, Radhabai gave birth to another child. But neither the mother nor the child survived.

After his B.A. examination, he gave private coaching to students to reduce the burden of his elder brother. Later he joined the Engineering College in Bombay. But soon he left it since students were dull. Then he decided to join the Indian Civil Service. And for this, he had to go to England to sit for a tough competitive examination and obviously success was not certain. Therefore, he decided to adopt law as his profession. He joined the Bombay University to complete law. In 1885, he passed the first part of the law examination and might have become a lawyer, or a judge. But a sudden and unexpected development altered the course of his life.

On 24 October 1884, the Deccan Education Society was formed to spread private education and bring it within the reach of children of even the lower middle class. An important landmark in the history of education in Maharashtra, it opened a new chapter in the life of Gokhale. Inspired by the ideals of the society, he joined in 1885 as a humble teacher in the New English School. In June 1886, he became a life member of the Society and promised that he would serve it for twenty years on a subsistence wage.

DISCIPLE OF RANADE

In 1885, Gokhale met Ranade for the first time at a function organized by the New English School. Impressed by his personality, Ranade appointed him as Editor of *Sarvajanik Sabha*, a quarterly Journal. It was a great honour for him as he was quite young and inexperienced. The editorship gave him his first lessons in political journalism and an opportunity to go through the problems of the educated mass.

Ranade, a close friend of A.O. Hume, Dadabhai Naoroji, William Wedderburn and Pherozshah Mehta, was held in high esteem by top ranking Congress leaders. Gokhale gained a lot because of his close contact with Ranade. It had a profound impact upon him. He remained as his disciple for nearly fourteen years.

A great Indian, Ranade was appointed as a judge at Poona in 1871, where he played an important role in the public life. When Gokhale came under his influence, he had already by then reached the pinnacle of glory. A leader of the rational, progressive and west-oriented educated class, he greatly admired the

English character and education. He believed that India would one day have a peaceful and constitutional evolution and like England would move forward along the road to progress. He felt that the British rule was blessing in disguise for India and it could be turned into an instrument of Indian resurgence. The Hindu society could be made free from all its blind beliefs and superstitions. But he was not a blind admirer of the West. He stood for representative institutions and a free press on the British model.

Gokhale's close contact with Ranade made him immensely happy. Proud of being associated with him for a long time, he had a strong reverence and awe for him. He considered him to be the chosen instrument of God to accomplish his mission in this world. Inspired by his patriotism, integrity, industry, perseverance and simplicity, he always acknowledged his profound gratitude to him. He came under his influence during formative years of his life. He faced a lot of ordeals during this period. But they proved to be a blessing in disguise for him as these made him more matured and more tolerant.

THE BUDDING POLITICIAN

In 1899, Gokhale opened a new chapter in his life by joining the politics of Poona and it was the beginning of his bright political career. It was also the last year of Bombay Governor Lord Reay's administration. Crawford, the Commissioner of the Central Division, abused his power by extorting bribes from his subordinates and took them to task if they did not oblige him. Punishments ranged from demotion to transfer to dismissal. Successive Governors did not take any action against him. But Lord Reay decided to prosecute him, and refused to accept the verdict of the British judges when they declared him "not guilty".

During the trial, the victimized junior Indian officers gave their witnesses against Crawford. But supporting the latter, his well-wishers demanded these officer's dismissal from service and Reay's callback to England. But, in Poona, there were many who supported these officers. On 1 September 1889, a meeting was held to express popular feelings on the case. Rich tributes were paid to Lord Reay for his courage and fair play. Speaking in this meeting, Gokhale moved a resolution denouncing the 'persistent and factious misrepresentations' of the Crawford case in the English Press (which demanded the dismissal of the junior Indian officers). His speech on the Crawford case exposing the misdeeds of the British bureaucracy and the Anglo-Indian Press was his first notable performance and brought him to limelight as a promising politician. He became a familiar figure in Poona politics in the 1890s.

In October 1896, Mahatma Gandhi met Gokhale. 'Love at first sight', was Gandhi's description of his first encounter with Gokhale who was senior to him in age only by three years. But this was not the only reason for the respect and reverence Gandhi had for him. In 1896, both of them were young; Gandhi was twenty-seven, and Gokhale thirty. While Gandhi was a little-known, diffident champion of the small Indian minority in distant South Africa, Gokhale was a prominent educationist, editor and politician in the centre of provincial and national affairs. Gandhi sought Gokhale's cooperation in raising the problems of the Indians staying abroad in the Imperial Council at Calcutta and in the House of Commons. The 1896 meeting was the beginning of a life-long collaboration and friendship between them which had a deep impact not only on their friendship and their political career but also on the history of India.

PROFESSOR GOKHALE

Gokhale started his career at the Fergusson College in Poona as a Lecturer in English Literature. He taught Literature, Mathematics, History and Political Economy. Being grave, conscientious, accessible and helpful, he commanded much respect from his students. His clear and eloquent exposition had a mesmerizing effect on them. He never considered that the study of history and economics would be merely an intellectual exercise, rather it would be a key to the understanding of contemporary problems. Therefore, students always considered him to be a source of great encouragement and inspiration. In 1895, he was elected to the Senate of the Bombay University, a rare honour for an Indian Professor. Though it was an additional burden to him, it gave much satisfaction to the Indian academic community which resented the virtual monopoly of examinerships by European Professors. Earlier in 1892, he became the Secretary of the governing body of the Council of the Deccan Education Society. It was a great honour and prestige for him.

ON THE CONGRESS PLATFORM

In November 1888, Gokhale attended the first provincial conference of the Congress at Poona, which elected delegates to the Allahabad session of the Congress. He was elected its Joint Secretary. But he could not attend the same. In 1889, when the Congress met at Bombay with Sir William Wedderburn in the chair, a large number of fifty-nine delegates including Gokhale from Poona attended the session. Gokhale delivered his maiden but quite inspiring speech on 27 December 1889. The young Professor–Politician had his own style of presenting the facts, acquired mastery over them and his logical arguments left a deep impact upon the educated Indians. His diction was elegant, but he did not hesitate to call a political spade a spade. He was outspoken and courageous while presenting the facts.

In 1890, when the Indian National Congress met at Calcutta, Gokhale spoke eloquently in favour of reducing the salt tax. As he spoke at length in the Congress sessions year after year on various aspects, he developed self-confidence and justified himself. Highly critical of the authorities, at the Allahabad Congress Session (December 1892), he spoke on the Indian share in the higher ranks of the administration. At the Lahore Congress (December 1893), he strongly criticized the Government of India for pursuing a policy of retrogression and for maltreating the educated mass. From 1889 onwards, he attended the Congress sessions regularly. At Nagpur Conference (1891), he was elected a Member of the "Subjects Committee", the inner forum for the selection of subjects and speakers for the plenary session of the Congress. In 1895, when the Congress met at Poona, he was one of the secretaries of the Reception Committee. The Poona Congress exposed the bitter rift in the body politic of Maharashtra, the reasons were more personal and social rather than political.

THE RISING STAR

The Indian National Congress was set up in 1885 under the leadership of A.O. Hume. He felt that petitions and protests did not serve any purpose. Hence, he decided to appeal to the public in India and England as it would certainly bring reforms. He wanted to agitate the public opinion. Stronger the public opinion, greater would be the reforms. Distinguished parliamentarians like Edmund Burke, Bright, Fawcett and Bradlaugh occasionally articulated Indian grievances, but to attract the attention of the British Press, Parliament and people on Indian view of Indian affairs, systematic efforts were necessary. Therefore, in 1888 Hume and his friends set up an "Indian Agency" in London. In 1889, the British Committee of the Indian National Congress was formed under the chairmanship of Sir William Wedderburn. For the next thirty years it carried on the Congress propaganda in Britain. Dadabhai Naoroji and Wedderburn, who were elected to Parliament in 1892 and 1893 respectively, formed the "Indian Parliamentary Committee". In 1893, it influenced the House of Commons to pass a resolution to hold the I.C.S. (Indian Civil Service) Examination simultaneously in India and England. In 1894, it demanded that there should be a parliamentary inquiry into Indian expenditure, and an equitable distribution of financial burdens between India and Britain. Following this, the British Government set up a Royal Commission to go into the aforesaid problems. It was headed by Lord Welby, a former Permanent Secretary of the British Treasury. The thirteen members of the Commission included M.Ps. as well as veterans of the civil and military services in India. The most heartening aspect was that the Royal Commission included members like Dadabhai Naoroji and two of his closest colleagues in England, namely, William Wedderburn and W.S. Caine.

It was felt that the views of the Indian nationalists should be effectively presented before the Commission and this could be possible if eminent persons were chosen. Naoroji, therefore, requested Ranade to come to London to present the case before the Commission. Ranade was ready to go and the Commission was ready to invite him but the Government of India blocked his way. Himself thwarted, Ranade decided to depute Gokhale as a representative of the Deccan Sabha. The Indian team also included D.E. Wacha, a representative of the Bombay

Presidency Association, G. Subramaniam Iyear on behalf of the Mahajan Sabha, Madras and Surendranath Banarjee on behalf of the Indian Association, Calcutta. Gokhale accepted the job as challenging and discussed economic and financial matters with G.V. Joshi and Ranade.

Just like a fish out of water, Gokhale felt suffocated during his first visit to England, as he could not adjust himself with English dress and manners. As he was strictly a vegetarian, he scrutinized the menu card very carefully before placing order for food, lest it did not contain anything like egg, meat or fish. He was also worried about his serious assignment.

Appearing before the Commission on 12 and 13 April 1897, Gokhale presented forcefully his written statement of the nationalist's views on the financial and economic problems of the British India: that the distribution of burdens between Britain and India was inequitable, that there was discrimination in favour of British industries, that there was a heavy 'drain' from India in the interest of the British garrison and capital. This was a familiar chargesheet against the British regime. While criticizing the British economic policies, he made use of the 'drain theory', but he did not make it the main issue of his argument. Besides discussing financial issues, he vehemently opposed the socio-economic and political policies of the Government of the British India.

Lord Welby, the Chairman of the Royal Commission, and Sir James of Perle grilled and cross-examined Gokhale on the sensitive issue of Indian poverty and famine. He boldly answered their questions, even though they did not agree with his views. Gokhale was not only successful in his mission but also did his job most splendidly. But, as he was very modest, he attributed all his success to his master, Ranade and friend, Joshi. He said that his role was no more than that of a conduit pipe and Edison's phonograph. No doubt, he got the required data from his mentors, but it was he who drafted the memorandum of his evidence which won him such high praise. Very much pleased and satisfied with his performance, Wedderburn saw in him a new ally for the British Committee of the Congress and found him to be able and earnest. Gifted with a capacity for brilliant exposition, he was quite at ease in the Committee room and on the public platform. He was confident and knew the art of telling: what, who, where, how and why. Wedderburn invited him to his residence at Meredith, acquainted him with British politics and introduced him to prominent British politicians and Anglo-Indian officials.

Praising Gokhale's success in England, Ranade described him as 'our rising man'. Gokhale's successful performance before the Commission, his interaction with British politicians, his participation in the debates and his deliberations and speeches made him bold, courageous and confident and provided him enough courage and strength to play a dominant role in Indian politics in future and influence the course of Indian history in the last quarter of the nineteenth century and the first quarter of the twentieth century.

A MAJOR SETBACK

When Gokhale left for England, India experienced a terrible famine in 1896–1997, affecting nearly 97 million people. In Western India, conditions deteriorated further when the region was affected by bubonic plague. To bring the situation under control, a Committee was set up by the Government of Bombay in March 1897 with W.C. Rana as Chairman and Lieutenant Colonel C.R. Phillips and Surgeon-Captain W.W.O. Beveridge as its members. It was authorized to handle the natural calamity effectively.

Sandhurst, the Governor of Bombay, informed the leaders of various political parties and communities of Poona about the measures taken to control the situation. These included the house-to-house search for patients for isolation and their treatment in hospitals. No one opposed these measures, though some apprehensions were there in Poona. Tilak's newspapers supported these measures and pointed out their real necessity to curb the epidemic.

The 'Operation Plague' started in Poona. The British soldiers inspected the houses while the Indian soldiers disinfected the buildings. Because the authorities feared that Indian soldiers would not be strictly impartial if they were asked to inspect. While making house-to-house searches, the British soldiers, as alleged, forcibly opened cash boxes, burned the personal belongings, account books and beddings of diseased persons. Complaints were made before Rand who simply ignored them. As a result, he incurred the wrath and displeasure of the public. When people failed to restrain the activities of the British soldiers through their representations, deputations and complaints in the press and platform, they submitted a memorandum on 20 May 1897 to the Governor of Bombay. The Deccan Sabha established in November 1896 under the inspiration of Ranade to serve as the mouthpiece of the moderate politicians of Poona, took the initiative. In the memorandum, it was pointed out that the British soldiers transgressed their limits when they shifted to the hospitals not only patients but even their relatives and passers-by. Men and women were publicly stripped off for "inspection". Socio-religious mores and ethics were blatantly violated. People were forced to open their houses and business premises and their belongings were destroyed without any reason. Even healthy women as well as women patients were not spared from sexual assault. Shocked and dismayed, Pandita Ramabai, a prominent social worker said: "God knows! How many young girls of good character have been obliged to go to the plague hospital and segregation camp and been ruined and lost for ever".

Gokhale read the memorandum in London during his lecture tour organized by the British Committee. By the time he read it, "Operation Plague" in Poona was over.

On 23 June 1897, a state banquet and reception was hosted in the Poona residence of the Governor to mark the sixtieth anniversary of Queen Victoria. Soon after the celebration was over, the guests left the party at midnight. W.C. Rand also left the place in his carriage. He had gone only two hundred yards when someone fired at him. But Lt. O.E. Ayerst, whose carriage immediately followed Rand's, was hit by the bullet. He succumbed to the bullet injury but Rand survived. The European community was deeply stirred. Authorities decided to take stringent action to suppress such activities.

Wedderburn was deeply moved by the developments in Poona as it was a matter of great concern. The question was not merely of providing some relief to those unfortunate victims harassed by famine, plague, home-searches and irresponsible and characterless soldiers but also to see that the Indian Press was not attacked and harassed. It was felt that if the Poona assassination could be shown in the local context of plague operations, then the harsh legislation against the Indian Press might be dropped off. Wedderburn decided that there should be a campaign for a public and impartial inquiry into Poona affairs. He convened a meeting of the Indian Parliamentary Committee on 1 July 1897 and invited four Indian delegates including Gokhale, who briefed the MPs on the background of events at his home town and demanded that there should be a public inquiry into these events. But it was rejected by the Government.

Strongly criticizing the Plague Administration in an interview, Gokhale alleged that the British soldiers misbehaved the women in Poona. But this could not be easily proved. Other allegations were unfortunately ignored. His critics branded him as an arch-liar slanderer. This gave him terrible mental pain and made him depressed. He could not substantiate his allegation as it was not easy to produce evidence two months after the completion of the plague operations. Meanwhile, Tilak was arrested. Punitive police was imposed on Poona. Natu brothers were deported. In such a situation, it was not easy to defy the authorities. Though it was difficult to legally prosecute him, he felt guilty. Therefore, he offered his apology to the Governor and others including the members of the Plague Committee and soldiers engaged in plague operation.

For Gokhale, the 'apology' was a bitter cup of humiliation. Some newspapers were highly critical of him as, to them, he compromised his reputation. But some other papers like *Indian Spectator* praised him for his absolute, frank and helpless self-condemnation. The *Marhatta* did not appreciate Gokhale's withdrawal of all the charges, since he failed to prove only one of them.

Lonely and unhappy, he wanted to retire from politics. In this regard, he wrote letters to Wedderburn, Caine, Naoroji and Hume. Extending all their support and sympathy to him, they were against his retirement from politics at the critical juncture of the national struggle.

Gokhale's sorrows and humiliations became worst compounded when the Brahmin community socially ostracized him for his foreign tour, since at that time it was considered to be a sin or a social crime if one went abroad. Frustrated and disappointed, he wanted to retire from position. But, later, he changed his mind. No longer he wanted to retreat from the battlefield as he prepared himself to face the onslaught of his opponents and the fickleness of public opinion with courage and confidence. The crisis in 1897 threatening his political career and which might have caused his political death, however, provided him enough strength for his spectacular comeback and for the important role he was to play in the political development of India.

THE CLOUD LIFTED

The year 1897, as stated above, saw the worst public humiliation and political eclipse of Gokhale. Undeterred and unperturbed, he wanted to contest to the Bombay Council from the District Boards of the Central Division. It was a bolt step and a courageous decision. The 'apology incident' made Gokhale tough and politically ambitious. Bal Gangadhar Tilak, his rival, was another contestant. Governor Sandhurst did not like Tilak and wanted to veto his election if he won it. He was also supported by Lord Curzon, the Viceroy. Besides, Gokhale was more popular with the voters in the districts and had an edge over Tilak. The latter, therefore, withdrew his candidature and supported another candidate, Garud. Gokhale won the election. His victory restored his earlier image, popularity, position and status. He got a platform to express himself. The "Rising Star of the Deccan" of former years began to shine to show light to others so that they could live happily with freedom.

As Gokhale's star was shining on the political horizon, darkness was descending over his domestic life giving him one of the most severe shocks in his life. His wife Radhabai died after giving birth to a son who died later, leaving behind two young daughters. Ranade also passed away on 16 January 1901. Gokhale tolerated his 'loss' with courage and fortitude. No loss, however grave and serious, could deflect him from his political career he had chosen. Elected to the Imperial Council in 1901, he became the President of the Poona City Municipality in July 1902, a honour bestowed on him in recognition of his significant service for the cause of the nation.

MEMBER OF THE IMPERIAL COUNCIL

On 20 December 1901, Gokhale became an "Additional Member" of the Governor-General's Council (Imperial Council). His thought-provoking address to the Council on 26 March 1902 during the budget session had a mesmerizing effect upon the Indian intelligentsia. Like Byron, he could have said that he woke up one fine morning and found himself famous. The *Amrita Bazar Patrika*, in its editorial, said that Indians had always an ambition that some Indian Member should openly and fearlessly criticize the Financial Statement of the Government. But this ambition was never fulfilled. When Members had ability, they had not the requisite courage. When they had the requisite courage, they had not the ability. However, for the first time in the annals of the British rule in India, a native of India not only exposed the fallacies of the Government, but also did it in an uncompromising manner. Both the British and Indian Press highly appreciated his budget speech. In recognition of his service, the Government of India announced the bestowal of a C.I.E. on him. It was well received in India. Many others had received this honour before. But Gokhale earned this distinction even though he was a strong critic of the Government.

Lord Curzon, the Viceroy, appreciated Gokhale's ability but not his patriotism. Praising his qualities, conduct and character and his role as a Member of the Council for five to six years, he said that by attacking the policies of the Government, Gokhale behaved like the Leader of the Opposition and in that capacity he (Gokhale) took him (Lord Curzon) to task. Curzon had never met a man of any nationality more gifted with Parliamentary capacities than Gokhale. He believed that Gokhale would have attained a position of distinction in any Parliament in the world.

From 1902 onwards Gokhale spent the best part of the winter not in Poona but in Calcutta, the seat of the Provincial and Central Governments and the commercial centre of the "Indian Empire". There he came in contact with great people like Motilal Ghose, Nilaratan Sircar, J.C. Bose, Prafulla Chandra Roy, R.N. Tagore and Sister Nivedita.

CONGRESS REINVIGORATED

The Nineteenth Session of the Indian National Congress held in Madras in December 1903 was a failure. Disappointed with the proceedings, the delegates had least interest or enthusiasm. Therefore, no province was prepared to hold the session in 1904. Hence, as a matter of compulsion, Pherozshah Mehta offered to hold it in Bombay in 1904 even though it was held there in 1902. At the turn of the century many Congressmen, while making self-introduction, were asking, "What the Congress has achieved?" It was repeated every year and, therefore, doubts were raised about the wisdom of its strategy. Young leaders refused to accept the British regime in India. Aurobindo Ghose strongly criticized the Congress leaders as they didn't have vision, courage and earnestness.

In 1902, Lala Lajpat Rai, a Punjabi politician, observed sceptically: a nation did not deserve any political status if it failed to distinguish between asking for political rights and claiming them. The British Government was very much delighted to see the waning of popular enthusiasm as well as the growth of scepticism among the Congress workers. All those, to them, were a welcome development. In 1896, Secretary of State Hamilton noted that the Congress as a political power had come steadily down during the last few years. In 1900, Lord Curzon said that the strategy of the Congress had failed and its fall was imminent. Its initial enthusiasm had worn off; it ceased to be interesting; its session was not even a three-day national festival; its influence did not penetrate into the district towns, more less into the villages; its leaders betrayed apathy and inertia between the annual sessions; many of its adherents vanished. Unfortunately, a small group controlling the organization from Bombay remained indifferent to the discontent in rank and file. It was afflicted by doubt and demoralization. Gokhale, therefore, suggested that Congress should be reorganized by inducting new faces. Instead of functioning like an academic institution, it should be work-oriented. In the Madras Session, it was decided to adopt a new constitution and set up a committee. Since Pherozshah Mehta did not want to share this power with a committee, he did not accept the proposal, hence rejected.

R.C. Dutt suggested that a full-time Secretary should be appointed to invigorate the Congress. Gokhale was ready to accept the office without any remuneration since it was, to him, an honour to work in that capacity. In 1903, Gokhale and Wache were appointed as Joint Secretaries. As Joint Secretary, his immediate task was to collect funds to save the British Committee from insolvency and also to reinvigorate the Congress Committee in the provinces. His friends including Wedderburn appreciated his fund-raising activity. They felt that he would give a new lease of life to the Congress and the British Committee in England from stagnation.

SERVANTS OF INDIA

As stated above, the influence of the Congress was declining as only a few members were seriously concerned about it. Others treated it as a part-time job. This should be their most important duty to perform. Gokhale felt that students after completing their courses should join the organization and work for the country. Effective steps were, therefore, to be taken to strengthen the Congress and one of them would be to motivate the students to involve themselves in the nation-building process. He was convinced that even a few of them with their commitment and dedication could change the image of the organization as well as of the country itself if they were really serious. To impart training to the graduates on various aspects for understanding nation-building activities, he set up a society in 1905 called the Servants of India and became its first Member. The trainees were paid monthly thirty rupees each and a full member got fifty rupees per month. They were supposed to act as full-time members to serve the country. Several members of the Society — G.K. Devadhar, A.V. Patwardhan, N.A. David, H.N. Kunjru, etc. carved out a niche for themselves in the public life of India.

CLASH WITH CURZON

Viceroy Lord Curzon felt that the Congress was moving away from the people. His indifference to the educated class and his hostility to their political aspirations created lots of misunderstanding and distrust in the minds of the enlightened citizens of India. The situation became highly volatile and sensitive when Curzon decided to introduce certain reforms in the universities. On 2 September 1901, he convened a 'private' conference of educational officers at Simla. Unfortunately, no Indian officer was invited to this conference. It was attended by top ranking white officials including the D.P.I., Principals, Vice Chancellors, etc.

The Simla Conference, which met for six hours daily for sixteen days, discussed in minute details the problems of Indian education. Lord Curzon took an active part in it. There was a strong demonstration in Calcutta against the Simla Conference as it was considered detrimental to the academic interests of the Indians and it would cripple the education system of the country. Demonstration disappointed Curzon since he never expected it. But he did his best in the Conference to protect and promote the education system. Terribly angry and annoyed, he strongly protested against the imputation of ulterior motives since he was merely trying to streamline university education as he had sought to streamline the departments of irrigation, railways and mining.

Government of India introduced a Bill on Education in respect of granting affiliation to of private colleges as well as of nomination of members to the Senates and Syndicates of the universities. Gokhale and other Indian Members of the Imperial Council protested against the Bill. This made Lord Curzon furious, angry and unhappy with Gokhale and others. No doubt, Gokhale lost the battle but won the war as he received wide acclamation from the intelligentsia. His patriotism made him great and a grateful country would never forget him for his services.

ENVOY EXTRAORDINARY

In 1904, the Conservative Government in the UK led by Mr. Belfour, was losing its ground. Hence, holding of general election became imminent. It was believed that the Liberal Party would replace the ruling Conservative Party. The Indian National Congress hoped that the new Government would be favourable and do something for the people of India. The Bombay Congress, therefore, unanimously decided to depute Congress representatives to put forth the claims of India before the electors, before the candidates contesting the election and before the political leaders in England. S.N. Banerjee, M.A. Jinnah, Lajpat Rai and Gokhale were to visit England as delegates. Gokhale was supposed to reach England by the end of May 1905. His departure was, however, stalled by Pherozshah Mehta, who interpreted the resolution of Bombay Congress to mean that delegates could leave for England only after the actual dissolution of the British Parliament. Gokhale, however, left for England when Dadabhai Naoroji, Hume and Wedderburn pressurized Mehta to give green signal for his departure. On 2 October 1905, he reached London. His main contention was that India should have a Self-Government. It was his new slogan. He addressed as many as forty-five meetings over a period of six weeks. He impressed everyone when he spoke with courage, confidence and conviction. His brilliant exposition and tremendous analysis of the problems confronting India had a strong impact upon his audience. It was felt as if the people were listening not to a politician but to an eminent statesman gifted with strong abilities, intellect and vision.

Gokhale said that India was passing through many ordeals, that the British people and Parliament failed to discharge their obligations and had been suffering from a guilt complex for grave dereliction of duty as they handed over the strings of Indian administration to a coterie of professional administrators, that the people of India had grievances which required immediate attention for their redressal as well as for fundamental changes. He blamed the British bureaucracy in India for the plight of India. The bureaucrats were arrogant, indisciplined, uncontrolled, apathetic, indifferent, devoid of vision and mission, bereft of zeal and had least interest or little incentive to undertake long-term measures for the permanent good of the country. As a result, the Indian economy was in a bad shape, village industries languished, the soil was exhausted, the peasantry was hopelessly in debt and the people were desperately poor. In other words, the socio-economic condition of the people was highly deplorable.

He offered certain concrete proposals for reform. It was proposed that 50 per cent seats of the Imperial Council should be reserved for Indians. The budget should be formally presented to the Council, Members be allowed to move amendments and the Viceroy could exercise his veto power. At least six seats should be allotted to India in the House of Commons so that it could have an opportunity to know at first hand the Indian view of things.

Gokhale's speech was highly appreciated in London. Lord Coleridge, the Liberal Peer, who presided over a meeting at the National Liberal Club, paid a rich tribute to him for his extraordinary moderate speech. He confessed that if he were in the same position as Gokhale, he would not have been so moderate. He wished that the House of Commons had members like Gokhale. He had no doubt that his arguments were reasonable, moderate and fair. Gokhale met in England leading political figures like Lord Rippon, Lord Reay, Herbert Gladstone, H.H. Asquith, Leonard Courtney, Arthur Godley, St. John Bradrick, Richard Huldave, L. George, Winston Churchill and John Morley. His mission was successful and this delighted him very much though he was very much exhausted.

The indomitable spirit with which he championed the cause of the country in Britain raised his stature and image. A friend wrote to him, "The whole Indian world is at your feet at present".

CONGRESS PRESIDENT

Gokhale was elected as President of the Banaras Congress just a few days before his departure to England. He stayed there for three months and during this period there was a sea change in the Indian political scenario following the partition of Bengal which insulted the Bengalis in particular and the Indians in general and which came into effect on 16 October 1905. The day was observed as the day of mourning; in Calcutta thousands did not take food, closed their business and walked barefoot to the banks of the river Ganges for a dip amidst deafening cries of 'Bande Mataram'. The boycott of British manufactures and the use of

'Swadeshi' (Indian) goods were advocated to bring the Government to heel. Traditional Congress policies were found to be least effective in the changed scenario. There was a strong demand for new methods and a new leadership. The reins of the movement were passing from the hands of the old guards like Surendra Nath Banerjee.

Lajpat Rai also believed that old methods of the Congress became obsolete and outdated. Like Bengal, other provinces should also ventilate their grievances by holding demonstrations against Lord Curzon. But Pherozshah Mehta and others in Bombay did not favour it, though Dadabhai Naoroji wrote to Gokhale from England on 26 November 1905: "Our way of emancipation is much nearer than many of us imagine". Wedderburn wanted the Benaras Congress to take full advantage of the great upheaval in the country.

Gokhale's task as President of the Congress was more difficult than what Wedderburn and Naoroji thought about it. The Bengal partition and its consequences made the extremist elements in the Congress of Bengal and their allies much strong and confident. They had also their counterparts in Punjab and Maharashtra. Gokhale felt that it would no more be possible to keep in tact the old traditional values of the Congress in the changing political scenario and follow the same methods as adopted in the past by the old guards of the Congress. He, therefore, felt that the situation would improve if Mehta attended the Congress session as he knew how to handle the dissidents and rebels. Earlier, Mehta had silenced his critics in 1903 at the Madras session of the Congress and shrewdly managed the Congress session at Bombay in 1904. But he refused to attend the Benaras Congress session as he did not like Gokhale, his speeches in London, his functioning as a member of the Imperial Council, his 'Servants of India' Society, his visit to England, etc.

Gokhale was given a warm, cordial and rousing reception by the citizens of Benaras. Moved by popular enthusiasm and aware of the latest developments in the Congress as well as in the country, he perceived the beginning of popularization of the Congress and emergence of a radical group which strongly opposed the old leaders and their slogans. The belligerent attitude of the Bengal Congress was shared and supported by the congress of the Central Provinces, Berar, Maharashtra and Punjab, which accounted for more than half of the delegates present at the session. The newly emerging extremist group urged that the Congress should henceforth act as the party opposition to the Government.

Against this political backdrop, Gokhale had to function and perform his role with much care and caution as his task was not only difficult but also quite delicate. Shrewdly adopting a position half-way between the Congress establishment and the new radicals, Gokhale in his presidential address made an appraisal of the political situation at the end of 1905, analysed the past and made a forecast of the future, criticized the monopolization of power by a hostile, self-centred and indifferent British bureaucracy in India. Self-Government was the only real and permanent remedy for the evils from which India suffered. He called even for a modest beginning in administrative and constitutional reforms:

enlargement of the size of the elective elements and powers of the Legislative Councils; appointment of Indians to the Councils of the Secretary of State, the Viceroy and the Provincial Governors; formation of advisory boards at the district level; separation of the judicial from the executive functions; reduction of military expenditure; and the expansion of education.

The Congress was virtually divided between the old guards led by Pherozshah Mehta and the radicals belonging to Bengal, Maharashtra and Punjab. But fortunately a close contest was avoided because of Gokhale's acumen, patience and tact. He succeeded in treading the tight rope between the old Congress orthodoxy and the new radicalism.

ADVOCATE FOR INDIA

Lord Curzon was succeeded by Lord Minto as Viceroy of India. During the last phase of his career, the former alienated large sections of Indian population. He was defamed and discredited for his measures including the partition of Bengal. Unlike Curzon, Lord Minto was cool and systematic to the Indian aspirations. In the Imperial Council, Gokhale, therefore, did not want to embarrass him. In his budget speech on 28 March 1906, he laid more emphasis on economic issues than on political affairs. An advocate of welfare state he favoured the reduction in the salt duty and land revenue at least in the famine-stricken areas; the amortization of rural debts; the funding of local bodies, particularly for water supply and drainage; the extension of primary education and the establishment of a technological institute.

Gokhale left for England on 14 April 1906. The paper he presented before the East Indian Association on 11 July 1906 was one of the most brilliant, clearest and forthright expositions of the Indian case for self-government which he had ever attempted. Three months' silent and strenuous diplomacy gave him maximum mental tension and this had an adverse effect on his health. He suffered physically and mentally. He lost his mental peace. Yet, his dreams remained unfulfilled. The reforms he advocated were never implemented.

GOKHALE AND HIS ECONOMIC THINKING

Gokhale's views on economics deserve special attention. He had a clear picture and a perfect vision of contemporary India and its economy. Expressing his anguish and shock over India's poverty, he warned that the economy would be in very bad shape unless major stringent steps were taken to improve it. A great exponent of public finance, he was against heavy taxation as it was regressive in character in a poor agricultural country like India. Too many taxes were imposed while per capita income was much low and, unfortunately, even the minimum amount of what was collected in form of taxes was not spent on welfare activities. Taxation, during the British regime in India, was a part of mechanism of the "drain" of wealth from India to the United Kingdom. This was a serious blow to the economic development of India as it prevented capital formation.

Gokhale complained that the Government's free trade policy severely affected the interests of the Indian industries and confined almost one half of the rural population in their land, because they had nothing else to do. Fresh employment opportunities could not be created because of lack of resource development. Addressing the Fabian Society in London on 9 October 1906, he said that people suffered from terrible poverty because of the drain of twenty to thirty million rupees annually to England. India was, thus, deprived of the capital which was so much essential for industrial development. The East India Company never wanted that India should grow in the fields of agriculture and industry. It produced raw materials only without factories to manufacture the same. This was the beginning of industrial decay in India.

SYMPATHY FOR THE WORKING CLASS

Unlike Gandhi, Gokhale supported mass production through or with the help of machines. Understanding the significance of the technological progress in advanced industrial countries, he emphasized the importance and urgency of technical and higher scientific education as well as mass education as they would be the instruments of modernization and technological progress. He, therefore, argued in favour of extending cooperation to the Government in the beginning stage of India's industrialization. He said that India had to depend for some time upon foreign countries for its machinery. He argued that the community as a whole should not be allowed to suffer for the sake of the narrow interests of the protected industries. Indiscriminate protection of industries either in the name of Swadeshi or tariff duties would certainly promote and enrich a few at the expense of the many.

Supporting the working class and though not a socialist in a partisan sense, he was certainly one of the earliest nationalists to protect the interests of labourers in mills and plantations. Moved by their plight, he moved in 1911 an amendment to the Clause 23 of a Bill in the Imperial Legislative Council to consolidate and amend the law regulating the factory labour.

During the pre-independence days, the poor villagers were forcibly taken outside the country to work on plantation firms. They did not know the country where they were asked to work. Deprived of their dues, they had to work like domesticated animals. No one was there to share their sorrows and sufferings. Strongly criticizing such conditions, he described it as "monstrous", "iniquitous in itself, based on fraud and maintained by force, wholly opposed to modern sentiments of justice and humanity". He rightly said that indenture labour replaced the slave labour that was abolished in 1834. He was shocked that while the emancipated Negroes refused to accept the indentured system because it was a thinly disguised return to slavery, Indians were victimized by the system.

A SUPPORTER OF THE PEASANTS

His approach to peasantry as a class was humane. He wanted that they should be free from the clutches of the rich landlords and zamindars who mercilessly and inhumanly exploited them. He, therefore, suggested that rural credit societies should be set up to improve their economic conditions.

SCIENTIFIC AGRICULTURE

A strong advocate of scientific agriculture, he sincerely believed that it was the irrigation of lands that would promote agricultural productivity in an agricultural society. Public irrigation systems must, therefore, be well developed. He was dissatisfied not only with the slow expansion of irrigation in India but also with the high irrigation rates.

FREE AND COMPULSORY EDUCATION

Education promotes and expedites economic development. Therefore, free but compulsory primary education should be provided to boys. He was very much shocked as the elementary education in Indian cities and villages was very poor and highly distressing.

It is unfortunate to note that the economic problems that the country faced in the first quarter of the twentieth century, still haunts the country. They are poverty, agricultural backwardness, rural industrialization, land tenures, irrigation development, scientific agriculture, drinking water, sanitation and public health; the role of public enterprise in social development; taxes as sources of development; democratic decentralization.

LAST DAYS

Gokhale's health condition deteriorated because of hard work and continuous and ceaseless political activities. In 1914, when he was in England his condition worsened and it became a matter of anxiety for his friends. He suffered from attacks of suffocation. It became fatal as on Friday, 19 February 1915 at 10.25 p.m. he collapsed and died. That afternoon he said with a smile: "I have been seeing the fun on this side so long, now let me go and see it at the other". One of the brightest stars on the political horizon of India disappeared for all times to come.

AN ESTIMATE

On 21 February 1915, *The Statesman*, an English daily described him as the greatest leader that India had ever produced. He was the greatest man, the greatest

Indian of his time. Recognizing and admiring his service and contributions to the Indian society, Mrs. Annie Besant once said him in 1914 that India could not spare him and a month or two of rest would mean years of work. Rabindranath Tagore said in December 1913 that for a man like him to live was in itself a service to the country — for his life was not merely useful, it was a light to others. In the words of Mrs. Sarojini Naidu, he had been a beacon light of hope to the young generation.

Born in a poor family, he had to struggle hard to reach the pinnacle of glory in public life. His outstanding qualities brought him prestige and eminence. He considered himself very fortunate for having worked with Ranade who taught him the principles of nationalism, as well as of Indian politics and economics.

Gokhale exerted a tremendous influence on the educated class as he spoke boldly, frankly and fearlessly. He was firm and courageous enough to criticize and condemn the anti-people policies of the Government. When the intelligentsia read or heard him, they felt that he was articulating their own innocent thoughts and aspirations. An embodiment of virtues, he was admired and appreciated by one and all, including his enemies and opponents.

Gokhale led a simple life and considered politics not as an instrument of power or influence but as a means for the regeneration and reconstruction of his country. He knew the British bureaucracy in India was well trained and organized, he felt that it would not be an easy task to challenge its monopoly of power. This could be contained if the nationalist ranks were well trained and disciplined. This was why he founded the Servants of India Society.

Utterly selfless, free from vices like vanity and self-advertisement, he never wanted to take slightest advantage of his office. He visited Madras in 1907 and when he was requested to lay the foundation stone of a new building there, he protested that he deserved no such honour, that too much was made of the too little done by public figures in India, and that men like him had to think that much more was to be done in the future than of the vast work that lies in front of them compared with what was done in the past.

Notwithstanding his dedication and devotion, his contributions were not only challenged by the British bureaucracy in India but also by his political opponents in Maharashtra, particularly in Poona. His political opponents called him a traitor, a coward. Such political abuse was the result of personal rather than ideological animosities.

Gangadhar Tilak did not like Gokhale. Languishing in jails and championing and defending the Hindu faith and orthodoxy, Gokhale had a charismatic personality which had a strong influence on the people of Maharashtra. The extremists were not happy with him.

Gokhale's bitter conflict with his political rivals in Poona tremendously strained his physical and mental health. He was elected as the Chairman of the Poona Municipality. Had he not been elected he would have left Poona and settled in Bombay in 1902. He was also elected to the Imperial Council. His influence crossed the boundaries of not only Poona and Bombay but also of the Deccan and Western India. He came to be respected as much in Calcutta and Madras as in Lahore and Allahabad. No other Indian politician of the time, with the possible exception of Dadabhai Naoroji at the turn of the century, commanded such high prestige among the Indian elite outside his own province.

Gokhale was one of the few Congress leaders who enjoyed confidence of the Muslim community. To H.W. Novinson, the correspondent of Manchester Guardian, he was a great statesman. To Sir Henry Cotton, a former Chief Commissioner of Assam, he seemed an ideal interpreter between England and India. G.P. Gooch, the British Historian and Liberal Member of Parliament recorded in his memoirs that in him he saw a great Indian, a citizen of the world.

Politics was the sole profession of Gokhale as he gave it his heart and soul. He did not get, because of his preoccupations, much time to go for physical exercise. He had little time for personal affairs. His two motherless daughters — who lived not far from the Home of the Servants of India Society — had little interaction with him. He neglected his family and ignored his personal needs.

A patriot of his order, Gokhale was averse to foreign domination and colonial rule. He fought for the removal of social and economic backwardness as well as of political subjugation. His political ideals were the ideals of the founding fathers of the Congress. He did his best to give the Moderate Congress ideology greater clarity, coherence and sophistication. He never defended the status quo in the sociopolitical and economic spheres.

POINTS TO REMEMBER

- A noble soul, Gopal Krishna Gokhale evinced a keen interest in journalism. Got the award: Knight Commander of the Indian Empire. Influenced by Ranade and Pherozshah Mehta.
- He along with Joshi founded a Quarterly to make the people educated and conscious. He was hated for his good qualities. His mission was to serve the people.
- He was born in 1866 in Kotluk. Mother: Satyabhama. Father: Krishnarao Gokhale. In 1876, his elder brother Govind and he went to Kolhapur for high school education. In 1879, his father expired. He wanted to give up his studies and share the burden of Govind who took up a job to maintain his family.
- His difficulties after his father's death: in 1881, he passed his matriculation examination. His education in Kolhapur, Poona and Bombay. Two wives: first wife, Savitri, was a leper, died soon; second wife, Radhabai, gave birth to two daughters. She along with her new (third) baby died soon after delivery.
- He took up law to become a lawyer. But could not complete the course. Joined as a teacher in 1885 in the New English School. Became a life

member of the Deccan Education Society. In 1885, he met Ranade, became the Editor.

- His contact with Ranade helped him a lot. Ranade's appointment as a judge in 1871 and his role in public life. He admired British character and education; was a champion of free press and representative institutions.
- He was grateful to Ranade. He joined the Poona politics. Crawford was a corrupt official. His prosecution by Lord Reay. Crawford's well-wishers protected him. In public meetings held in Poona, he was denounced by Gokhale.
- His speech against Crawford brought him to limelight in Poona politics. In October 1896, Mahatma Gandhi met him. Their lasting friendship and its impact on Indian politics. Gokhale joined the Fergusson College in Poona.
- He was a very successful teacher. In 1895, he was elected to the Senate of the Bombay University, a rare honour. In November 1888, he attended the first provincial conference of the Congress at Poona. Gokhale's maiden, but inspiring speech.
- He attended the session of the Congress in 1890 held at Calcutta. He spoke on reducing the salt tax. His address in the Congress sessions made him confident. He spoke on various subjects.
- Protests and demonstrations were of no use in redressing grievances and achieving the goal. Hence, public opinion was to be agitated. 'Indian Agency' was set up in 1888.
- The Royal Commission was set up. Ranade was to present his views before the Royal Commission. But he was not allowed to leave India. Hence, Gokhale, along with others, was chosen to go to England to present the facts before the Royal Commission. He felt like fish out of water in England.
- He appeared before the Commission in 1897 to present his views on finance and other matters. He did a splendid job.
- Wedderburn's interaction with Gokhale was quite cordial, exciting and fruitful. Ranade's praise for Gokhale. Terrible famine in 1896–1897. A Committee was set up in March 1897 to deal with it.
- Measures adopted by the Committee were informed to various political parties. Tilak's support to those measures. 'Operation Plague' in Poona.
- His memorandum exposing the misdeeds of the British soldiers during the 'Operation Plague'. Their harassment and sexual assaults against innocents were condemned by Gokhale. Attempt to murder Rand failed but Ayerst succumbed.
- Wedderburn was disappointed with Poona developments. His demand for an inquiry into the 'Plague Operation'. His briefings to the MPs on

the background of events. There should be a public inquiry into these unfortunate incidents.

- His allegations that women were misbehaved, could not be proved. He cut a very sorry figure and suffered from a 'guilt complex'. His apology to the Governor. He was taken to task by the Press.
- A part of the Press was in his favour. His praise for the activities of the leader. He wanted to retire from politics. He was ostracized by the Brahmin community for his foreign visit. He changed his mind and continued to remain in politics. Gokhale's contest to the Bombay Council. Bal Gangadhar Tilak was another contestant. He was not liked by Sandhurst and Lord Curzon. He withdrew his candidature. Gokhale won the election.
- He lost his wife, and Ranade in 1901. He was elected to the Imperial Council in 1901 and became the Chairman of Poona Municipality in 1902. His contributions as an Additional Member of the Imperial Council.
- C.I.E. was conferred on him even though he was a critic of the Government. Lord Curzon's appreciation for Gokhale's deeds. Madras session of the I.N.C. was a failure. No province came forward to hold the session in 1904. Pherozshah Mehta's proposal to hold it in Bombay.
- Emergence of young leaders in the Congress. They challenged its strategy. Its enthusiasm was declining. Leaders were sceptic about its success. Gokhale's suggestion: it should be work-oriented.
- In Madras Session, it was decided to adopt a new constitution and set up a new committee. Pherozshah Mehta did not accept this. Gokhale was appointed as a Joint Secretary. He collected funds to reinvigorate the Congress. His fund-raising capacity was appreciated.
- Steps to be taken to involve the students. He set up a society called Servants of India and became its first Member. Society was to impart training to the graduates and the trainees were paid monthly. Lord Curzon's impression about the Congress, educated class. He convened a conference in Simla.
- Strong protests against the Simla Conference, against Lord Curzon. Curzon was disappointed and angry. Education Bill was introduced. 1904: Elections in the UK became imminent.
- His visit to England to put forth the Indian claims. Addressed forty-five meetings in six weeks. His brilliant performance impressed the intelligentsia of the UK. He offered certain concrete proposals. His brilliant speech was highly appreciated, met leading political figures in Britain. His image went up. He stayed in the UK for three weeks.
- Partition of Bengal in 1905 and its impact: demand for new methods, new strategies, new leadership. Leaders were divided on the issue of holding demonstrations. Gokhale felt that extremist elements, which were raising their heads following Bengal partition, were becoming strong and strong

and old Congress values were to be replaced. Gokhale wanted that Pherozshah Mehta should attend the Benaras Congress Session to silence the critics. But, the latter declined his offer as he did not like him and his activities. Gokhale's task in the Benaras Conference Session became delicate because of the emergence of extremists within the Congress.

- His constitutional and administrative proposals. Congress was divided.
- Lord Curzon became unpopular for his measures. He was succeeded by Lord Minto who was cool and systematic. Gokhale's visit to England in 1906. He was tired. He became ill. His ideas on economics were sound.
- During the British regime in India, wealth was drained in form of taxes. Even minimum of it was not spent on welfare activities.
- He was in favour of large-scale industrialization. He argued that India should depend upon foreign countries, developed and industrialized for her industrial progress. Progress should not be stalled in the name of protection to local industries. A supporter of labourers and their interests.
- He was against the slavery, for the cause of poor peasants, an advocate of strong scientific agriculture. Irrigation facilities must improve.
- His views on education: it should be compulsory and free. He died in 1915 (19 February).
- He was a bright star, a light to others, a beacon light of hope. Born in a poor family, he achieved the highest distinction. His contact and association with Ranade was remarkable and significant.
- He was an embodiment of virtues, led a simple life, never considered politics as an instrument of power and influence, but as a means of service. Selfless, free from vanity and self-advertisement. He did not lay the foundation stone of a new building as it was too much an honour for him.
- His enemies and critics called him a traitor. He was widely an acclaimed figure in India. Apart from Dadabhai Naoroji, there was no one who could be made comparable to him.
- He enjoyed the support and confidence of the Muslims. He was a great statesman, a great Indian, a citizen of the world, a patriot of high order. He was opposed to colonial rule, a follower of the rules laid by the Congress.

8

Shri Aurobindo (1872–1950)

INTRODUCTION

An ardent lover of mankind, a self-realized saint, an outstanding political prophet, an eminent poet, a seer of high order, a significant interpreter of Indian history, culture and philosophical idealism, a great metaphysician, a renowned patriot, Shri Aurobindo was a dedicated and divine soul. Considered by Romain Rolland as the highest synthesis of the genius of Asia and the genius of Europe, he heralded a new era in the sphere of spiritual poetry through his monumental work *Savitri*, his epic poem. One of the most systematic and learned thinkers of India, he was a versatile genius and left an undying influence on the Indian mass through his moral, spiritual and intellectual accomplishments. Sending a spiritual message to the humanity, he was a political thinker, a social reformer, a man of action and who played a very important role in the history of Indian nationalism and Indian Renaissance.

In the monumental works like *Savitri* and *The Life Divine*, he presented the gospel of spiritual transformation of the world. Guided, motivated and inspired by his spiritual realizations, he wrote commentaries on some of the Vedic hymns, the *Isha* and the *Kena Upanishads* and the *Gita*. His important works are: *The Life Divine*, *Essays on the Gita*, *The Synthesis of Yoga*, *Savitri*, etc.

Aurobindo, through his writings, moulded the political future of Bengal and purity of India. His writings had a profound impact on Subash Chandra Bose. Gifted with unsurpassing intellect, he played a key role in the Indian Renaissance Movement. Critics as well as the students of the East and West recognized his importance in the fields of psychology, philosophy, yoga and literature. In the history of Indian nationalism and freedom movement, Aurobindo's position was as high as that of Tilak, Pherozshah Mehta, Dadabhai Naoroji, Surendra Nath

Banarjee, Gokhale, Lala Lajpat Rai, Shraddhananda, Bipin Chandra Pal and other great leaders of the early years of the freedom struggle.

EARLY LIFE

Aurobindo was born in Calcutta on 15 August 1872 to Krishnadhan Ghose and Swarnalata Devi. His father, a highly qualified doctor with a training in England, was very much influenced by the Western way of life. Krishnadhan, therefore, wanted to westernize his children. He sent them to an Irish nun's school in Darjeeling for education and then to England in 1879. Looked after by an English clergyman, they were not allowed to interact with Indians. He kept his children away from India and its culture.

Aurobindo was brought in an atmosphere which made him absolutely ignorant about Indian social system — its politics, its society, its culture, its economics, its past and present, its heritage, etc. At the age of seven, he stayed with and tutored by the Drewett family at Manchester. When they left for Australia in 1885, he was sent to St. Paul's School in London. Then he joined King's College at Cambridge where he excelled in English literature for which he was awarded prizes. He also passed the I.C.S. Examination in 1890 while he was at Cambridge. But he could not join the service as he failed the riding test. He had a strong disliking for the service and failed deliberately in the examination. By doing so, he killed two birds in one shot: he did not displease his parents and, at the same time, achieved his goal. He was destined to realize himself, seek after the Truth, know about God and guide the spiritual destiny of millions.

Aurobindo stayed in England for a pretty long period of fourteen years. During this period, he studied at Manchester, London and Cambridge. He read thoroughly the Greek classics of Homer, Goethe, etc. He also read English and French literature and learnt Spanish, German and Italian languages. Thus, at a tender age, he acquired mastery over English and other European languages. He had his mastery in the languages. But he learnt Bengali at the age of twenty-four after his return to India from England. While he was in Baroda, he studied *Upanishads* and *Gita*. The Vedantic synthesis of Rama Krishna and of Vivekananda also profoundly influenced him. During 1905–1910, he not only actively participated in the freedom movement in Bengal but also deeply studied the Hindu scriptures and experienced wonderful mystic visions during his imprisonment in Alipore Jail. As a brilliant writer on philosophy, he brought a synthesis of the ancient Vedantic and modern European political philosophies. He discussed the reconstruction of the social and political life of a dependent nation in his work *Political Vedantism*.

POLITICAL INFLUENCES

Shri Aurobindo's father did his best to anglicize his children. But soon he became disillusioned with the functioning of the British Government. In his letters to Aurobindo, he denounced the Government for its cruelty. He also sent him copies of *The Bengalee* newspaper in which news items relating to insult and humiliation meted out to the Indians by the foreign rulers were published. All this had a great influence upon Shri Aurobindo and he was attracted towards Indian politics. In 1891, he came in contact with the Indian Majlis at Cambridge. He took an active interest in its affairs and delivered anti-British and anti-imperialist speeches and also became its Secretary. Aurobindo later joined a secret society called "The Lotus and Dagger" formed by some enthusiastic young Indians at Cambridge. The members of this organization had to take an oath that they would do their best to liberate India from foreign domination. As an organization the Majlis was not that active as it should have been. But this gave a clear picture about the activities of its members including Aurobindo. The secret society had a tremendous impact upon the later activities of Aurobindo, particularly his role in the freedom struggle.

Aurobindo was influenced by Mazzini's Risorgimento and the Irish patriotic movement. He expressed his feelings for his mother country through poems: *Lines to Ireland*, *Bande Mataram* and *Karmayogin*.

He returned to India after spending fourteen years of his formative period in England. Soon after his return, he got a job in the court of Maharaja Sayaji Rao Gaekwar of Baroda. He read a lot on various aspects of the East and the West: their culture, philosophy, tradition, literature, etc. It is because of this and his spiritual practices, he could reach at the Truth.

POLITICAL GOAL AND TECHNIQUE

Aurobindo laid down a three-point programme as an alternative to that of the Congress: open propaganda against the British rule, preparation for secret armed struggle and total boycott of foreign goods. He had a strong desire to see India free from the British regime and this could be achieved only through a revolutionary movement involving violence and terrorism.

It was necessary to adopt violent means because the purpose of the terrorist movement was not terrorism but to install a national government. The terrorists had two objectives: to destroy national property like bridges and buildings, and to kill selected British officials. By this, they wanted to demoralize the British administration and rekindle the spirit of patriotism in the minds of the people who would come forward to overthrow the British regime. Because of his dream to set India free, Annie Besant rightly called him "Indian Mazzini".

Aurobindo transformed the Congress organization into a nationalist one; replaced the term 'Swaraj' by independence and believed that political freedom constituted the fundamental core of a country and it could not be compromised for anything. When the anti-partition movement, following the decision of the Government to partition Bengal in 1905, passed into the hands of the militants, they gave a clarion call to the people to resort to passive resistance, observe Swadeshi, adopt boycott, and not to cooperate with the Government by boycotting government services, the courts, and the academic institutions run by the Government. Aurobindo and other militants wanted to paralyse the administration by creating favourable conditions. Through Swadeshi and anti-partition movement, he wanted to make the people conscious of socio-economic and political issues and asked them to sacrifice everything for the sake of the country. It was because of him the nationalist movement acquired a new image and gained much momentum.

The Congress met at Surat in 1907. It was a landmark in the national movement of India. Aurobindo presided over the meeting of the extremists at Surat and the Nationalist Party was inaugurated. The extremists could not succeed in bringing the Congress under their control because of their insignificant strength, but they gave a new direction to the Congress. During 1907–1908, the Nationalist Party gained in strength and Aurobindo played a major role in this direction.

Following the Surat session in 1907, Aurobindo was arrested by the government for his revolutionary activities. But later he was released. Again in 1908, he was arrested and spent one year in jail as an under-trial prisoner. He was arrested for the third time in 1910. On receiving information from Sister Nivedita that he might be deported from the country, he left Calcutta under disguise for Pondicherry and settled there for rest of his life, seeking after the "Truth". Since he lived in Pondicherry, a French colony, he could not be harassed and prosecuted by the British Government. Following his disassociation from and non-involvement in the Indian politics, his revolutionary movement suffered a setback. Opening a new chapter in his life at Pondicherry, he practised deep meditation and concentration to realize God. Ultimately he succeeded in his mission on 24 November 1926 when he realized himself.

Convinced that God would certainly help for the liberation of India and that India would one day certainly achieve her independence during his lifetime, he felt that after independence, a new India would emerge and its basis would be "Dharma", which would ensure an ideal living and not be merely a religious creed as expressed by West.

Aurobindo's political life covered the period from 1902 to 1910. Though he was in politics for a very small period, he played a very important role in this field and exerted a tremendous influence upon others. Notwithstanding his recourse to terrorism, he made it spiritual and moral in nature. Therefore, his method was considered patriotic.

METAPHYSICS

Aurobindo brought a reconciliation between the Indian idealism and Western materialism. While the former laid more emphasis upon abnegation and renunciation, Mayavada and Salvation, the latter attached more importance to materialism and enjoyment of the matter. Believing that both India and Europe laid emphasis upon the extremes, hoping that a harmony could be brought out and maintained between the Indian idealism and the European secularism arguing that this could be possible only when equal importance would be given to spirit and matter.

He observed that "the supreme reality was spiritual principle. It was supreme and real and not a mere static, transcendental and immutable entity. It contained the potential seeds of dynamic mutation and multiplicity. Therefore, diversity was as real as unity. The external universe was the real creation of a real being and it was not simply a figment of imagination. Hence, the claims of matter and life should not be negated. He was of the opinion that matter was a veiled spirit. For the purpose of cosmic evolution, the spirit assumed the form of inconscience by a total limitation of its consciousness. Out of the inconscience, the evolutionary progression started through the successive and graduated emergence of matter, life and mind. Thus he succeeded in reconciling spirit and matter and creating a metaphysical synthesis. His concept of metaphysics rests on the fusion of Eastern and Western ideas".

AUROBINDO'S PHILOSOPHY OF HISTORY AND CULTURE

As a political philosopher, Aurobindo believed that the spirit determined the course of history. Through history the divine plan unfolded itself, the Brahman manifested Himself, revealed Himself. He argued that the course of Indian National Movement was determined and influenced by God. It was He who wanted that India should develop as a new nation and before that it should be ruled by Great Britain so that the Hindus could be trained in the art of self-discipline. It was Kali, the Divine Mother, who wanted that there should be French Revolution. Therefore, it occurred in 1789.

His concept of cyclical evolution of human cultures and civilizations was influenced by Karl Lamprecht, although the concept could be found in the Vedanta and Puranas. Lamprecht argued that five stages could be traced out in Germany's political evolution. They were:

1. The primitive Germany.
2. The early middle ages.
3. The later middle ages.
4. The individualistic age from the Renaissance to the Enlightenment, and
5. The subjective age starting with Romanticism.

Aurobindo in his book *The Human Cycle* considered the Vedic Age to be the symbolic era of Indian history. To him, Varna was a typical social institution and caste structure and form as a conventional social form. He was disappointed to see Indians becoming more and more materialists because of the impact of the West. But he was very much confident that this age of materialism would soon be replaced by the spiritual age when the course of evolution of man would be guided by the human spirit which constituted an external part of the Divine.

Lamprecht considered the present age to be an age of nervous tension. Thus, while Lamprecht's philosophy of culture was psychological in nature, that of Aurobindo was both psychological and spiritual.

THEORY OF NATIONALISM AND HUMAN UNITY

Aurobindo felt that a country could be great or achieve greatness if its people were patriots, altruists and selfless. In an article in the *Bande Mataram*, he wrote nationalism was simply the passionate aspiration for the realization of the Divine Unity in the nation, a unity in which all the component individuals were really and fundamentally one and equal. The individuals, however, might play different and apparently unequal functions in socio-economic and political life of the society. The Indian nationalism would promote equality between man and man, between caste and caste, between class and class. All beings were different in terms of wealth, education, social status, caste, language, religion, sex, etc. But they were equal and united parts of the *Virat Purush* as realized in the nation.

Nationalism as an ideology was of Western origin, although there existed in India a sense of "cultural self-consciousness and political anti-foreignism". Nationalism, as a religion, was spiritual but not fanatical and narrow in character. Embracing cosmopolitanism, it was in the political evolution of man only an essential phase, a necessary stage. Ultimately all the peoples of the world would be united through a world union and the spiritual foundations of such unity could be laid down by a religion of humanity and the feeling of oneness.

The contemporary world witnessed clash and confrontation rather than cooperation. Notwithstanding this, there would be a world union as it was inevitable and unavoidable. The compulsion of circumstances, the urge of nature and the need and necessity of mankind would certainly force the people to have a world union. They would certainly form a world-state. There would be a federation of free nationalities and there would be no subordination of one to another. Inequality would also disappear. All would have an equal status. If they formed a confederation, there would be maximum freedom. But this might give rise to divisive tendencies. Therefore, a federation should be formed. This would continue to exist for a long period or for ever.

POLITICAL IDEAS

Utilitarianism

Jeremy Bentham's utilitarianism, which stands for the "greatest happiness of the greatest number", has been strongly criticized by many including Aurobindo for ignoring the interests of the minority. Aurobindo felt that the ultimate reality was the spiritual being. Therefore, every individual should try to achieve the good of all living beings.

Capitalism

He criticized modern capitalism as he was opposed to the concentration of wealth in a fewer hands. He also did not accept and appreciate socialism as it would make the state an authoritarian one. However, he accepted the socialist ideal as a starting point. He highly appreciated and praised the lofty principles of socialism like equal opportunity and economic and social freedom (i.e. right to work, etc.).

Spiritual Freedom

He asked every individual to be free spiritually as it was the basis of his economic, political and social freedom. He must obey the laws of God, of one's being. Here he was influenced by *Bhagavad Gita*. He advocated a spiritualized collectivism which would "reconcile the claims of the individual being and those of the collective being". Hence, his "spiritual anarchism".

Aurobindo observed that society had become polluted, perverted and degenerated over the years. As a result, everywhere there was social and political deprivation, despondency and depression. To remove all these from the society and make it pure, the people should cultivate virtues, be highly spiritual in their outlook. Mere economic development and political freedom would not help the regeneration of the society. In order to construct a perfect society, the people should be perfect. A "spiritualized society" would provide a beautiful life to all and would rely on the spiritual sources of governance. Man should evolve beyond mind to supermind. So that a new race of beings would be born. These newly born beings would be far better than the present people who were far better than the animals. The day would come when social and political discords, conflicts, contradictions and struggles could be eliminated from the society and there would be mutuality, harmony and unity.

The "Phenomenology" of Political Values

Aurobindo, a political lieutenant of Bal Gangadhar Tilak for some time and who demanded as early as in 1907 and in 1909 complete independence for India, believed that certainly there would be renaissance in India. Advocating for human unity, he observed that civilization would be doomed unless human nature was spiritually oriented. An exalted and inspired patriot, he refused to acknowledge the superiority of the West and argued that the Indian nation was the "manifestation of the divine being". His concepts of metaphysics, philosophy of history and culture, nationalism, freedom and spiritualized collectivism reflected a synthesis between the ideas, ideals and values of the East and the West. He who believed the power of the spirit was highly influenced as he got a good message for him. He brought a harmony between the insights of the East and the theoretical generalizations of the West. Hence, the intellectuals of the West and the East, visualized a greater harmony and reconciliation of the intellectual traditions of the two worlds. Aurobindo stood as a great intellectual and spiritual force asserting the creation of a phenomenology of political values.

PHILOSOPHY OF POLITICS

Creative Synthesis

Aurobindo, whose philosophy was a product of the contemporary renaissance movement in India, played a great role in guiding the political destiny of India. He propagated the idealistic aspirations of India, interpreted Indian philosophic idealism and historic culture and synthesized the moral, spiritual and aesthetic traditions of the East and the West.

Influenced by *Bhagavad Gita*, Aurobindo built up a "gigantic intellectual structure" in his political philosophy. In his writings, he was very much close to Heraclitus, Plato, Dante, Kant, Hegel, Mazzini, Nietzshe, Karl Lamprecht, Bergson, Dayananda, Vivekananda, Tilak and others. All his writings stressed "spiritual freedom, nationalism, internationalism, antiutilitarianism and the importance of moral–spiritual values in the social and political structure".

Historical Structure and Cultural Causation

With much enthusiasm, faith and conviction, Aurobindo believed that the day would come when the whole society would be spiritualized. The present civilizational crisis was a prelude to some great cosmic crisis. It appeared that nature was in travail, waiting for the descent and dawn of super-mental wisdom. Here his philosophy was very much similar with that of *Bible* which believed in the coming of David or Christ and the "inevitable crystallization of the divine kingdom on earth". Aurobindo argued that history was not an "aimless, purposeless random conglomeration of mechanical forces; there is an inward spiritual purpose running throughout the historical structure". Earlier, Aristotle, Hegel, Karl Marx also believed like this. To Aurobindo, mankind would realize peace and freedom throughout the "supramental progression of history and evolutionary nature".

Aurobindo's philosophy of history certainly made a theoretical advance. For the first time in India, a mystic and metaphysician focussed upon social, political and artistic achievements of the Indians. His philosophy of history covered the Vedantic concept of the ultimate reality; Hegel's justification and rationalization of evil, war, hatred and sorrow as forces in history; the concept of superman by Nietzsche; the Vaishnava concept of "lila" or Brahman, the Tantric concept of Kali, etc. "All these have been integrated in a theoretical philosophic structure showing scholarship, a deep religious mysticism and a romantic imagination". He made a synthesis between the absolute and the world, spirit and life, mysticism and politics.

Nation Building

Aurobindo's theory of an exalted, purified and sanctified nationalism was a great contribution to the modern Indian political thought. In 1907, he boldly declared that there should be an absolute democratic Swaraj for India. He never considered the concept of nationalism as a narrow creed or chauvinistic cult. He wanted that fundamental values of Indian ethics and culture — Dharma, Tapasya, Jnanam and Shakti — should constitute the forces of Indian nationalism and the Indian leaders should follow the pure means to attain their objectives. He not only wanted the political freedom and of man but also the goal of an inner oneness of all human beings. All the barriers which challenged unity must be removed or broken and man is to be united with others in an atmosphere of fraternity. Cooperation, fellow-feeling, mutuality, trust, confidence, faith, reciprocity, love, forbearance, etc. should be the key factors in moulding the life of man.

An individual should be guided by moral and spiritual values as it ensured his political success, purified his soul and helped him in realizing his own. He made politics highly spiritualized. India could achieve its glory and prestige and rise to great heights in terms of science, technology, philosophy, arts, literature, etc., if its socio-political life was influenced by spiritual values.

AUROBINDO'S CONCEPT OF STATE

Aurobindo's concept of state differed from that of the British and German idealists like T.H. Green, Bosanquet, Hegel, Bradley, etc. They made the state absolute. State gave a meaning to the social institutions like family, church, university, trade, etc. These institutions found their fulfilment in the state. But Aurobindo observed that the social institutions had their own importance and did not depend for their significance on the state. The society was organic and had a soul. The individual was also a spiritual self. The community was also a formation of Reality. It could apply force against any individual if the latter committed any error or did anything wrong but it had no right to punish a spiritual person on the ground that he did not obey the state. Swaraj was not enough. All must be equal and they must have an equal opportunity. Like Bosanquet, Aurobindo also realized the worth of the nation state.

AN ESTIMATE

A great dramatist, a renowned poet, a genius, a classical epic writer, a master of prose writing, an eminent littérateur, a philosopher of high order, Aurobindo was a great source of inspiration to the national freedom fighters in the early years of the twentieth century and his writings were a deep gospel to the frustrated and anguished Indian nation in the early part of the twentieth century. A major and an outstanding figure and personality in the history of Indian renaissance and Indian nationalism, his works reflected a new rising soul of India and delivered a spiritual message for humanity.

POINTS TO REMEMBER

- Aurobindo: a divine soul, author of *Savitri* and other brilliant works, a systematic and learned thinker.
- Born in 1872 (August 15). Father: Krishnadhan Ghose. Mother: Swarnalata Devi. Father: a doctor, influenced by the Western way of life, wanted to westernize his children, sent them to Darjeeling and then to England, children not to interact with Indians and to remain away from Indian culture.
- Aurobindo's education in England: passed the I.C.S. Examination, failed the riding test deliberately, could not join the I.C.S. service, had a strong disliking for it, achieved by doing so his goal. His mastery over several languages. Studied Western and Eastern philosophies. His mystic vision in Alipore Jail.
- Aurobindo's father: disillusioned with the British Government, for its cruelty and anti-people measures, he sent his newspaper publications depicting the cruelty of the British Government. His contact with Indian Majlis at Cambridge and with a secret society "The Lotus and the Dagger".
- Majlis: its purpose: to liberate India from foreign domination. Its impact upon Aurobindo was tremendous. He returned to India. Got a job in the court of Satyaji Rao of Baroda. His agenda was an alternative to that of the Congress. His desire to see a free India.
- He adopted violent means to achieve the goal: to destroy bridges and to kill British officials. He was called Indian Mazzini. He changed the image of the Congress, replaced 'Swaraj' by 'Independence'. Political freedom not to be compromised. Impact of 1905 Bengal partition.
- The Surat Session of the Congress in 1907: He presided over the meeting of the extremists at Surat. Inauguration of the Nationalist Party. His arrest in1907 after the Surat session. Again arrested in 1908 and in 1910. To avoid deportation, he left Calcutta under disguise for Pondicherry. His self-realization on 24 November 1926. He had a vision that one day India would be free and God would help her in achieving freedom. His political life (1902–1910).
- Spirit determined the course of history. India to develop as a new nation and before that to be ruled by Britain.
- French Revolution took place because Goddess Kali wanted. His concept of cycle was influenced by Karl Lamprecht.

- Nationalism: a religion, an ideology of Western origin, cosmopolitan, not narrow and fanatical. Lot of clash and confrontation in the society, but there would be world union. Formation of world-state, a federation of nationalities and no subordination of one nationality to another.
- Formation of a confederation: federation better than confederation. Aurobindo: against utilitarianism. Criticised modern capitalism and socialism, but appreciated some principles of the latter. Everyone to be spiritually free.
- "Spiritual anarchism". Society polluted, people to be spiritual, to cultivate virtues, spiritualized society to provide a beautiful life.
- Renaissance of India. Built up a gigantic intellectual structure. He was a great intellectual, spiritual force. His creative synthesis.
- He was influenced by *Bhagavad Gita*. His stress on moral values. History not a conglomeration of mechanical forces, has a spiritual purpose. Man to enjoy or realize peace and freedom throughout history.
- His nationalism: a significant contribution. In 1907, he declared for India a democratic Swaraj.
- His concept of state: he differed from the Western philosophers like T.H. Green and others. They made the state absolute and the institutions found a fulfilment in it. Aurobindo rejected this theory. To him, social institutions had their own importance and did not have to depend upon the state for their survival. The society, to him, organic with a soul. Moral and spiritual values must guide the activities of the people. Socio-political life to be spiritualized.
- State: no right to punish a moral person. Besides Swaraj, there must be equality.

9

Mahatma Gandhi (1869–1948)

INTODUCTION

People come to this world with a purpose, spend sometime here, then go back to their permanent abode soon after completion of their job. As long as they are here, they do something: either good or bad. If it is bad, they are criticized, censured and condemned. They are treated with contempt and scorn, distrust and suspicion. If they do something good for the nation, for the country, for the people, they are appreciated, admired, respected and honoured. They have a strong faith in the principle, "ask not what your country can do for you, ask what you can do for your country" (John F. Kennedy, the late President of the U.S.A.). It is because of their sacrifice, devotion, dedication and commitment they are known as the Mahatmas. Mohan Das Karamchand Gandhi was such a Mahatama, the venerated "Father of the Nation".

In the year 1915, Nautanlal B. Mehata organized a meeting in a village known as Jaitpur in the state of Bombay to felicitate Gandhi after his return from South Africa to India in the same year. In that meeting, Mehata addressed Gandhi as Mahatma (Mahan Atma: Great Soul). Later, Rabindranath Tagore also addressed Gandhi as Mahatma. Since then Gandhi is known as Mahatma Gandhi. He is also called the "Father of the Nation". It was the Netaji Subhash Chandra Bose who first addressed him as such in his condolence message to the Mahatma on the demise of his wife Kasturba Gandhi. In the wake of the Quit India Movement Gandhi and Kasturba were interned at Aga Khan Palace in Poona (now known as Poone). Here Kasturba passed away on 22nd February 1944. Shocked, Bose sent the following message to the Mahatma on Azad Hind Radio on 4th June 1944:

> Nobody would be more happy than ourselves if by any chance our countrymen at home should succeed in liberating themselves through their own efforts or by any chance, the British Government accepts your "Quit India" resolution and gives effect to it. We are, however, proceeding on the assumption that neither of the above is possible and that a struggle is inevitable. Father of our Naiton in this holy war for India's liberation, we ask for your blessings and good wishes.

It may be noted here that like Gandhi leaders of other countries are also credited with the title "Father of the Nation". Fathers of the Nations belong to two categories: some hold office like President or Prime Minister after achieving success in the liberation struggle or in the unification of the country, while others shy away from power and all other temptations of office. To the first category, among others, belong: George Cadle Price of Belize, Thomas Garrigue Massaryk of Czechoslovokia (now Czech Republic and Slovok Federal Republic), Sukarno of Indonesia, Jomo Kenyatta of Kenya, Ibrahim Rugova of Kosovo, Tunku Abdul Rahman of Malaysia, Sir Seewoosagur Ramgoolam of Mauritius, Sam Nujoma of Namibia, Einar Gerhardsen of Norway, Mohammad Ali Jinnah of Pakistan, Sir John Compton of Saint Lucia, Don Stephen Senanayake of Sri Lanka, Johan Ferrier of Surinam, Julius Nyerere of Tanzania, Sheikh Zayed Bin Sultan Al Nahyan of United Arab Emirates, George Washington of the USA, El-Quali Mustapha Sayed of Sahrawi Arab Democratic Republic. To the second category, among others, belong: Ahmad Shah Durani of Afghanistan, Don Jose de San Martin of Argentina, Sir Henry Parkes of Australia, Sir Lynden Pindling of Bahamas, Ante Starcevic of Croatia, Carlos Manuel de Céspedes of Cuba, Charles IV, Holy Roman Emperor (Karel IV) of Czech lands, Frantisek Palacky of Czech lands, Miguel Hidalogy Costilla of Mexico, William the Silent of Netherlands, Sir Michael Somare of Papua New Guinea, Peter I of Russia, Mustafa Kemal of Turkey, Jose Gervasio Artigas of Uruguay and Mahatma Gandhi of India.

LIFE SKETCH

A political saint, a "Karma Yogi", a bold, dashing and powerful personality who set India free from the British regime which ruled the country for nearly two hundred years by dint of his hard work, sincerity, sacrifice, dedication and devotion, and by a means unknown to anyone earlier, Mohandas Karamchand Gandhi would go into the annals of history as the greatest political actor in the contemporary world. He surpassed all his contemporaries both in India and abroad and achieved something which no one had ever dreamt of, which no one by any stretch of his imagination could have ever thought of. His was an extraordinary life, as it saw the fusion of ancient Hindu religion and culture, and modern revolutionary ideas about politics and society in his formidable personality. Born on 2 October 1869 in Porbandar in Gujarat, he was the third son and fourth child of Karamchand and Putilibai Gandhi. When he was about twelve-year-old, his parents considered him old enough to marry, and they made the necessary arrangements. His bride, Kasturbai Makanji, was the daughter of a merchant of Porbandar. After passing the matriculation examination in third division in 1887, he was admitted in 1888 into Samaldas College in Bhavnagar. As he was averse to college education, he gave up his studies in the same year and left for England in October 1888 with a desire to become a barrister. And for this no degree was needed. In December 1890, he passed his final examinations.

Gandhi returned to India in July 1891 with a sense of satisfaction and joined the Bar at Rajkot. As he was ignorant of Indian law and history, he suffered from diffidence and was afraid of being exposed. Therefore, he left Rajkot for Bombay for further study and acquired practical experience. He lived there for six months. During this period, he could get only one case. He thought of giving up the legal profession and becoming a teacher. He applied for the post of teacher in a school, but his application was rejected as he did not have the required qualification. Discouraged, he returned to Rajkot.

In 1893, he came to know about a job in South Africa. A Muslim merchant Dada Abdulla Seth from Porbandar was involved in a civil suit with Seth Tyed Haji Khan Muhammed. The local Indian lawyers working on the case were so deficient in English that they could not even carry on the necessary legal correspondence, and the merchant decided that he should bring a trustworthy person proficient in English from Porbandar, to teach them English for about a year. Gandhi felt that the job was more suitable for a clerk than for a barrister. He also did not like living in Rajkot. However, he changed his mind and in April 1893 he left for South Africa.

Gandhi stayed in South Africa for more than twenty years and his political career started there. There the Indians were ill-treated and discriminated. They were not allowed to travel in the railways with the Europeans, nor to enter into the hotels and clubs meant for the Europeans. The Government also denied them the right to vote and subjected them to other humiliating laws. They had to register themselves, fix their thumb impressions, were forced to pay unjust taxes and treated like coolies and criminals.

Gandhi challenged the unjust and inhuman laws boldly and non-violently. For this, he had to pay a heavy price. He was tortured, beaten mercilessly and arrested. But he remained firm. Demoralized, the Government had to accept most of his demands. Tremendous success made him self-confident to lead a non-violent struggle through Satyagraha.

Gandhi returned to India in 1915 and worked for its freedom and socio-economic development. On 9 January 1917, he launched a Satyagraha in Champaran, demonstrated a hartal against the Rowlatt Bill in 1919, launched the Non-cooperation Movement in 1920–1921 and Civil Disobedience Movement from 1930 to 1934. In 1930, he also undertook the famous Dandi March against the salt law of the British Government. In 1942, he proclaimed the famous Quit India Movement.

It is because of his significant contributions to the freedom struggle and to the cause of the nation, he has been rightly called the "Father of the Nation". But, unfortunately, he was assassinated on 30 January 1948 by Nathuram Godse, and became a martyr. With his sad demise, the country lost a great and noble soul, a dedicated worker, an astute politician, an idealist, a pragmatist, a reformer, a statesman of high order, an ardent nationalist, a prophet and a philosopher. Condoling his death, George Bernard Shah rightly said that "it is dangerous to become too good".

An apostle of non-violence, a votary of truth, an embodiment of love, a propounder of divine faith, a lover of mankind, Mohandas Karamchand Gandhi, popularly called "Bapu" and reverently addressed as "Mahatma", is no more with us. But his principles and precepts will always guide like the North Star and inspire the future generations in establishing a rosier world where hangovers of devastation and destruction, denial and deprivation will be unknown.

SATYAGRAHA

Satyagraha is more than the passive resistance as it goes beyond it. It denotes the method of securing rights by personal suffering; it is opposed to resistance by arms. A cardinal concept of Gandhian political theory, it means a deliberate and conscious assertion of truth and right against the vested interests. Elaborating the concept, Gandhi wrote:

> When I refuse to do a thing that is repugnant to my conscience, I use soul-force. For instance, the Government of the day has passed a law which is applicable to me. I do not like it. If by using violence I force the Government to repeal the law, I am employing what may be termed body-force. If I do not obey the law and accept the penalty for its breach, I use soul-force. It involves sacrifice of self. Moreover, if this kind of force is used in a cause that is unjust, only the person using it suffers.

The practical application of non-violence in life is Satyagraha or soulforce, which is rooted in the inward strength of the soul. It is not merely abstaining from violence, but doing good. If one hits one's adversary, that is, of course, violence; but to be truly non-violent, one must love him and pray for him even when he hits. Love forgets and forgives evil, wrongdoing, injustice or exploitation. It does not evade the issue but fearlessly faces the wrongdoer and bravely resists his wrong with the force of love and suffering.

Satyagraha is the "soulforce" or "truth-force"; the non-violent resistance to evil with all the moral and spiritual force; the use of moral force or firmness in the vindication of truth; and to fight injustice, exploitation and oppression. Trust and suffering being its attributes, it does not harm the opponent but overwhelms him by love and innocence; it is over-coming of evil by good; a positive, but not a negative attitude; not non-resistance or submission to evil; resists it through love; a belief in truth and love; to overcome evil through self-suffering and self-sacrifice. A Satyagrahi never considers his adversary an enemy and always appeals to his reason and conscience to mend his behaviour.

The concept of Satyagraha was Gandhi's own. He coined it when the Transvaal Government introduced in 1906 an anti-Indian legislation in the local legislature: the Asiatic Registration Bill, seeking to prevent Indians, who had left the Transvaal during the Boer War, from returning and to prevent any future Indian immigration; forcing all Indians (around thirty thousand in number) living in the Transvaal to go for fingerprinting and receive from the Government registration certificates. They were supposed to carry these certificates with them whenever and wherever they went. Otherwise, they would be fined, imprisoned or deported. The Bill, as expected, was strongly opposed as the Indians feared that if it was passed, it might one day be used to drive them out from the Transvaal as well as from the whole of South Africa. Under Gandhiji's leadership, the Indians living in the Transvaal unsuccessfully opposed the Bill. It was against this background Gandhi coined the term 'Satyagraha'.

Gandhi believed that soul was superior to body. Hence, he advised the people to oppose any law that went against their moral code of conduct. It was the voice of Atman — the inner conscience — that should be taken into consideration as it was supreme. The dictates or commands of the Government were to be strongly resisted if they prevented the people from discharging their higher obligations. Gandhi was not opposed to Satyagraha in a democratic set-up. He did not have full confidence in a parliamentary democracy nor could he accept, unlike Locke, the axiomatic superiority of the majority will represented in parliament. Like J.S. Mill, he believed that one single individual might be absolutely right in resisting the anti-people laws of the state. He said that even if he were in a democracy, he would fight against the evils because non-cooperation with evil would be a sacred duty.

The ethics of Satyagraha, thus, does not go together with that of democracy, which rests on numbers only. Satyagraha is in no way related with numbers participating in it. In democracy, people are influenced or misguided, or lured by passion, prejudices and petty considerations. But a Satyagrahi is free from all these. Satyagraha refutes anything that is repugnant to the soul. Even if a Satyagrahi is a lone individual, he should boldly confront any challenge to the higher law of the Atman. While fighting for justice and the truth, he prepares himself for any kind of sufferings and sacrifices.

Satyagraha is an inherent birthright of a person, a sacred right, a sacred duty. If the Government tramples the rights and freedoms of the people; denies them their due share in the process of the Government; deprives them of their independence; protects social exploitation; promotes economic inequality; encourages indiscipline and rests on force, it should be challenged, disobeyed, resisted and overthrown. And any one who opposes such type of Government and tries to vindicate his rights must be prepared to invite all kinds of wrath from the Government. He may be fined, tortured, imprisoned, persecuted, prosecuted and, if necessary, eliminated.

Techniques of Satyagraha

There are different techniques of Satyagraha:

(i) *Fasting*: It is applied only against those who are bound by ties of close personal affection. Fasting is nothing but prayer. It crucifies the flesh, elevates the soul, cleans the body and mind, and influences the people morally. It is the voice of God, conscious self-suffering and makes a strong appeal to one's emotion and reasoning power. It is never a coercion but always persuasion; is not hunger strike; never puts any pressure on the Government; not a moral coercion; is in accordance with an inner voice and not "against anybody in particular". "It is particularly against myself". Gandhi advocated both private and public fasts; but they should undertake selflessly, without any expectation and for the sake of truth, love and renouncing or abjuring earthly possession and ambition. At times, he resorted to fasting when he found impurities in his followers.

(ii) *Voluntary migration* (*Hijrat*): It is adopted as a last resort. "Tyranny is a kind of plague and when it is likely to make us angry or weak it is wise to leave the scene of such temptation". Gandhi advised *Hijrat* to the Satyagrahis of Bardoli in 1923, of Limdi, Junagad and Bathalgad in 1939, and the Harijans of Kaitha as a result of oppression by the caste Hindus.

(iii) *Non-cooperation*: It is another powerful technique adopted to get justice from the Government.

(iv) *Hartal* (*strike*): It seeks to paralyse the administration through peaceful means. Violence in any form should not be resorted to during hartal.

Satyagrahi: His Qualities

Satyagraha as a technique never stands for social or political disintegration. A Satyagrahi initially obeys the laws of the State. It makes him self-disciplined and helps him to judge as to which particular rules are good and just and which unjust and iniquitous. Only then he has the right to disobey the civil laws in well-defined circumstances.

A Satyagrahi, who believes that the soul can be saved from the evils, always practises Ahimsa and gladly accepts all kinds of sufferings, which may result from his truthfulness. Gandhi felt that a Brahmachari (celibate) free from worldly desires and attachments was most capable of practising Ahimsa (non-violence) and Satyagraha. The Gandhian philosophy of Satyagrahis springs from the supreme concept of the Truth, the ultimate reality, and every thing other than the Truth fades into oblivion. Therefore, a Satyagrahi should do his best to safeguard the criteria and foundations of the Truth.

Canons for a Satyagrahi

A Satyagrahi should strictly observe certain canons of moral discipline. He must be

- moral, spiritual and virtuous;
- a man of moral courage and strength to fight the evils of the society;
- endowed with qualities like determination, commitment, dedication, devotion, courage, endurance and perseverance;
- obedient to the leader of the Satyagrahi unit;
- strong and stout and practise brahmacharya and hathayoga;
- absolutely firm in his resolve; reasonable and rational in his approach;
- pure in his mind, clean in his heart and just in his deeds;
- away from all vices like anger, passion, lust, greed, selfishness;
- a man of principles, learning, culture and should not deviate from the path he has rightly chosen.

Satyagraha, based on personal purification, a criterion of political power, is a great contribution of Gandhi to political thought. It is a pure means adopted to achieve a righteous end. A Satyagrahi, according to Gandhi, must always read *Bhagvad Gita* and *Ramcharitmanas* of Goswami Tulsidas so that he can acquire all the required qualities which will ultimately help him in attaining the desired goal. He need not always be a man of scholastic learning, he should strictly follow celibacy, observe austerity, follow truth, cultivate fearlessness and give up the last vestige of cowardice.

Forms of Satyagraha

There are different forms of Satyagraha. Non-cooperation with the evil-doer is a mild form of Satyagraha. But civil disobedience of the laws of the Government is a strong and extreme form. It should be resorted with a sense of discrimination, civility, discipline and non-violence. There can be individual as well as mass civil disobedience. In case of the latter, the masses will have to be in the beginning rigorously trained for action. Gradually, they will learn this art. Complete civil disobedience, a very powerful movement, can be more dangerous than an armed rebellion, because the untold sufferings and miseries of the people make them bold enough to destabilize the Government.

Satyagraha and Passive Resistance

Mahatma Gandhi's experiment with non-violence involves four successive stages. They are:

1. Passive resistance (in South Africa).
2. Non-cooperation (1920–1921).
3. Civil disobedience (1930–1931), and
4. Satyagraha (1940–1941).

Gandhi's Satyagraha is a spiritualized and moralized form of the concept of resistance. Some Western political philosophers too advocated resistance.

John Calvin advocated partial resistance by "inferior magistrates". Thoreau was arch-champion of civil disobedience. During the Swadeshi Movement, Tilak, Aurobindo and the extremists also advocated passive resistance. Sometimes the Gandhian Satyagraha is confused with the passive resistance. But both are quite different. Their features are given here.

Features of Satyagraha and Passive resistance

Satyagraha	*Passive resistance*
• A dynamic force.	• Compatible with internal violence towards the enemy.
• Non-violent action to resist injustice.	• Mainly contemplated in political sphere.
• Practised at all levels — domestic, social and political.	• Governed by jealousy.
• Goes beyond passive resistance.	• Force is applied against the enemy.
• Stresses continuous cleaning of the mind.	• Action against the enemy. It involves punishment, coercion, etc.
• Emphasis on inner purity.	• Punishment to the enemy.
• Stress on a spiritual and moral teleology.	• A political technique of limited application.
• Motivated by principles like love, charity, sacrifice and suffering.	• Sometimes it meant Swadeshi and boycott or disobedience of unjust laws.
• Seeks to bring about changes in an opponent.	
• No action against the enemy.	
• Infliction of suffering on one-self.	
• A moral force.	

Satyagraha never supports the application of force. This sounds good. But under certain circumstances, force may be used to resist force. Physical force, Gandhi says, is better than moral cowardice. Satyagraha is far more comprehensive than the passive resistance as advocated in India during 1906–1908. Tilak and Aurobindo supported violence on moral grounds. But Gandhi believed Ahimsa in absolute sense. As a philosophy of life and politics, Satyagraha contemplates mass action for sounding the death knell of the despotic Government.

SARVODAYA (THE GOOD FOR ALL)

Based on the concept of the unity of existence, Sarvodaya (the good for all or the emancipation of all) implies a constant fight against cruelty to human beings and animals. It has its roots in the famous Mantra of the Yajur Veda — *Isavasyamidam Sarvam* — the entire universe is permeated by the Supreme God. Gandhi's Sarvodaya has its roots in the Vedantic concept of the spiritual unity of existence and the Gita–Buddhistic concept of *Sarvabhutahita* or the good for all living beings. Its idealism being more comprehensive, it does not agree with John Locke's theory of majoritarianism, Karl Marx's concept of class struggle and Jeremy Bentham's principle of the greatest happiness of the greatest number.

With a sacrosanct character of human spirit, Sarvodaya includes the values of freedom, equality, justice and fraternity and opposes the state machinery. State is not created by God. An instrument of coercion and exploitation, and based on force and organized violence, it protects and promotes the interests of those who have manipulative skill and capacity to influence and control the government machinery. Sarvodaya seeks to replace the politics of power by the politics of cooperation. Moral in character, it has been to a great extent influenced by Ruskin, who in his work, "Unto This Last", said that the people should have freedom and equal opportunity for their spiritual growth.

Ensuring good life to all in every sphere of life — social, economic, political and cultural; symbolizing the greatest good for all the people; rejecting Bentham's theory of greatest happiness of the greatest number; seeking to provide social justice, economic equality and political rights to the people; and rooted in love, faith, kindness, help, goodwill, Sarvodaya shuns violence as violence breeds counter-violence.

Sarvodaya aims at the realization of happiness of all and the elevation of all. At the political level, it has two significant implications: repudiation of the theory of class struggle and safeguarding the interests of the minority. As stated earlier, it seeks to maximize the good of the entire community. Discouraging and denouncing the lust for power and wealth, it emphasizes disinterested service. Dedication, service and the realization of common good are its features.

Both Sarvodaya and Communism have faith in social equality. But there is a difference between the two. The former rests on truth and non-violence and aims at establishing a regime ensuring liberty, equality and justice through love and non-violence. Opposing majoritarianism and giving importance to consensus, Gandhi stood for the village commonwealth and criticized Western democracies as they adhered to the principle of violence.

SWADESHI

Gandhi's Swadeshi was a weapon to drive out the British from India. It was his watchword. By using the Swadeshi goods and boycotting foreign goods, he wanted to challenge the English trade and commerce and teach the British a lesson. He knew that the Great Britain was a merchant nation and the British and the East India Company came to India for trade purposes. In case the trade was not profitable, they would never stay here. Therefore, he advised the people to boycott the foreign goods. Inspired, not only they boycotted the foreign goods, but also burnt them at different places. By purchasing the goods manufactured in India, they encouraged Indian industries and gave them a new lease of life. The Indian workers also got jobs and Indian money stopped flowing out of the country. All these greatly improved the Indian economy.

He encouraged the use of "Charkha" and "Khadi" to improve the lot of the poor in India and inspired the people to use "Khadi". With Charkha and Khadi, he wanted to bring a great change in the village economy and finally in the Indian economy. He stood for the decentralization of production and wanted every village to produce and use all its necessities so that it could become self-sufficient. In addition, it should produce something more to fulfil the requirements of the cities. Heavy industry would necessarily be centralized and nationalized. Opposing industrialization on the lines of the West, he did not favour industrial economy as it did not recognize the dignity of man. Rather it made him a slave, a soulless machine. He ruled out the organized industries not because they did not require any special support. For instance, the West had yet to discover anything so hygienic as the Indian tooth-stick. This was cent-percent Swadeshi giving a tremendous satisfaction to the people. He favoured cottage industries as it gave employment and removed poverty in the countryside. He launched the Swadeshi Movement because political freedom was meaningless without economic freedom.

NON-VIOLENCE

Ahimsa, otherwise known as non-violence, means no torture to any one's life. No one should do anything evil against any one. One should love all the living and non-living beings. This can be possible only when one is pure and divine. This can be done either by withdrawing from the world or by fighting the evil by doing good deeds in the world. Ahimsa is not merely being harmless to others but is a positive state of love, of doing good even to the evil-doer. He believed that only love or non-violence would conquer evil wherever it was found — in people or in laws, in society or in government. He who practises non-violence should not only be good to all the living beings, but also not to hurt even those who are unjust. He must love them. But he would oppose the tyranny whether of parents or others, but never hurt the tyrant.

About his practice of non-violence, Gandhi often used to say, "Truth was inborn in me, non-violence came to me with great effort." His greatest contribution to politics in particular and life in general was his teaching and practice of non-violence. On 14 August 1920, he wrote in *Young India* that non-violence was a perfect state. It was the real towards which all mankind moved naturally, though unconsciously.

Non-violence as a concept did not originate from Gandhi. But certainly he was the first to apply it on a huge mass scale and in the arena of politics. If Bismark unified Germany through the policy of blood and iron, it was Gandhi who adopted non-violence as a means to get independence for the country. Emphasizing it, he once said that his interest in India's freedom would cease if she adopted violent means, for the fruit would be not freedom but slavery in disguise. For him, non-violence was not a mere philosophical principle. It was the rule and breath of his life. It was a matter not of the intellect but of the heart.

Condemning violence, and recognizing the importance of liberty and love over it, Gandhi said that non-violence must have universal application, transcending time and space. Applied in both war and peace, it had lasting service. The more one practised it, the more he become perfect, disciplined. One attained divinity to the extent he practised it. By doing so, he could attain *moksha*. Gandhi said:

> The basic principle on which the practice of non-violence rests is that what holds good in respect of one-self equally appeals to the whole universe.

His dictionary did not have such expression as violent fight. Apparently, non-violence might appear to be ineffective but, in fact, it was not. The effects of Buddha's non-violent action persisted and were likely to grow with age, while that of the Caligula's slaughter not. Whatever was needful and could be gained by political power could be more quickly and more certainly gained by non-violent means.

Non-violence Rooted in Ahimsa

Non-violence, taught and practised by Mahatma Gandhi and rooted in the Indian doctrine of Ahimsa or non-injury, meant not to cause any harm to any one by inciting any injury either consciously or unconsciously under any situation or to take away one's life; avoiding injury to anything on earth in thought, word and deed; avoiding harsh words, harsh judgements, ill-will, anger, spite and cruelty. It meant pure in thoughts and deeds; avoidance of uncharitable thought even for the enemy; opposition to evil, not by another evil but by good; overcoming of evil by good. According to Gandhi:

> The injunction 'love your enemies' is not only the noblest idealism, it is also the most practical politics.

It meant infinite love for every living being and this, in turn, meant infinite capacity for suffering. It was omnipotent, infinite and synonymous with God Himself; an effort to abandon violence that was inevitable in life.

Non-violence: Weapon of the Strong and Weak

To Gandhi, non-violence, the weapon of the strong and of the weak, could be adopted by an individual physically and morally strong or physically weak but morally strong, as a means to achieve end. But if morally weak but physically strong, he could not resort to it. When brought under strong influence, non-violence could be used by women and children and by illiterate and others regarded as weak.

Gandhi cautioned that a coward could never practise non-violence and it should never be used as a shield for cowardice. To him, retreating from the battle ground was an act cowardice and unworthy of a warrior. He said that in a situation if he was asked to choose one between two alternatives — cowardice and violence, he would certainly choose violence. Non-violence was Gandhi's "first article of faith and the last article of his creed".

Non-violence is not Passivity

Non-violence or Ahimsa does not mean that one will be submissive to the wrongdoer. It is his resistance to the evil with full moral and spiritual force. It is not a negative force, but a dynamic and constructive force more positive than electricity and more powerful than even ether. The highest violence can be met by the highest non-violence. It is the principle for which Gandhi lived, for which he desired to live, and for which he believed he was equally prepared to die. Stating that Ahimsa should be the practical rule of life, he said that if one did not practise non-violence (which, elsewhere, he spoke as the 'maturest fruit' or Truth) in one's personal relations with others, and hoped to use it in bigger affairs, he was certainly mistaken. Non-violence, like charity, must begin at home. One's non-violence would be put on trial when his action was resisted by others, as living amongst descent people, his conduct might not be described as non-violent. Mutual forbearance was non-violence. Therefore, Gandhi believed that non-violence was the law of life. He had to practise it to those who acted violently towards him and the law must apply to nations as to individuals. Training was, no doubt, necessary. And beginnings were always small. But if the conviction was there, the rest would follow.

Truth: The Basic Principle of Non-violence

An apostle of Truth, Gandhi identified Truth with God and believed that it could be realized by love or Ahimsa. One could not know about the truth and practise love, unless he was pure at heart. Discipline, austerity and tapas made one pure. Truth, the fundamental basis of non-violence, the sovereign principle, quenched the untruth. Love quenched anger, self-suffering the violence. This eternal rule was a rule not for saints only, but for all. Truth was Gandhi's highest "Dharma" and non-violence the highest duty. He never wanted that violence should be applied to achieve a goal. In 1909, Madanlal Dhingra shot down an English officer and was hanged to death. Without expressing his anger or surprise over the incident, Gandhi remarked, "Dhingra was a patriot, but his love was blind. He gave his body in a wrong way, its result can only be mischievous". Praising non-violence, Gandhi said that India's ills could not be removed by the violence as India's civilization required the use of a different and higher weapon of self-preservation. In his message to the Indian National Congress in 1909 he said violence in any shape or form was to be given up. Neither Swaraj could be won nor any benefit the country would get by violence and terrorism. Anger was to be conquered by non-anger and evil by good.

Non-violence, to him, was a struggle for truth. An individual, while waging a non-violent struggle, should strictly follow the principle of truth without any deviation. In case he deviated, he must have courage to confess his guilt and renounce everything that he gained. Gandhi himself called off one of his non-violent movements (1922) when he was on the verge of attaining success saying that he had committed a great blunder. A Satyagrahi should lay more emphasis on truth rather on victory. Non-violence was a means as well as an end and it should not be taken lightly. To follow the truth meant taking refuge in God and a Satyagrahi should not be afraid of the adverse consequences. Ignoring them, he must remain firm and steadfast.

Appeal to the Moral Sense in a Spirit of Love

Gandhi believed that God resided in every being both animate and inanimate. Hence, everything was divine. Therefore, an emotional appeal could be made even to an enemy through love and conscious suffering. Suffering strengthened those who suffered and weakened those who inflicted suffering. Through love truth was realized. Love was the means and truth the end. Non-violence could "melt even the stoniest of hearts". An enemy could be won by persuasion, not by coercion. Gandhi hated the evil but not the evil-doer, the British imperialism but not the Briton. He fought against British imperialism, but not the British or the Englishman or anybody. They were his friends. He also said:

> If my love is sincere, I must love the Englishman in spite of my distrust.

To Gandhi, Ahimsa was the greatest love, the largest charity. Love never claims, it ever gives, ever suffers, never resents, never revenges itself. In the practice of non-violence, truth is the foundation and love the weapon. Writing on self-suffering, Mahatma Gandhi said: "A nation that is capable of limitless sacrifices is capable of rising to limitless heights. The greater the sacrifice, the quicker the progress". He never supported violence. Those who used force overlooked the fundamental distinction between the animal and the human worlds and "exalted a biological generalization into a doctrine of human destiny". Adoption of violent resistance in a world where it did not belong posed a threat to human life and degraded it to the level of animal existence.

Non-violence: A Total Philosophy of Life

Gandhi's non-violence, a total philosophy of life, is made applicable to every aspect of life but not to certain isolated incidents or acts. It is applied to both private and public spheres of life. In economic field, it stands for decentralized village economy opposed to both capitalism and communism which stand for exploitation. In political field, it means a federation of autonomous village republics. In international relations, it means negotiation, arbitration and adjudication. In its relation to other faiths, cultures and ideologies, it means the toleration of others' faith, mutual sympathy, humanity and understanding. It is also applied to caste, class and racial conflicts. Nay, it can be applied to the whole creation.

A man who believes in non-violence feels that he has conquered the whole world. He expresses his love — Ahimsa — in such a manner that it impresses his enemy so much that he reciprocates his love. Therefore, there is no room for organized assassinations, murders or any violence for the sake of one's country or even for guarding the honour of precious ones that may be under one's charge. After all, that would be a poor defence of their honour.

Non-violence as a doctrine gives us a message that he who adopts it as a principle guards others' honour even at the cost of his own life. And that requires more courage than delivering the blows. If he does not retaliate and stands by his principle, he may receive blows from his enemy. But that does not deter him from his chosen path. Non-violence does not recognize patriotism that justifies wars.

Non-violence Graded

A student of Gandhi's philosophy may pose a question: whether his concept of non-violence is absolute and unlimited. Opinions vary in this regard. Persons like Maulana Abul Kalam Azad thought that it was absolute, while the general opinion seemed to be just the opposite. Gandhi believed that those who did not have faith in absolute non-violence might resort to such force as they had. Even in the conflicts between nations, he did not always teach passive resistance. In the 1930s and 1940s when Japan was engaged in an aggressive, ruthless and unprovoked warfare with China, Gandhi thought that China was relatively right in fighting against Japan. Similarly, he supported Poland when Germany attacked her in 1939. Physical resistance in those cases, to him, was the nearest approach to non-violence. At the same time, he refused to consider non-violence as a mere expediency and insisted that it should be observed in thought, word and deed.

As said earlier, Gandhi was highly religious, spiritual and laid emphasis on moral values which every one should practise. It was this strong conviction that helped him in adopting non-violence as an instrument to liberate India.

STATE

Philosophical Anarchism

It has been argued by some that state is an evil, a necessary evil as it restricts the freedoms of an individual, while others opine that state protects one's freedom, promotes his welfare and creates an atmosphere for him so that he can develop to his best self.

Political philosophers, thus, differ from one another with regard to the purpose of the state. While some favour its abolition, others want to make it strong and powerful; some restrict its scope, while others try to widen it. Gandhi, a philosophical anarchist, said that Government was best which governed least. Restricting the activities of the state to minimum, he firmly believed in self-directed activity. Emphasizing voluntary cooperation at the village level, he realized that undue state action killed or suppressed one's initiative as it gave rise to nepotism and bribery. Like other philosophical anarchists, he believed that the compulsive nature of the State robbed individual action of its morality. Men were not machines, and when they were forced to act as automations, there could be no question of morality. Like Thoreau, he considered the state to be a soulless machine. He said that stateless democracy was the most ideal society. On 2 July 1931, he wrote in *Young India*: in such a state of enlightened anarchy, everyone was left to himself. Everyone was his own ruler. There was least interference in his activities from outside. He ruled himself in such a manner that he was never a hindrance to his neighbour. In the ideal state, therefore, there was no political power because there was no state.

Gandhi wanted that the State should enjoy minimum power and its role be minimum and limited. Voluntary associations should enjoy more power than the state. State should not be coercive; be people-oriented and welfare-oriented; be least arbitrary and least authoritative and coercive. To him, there was a close link between the individual and the state. Both were inseparable. In other words, the people were the roots and the state was the fruit. If the roots were sweet, the fruits were bound to be sweet. An instrument of exploitation, the state let loose an organized violence against the poor, weak, docile, meek and mild. Supporting the rich, it oppressed the poor, restricted their scope and always rest on force and fraud, coercion and intimidation. In a non-violent society, the state governs the least and applies minimum force. He believed that in the ideal state of Ram Raj or the kingdom of God upon earth moral authority of the people reigned supreme and the state would collapse and perish in time. But, at the same time, he did not want its immediate abolition. The increasing performance of the state should be the immediate goal although the ultimate aim would be philosophical and moral anarchism. His hostile attitude towards the State could be attributed to his bitter experience in South Africa and India under the British regime.

WELFARE STATE

Gandhi belonged to the schools of liberalism, philosophical anarchism and collectivism, and had profound faith in the socialistic thought which stands for sharing of good things. If he were alive today, he might have supported the socialist measures adopted by the state to improve the living conditions of the poor and the backward, and all its welfare activities had they been proposed by the people themselves as it was for them the state existed, and it was they who counted much in their relation to the state. He might have outright rejected all the state actions that were responsible for corruption nepotism, favouritism, and laziness.

SWARAJ

Swaraj for Gandhi was part of the Truth which was God. In the field of politics or political freedom, it could be obtained only through intense suffering and continuous struggle. It was by no means a gift to be conferred on the people, but something to be achieved through hard work and sincere efforts. And it required a moral courage, physical endurance and a strong conviction. Accepting the Tilak's slogan "Swaraj is our birth right", believing that the people were entitled to freedom because they had fought for it and had to pass through a number of ordeals; arguing that people should be free because of their immense sufferings they had suffered for freedom; emphasizing that his Swaraj stood for the downtrodden and starving millions; he felt that if the state failed to ensure a good life for its citizens must be resisted peacefully.

Swaraj was not the replacement of the white bureaucracy by the brown. It was the total recasting of life in India. There should be unity in diversity and communal harmony. The society should be free from regional imbalances and rural–urban dichotomy. Freedom, personal and civic, was the foundation of Swaraj. He considered it as a whole. It could be moral freedom (emancipation from the slavery of passions), national freedom (emancipation from the bondage of alien rulers and exploiters) and spiritual freedom as realization of truth. Dedicating every moment of his existence to the cause of the Swaraj, the birth right of Indians, he said that they should not be deprived of it. Swaraj for him meant freedom for the meanest of our countrymen. He was not interested in freeing India merely from the British yoke, but from any yoke whatsoever.

Swaraj meant self-rule or Ram Raj, or the Kingdom of God on earth. He had a strong desire for Ram Raj. As God did not reside in heaven, He had to be realized on earth. One need not think of the world beyond. If he could do his duty with all sincerity, God would take care of him. This necessarily included political independence.

On 9 March 1922, he published an article in *Young India* drawing a distinction between the ideal society and Swaraj. The former could be characterized by the absence of railways, hospitals, machinery, army and navy, and laws and law courts. But under Swaraj, these five categories would function. Law and law courts would, however, protect the people's liberty and they could not be the bureaucratic instruments of oppression. He believed that people in Ram Raj should lead a happy life, without any hangovers and discrimination on the basis of caste, race, religion, sex, etc. On 15 November 1928, he wrote in *Young India* that in the Swaraj of his dreams, the poor people would have the same facilities as the rich had been enjoying. In 1931, he wrote that the Swaraj of his dream was the poor man's Swaraj. Once this goal was attained, there would be no exploitation. People should shape their own destiny according to their choice and liking. Unity among different sects would help in achieving Swaraj. Hence, his emphasis on Hindu–Muslim unity. And for this, the Hindus must come forward as their responsibility was greater than that of Muslims, the latter being in minority. It was argued by some that Indian Swaraj would be the rule of the majority community, the Hindus. They were certainly mistaken. There could not be greater mistake than it. If it were to be true, Gandhi said that he would not call it Swaraj and fight it with all its strength at his command, for, to him Hind Swaraj was the rule of all, the rule of justice. Whether under that rule, the minorities were the Hindus or Musalmans, they had to do justice. No community in India should develop an apprehension that Swaraj would be monopolized by a community. Swaraj would be real Swaraj only when there would be no occasion for safeguarding such rights. Therefore, necessity of separate electorate for different communities did not arise. His Swaraj, a comprehensive concept embracing various aspects of life, rest on Indian way of life. Addressing the delegates at the Karachi session of the Congress, he said that the critics must bear in mind that poor man's Swaraj was soon coming and let them not be found unrepresented when it actually came. Advocating the economic Swaraj, he said that let every one including the poorest among the poor prosper in the society.

Swaraj, to Gandhi, was freedom that one enjoyed in every sphere. It was complete independence of alien rule and complete economic and moral freedom. While political Swaraj necessarily meant the removal of the control of the British army in every shape and form, economic Swaraj meant freedom from the British capitalist, as also their Indian counterpart. Moral Swaraj meant replacement of the British army by national army of occupation. By political independence, Gandhi did not mean a mere imitation of the Europeans or Americans. They had systems suited to their own genius. Indians must choose that which would be most suitable for them. He described it Ram Raj, which meant sovereignty of the people based on moral authority. Indian economic independence meant to him the economic uplift of every individual by his or her conscious effort. People must lead a good life and maintain a decent standard of living.

Swaraj could be possible through intensive socio-economic reforms. It ensured harmony and improved the economic condition of the masses. India's end could be achieved without political power. Swaraj did not depend on jail going. If it did, there were thousands in jails; it depended on everyone doing his or her own task.

Therefore, he urged the people to go to villages, identify themselves with the villagers, with untouchables and give a meaning to the Hindu–Muslim unity. They should do menial jobs like scavenging. After getting Swaraj, they could go to sleep, unconscious, unmindful of various problems confronting them. Swaraj was not absence of rule. The people should strive hard to make it success. It recognized no race or religious distinctions. Nor was it to be the monopoly of lettered person, nor yet of the rich men. It was to be for all including the farmer, the maimed, the blind and the starving toiling millions. A stout-hearted, honest, sane, illiterate man might be the first servant of the nation. Swaraj did not lie in the cities but in the villages. If India was to attain true freedom, the people should live in villages but not in towns; in huts, not in places to accommodate crores of people. An ideal village would be self-sufficient in nature, free from social evils like untouchability and caste and race exploitation.

Swaraj should be enjoyed by teeming millions who were poor, backward and ignorant. If the people at bottom were uneducated and not conscious of their rights, they would be exploited. It must stop. This could be possible only with education that would remove ignorance and illiteracy. Hence, his insistence on national education.

ECONOMICS

The Gandhian economy aimed at applying the principle of non-violence to the economic life of man and saw clearly that industrial revolution gave rise to, as a consequence, the worst type of materialism as well as anarchism, individualism, socialism and idealism. Opposing capitalism and all sorts of exploitation, emphasizing humanitarian and cultural values, it sought to establish a system in which an individual would be given maximum opportunities to operate in any manner that he liked. Self-sufficiency, decentralized production and equitable distribution — these were the three fundamentals of Gandhian economics. It does not encourage large-scale production through machines. However, certain goods and services could be looked and managed by a few private individuals. But they would be answerable and accountable to the state. The state would exercise its control over the postal and telegraph systems, roads and other means of communication, railways, forests, mines, irrigation, heavy industries, etc.

International trade and commerce would be minimized as surplus goods only would be exported. Commodities necessary for health and well-being of the people should not be exported for the time being. Gandhi believed that in due course of time the gulf between the rich and the poor would be reduced and there would no more be any exploitation of an individual by another or of a class by another.

He was against the use of machines as means of production and opposed very much the machine age. He, however, believed that machine was good if it served man, but not when it sought to make him a slave. He never opposed small-scale machinery like sewing machine. Rather he welcomed it as it provided relief to an individual who used to stich with his own hands. Industrialization, to him, might lead to greater production of goods, but not necessarily to greater moral progress. Social necessity, rather than the personal whim, would determine the character of production.

He never wanted that a peasant society would be deprived altogether of the benefits of the machine. He was not against large-scale production. When he was asked whether there could be a harmony between cottage industries and large-scale production, he wrote on 28 January 1939 in *Young India*, "Yes, if they were planned so as to help the villages". Key industries, which the nation needed, might be centralized. Under his scheme, cities would not be allowed to produce the items which the villages could. The proper function of cities was to serve as clearing-houses for village products.

Gandhi believed in the ideal of trusteeship. To him, the property including landlord's land and the rich man's wealth belonged to God, Who had appointed them as His trustees. Considering themselves to be trustees, they should use property for the good of the community. Christianity preached that nobody owned wealth; it was only God's gift to him. Gandhi said that the rich people were not expected to throw away their wealth, but they should not have any attachment or lust for it. Instead, they should use only as much as they needed for themselves, distributing the remaining among the poor. He opposed accumulation of wealth and economic inequality. He preferred the interests of the society to those of an individual.

Gandhi felt that riches were always a hindrance to real growth. To solve this, he evolved a trusteeship system which would transform the present capitalist order of society into an egalitarian one. It did not recognize any right of private ownership of property unless it was permitted by society for its own welfare. The rich must act as trustees of the people. Capital and labour would coexist — capital as trustee of the society. In his socialism, the prince and the peasant, the wealthy and the poor, the employer and the employee were all at the same level. This would ensure perfect unity in the plurality of designs.

Strongly criticizing gross economic inequality existing in the contemporary society, Gandhi said that the basis of socialism was economic equality. There could be no Ram Raj in such a society if inequalities existed and the people did not have enough to eat.

Gandhian economy was essentially village economy. It stood for improvement of the economy of the rural poor with the help of cottage and indigenous industries like spinning and hand-weaving, gur-making, paddy-dehusking, oil-processing, paper-making, leather work, basket-making, and the like. Gandhi was not an agrarian reactionary when he opposed urbanization, machinization, large-scale nationalization, and capitalism. The only way to harness the large manpower was to strengthen cottage industries.

Gandhi wanted India to become a network of self-governing and self-sustaining village republics, each village or group of villages having its own industries and each of them living an autonomous existence.

Gandhi was not a socialist in the usually accepted sense of the term. If at all he was a socialist, his type of socialism was village socialism. Like other socialists, he did not believe the principle of state ownership of the means of production. In an interview with Louis Fischer, answering the question what he meant by socialism, Gandhi said that his socialism was ever-lasting. He did not want to rise on the ashes of the blind, the deaf, and the dumb. He wanted freedom for full expression of his personality. Under other forms of socialism, there was no individual freedom. One owned nothing, not even his body.

Gandhi's views on economy could be summed up: "decentralization of production and regional self-sufficiency; avoidance of the extremes of wealth and poverty; equal respect for all religions; removal of the sense of high and low in the social scale; acceptance of wealth as a trust for the betterment of the whole humanity; raising of the moral standards of life by reducing the material standard of luxurious living; renunciation of all vindictive punishments and reprisals; and reducing the use of physical force to its minimum in the task of maintaining law and order".

Gandhi differed from Marx. Marx, a dialectical materialist, an exponent of class struggle, believed that religion was the opium of the people and wanted to achieve his goal through violence and revolution. On the other hand, Gandhi, a propounder of class cooperation, a philosophical idealist had tremendous faith in religion which was a part of his life.

RELIGIOUS BASIS OF POLITICS

Politicians hardly have any interest in religion. But Gandhi was an exception to it. His devotion to Truth inspired him to join politics. He said that those who believed that religion had nothing to do with politics did not know what religion meant. He had no desire for anything in this material world since everything was subject to decay and death. He strived for the kingdom of heaven. This could be possible only through continuous hard work, constant sacrifice and selfless service to the cause of the humanity. He treated equally both his friends and foes. His patriotism, his faith in God, his strong moral conviction — all these would take him to the land of eternal freedom and peace. Thus, there was no politics without religion. Politics bereft of religion was a death-trap because it killed the soul.

For Gandhi, service to mankind was service to God and work was worship. There was no religion apart from human activity. God, to him, was Supreme and Absolute Reality. It was his faith in God that had created in him a new man. He wrote in *Young India* on 11 October 1928 that there was an unseen, indefinable and mysterious power that pervaded everything. He felt it, though he did not see it. It could be felt, but could not be proved. It was something different from other objects which could be perceived through his senses. Such unseen power cannot be proved by any external factor(s) or phenomena. This is something to be felt within. It is evident when we look at the sages and seers cutting across countries and continents. The lustre on their faces, their virtues, their conduct and character—all these indicated they were the self-realised souls. Does it not prove that there existed an unseen power? To reject this evidence was to deny oneself.

On 16 May 1938, he wrote in *Harijan*, it could never be a matter for argument. He was very much sure of His existence and it was as true as his sitting in the room. He could live without air and water, but not without Him. One could remove his eyes, but that would not kill him. One could chop off his nose, but that would not kill him. But he would be no more alive and die soon if his belief in God was shaken.

AN ESTIMATE

It is not easy to evaluate a great personality like Gandhi. A Mahatma, a Great Soul, a statesman, a reformer, a saint, a prophet, an enigma and an outstanding political leader, he influenced the course of Indian politics during the first half of the twentieth century. Modest, gentle, quiet, soft and kind, he had an indomitable spirit and iron will. An advocate by profession, a peasant both in his body and mind, he wore dress, like a farmer, that covered half of his body. It was a living testimony to his simplicity. Identifying himself with the poor and deprived, illiterate and ignorant, uneducated and uncivilized, he led an ascetic life.

He loved both his friends and enemies equally and strongly, and argued for abolition of any distinction between men and women. A man of rare virtues, a champion of universal love and peace, he symbolized the ambitions and aspirations of Indians; gave a new dimension to Indian politics, revived and refreshed the value of religion in politics.

The greatest personality of India, an irrepressible champion of her liberties, he taught the world at large and his own people three things: not to harbour animosity and practise love; to shun violence; and to work hard. His philosophy, his actions and his approaches to issues and problems distinguished him from others. His name 'Gandhi' is no more the name of a person. It means something else, something more than a name. It means a way of living in this troubled and modern world. Gandhism now stands for a way of life, for courage to fight against injustice in the world.

A unique personality, he made the impossible possible when he declared that 'Independence' could be possible without using arms, ammunitions and any kind of violence. He revealed to the world that it would be foolish on the part of statesmen and rulers to rely upon force to achieve their goals. To him, the tyranny of the state could be challenged through non-violence. Not only he said this with force and vigour but also implemented it with all his sincerity and seriousness.

Gandhi's truth and non-violence as means to achieve an end are more powerful than the sword. This was his ideology which symbolized peace. The whole world appreciated his ideology though most of the leaders were doubtful about its use in practical field. They admired him for his unique ideology.

Gandhi had no possessions, nor he held any position. Clad in a 'dhoti', he was a half-naked 'fakir'. Without any force at his back, without even a stick or stone, without power or patronage, he pulled down the pillars of an empire and brought freedom to the subcontinent of 400 million unarmed people.

Unimpressive and unassuming in appearance, he proved himself to be one of the greatest heroes and there is none who can be made comparable with him. He was admired for his courage and confidence, fire and fervour, purity and resolve, conviction and control over senses. People admired him for his strong, unique and marvellous political leadership. The influence he had on people cutting across various continents was beyond one's calculation. One might differ from him on several aspects, but cannot withhold his sense of indebtedness to him.

A strong follower of the Truth, a symbol of rising nationalism, a propounder of socio-economic and psychological transformation in the country, he gave a new dimension, a new image, a new direction to the freedom struggle. He provided a very effective and successful leadership to the freedom struggle.

The greatest revolutionary of recent times in India, a unique personality in Indian politics, he developed a new and humane technique called non-violence for the liberation struggle of an oppressed people and applied it with greatest accuracy and precision. He was a Mahatma (Great Soul), great among all the great persons and leaders that the world has had ever produced. But, at the same time, he was also a man of ground reality. A man of vision and foresight, he was simple in his attire, secular in his approach, pure in his mind and open in his heart. He did wonders and achieved the highest in his life.

His achievements were unparallel and unbelievable in the history of the world without commanding any force and conquering any territory. He exerted a tremendous influence on the mankind. Whatever he achieved was beyond one's comprehension. By no stretch of imagination one can ever think about him that a lean and thin man weighing a few pounds could pull down the pillars of the British regime in India. He would go down in the annals of history as a great liberator of 'untouchables' from their bondage of affliction — a work to be always remembered as the greatest act of human emancipation ever known to history of mankind. His tremendous success in this regard gave a new image to Hinduism and it was his one of his greatest contributions to the progress of humanity.

He transformed the principle of non-violent resistance into an instrument to achieve peace, liberty and justice. To many, it was a personal discipline, but to Gandhi it was a social programme to set the world free from bondage. He lived a great life of devoted service to a great ideal and demonstrated in his own life the mighty strength of passive, non-violent resistance against every form of evil, exploitation, injustice and wrong-doing.

A man of rare virtues and of impeccable character, he gave the Indians a new spirit, a sense of self-respect and a feeling of pride in their own culture and civilization. He was something more than a politician.

He practised what he preached. He presented to this unbelieving world all that was noblest which could be achieved by every one if he moved in right direction. He is no more with us as his physical body was assassinated and consigned to flames, but the spirit in him, which is sublime, constant and eternal will encourage and inspire countless generations for nobler living. A very great man, he was the greatest of the twentieth century. An Indian of the Indians, he is revered, respected and honoured by one and all who are sensitive to his deeds and contributions.

POINTS TO REMEMBER

- Gandhi's birth: on 2 October 1869 in Porbandar, Gujarat. Parents: Karamchand Gandhi and Putlibai Gandhi. Wife: Kasturbai Makanji Gandhi. Passed H.S.C. Examination in 1887. Least interest in college education. In 1888, he left for England for Bar-at-Law training. He joined the Bar at Rajkot in 1891. He left for Bombay for further study and stayed there for six months.
- He wanted to be a teacher, but could not as he was not qualified. A job in South Africa. He stayed there for more than 20 years. Indians' plight in South Africa, Gandhi challenged South Africa Government's policy against the Indians. He had to pay a heavy price for it.
- Gandhi's return to India in 1915. His political activities during 1915–1948. His assassination in 1948.
- Satyagraha: it is more than the passive resistance, securing rights by personal suffering, assertion of the truth, application of non-violence: not only abstaining from violence, but also doing good. Soulforce: it is non-violent resistance to evil, no harm to the wrongdoer, to hate the wrongdoings but not the wrongdoers. It is his own creation. He coined it in 1906 following an anti-Indian law passed by the Transvaal Government. It was the Asiatic Registration Bill.
- A Satyagrahi to oppose any law if it was immoral. His protest was the voice of the Atman. Dictates to be opposed.
- He differed from Locke, was close to J.S. Mill. Satyagraha and democracy may not go together. Satyagraha: a sacred right, a sacred duty; to challenge Government's misdeeds.
- Techniques of Satyagraha: fasting, voluntary migration, non-cooperation, *hartal*.
- A Satyagrahi's qualities: law-abiding, practises Ahimsa, accepts sufferings. Cannons for a Satyagrahi: endowed with virtues. Forms of Satyagraha: non cooperation, civil disobedience, Satyagraha and Passive Resistance.
- Sarvodaya: good for all, no violence against any one (human beings and animals). It goes against the theory of John Locke and of Jeremy Bentham. It includes values like freedom, equality, justice, etc.
- State: not created by God, an instrument of manipulation and exploitation. Sarvodaya: emphasis on politics of cooperation. Moral in character, it is influenced by Ruskin's thought. It rejects violence, class struggle and defends minority rights. It agrees and disagrees with communism.
- Swadeshi: a weapon to drive out the British from India, to boycott the foreign goods, to bring a change in the village economy. Centralization and nationalization of heavy industries. Industrial economy made human beings slaves. Gandhi favoured cottage industries.

- Ahimsa (non-violence): no torture to any one, to harm to others. To right the evil through good deeds; to oppose the tyranny, not the tyrant. It never originated with Gandhi, but it was he who applied it on a huge mass scale and in the arena of politics. 'Violence' was never found in his dictionary. Not to harm anyone in thought, words and deeds.
- Non-violence: positive and negative meanings. Negative: not to harm anyone. Positive: to love everyone. It is a weapon of the strong and of the weak. A coward cannot practise it. Gandhi would prefer violence to cowardice. It is not passivity. One need not be passive to the wrongdoer.
- Non-violence: law of life, a whole philosophy of life.
- Truth was Gandhi's highest 'dharma' and non-violence was his highest duty. Violence: not a remedy for ills.
- Non-violence: a struggle for truth; a means and an end. It is a total philosophy of life and made applicable to different fields.
- Non-violence does not recognize any kind of patriotism that justifies wars. Whether it is absolute or unlimited? Opinions vary. To Maulana — it is absolute. General opinion — not absolute. A non-believer in non-violence fights with his own force. Gandhi's support to China when Japan attacked her, to Poland when Germany attacked her. Their physical resistance was close to non-violence.
- Non-violence: spiritually, morally motivated to adopt it as an instrument to liberate India. State: an evil, not an evil; some for its abolition, some for making it more powerful. Gandhi: a philosophical anarchist. Too much state action killed one's initiative.
- State, to Gandhi, a soulless machine. He favoured stateless democracy, enlightened anarchy — a society where everyone is left to himself. State to have minimum power, to play limited role. Voluntary associations to be more powerful than the state. State not to be coercive, to be welfare-oriented and people-oriented. In a non-violent society, it governs the least.
- Gandhi not in favour of immediate abolition of the state. He favoured philosophical and moral anarchism, a Welfare State. To him, Swaraj was part of the Truth.
- Political Swaraj to be obtained by hard work. State to be resisted peacefully when failed to protect its people. Swaraj: to recast the life in India; unity in diversity, communal harmony. Gandhi's importance to freedom. People: not to be deprived of their Swaraj.
- Swaraj meant self-rule or Ram Raj or kingdom of God on earth. His distinction between ideal society and Swaraj.
- People to shape their own destiny, unity among various sects. Swaraj: not the rule of the majority. Every community being equal with other

communities, influenced by Indian way of life. It is poor man's Swaraj. Economic Swaraj: a must. Types of Swaraj: political, economic and moral.

- Swaraj does not mean absence of rule. Swaraj lies in the villages. Poor, ignorant and illiterate people should have it.
- Gandhian economics: application of non-violence to economic life. State's control over various departments. Minimum international trade and commerce. A society free from exploitation, no difference between the rich and the poor.
- He was against heavy industry; favoured small machines like sewing machines, machines should not enslave men. Emphasis on village, village needs, village industries.
- Trusteeship: property belongs to God and it was a gift of God to him. A rich man was simply a trustee of his wealth; he should not overspend for him, he should spend for the poor. Gandhi favoured an egalitarian society.
- Inequalities in the society would not bring Ram Raj. Gandhi encouraged cottage industries. Villages were to be self-sufficient. He was a village socialist. No state ownership of the means of production.
- Gandhi differed from Marx.
- He had tremendous faith in religion.
- He was a Mahatma, a great soul, noble and virtuous, a champion of love and peace; he gave a new dimension to Indian politics by spiritualizing it. The whole world appreciated his policy of non-violence. A unique personality, a great exponent of truth, a revolutionary, a man of vision, of rare virtues.
- His achievements were unparallel. He practised what he preached. He was the greatest personality not only of the twentieth century, but of the millennium. A formidable personality, he was admired by one and all.

10

Manabendra Nath Roy (1886–1954)

INTRODUCTION

Manabendra Nath Roy (M.N. Roy) will go down the annals of Indian history as a great freedom fighter, a writer of unusual brilliance and an original thinker of the highest order. His admirers appreciated him and held him in high esteem for his views and ideas while his critics severely criticized him for the same.

Born on 6 February 1886 in a small village named Urbalia in Bengal, he was known as Narendra Bhattacharjee in his childhood stage. But later he changed his name in the U.S.A. and was known to the world as Manabendra Nath Roy. His father was a priest. So it was expected that he would also become a priest. But he followed a different course of life and became a great and important politician and philosopher of the country.

In his early years, he was influenced by Swami Vivekananda, Bankim Chandra, Swami Ramtirtha, Dayanand Saraswati and Jatin Mukherjee, a revolutionary leader.

At the age of fourteen, he joined the revolutionary movement which aimed at removing the British from the Indian soil. In the Bengal Partition Movement (1905), he actively participated. He was arrested in 1907 in connection with a political dacoity that was committed at the railway station at Charingpota, 12 miles from Calcutta, and in 1910 in connection with the Howrah conspiracy and the Garden Reach Dacoity case.

He left for Germany in 1914 to seek support and cooperation which would help India in attaining her independence. However, because of changed circumstances he was frustrated and disappointed. Again in 1915, he left for abroad and stayed there for a long period of sixteen years. He did not return to India with arms and ammunitions for sedition but returned as one of the most important philosophers, widely known and highly acclaimed and at the same time severely criticized.

During his study abroad, he visited a number of countries like Dutch Indies, Java, Philippines, Korea, Manchuria, the U.S.A., China, Japan, Mexico, etc. He assumed different names. He was known for some time as Father Martin. In 1916, he reached Mexico, "the land of his rebirth". His stay at Mexico profoundly influenced his career. It was here at Mexico he made his first literary contribution. He opened a new chapter in his life by publishing his first article entitled "The Way to Durable World Peace".

He formed the Communist Party in Mexico, the first in America and outside the European continent. It was, for him, a sudden jump from diehard nationalism to communism. And he forgot the original cause (to get help from other countries to oust the Britishers from India) for which he had left India.

In Mexico, he realized that most of the economic and political problems could be attributed to nationalism and its only panacea would be socialism. Here, he was influenced by Borodin, a Marxist. He attached more importance to social justice and economic freedom. No more he wanted to have political agitations to achieve the goal.

During his stay in Russia from 1919 to 1926, he was influenced by communist philosophy and by Lenin. Although he accepted communism in principle, he differed from Lenin on many points and issues including colonial question. At the end of 1926, he visited China along with Borodin and Blucheer. He made deep and detailed study on the problems of China in his work "Revolution and Counter-Revolution in China". He also advised the Chinese Communists to wage an agrarian revolution in order to extend and expand their social basis. But the Communist Party of China ignored his advice. He felt very unhappy as it was a betrayal of the peasants as well as of the proletariat.

He soon returned to India in 1930 and moved for some time in disguise and was known as Dr. Muhammad. But he was arrested in connection with Kanpur Conspiracy case and sent to jail for six years. In 1936, after fifteen years' exile and six years' in prison, he joined the Indian National Congress. At the Karachi Congress, he came in close contact with Jawaharlal Nehru and Subhas Chandra Bose and he was the moving spirit behind the adoption of resolutions on economic and social objectives by the Congress. This was the first commitment of the Congress for a socio-economic programme.

As a member of the Indian National Congress, he did not agree with Gandhi on many issues. To him, Gandhi was a hypocrite and Gandhism lacked an economic programme to win mass support and which sought to unite all sections of people: landlords and capitalists, who exploited the common poor people, with peasants and workers who were exploited. It would be, to him, wrong to give too much importance to religion, particularly in the sphere of politics. It would certainly mislead and misguide the ignorant masses. He did not have confidence in the ability or capacity of Gandhi in giving right direction to freedom struggle. In 1939, he formed the League of Radical Congressmen. And in 1940, he contested the Presidentship of the Indian National Congress, but lost to Abul Kalam Azad. His defeat and growing differences with Gandhi forced him to leave the Congress in September 1940 and in December, he formed the Radical Democratic Party. He supported the War against the Fascist forces. As a result, he was branded as an anti-nationalist and pro-British.

When he realized that the Radical Democratic Party would no more serve any purpose as it had become inconsistent with the type of democracy he was advocating for, he dissolved it in 1948. After that he did not join any political party nor did he profess any party politics. He became the Founder Director of the Indian Renaissance Institute, Dehradun, and spent much of his time in writing and thinking. On 25 January 1954, he left his mortal frame, immortalizing himself for the thoughts and deeds and would always remain as a constant and undying source of inspiration for many.

FREEDOM

A part of human personality and a product of culture, to him, freedom should be understood in the context of happiness. It promoted happiness and shaped human personality. It was not a gift to the individuals by the authority, it was rather achieved by them a beautiful castle not built in the air of imagination, its pillars were humanism, individualism and rationalism.

He did not want that individuals should enjoy absolute and unlimited liberty as this would go against the basic purpose of the human society. He allowed the state to interfere in their affairs provided it promoted the welfare of the community.

He considered freedom as the supreme value, the source of all human values. His close association with the socialist thinkers influenced him to think about economic freedom. It was not the only freedom but much of life depended upon it. He strongly believed that socialism alone could bring and ensure it. He also felt that freedom and progress in the society could be assessed and measured in terms of freedom and progress of the individual.

Freedom, a positive quality of human behaviour, made an individual a useful citizen. In his theory of freedom, he did not have any place for religion or for any supernatural values as the latter deprived him of his intellectual freedom.

RADICALISM AND MARXISM

Roy's childhood days were neither happy nor remarkable. A kind of deprivation during the formative period of one's life normally makes one a radical and rebel. As expected, he became a revolutionary. But later, he became a communist out of necessity though he was not very much attached towards communism in the beginning of his career. Had it been so, he might have desired to go first to Russia rather than to Germany.

During his stay at Mexico, he was deeply moved by the sufferings of the people. American economy had a tremendous impact upon their socio-economic and political aspects. This made him to think in terms of the welfare of the society as a whole. In 1917, Russian revolution and the capture of power by the Bolsheviks inspired and encouraged the people across the Atlantic as it gave them hope and confidence that the days of their sorrow would be over soon. All left wing socialists expected that things would change. They were all would-be-communists. But in case of Roy, the influence of revolution did not make him a greater revolutionary than what he was before, but it saw a sudden political evolution in him; a sudden jump from die-hard nationalism to communism. This unexpected influence profoundly influenced his career and made him a different man with a different mission. His ardent nationalism took a dramatic turn towards communism.

Roy became so much interested in communist movement in Mexico that he rendered financial assistance to it and became the first Secretary of the Communist Party of Mexico. Marxism inspired him very much. He wanted that the idea "live and let live" should have a wider space in the society. Marx's concept of freedom appealed him very much. He felt that though Marxism became a totalitarian theory, Marx was an advocate of freedom; and as a Humanist, he stood for the freedom of the individual. Marx talked of socialism as the protector of freedom and man would control his social environment. Like Marx, Roy believed in the essential goodness of man. Both of them believed that man would give up ultimately all his irrational forces and become good, perfect and rational.

With the passage of time M.N. Roy, however, differed from Marxism and Communism (which include the thoughts of Marx, Engels, Lenin, Stalin and Trotsky). Marx believed that the middle-class would perish in due course of time and there would be only two classes in the society, i.e. haves and have-nots. Roy found the contrary in the reality. He found that the middle-class played a very key role in moulding the history of many countries. Marx said that surplus value resulted in social injustice and degradation. Unlike Marx, Roy argued that surplus value brought in social progress and cultural development. He made "positive good of a negative concept in Marx". He believed that surplus value would be everywhere, in every country irrespective of its nature of political system. Marx opined that the course of history was determined by the economic laws of demand and supply. To Roy, besides economic factors, there were other forces like ideas, beliefs, aspirations which determined the course of history. Marx's thesis on 'Matter' was also not acceptable to Roy as the former gave too much importance to material aspect of life.

Marx emphasized the economic aspect of life and progress. Roy believed that this approach to history was not comprehensive. Along with economic consideration, there were social and ideological ones, whose importance could not be ignored in the study of development of history. He argued that religion, culture, politics, sympathy, humanitarian considerations and a number of other factors shaped and rebuild a society. He believed that Marxist concept of freedom enslaved the individual. Civil and political liberties were considered by Marx as untrue, imaginary and unnecessary. To him, individual could not survive without society. In other words, an individual had to identify himself with it. But, on the other hand, Roy argued that individual should not be considered as a means to an end. Unlike Marx, Roy was an exponent of moral, social and intellectual freedom of individual. And it could not be suppressed. Marx and Engels were ardent supporters of Germany and anything that was German. Such an idea of racial or national superiority was unthinkable for Roy. His aim was always to set an international society.

POLITICAL SYSTEMS

Roy had strong faith in democracy, but never believed it blindly. It was anti-totalitarianism. In a totalitarian system, the life of an individual in totality was controlled by the state. He loved democracy as it was a part of his faith in humanism and the essential goodness of man. It offered absolute freedom of mind and intellect. He set up a linkage between democracy and humanism, the two noble dreams of the mankind. Arguing that democracy is the social and institutional expression of humanism, he emphasized that humanism entailed confidence in man, and democracy was born of that confidence.

Roy and other radicals found certain defects in the existing democracy. Therefore, they evolved a new form of democracy called *Radical Democracy*. Ellen Roy, his constant co-worker, explained the meaning of Radical Democracy. Derived from the Latin word "radix", the term 'Radical' stood for "from the root". If there was anything wrong with democracy, one must dig deeper to the roots of the concept and find out what was wrong and try to rectify that. Democracy must be radical or it was no democracy at all. Roy said that Radical Democracy, the real democracy, would not have any political parties to function. In case they existed, they would wither away. As a result, people would have more freedom. In democracy, individuals were expected to play a major role in the political process. But they did not. Instead of being active, they became dormant. He, therefore, suggested that political parties should be replaced by professional groups of engineers, doctors, jurists, teachers, etc. to articulate the public opinion.

He asserted that ignorant and immature people did not deserve democracy. It could be a way of life only if they were free, rational and morally responsible.

Radical Democracy never gave any importance to right to vote. It sought to raise the people to a higher standard of existence. It aimed at increasing production so that the demands of the people could be met and a higher standard of living for them could be created.

Roy never considered democracy as a mere method of political administration. To him, it was a way of life. His faith in democracy reflected his love for mankind.

Opposed to dictatorship and fascism, he observed that fascism was not only an enemy of democracy but it was the most dangerous enemy of civilization as it laid overemphasis on state and considered the individuals as mere cogs who could be sacrificed for the group or the state.

MAN AND MANKIND

"Individual" occupied a very important place in Roy's philosophy. Progress, prosperity and worth of the society depended upon that of the individual. If individuals were good, the society must be good. During the first phase of his political career, as he was a communist then, he laid emphasis on "duties". However, he changed his mind later since duties alone would turn individuals to slaves. He would be enslaved by the state. Hence, his emphasis on liberty of the individual.

Reconciling liberty with authority, he never made the liberty absolute, nor the authority unlimited. Every individual must enjoy freedom and fulfil social obligations.

In the beginning, he also, like Marx, believed that the state would wither away. However, subsequently he changed his views realizing that the state could be an end in itself, nor it should strive for its welfare. Rather it should promote the happiness of the individuals. To him, the state was not a necessary evil, nor would it wither away. Limiting the powers and functions of the state, he observed that it would be simply an instrument to attain common interest of the individuals. He argued that a Radical Democratic State would not only eliminate the lapses of formal parliamentary democracy but also be conscious of the dangers of dictatorship of any class or elite. Like others, he also believed that society was the product of human efforts. For the sake of self-defence and self-development, it was created by the individuals. God did not play any role in such creation.

Emphasizing world unity, he thought that mankind would continue to suffer as long as people were not united. The present world was passing through one of the darkest phases because of too much emphasis on nationalism. Never it was perceived that the whole world was a unit. Narrow national ambitions should not be encouraged as this would encourage conflict, confrontation, discord and wars in the society. It would be detrimental to the interests of the mankind if people were guided by their parochial interests, but not by those interests which would promote nationalism. He supported internationalism as it eliminated international rivalry in economic sphere. National considerations, when extended to economic field, would result in imperialism.

He believed that international society was an organic unit as well as a necessity. Society would be free from all problems like poverty, unemployment, war, famine, drought, flood, etc. if the entire world would be considered as a unit and the nation states were dissolved. In his philosophy, there was no place for militant nationalism. He had a strong conviction that radicalism was essentially a path to attain internationalism.

SCIENTIFIC POLITICS

Scientific politics as explained by Roy differs from that of Thomas Hobbes and Spinoza. They laid much stress on scientific methodology as they modelled their theory on the patterns of Geometry. But Roy gave much importance to the social foundations of scientific propositions. To him, scientific politics covered a set of political propositions which recognized the class character of the exponents of the divergent ideologies.

Spiritualism

Since time immemorial, religion has been playing a dominant role in shaping the history of mankind. This may be attributed to the people's ignorance. Lack of exposure to education and to modernization made them irrational and they condoned all their misdeeds under the pretext that religion was the guiding spirit of all their actions. This position continued until the outbreak of Renaissance. Religion formed revolution, but in the long run it enslaved the human mind. Roy agreed that in the first phase of their career, Buddha, Christ and Mohammad were the torchbearers of the revolution. They gave a new meaning and a purpose to life and opened a new vista of vision.

In the East as well as the West, Roy believed, the religious institutions were the centres of learning, playing a key role in the promotion of education. Without them, it would have been certainly delayed. The monasteries were the centres of learning and scholars from different places came here to study, exchange their thoughts, share their ideas, and widen their outlook. Besides imparting knowledge, they were the main centres of economic interest. As they owned much land, the common man depended on them for his survival and growth. Taking its advantage they exploited him mentally and intellectually, certainly a great disservice to the mankind.

He observed that the Reformation Movement, a product of Renaissance, brought about a change in the attitude of man towards God and religion. The Renaissance opened a new chapter in the history of mankind as it was the beginning of man's struggle for intellectual freedom and the quest for truth, of his revolt against superstitions and supranatural forces, of his freedom from bondage by offering rational and natural explanations for different natural phenomena as against spiritual dogmas.

Roy opposed all religions as they were intoxicants and stifled the growth of human mind. They never induced the people to fight against evils. In other words, it made them dull, lethargic and indifferent but never action-oriented. But all attempts to reform it ended in dismal failure.

Materialism

Materialists argued that everything could be reduced to matter. Everything including mind emanated from it. Except matter everything was false. In other words, it was the only Truth. All other appearances were mere transformations of the matter. Like Heraclitus, Roy, a staunch materialist, believed that whatever was common was true; the exception was false. Anything that was beyond the comprehensions of the mind was not true, but an illusion. There was no question of Utopia or heaven; no scope for miracles, supernatural powers, etc.; Truth was not the Truth if it was not accessible to the senses. Matter gave strength and sustenance to the individuals and other living beings. All of them required food, water, shelter, clothes, etc. for their existence. Without matter they would be no where and might perish in no time.

Socialism

Roy firmly believed that socialism would bring to an end economic exploitation, social slavery, cultural backwardness and spiritual degradation. It would create better conditions for the people and usher in a new era for them.

Disappointed with the methods of existing types of socialism, he evolved a new type of socialism called *Cooperative Socialism*. It treated the individuals as independent units of the society. There was no domination of any kind. He was not under dictation or domination, not subject to any kind of bondage and would gain much by being a member of Cooperative Socialism.

As a contrast, socialism as explained by Marx and his followers did not offer the individuals freedom in many sectors. They simply assured them of economic freedom — there would be no problem for food. But in Cooperative Socialism, food would be there — not because it was a price for freedom, but because he would make an effort, along with other human beings, to get it. Neither compromises, nor sacrifices were to be made. There was also no loss of individual thought in moral, cultural, intellectual, political and social sectors.

His Cooperative Socialism combined the advantages of a liberal philosophy with the benefits of an organized society. This gave a new dimension to the history of world socialism, having an ethical-spiritual value. A name for a social philosophy, it did not mean only forms of enterprise or political institutions. An alternative to orthodox liberalism as also to recent varieties of cooperativism and communism, it was not a mere method of economic attainment. It was, in a way, a way of life and living. Needless to say, once it became strong, it would ensure individual's freedom and shower benedictions and benefits on him.

THE INDIAN PROBLEMS

Economic Aspects

Roy realized that India passed through a serious economic crisis. The years of colonial rule had drained its economic resources and made it a pauper. He felt a revolution in economic sector could be possible once the peasants were well organized and well protected.

He made a deep and thorough analysis of the agricultural problems in India and strongly argued that the government should be held responsible for economic development. He believed that the problem of the price level was one of the greatest difficulties in the Indian economy. This was more important than the problems of production and consumption. To him, it was not the lower production but lack of sufficient control over the price line that was responsible for economic crisis.

He was conscious of the role played by the Indian traders who were not only the monopolists but also the instruments of exploitation. He, therefore, suggested that the consumers must organize cooperatives to prevent or check influence of the traders.

He was very much opposed to the first Indian economic plan otherwise known as the Bombay Plan, because it sought to industrialize India to help the capitalists and capture the international market. He, therefore, appealed the middle-class in India to adopt new economic measures. Otherwise, their survival would be in danger. He urged upon the people to bring the feudal social relations to an end so as to bring a new era in their economic life.

In the first phase of his career, he had little consideration for economic freedom. He always thought in terms of political and intellectual freedom. But in course of time, he changed this opinion and considered economic freedom to be more important than the other two.

He was in favour of the nationalization of the basic industries. The state should take initiative to set up major industries through cooperatives. There must be land reforms. The remnants and traces of feudalism must be abolished.

He suggested that adequate remuneration and wages should be paid to all the workers and labourers so that they have a reasonable living. No body should be asked to work for more than eight hours a day and benefits like leave, promotion, pension, etc. be provided.

He felt that progress of a society depended upon the emancipation of the workers and tillers of the soil. With this view in his mind, he formed the Indian Federation of Labour and tried to organize the labour force of the country. He made a significant contribution to the Trade Union Movement in India.

SOCIAL ASPECTS

Roy felt that a society could not develop unless the social maladjustments were removed. He admitted that social stagnation was primarily responsible for the backwardness of the country. Social life in India was influenced by many superstitions and prejudices. The age-old notions and traditions limited the scope for radical thinking and progressive ideas. He wanted to reform the Indian society with practical experience. He felt that social reforms were more essential than political and economic as man lived more on the social plane. Without social freedom, an individual lost his significant distinction; his rationality being stultified, he lost his moral equilibrium and other modes of freedom became merely empty words. He challenged some of the ideas of Gandhi like ahimsa, non-violence, satyagraha, etc. as these were considered by him as "a bundle of hypocrisy" and these would make the country a backward one in the world.

Roy, therefore, urged upon the people to revolt against all attempts of submission — physical, spiritual and mental. He also asked them to accept the better and the nobler aspects of the Western world.

He believed the scientific approach and went to the roots of the problems. He felt that a mere political revolution would not liberate the people of India — there must be a philosophical revolution as well. In the social revolution, both the workers as well as the intellectual class should participate.

POLITICAL ASPECTS

In India, most of the people were not politically conscious. The degree of their political awareness and understanding was very low. Those who worked in government offices and other organizations were not serious about politics. Politics in India was not a serious affair as it was in advanced countries.

In India, he felt, political decisions were influenced more by passion and prejudice than by reason. He wanted that reason should play a dominant role in the decision-making process. He organized the intellectuals of the country to create a new political set-up with new ideas and ideals.

HUMANISM

Roy realized the importance of a new kind of socio-economic and political philosophy. He was aware of the dangers of Marxism on one side and lapses of the parliamentary form of government on the other. To overcome this, he formulated the philosophy of "Radical Humanism" or "New Humanism". His weekly journal, *Independent India*, which started in 1937, was renamed as *The Radical Humanist* to propagate his views on society and social reconstruction.

The word 'humanism' is derived from the Latin word "Humanus", which refers to a system of thought concerned with human affairs in general. It does not refer either to God or individual, or nature. Humanism is an attitude which attaches primary importance to man and his faculties, affairs and aspirations.

Humanism, as a concept, means different things to different people. For example, to some, it means reasonable balance of life and social reality.

To some, it simply refers to the study of humanities and literature. To others, it is an understanding of freedom from religious bondage and dogmatism. But to majority of the humanist thinkers, it simply means the study of man. Humanism can, therefore, be defined as an attitude of mind which gives primary importance to man and his faculties. God, therefore, does not have any importance or relevance as He is relegated to background. Roy felt that the idea of God might have been a lever for humanism. It was not for the sake of God that God was created, and worshipped. It was rather for the sake of man himself that God was made. When an individual faced crises or was passing through a bad phase in his life, he could get solace by worshipping God. He used God as an instrument for securing peace, pleasure and happiness.

The principles of humanism are as follows:

1. Man by nature is good and capable of becoming perfect.
2. There exists no barrier to future progress of human civilization. All the evil forces on the path are to be eliminated.
3. An individual makes use of liberty for the development and betterment of the society.
4. An individual should identify himself with the human society. Interests of the society are more important than those of the individual.
5. Once an individual becomes rational and enlightened, he is no more influenced by superstitions. His scientific knowledge influences his social, industrial and economic aspects of life.

Roy realized that it would be difficult to have real humanism unless religion and superstitions were given up. He, therefore, formulated New Humanism. Going into the genesis of man and examining the origin of his background, he formulated his New Humanism based on fundamental experience of life. It was to grow from the experience of perennial crisis which affected the entire existence of man. It was this crisis in every aspect of human life that motivated him to create a new kind of philosophy for the future of mankind so that man would not lose confidence in himself and be lost for all time to come. New Humanism was a product of such kind of experience and thinking. The mystery of man has been solved by modern sciences partially by modern biology. He is the outcome of biological evolution. Roy further argued that every individual by nature and as a biological organism was moral and rational, and as such, he was capable of living with others in peace and harmony.

The New Humanism wanted to inspire every one to strive for and attain higher ideals and higher position in his life. He should shape his own destiny. It aimed at making him confident and courageous.

New Humanism, based on scientific knowledge and experience, explained man in the context of his socio-political and economic life, and also the whole universe in the light of an integrated picture of knowledge, experience and intuition. Therefore, New Humanism is called *Integral Humanism* or *Scientific Humanism*. It is also known as *Radical Humanism*, because it tried to explain the problems from the roots.

Scientific Humanism or New Humanism while emphasizing scientific outlook and maintaining that there could be rational understanding and perfect harmony among individuals and social organizations through knowledge, education and spirit of cooperative living, emphasized that man and the universe were integrated in a cosmic system.

Roy observed that New Humanism did its best to solve the problems of ethics and hysterology, and to synthesize the humanist, the materialist and the rationalist so as to coordinate the philosophy of value with a social philosophy and ethics. Based on certain premises of social absolutes, it considered man as

- not born social after the pattern of the bees or the ants;
- a family animal, only circumstances forced him to be social;
- a hunting animal wishing to live on the weaker;
- a selfish animal;
- a rational animal, enlightened but selfish;
- a freedom-loving animal, imaginative and creative.

New Humanism emerged as a philosophy of the modern man without bondage. Whether it can stand the test of time or not, it is left to the future. But one thing is certain that Roy made significant contributions to political philosophy through New Humanism.

Dedicated and devoted to his nation, he did his best to reconstruct, rebuild and remould the human society. All his suggestions in this regard are powerful, relevant and thought-provoking. One could see in his work the reflection of his vast experience and tremendous insight.

AN ESTIMATE

An erudite scholar, he made a brilliant exposition of ideas on Indian politics and philosophy. An author of several books including *Materialism*; *Reason, Romanticism and Revolution*; *The Philosophical Consequences of Modern Science* said to be one of the most voluminous books containing six thousand pages. He was, as said earlier, a staunch materialist. To him, materialism was a revolutionary philosophy as it allowed man to fulfil his material desires. But the people of the East do not subscribe to such ideas as they believe in renunciation, denunciation and abnegation but not in enjoyment. Sacrifice is more important than enjoyment. But Roy's emphasis on materialism was highly thought-provoking and one should review and rethink it afresh.

Roy's New Humanism rests on the premise of values. To him, a society becomes pervert once its values are eroded and erosion of values can be prevented when the administration is looked after by men of eminence, character and integrity, and other virtues. His value-based politics attaching importance to freedom, knowledge and truth is said to be his most significant contributions to behavioural political analysis.

Earlier, Roy was a Marxist, a revolutionary in spirit, as he believed in the forcible seizure of power. But later, he gave up such ideas and argued that moral renaissance would free the society from its turmoils. It is ethics which guides a government properly and its functioning depends upon adoption of ethical principles as guiding factors. From a Marxist, he became an ethical revisionist and from an atheist, to a theist.

It has been argued that his New Humanism is not a new or novel contribution but a restatement of Marxism. Like Edward Bernstein, a Left-wing German revisionist, and Adler, he supplemented materialism with humanist ethics by emphasizing freedom, reason and human social values and ethics. His insistence on materialism, as the only possible philosophy, showed his blind faith in Marxism. There are modern schools like Organism, Neutralism and Existentialism. It does not serve any purpose if it is argued that all non-materialistic systems are wrong or manifestations of religious revival.

Roy was a hedonist as he propagated Bentham's hedonism in the name of New Humanism. His belief in hedonism could not endear himself to the people of the East as they were more amenable to the ideas of ethics, values, virtues like abnegation, renunciation and denunciation of worldly desires, etc. But, of late, they have been moving in the direction of the West and become more materialists than the Westerners.

Roy tried to give a sociological interpretation of Indian culture. As he was a disciple of Marx, he ignored diverse social forces responsible for emergence and maintenance of social values. Like Marx, he also believed that it was economics, not the ethics or values, which constituted the substructure.

His exposure to Western philosophy developed in him a superiority complex. Therefore, he never suffered from guilt complex when he criticized Gandhism as medievalism and denounced the Gandhian mode of living as 'primitive'.

He left India and was in exile for fifteen years (1915–1930). He spent six years in jail from 1930 to 1936. Away from the country, imprisonment took him away from Indian culture, ethics and values. As a result, he strongly criticized Hinduism and Indianness. To him, nationalism was an "antiquated bourgeois separatist creed".

A modern philosopher, he resented primitivism and medievalism of Indian culture and Gandhism. A materialist, he argued that religion and spiritual philosophy was based on fantastic ignorance. He indulged in satires against the spokesmen of ideologies and views different from his own.

Treating nationalism as an "antiquated cult" and equating it with "thoughtless emotionalism", he argued that Indians, who were under the intoxicating influence of nationalism, were not allowed to support the Allies against the Axis powers. Equating nationalism and the philosophy of Gandhi with fascism, he urged upon the British Government in India to suppress the national movement.

'Critical' rather than 'constructive', Roy failed to give any new thought-system, and contribute an integral system of thought either to political science or to political philosophy. However, he tried to "synthesize different elements of thought and bring to a common focus the elements of rationalistic renaissance, physical realistic cosmology, humanistic ethics and a passionate quest for freedom." But the synthesis as it finally emerges is neither very "profound nor original". Notwithstanding all these deficiencies and weaknesses with Roy, he can be very rightly said to be the most learned, outside the universities, scholar among the writers on Indian political philosophy.

POINTS TO REMEMBER

- M.N. Roy, a great freedom fighter and an original thinker, was born in 1866. He was influenced by many thinkers and scholars. His active involvement in politics during his early period of life. He was arrested in 1907 and 1910.
- His visit to foreign countries: formed the Communist Party in Mexico. Influenced by Borodin. His emphasis on social justice. His stay in Russia (1919–1926) and influence of Lenin on him. His visit to China in 1926. His return to India in 1930. Arrested in 1936 and imprisoned for six years. He joined the Congress in 1936.
- His influence on the Congress in adopting socio-economic resolutions: his close contact with Subhash Bose and Pandit Nehru. He differed from Gandhi. To him, Gandhi did not have any economic programme. His least importance to religion. Formed the League of Radical Congressmen (1939).
- His contest for the office of the Congress President in 1940: he lost to Abul Kalam Azad. He left the Congress in September 1940 and in December 1940 formed the Radical Democratic Party (R.D.P.). His support to the British Government during the Second World War. Dissolved the R.D.P. in 1948 and gave up politics. Set up the Indian Renaissance Institute at Dehradun. In 1954, he passed away.
- Freedom: shaped personality and promoted happiness; not a gift but an achievement; not absolute; state not to interfere in the affairs of individuals if it is harmful to them; supreme value; economic freedom; socialism brings economic freedom; freedom of individual linked to the freedom of the society.
- Freedom: a positive quality, makes an individual conscious of his rights and duties.
- Radicalism and Marxism: childhood days not happy, deprivation made him a rebel, a revolutionary, a communist. Influenced by the living conditions of the people in Mexico and the 1917 Russian Revolution. He was the first Secretary of the Communist Party of Mexico. Like Marx, he believed in the essential goodness of man. Later, he differed from Marx in respect of existence of or elimination of Middle-class, Supreme Value

and the matter. To Roy, besides economics, other factors also influenced one's life.

- To Marx, society is more important than the individual. To Roy: individual not a means.
- Democracy: he had strong faith in democracy as it ensured freedom to individuals. He had also faith in humanism and essential goodness of man. He found certain defects in democracy. Evolved a new form of democracy called Radical Democracy. No political parties in it. They must wither away. Political parties to be replaced by functional groups.
- Democracy not suitable for all the people. Radical Democracy — no importance to vote. It ensured a higher standard of living. It was a way of life. He opposed dictatorship and fascism because they sacrificed the interests of the individual.
- Man and mankind: men and society: their progress and prosperity interlinked. He reconciled liberty and authority. State will wither away. But changed his views. State an end in itself. State to promote the happiness of individual. State — not a necessary evil.
- Society: a product of human efforts. People to be united to avoid conflict and confrontation. He was an internationalist. Nation States to be dissolved. No place for militant nationalism.
- Scientific politics: Roy's scientific politics differed from that of Hobbes and Spinoza.
- Spiritualism: importance of religion in the lives of individuals.
- Religious institutions: centres of learning and economically sound. Common man depended upon them for his survival. He was exploited.
- Reformation movement and renaissance: religions were intoxicants.
- Materialism: the only truth. No utopia, no heaven, no supernatural powers, no miracles. Matter gave strength and sustenance.
- Socialism: exploitation should stop. Socialism would give people new hopes, new aspirations. Existing varieties of socialism disappointed him.
- Cooperative socialism: individuals were independent units. No domination. To Marx, socialism never guaranteed freedom, cooperative socialism was an alternative to orthodox liberalism. A way of life and living.
- The Indian problems: economic aspects — India passed through a crisis, peasant revolution was a must. Government responsible for economic development. To maintain the prices of commodities — an important task of the Government. Indian traders were exploiters. He opposed the Bombay Plan.
- To Roy, economic freedom was more important than political freedom. Nationalization of industries. Cooperatives to set up industries. Labourers to be adequately paid. Emancipation of the workers.

- Social aspects: social evils to be eradicated. Social reforms more important than political and economic reforms. He challenged Gandhi's ideals. He urged upon the people to revolt against submission. He was scientific in his approach.
- Political aspects: people's political awareness was very low. Politics not a serious matter. Reason's role in politics. One should be above biases and prejudices. He wanted a new political set up with new ideals and ideas.
- Radical humanism: he was aware of dangers posed by Marxism and parliamentary form of government.
- Humanism means different things to different people. It is the study of man. An attitude of mind: man is good. He should seek the development of the society and identify himself with society. He lives peacefully with others.
- Humanism encouraged and inspired one to go for ideals, to shape his own destiny. New Humanism is also known as Integral Humanism, Scientific Humanism and Radical Humanism. It wanted to solve the problems of ethics and hysterology.
- Humanism explained 'man' from different perspectives. Man was not a social animal as bees and ants were. Selfish, though rational, enlightened and freedom-loving; he loved hunting.
- He was a brilliant scholar. His emphasis on matter. His views went against the philosophy of the East. His philosophy rests on values. Perversion may be attributed to erosion of values.
- His value-based politics: men of character to be in power. Earlier, a Marxist. Changed his views. Moral Renaissance to set the society free from evils. His emphasis on reason, freedom and social values. His insistence on materialism showed his blind faith in Marxism.
- A hedonist: his hedonism was opposed to the Eastern philosophy. He explained Indian culture in the light of social forces. Away from India for a long time made him a "non-Indian" in approach.
- He criticized Indian culture and Gandhism. To him, Gandhi was a fascist. He was the most learned scholar among the writers on Indian political philosophy.

11

Jawaharlal Nehru (1889–1964)

INTRODUCTION

If Mohandas Karamchand Gandhi is rightly described as 'Father of the Nation', Pandit Jawaharlal Nehru can be rightly said to be the Architect of Modern India. While the former liberated India from the British bondage and made her free and independent, the latter guided her destiny with all his sincerity and seriousness for nearly eighteen years. One 'created' a country while the other 'made' it great in the eyes of international community. A dedicated soldier in the freedom struggle, a trusted lieutenant of Gandhi, Nehru occupied a significant position in the history of national struggle for independence. A man of foresight, knowledge, wisdom, of ideas and action; a statesman; a philosopher, he laid the foundation of a strong, united, democratic, secular and socialist India. Influenced by his father Motilal Nehru, he was a staunch nationalist and an ardent patriot. Occupying the office of the Congress President in 1929, 1936, 1937 and 1946, he, along with Gandhi and other eminent leaders, worked hard to liberate the country from the British regime.

Author of *Glimpses of World History, Autobiography* and *Discovery of India*, Nehru like his father, was a "realist" as well as a "rationalist". He had no feeing for any transcendental Being. He was not dogmatic, nor a militant atheist, nor a materialist. But, at the same time, he was never a spiritualist like Gandhi, who was a devout and prophetic personality and with whom he spent most of his time to liberate India. He had a tremendous attachment and regards for Gandhi. He met him in 1916 at the Lucknow Congress session and came under his influence in 1920. The personality and principles of Gandhi had tremendous influence on his thought and action. Gandhi's approach and methods appealed him most.

Influenced by the writings of Peter, Oscar Wilde, Bertrand Russel, George Bernard Shaw and others, he was a keen student of history; an ardent nationalist;

a socialist and an intellectual of high order. He stood for a casteless and classless society and for freedom, social justice and equality.

In his life time he was exposed to and influenced by various ideologies as they appealed him and made him matured. He was influenced by classical liberalism with its emphasis on individual rights; by fabian socialism at Cambridge; Gandhism, which believed in non-violence and the purity of means, and in the late 1920s and 1930s by Marxist theory and the gospel of a classless society. He was also attracted to the ethical norms of Western humanism, and later when he was imprisoned, to the precepts of Vedanta, the ancient system of Hindu philosophy.

EARLY LIFE

It has been believed that in January 1889 Motilal Nehru, who had lost his first son and did not have any child then and who had a strong urge for a son, visited with his friends Madan Mohan Malaviya and Pandit Din Dayal Shastri, the holy city of Rishikesh in the Himalayas. One evening they met a yogi and with folded hands Malaviya prayed him to shower his blessings on Motilal so that he could have a son. Looking at Motilal with his deep and penetrating eyes, the yogi told him that he was not destined to have a son. But Din Dayal said that for a yogi nothing was impossible. He could do and undo anything if he so desired. With these words, he once again prayed the yogi to shower his benediction. The yogi then went into a trance and after some time sprinkled water from his pot at Motilal, went pale and told Motilal that his desire would be fulfilled. The next day the yogi passed away. Ten months later Jawaharlal was born on 14 November 1889. Nehru himself dismissed this as a myth.

The ancestors of Jawaharlal Nehru migrated to Delhi from Kashmir. Nehru himself discussed this event in his Autobiography (1930). Farrukh Siyar, the Mughal Emperor (1713–1718) during his visit to Kashmir came in contact with Raj Kaul, an eminent Sanskrit and Persian scholar and requested him to settle in Delhi. Kaul readily accepted this proposal and came to Delhi in 1716 and the Emperor gave him an estate situated by the side of a nahar (canal). The Persiah term for 'canal' is nahar. To please the Emperor, he changed his surname from 'Kaul' to 'Nehru'. And so Raj Kaul adopted the title "Nehru".

But history is silent over the visit of Siyar to Kashmir. 'Nehru' is not a title which a Kashmiri Pandit needs to acquire. It is one of the regular surnames of people belonging to a particular caste living around either of the two villages in the valley from where the Nehrus are believed to have migrated, Noar or Naru in Badgam district and the other near the small town of Tral. There is another story which says that the family came from the Rainwari area on the outskirts of Srinagar. However, it is certain that the Nehrus adorned the Mughal court and enjoyed Zamindari rights over a few villages.

EDUCATION

At the age of sixteen, he went to Harrow in 1905 for his education. Prior to that, he never attended any school as he was educated at home by private tutors and English governesses. He left Harrow in October 1907 since he could not adjust himself there. But he managed to spend two years there as study and extracurricular activities kept him busy. He had always a feeling that he did not belong to his classmates. He was mentally isolated from them.

While he was at Harrow, he never forgot India as he was constantly observing the events taking place in his own country. Information provided to him on various problems and issues made him restless. During this time, Lala Lajpat Rai and Ajit Singh were deported and Bengal was in turmoil and there was Swadeshi and boycott. All this agitated him deeply. He left Harrow and joined Cambridge, Trinity College. He spent there three years. In 1907 and 1908, Indian politics was passing through a crucial phase and he wanted to be a part of it but could not decide what to do.

JOINED THE BAR

He left Cambridge after taking a degree in 1910. He also completed Law. On 19 June 1912, he was admitted to the Bar by the Inner Temple and in the same year he returned to India finally after a stay of over seven years in England. In 1912, he joined as a lawyer in Allahabad High Court.

MARRIAGE

On 8 February 1916, he married to Kamala who was about seventeen years old at that time. She hailed from the Kaul family of Kashmir, who had settled in Delhi. She was the daughter of Pandit Jawaharam Lal Kaul, a businessman of Bazar Sitaram, and the owner of a flour-mill. Born on 1 August 1899, Kamala was only thirteen when the decision about her marriage with Jawaharlal was taken. Educated at home, she knew only Urdu and Hindi. Since Bazar Sitaram was hardly London, she was trained by the European governess so that she could adjust herself with the members of the anglicized Nehru family.

POLITICAL CAREER

As he was not happy with his profession, he evinced a keen interest in politics. As a result, he was irresistibly attracted by the charming personality of Gandhi who had a mesmerizing effect on him. He began to play an active role in politics and became a close follower of Gandhi whom he met in 1916 at the Congress session held at Lucknow. He had tremendous respect and regards for him. Gandhi also loved him very much. The relationship between them lasted for more than three decades. He became very active in politics in 1920 when he participated, for the first time, in a district conference of the Congress held in February and by July assumed the office of Vice-President of the Allahabad Unit. His active political career spanned over a long period of more than four decades. Apart from playing an active role along with Gandhi and others for attaining India's freedom, he also shaped and guided its destiny as its prime minister for nearly two decades.

He began his political career by joining the Home Rule League established by Bal Gangadhar Tilak and Mrs. Annie Besant. He participated in the Non-cooperation Movement and was imprisoned. An advocate of the theory of complete independence, he along with Srinivasa Iyengar and Subhash Chandra Bose sponsored it as the goal of the Congress. He opposed the ideal of Dominion Status which was, however, accepted by majority of top leaders of the Congress as well as by the All-Party Committee of which his father Motilal Nehru was the President. With the blessings of Gandhi, he became the President of the Indian National Congress at Lahore in 1929. The presidency of the Congress was the highest honour which the country could bestow. On the midnight of 31 December 1929, the historic independence resolution was passed. He was the President of the Congress again in 1936, 1937 and 1946. He formed the Interim Government in India and became the Prime Minister of Independent India on 15 August 1947. He occupied this office till his death on 27 May 1964.

SOCIALISM

During his student career in London (1907–1912) Nehru developed a liking for Fabian socialism as advocated by George Bernard Shah and Webbs. But he was not serious about it as he took it on humanitarian ground. His interest was purely academic. He was interested in it but not highly impressed by its ideas. He had also some problems with socialism as is evident from his incomplete review of Bertrand Russel's book *Roads to Freedom*, published in 1918. In that review (1919), he wrote that it never gave much hope to the people, one could draw a conclusion from the war that an all-powerful state was not in favour of individual liberty. It was the heaven for the bureaucrats, who in the West and in the East, did not tolerate any wind of criticism and were averse to any progress. Life under socialism would become miserable and be a joyless and soulless thing, subject to rules and orders framed by the all-powerful official Cortes. Nehru did not complete the review because by the middle of 1919 he could not decide as to what the course between these two options should be like.

He favoured agrarian socialism as it could contain and challenge feudalism that exploited poor peasants. During his visit to Europe (1926–1927) not only he appreciated and applauded the theory of social and economic emancipation but also condemned imperialism in the meetings of the League of Nations held in Brussels. When he visited Russia for a very short period, he was impressed by Lenin's Communism. In 1928, as the President of the Indian National Congress and of the Indian Trade Union Congress, he announced his commitment to socialism and republicanism. As the President of the Lahore session of the Congress, he declared in December 1929 his commitment to socialism and republicanism.

In 1930, he made it clear that he did not accept Robert Owen, Fourier and St. Simon's views on socialism. However, he praised it for being a panacea for all kinds of evils like exploitation and oppression of the poor, deprived. He appreciated the basic and fundamental aspects of socialism like state ownership and control of the basic means of production and distribution.

A supporter of political rights, he opposed liberal economy, rejected the Physiocratic School of Economics and denounced Ricardo and Smith's principle of non-interventionism. A socialist in his own way, his ideas on socialism were close to those of Wagner and Schmoller. He implemented them when he became Prime Minister by extending government help to industries and encouraging industries in private sector.

Socialism, to him, was a way of life, a philosophy of life, but not merely a formula for economic construction. As the President of the Indian National Congress in 1936, he was categorical when he considered socialism from the economic point of view. He was not a Utopian Socialist. Having faith in ethical socialism, he believed that it could emancipate the poor, the oppressed, liberate them from bondage and slavery, eliminate feudalism, autocracy and private property, remove and replace greedy acquisitiveness with cooperative service. To him, this could help in bringing a change in man's "instincts, habits and desires", and give birth to a new civilization. In 1929, at the Lahore Congress session, he reiterated his faith in socialism and republicanism.

Nehru was averse to fascism, as it made him sick at heart, and was repelled by its crudity, vulgarity and violence. In 1927, he returned from Europe as a matured and serious socialist with a strong faith in socialism and with a belief that it was not a vague humanitarianism creed but a strong scientific economic philosophy which could be translated into action that could bring in vast and revolutionary changes in India's political and social structure. In 1936, he declared in Lucknow that socialism, to him, was not merely an economic doctrine but also a vital creed which he held that with high esteem. He worked for Indian Independence because the nationalist in him could not tolerate foreign rule. He worked for it even more because, to him, it was the inevitable step to socio-economic change. He wanted that the Congress would become a socialist organization and join hands with other forces in the world who were working for the new civilization. But he realized that the majority in the Congress might not agree to go thus far. He stood for socialism and hoped that India would stand for socialism and that would go towards the constitution of a Socialist State and he believed that the whole world would have to go that way. What form of socialism it would cause is another matter.

On 9 November 1954, at a meeting of the National Development Council, Nehru said that he had in his mind a complete, perfect, definite and absolute socialistic picture of society. By it he meant largely that the means of production should be socially owned and controlled for the benefit of society as a whole. There was plenty of space for private enterprise provided the primary goal was achieved.

At the Avadi Session of the Congress (January 1955) which met under his leadership, the ideal of socialistic pattern of society was accepted. Such a society would promote social ownership or control of the principal means of production, acceleration of national production and the equitable distribution of wealth of the nation. The word 'socialism' had its origin in the West. In Europe, it was connected with class war, but the same was not the case in India. Of course, every society is prone to change and, as a matter of fact, it experiences difficulties when it undergoes change. The actions of the government, to him, should be governed by the ideal of a socialistic society and, by no means, socialism could be achieved by resolutions, even by decree, or by saying that there was socialism. This could be achieved by hard work, by increasing our production and through equitable distribution. His socialism was, in strict sense of the term, Indian socialism and influenced by the Indian conditions.

Though Nehru was convinced that socialism was a powerful and valuable panacea for the Indian problems like poverty and degradation, he was interestingly, not serious about it. He discussed it elaborately to make people conscious so that they could take a right decision when the issue came up. Socialism could not be thrust upon India. He hoped that it could be realized with the support of the vast majority and without any harm to anyone. Some compensation should be paid to propertied and vested benefits. However, there might be upheavals if socialist measures were opposed. He hoped that the rich in India were wise enough to avoid this.

His views on socialism were, as expected, strongly opposed by the rich and the industrialists, as those did not serve their interests. Twenty-one leading businessmen issued a manifesto condemning his 'destructive and subversive programme', as it would create disorders and check the progress of the government. Strongly criticizing them, he said that he supported socialism because it would remove the glaring economic inequality of the Indians, solve their unemployment problem and check their progressive deterioration. Deploring the existing conditions in India, he observed that it was these affluent persons who opposed his views. But, by no means, they could check these ideas as they were essential and fundamental. India would have to accept all these views in future.

Nehru was criticized for his views by the rich class and by the eminent leaders of the Congress like Vallabhbhai Patel, Rajendra Prasad, Rajagopalachari and Gandhi. But, they could not openly oppose his socialist views. Criticism and resentment could not deter him from presenting his views on socialism. To him, after Independence, socialism was bound to come. While addressing the Lahore Session of the Congress on 3 June 1936, he said that the whole economic structure would collapse. The capitalist system had to go along with it. This was how he visualized the happenings in future.

As Nehru had differences of opinion on socialism with other important leaders of the Congress, he believed that after Independence socialism could be adopted in India if the people wanted it. On 23 May 1956, he said in the Lok Sabha, since socialism would usher in a new era characterized by equality, absence of disparity every individual would lead a good life in the society. He favoured state trading in food grains and cooperative farming. But it was strongly criticized by the opposition and the press. In 1963, the All-India Congress Committee met in a session at Jaipur where Nehru urged for implementation of the socialist programmes. The Congress, which met at Bhubaneswar in 1963 under his leadership, adopted a resolution to make India Socialist State. Emphasizing individual dignity and democracy, the Congress also accepted the ideology of social justice and the social and economic revolution.

Nehru did not believe that production would go up with electrification and nationalization of industries. In the Lucknow session of the Congress, he forcefully argued that Khadi and rural industries would bring a radical change in economic scenario of the country.

Unlike the British Fabians, Nehru believed that socialism could be realized immediately. Application of science and technology would boost production. He stood for nationalization, increase of productive resources and full employment, development of new industries. He was against purchasing of old machines and factories, and the nationalization of old industries. He encouraged river valley projects as these would generate hydroelectric power and also favoured the heavy and basic industries by the government, and they should be done not at the cost of private sector. He thus favoured a mixed economy as well as a Welfare State which could be realized through cooperative farming.

DEMOCRACY

Nehru had a tremendous faith in Parliamentary democracy and it could be successful only when people cultivated virtues like discipline, sacrifice, etc. They should be self-resistant but not self-seekers.

Condemning violence and authoritarianism, criticizing war as it destroyed all the values for which democracy stood, he said that democracy was, in fact, a casualty of war in the world. As a result, it became ineffective and did not function properly any more as was evident from the tragic consequences of the last two World Wars and something infinitely worse was likely to happen if there was another war.

Criticizing Fascism, Nazism and Regimentation, he always dreamt that India should develop fast in the field of industry and carve out for itself a place in the industrial map of the world. India must advance in the field of science and technology so that it could be equal to any of the advanced countries of the world. His long association with nationalists and freedom fighters as well as his deep involvement in freedom struggle strengthened his love for civil liberties of which he was a great champion. A passionate and ardent supporter of freedom, he said that opposition or contrary opinion should not be suppressed or crushed. To do so would be like cracking the skull of an opponent because his actions were disapproved.

A charismatic leader, a towering personality, Nehru as a leader had a mass-base and was extremely popular with his people. He was their undisputed leader. His tremendous popularity and dynamic personality was an asset to Indian democracy. He asked his people to maintain perfect discipline and brotherliness. This was certainly aimed at strengthening "the sense of community" which, to McIver, was the foundation of the democratic mechanism.

An exponent of individual liberty and equality, Nehru's ideas were deeply rooted in western liberalism. Democracy as was in practice in the West had a strong bearing upon his political beliefs and principles. Democratic ideas were germinated in the eighteenth century in France. The American and French Revolutions made them very popular. To millions who were oppressed and exploited, they brought a thrill and a message of good will, progress and prosperity.

Absolute equality, to Nehru, was a misnomer. Certainly, there would be inequality in different spheres of human activities. But attempts should be made to establish a society where a reasonable equality and tolerable inequality existed. Admitting the existence of physical, intellectual, social and economic inequality, he said that given an opportunity and basic training, everyone could improve his conditions and there would be far less inequality than what it was before. Democracy admitted that men were as a matter of fact unequal, they should be treated as having an equal social and political value. They elected their representatives to the assembly or the parliament by casting their votes. Their votes were the symbol of political power and it was assumed that if everyone had a vote, each such person would have an equal share in political power.

Shocked at the decadence, deterioration and degeneration of democracy over the years, Nehru felt that neither the people nor the leaders behaved properly. The people found it difficult to choose the right persons to represent them and promote their interests. To him, democracy was not a gift to be conferred but a virtue to be practised, a habit to be acquired. Mere pious declarations would not enable the people in realizing liberty and equality. A proper climate was to be created so that these ideals were put into practice, failing which democracy would degenerate into mobocracy and oligarchy.

Nehru believed that democracy was the best form of government as this helped an individual to realize his best self. Like J.S. Mill, he always opposed the suppression of minority by the majority through its voting strength.

SECULARISM

Secular in thought, deed and action, and influenced by Ferdinand T. Brooks, his tutor, Annie Besant and others, he laid emphasis on secularism. He never accepted anything blindly. Free from religious dogmas, convictions and prejudices, he laid stress on harmony among the people belonging to different languages, religions and races. He felt that it was secularism that could bring unity and integrity to the Indian society which was torn asunder by casteism, linguism, regionalism, chauvinism and communalism. A humanist and pragmatist, he knew that divisive and subversive forces would threaten the very existence of the Indian community. He asked the people not to mix up religion with politics. To save them from becoming a prey to communal and fundamental forces, he had to strive hard in inculcating the spirit of secularism in their minds.

As he was educated in Britain, he found himself more comfortable in the company of Bertrand Russel than the Scriptures. He felt very uneasy when Gandhi made use of religion in the Khilafat Movement. He wrote in his Autobiography that he was not happy and felt deeply hurt when he saw politics being influenced by religion — whether it was Hinduism or Islam. He did not appreciate what the Moulvies, Maulanas and Swamis, and the like said in their public addresses as they were biased, prejudiced, narrow and mean. He even did not appreciate Gandhi's frequent reference to Ram Raj which would be established in India in future. He was also averse to the idea of the theocratic State and of the view that such kind of concept should not have any place in the modern world.

He firmly believed that secularism should be the basis of Indian polity. The Karachi Session of the Congress held in 1931 gave the official expression for the first time to his concept of secularism. At his behest, a resolution on "Fundamental Rights and Duties" was passed by the Congress. It explicitly stated that the state should observe neutrality in regard to all religions.

To him, secularism did not mean hatred for any religion. Nor it ever tried to undermine the importance of religion in one's personal or private life. On the contrary, it gave equal importance to all religions and stood for perfect harmony among all the religious sects. Religion had no place in politics, nor had it any role to influence the latter. Depressed by the wave of Hindu–Muslim riots, he was bitter against the role of religion in the country's politics. Commenting on religion and politics, he observed that the less we talked of and worried about the 'next world', the more good we are likely to do to our fellow countrymen and country.

The essential spirit of secularism was tolerance of all religions, all ideologies and all forms of government.

FOREIGN POLICY

Foreign policy, to Nehru, was to be shaped and influenced by the principle of enlightened self-interest. He reiterated it openly on several occasions. On 4 December 1947, he said it in the Constituent Assembly that whatever foreign policy the Assembly might adopt, it should seek to protect and promote the interests of the country and there should be no compromise on it. It might talk about peace and freedom and earnestly mean what it said. But in the ultimate analysis a government functioned for the good of the country it governed and no government could dare to ignore the interests of that country. Therefore, whether a country adopted imperialism or socialism, or communism, its Foreign Minister thought primarily of the interest of that country.

Nehru's foreign policy was, thus, basically guided and governed by the needs and interests of the country and influenced by its history and background. The doctrine of *Panchshila* might be considered as old as the Buddha whose gospel of peace was enshrined in the rock edicts of Asoka and echoed more than two thousand years later in the teachings of Gandhi.

A pertinent question may be raised here. Is national interest, as advocated by Nehru, to be the basis of foreign policy, opposed to the interests of other nations? No doubt, the policy which respects the interests of other nations has been considered to be a progressive one. Nehru's views on the reconciliation of national interest with the interests of other nations reflect the progressive view which has been appreciated by modern thinkers. Some give emphasis on the interests of their own country, without taking into account the consequences of their action. While others think that in the long-run policy, the interest of another country is as important to them as that of their own country. Self-interest may also motivate a country to extend cooperation to other nations, cultivate goodwill with them. Nehru warned that adoption of a narrow and selfish national policy might excite and provoke, satisfy and appease the people for the moment. Such a policy would be just like a communal cry exciting or satisfying their passions. But it would be bad for the nation and also for the whole international community because the ultimate good was ignored. Therefore, India's interest, to Nehru, should be looked in the context of world cooperation and world peace, and it should be so oriented to promote and preserve world peace.

Nehru's foreign policy was, thus, governed by India's long-term interests as well as by those of the international community. But in case there arose a conflict between India's self-interest and interests of other nations, he said that he would support the interests of his own country and not bother for the consequences.

Protection of national interest through rightful means was the most important goal of Nehru's foreign policy and the latter is to be viewed from the perspective of world cooperation. This goal was reflected in his first broadcast speech to the nation on 7 September 1946, five days after the Interim Government assumed office on 2 September. He said that India should participate in international conferences as a free nation with its own policy and not merely as a satellite of another nation. It should interact with other nations and extend its support and cooperation to them to promote world peace and freedom. If they are threatened in any part of the world, it will have adverse impact on other parts of the globe, causing conflict and war. India's interest in the liberation and development of colonial and dependent countries and peoples, and in recognizing in theory and practice the principle of equal opportunities for all races were the fundamental principles of Nehru's foreign policy. He repudiated the Nazi doctrine of racialism, wheresoever and in whatever form it might be practised.

Nehru stood for territorial integrity of India and freedom of policy. In his inaugural address to the Asian Relations Conference held on 23 March 1947, he observed that India (and other countries of Asia and Africa) had been used as pawns by other nations in their international game. The developed countries should encourage the newly independent nations to stand on their own feet to formulate their own policies and play their role in the maintenance of peace. His foreign policy, as said earlier, aimed at promoting international peace. As war brought untold miseries, pains and sufferings to the mankind, it would be suicidal on the part of the people to have another World War. Apprehending its worst and painful consequences, he made it a mission to reduce international tensions, have nuclear tests suspended, and achieve complete disarmament. He always wanted that India's security should not be threatened and it must achieve its economic progress and prosperity. And this could be possible only when there was no war.

Nehru's foreign policy aimed at achieving freedom for dependent people, eliminating racial discrimination, and protecting the interests of the people of Indian origin aborad.

Most of the countries in the world have condemned, at least in theory, the policy of racial inequality and accepted racial equality as a principle, though there was a wide gap between theory and practice. The architect of foreign policy, he strongly criticized racial discrimination, a cause of potential world conflict. Addressing the Indian Council of World Affairs on 22 March 1949, he observed that the future of mankind would be grim if racial discrimination was allowed to continue as it was an affront to the mankind, to their dignity and they would not tolerate it. It would not be confined to particular areas in South Africa or elsewhere; it would affect peoples in vast continents. He, therefore, strongly denounced the apartheid policy as practised in South Africa.

A large number of people of Indian origin have been living abroad as citizens of the countries in which they have settled. They have settled in more than fifty-eight countries across all the continents. Their forefathers migrated from India in search of jobs. Poverty, unemployment and backwardness in India might have forced them to leave the country and settle in foreign lands for their bright future. But very often they faced problems either from the natives or from the governments of respective states. Therefore, they appealed the Government of India to help them.

In 1957, Members of the Lok Sabha brought into notice of the government the disabilities suffered by the people of Indian origin in foreign countries. They not only elicited more information from the government on the issue but also wanted to know what steps it had taken to redress them. Responding to them, Nehru said that the Government of India had left it to the Indians abroad whether they would continue to remainas Indian nationals or adopt the nationality of the country they had settled in. If they chose the latter, they must enjoy all the rights enjoyed by the citizens of that country. India would in no way be concerned about their socio-economic and political rights, but she would continue to have her emotional bondage with them. However, if they remained Indian nationals, then all that they would be getting was favoured alien treatment. They became aliens and they should get as good a treatment as any other alien. Since aliens had no right to vote, they too could not vote. But they should be allowed to enjoy all other civic privileges.

Indian settlers should closely interact with the people of the country they had adopted and should not exploit them. Instead, they should be friendly to the people of those countries, cooperate with them and help them, while maintaining their own dignity and self-respect. That was not only a policy which Nehru considered right but the only practical policy, because if Indians did not do that abroad, they would have to pay a heavy price, they might be crushed by the local population and the foreign elements from Europe and elsewhere.

Non-alignment, which constitutes the core of foreign policy, aims at not entering into military alliances with any country, and in particular with any country either of the Western or of the Communist bloc. Another feature of non-alignment is "acting according to our best judgement". It is an independent approach to foreign policy and not to be influenced by any particular line of action because of the membership of any power bloc. It seeks to maintain friendly relations with all countries, whether they are members of the military blocs or not. It is not a negative policy, but a positive one, a definite one, a dynamic one. It does not mean neutrality which implies a refusal to express positive views and take positive actions on specific issues that divide the blocs. But on no important issue has India ever hardly refrained from expressing a definite point of view or helping to implement it. India's attitudes, policies and actions on various international issues, particularly relating to war and peace, hardly reflect neutrality.

The basis of formulation or formation of the policy of non-alignment was the circumstances of India, her past thinking, her mental outlook, conditioning of her mind during her struggle for freedom, and the present circumstances. Highlighting the importance of the policy, he said that there was no other policy for this country to adopt with the slightest advantage.

Would non-alignment ensure or guarantee territorial integrity? Would it protect the country from external invasion or aggression? Nehru did not have any direct answer to these questions. He stated if India did not involve in the affairs of the power blocs, her involvement in wars would be much less. But, at the same time, he said that it was difficult to remain neutral in world wars. However, India could join, without being tied to any power bloc, the side if it protected her interest.

PLANNING

Nehru visited Soviet Russia in 1927, read Karl Marx and was impressed by the progress of the Soviet Five-Year Plans. In 1938, he persuaded the Congress, which came to power in all but three of India's provinces — Bengal, Punjab and Sind — to set up a Planning Committee which adopted a Ten-Year Plan to promote socio-economic welfare of the people.

Nehru as the Prime Minister and the architect of modern India, inaugurated the Five-Year Plans as it would help in opening a new chapter, realizing some of the fundamentals of the socialist structure could be limiting the acquisitive factor in society and removing the barriers of growth. All this would be beneficial to the common man. His standard of living would go up and he would lead a good and peaceful life.

NATIONALISM

Nehru, a great nationalist, was certainly not an exponent of theory of nationalism. Even though there were cultural diversities in India, there existed fundamental unity among its people. Inspired by the concept of cultural pluralism and synthesis, and influenced by Rabindra Nath Tagore's "synthetic universalism", he rejected the "assimilative–integral religious approach" to nationalism as advocated by Dayananda, Vivekananda, Bipin Chandra Pal and Aurobindo. Recognizing the emotional aspects of nationalism and considering it a noble phase of self-magnification, he observed that it was essentially a group memory of past achievements, traditions and experiences, and "it was the stronger today than it had ever been". Whenever a crisis had arisen, it had emerged again and dominated the scene, and people sought and found comfort and strength in their old traditions.

Nehru's concept of nationalism was influenced by the racial arrogance of the British rulers, grim poverty and ruthless exploitation of the Indians and the administrative and political decisions of the British Government. He was neither a Gandhian, nor a Marxist, nor an orthodox. But in his heart of hearts, he was a Gandhian. Committed to the society and its people, he was a staunch nationalist as is evident from the fact that he declined politely but firmly, unlike other leaders, the British offer to become the education minister in the provincial government of Uttar Pradesh. Soon after his release from the prison, Sir Grimwood Mears, the then Chief Justice of the Allahabad High Court, offered him the job. The British Government could successfully entice earlier other leaders like S.N. Banarjee who left the Congress to become ministers. Banarjee was a minister in Bengal (1921–1923). These leaders were not only selfish but also anti-nationalists.

AN ESTIMATE

Nehru's contributions to freedom struggle in India, his fight against the British imperialism, his services as the architect of modern India were monumental, and unparallel. Loved and admired by his own people as well as the peoples of other countries he shaped the history of his own time. He was more than a person; he was a nation in himself. A lover of democracy, an advocate of human rights and freedoms, he mastered history, wrote history and made history.

A humanist believing in scientific humanism, he was a champion of the liberation fighting for the cause of colonial world, a socialist seeking to promote the socio-economic welfare of the people on the basis of socialistic pattern of society, a democrat strengthening the foundations of Indian Parliamentary democracy and emancipating the women legally and socially, a staunch advocate of nationalism, and a sworn enemy of communalism. Thorough in international issues, he analysed them in proper perspective and sensitive to international developments, he wanted that India should give up the policy of isolation.

A man of indomitable courage and invincible spirit to fight against injustice, exploitation and oppression; of uncompromising loyalty to the cause of the nation, he used to be very much emotional and sentimental and could not suppress the feelings. One could read his mind, feel his feelings. He wept like a child when he was in the company of Gandhi (as he did when accusing the Mahatma, following the Irwin Pact, of betraying the nation). He used to lose his temper in public life if he felt that justice was denied to the people or when there was any bias and prejudice against any one.

Nehru, to Rabindra Nath Tagore, was a person "greater than his deeds and truer than his surroundings". So indispensable was he for India that everyone had one and the same question in mind: After Nehru, who? Who would guide the destiny of India after him?

POINTS TO REMEMBER

- Motilal Nehru and his friends met a yogi in 1889 in Rishikesh. Jogi's benediction on Nehru and ten months after the incident, Pandit Jawaharlal Nehru was born on 14 November 1889. The latter dismissed this incident as a myth. Raj Kaul, Jawaharlal's grandfather, on the request of the Emperor left Kashmir and settled in Delhi. He changed his surname from 'Kaul' to 'Nehru' to satisfy the Emperor. This theory is, however, subject to controversy.
- Education: no formal education until 1905 when he joined Harrow. Left it in 1907. Could not identify himself with his classmates. He felt restless with the developments taking place in India.
- Joined the Bar in 1912 in Allahabad High Court.
- Marriage in 1916, with Kamala.
- Political career: Met Gandhi in 1916, was influenced by him, his strong powerful and formidable personality. Vice-President of the Allahabad unit of the Congress. His role in politics spanned four decades. Joined the Home Rule League. Opposed 'Dominion Status'. In 1929, he became the President of the Indian National Congress in 1929.

- He was the President of the Congress in 1929, 1936, 1937 and 1946. Formed the Interim Government in India and became the first Prime Minister of India on 15 August 1947.
- His views on agrarian socialism; he challenged imperialism, feudalism, supported social and economic emancipation; impressed by Lenin's communism, his commitment to republicanism, opposed the views of Robert Owen, Fourier, and St. Simon, supported the fundamentals of socialism like state ownership and control of the basic means of production. He opposed fascism, liberal economy, supported socialism.
- He was in favour of a socialist state.
- His socialism was opposed by the rich class, the industrialists and leaders of the Congress. India would have to adopt socialism after independence.
- Democracy: its success depends upon peoples' virtues.
- He criticized Nazism, Fascism and Regimentation. His emphasis on industrialization of the country. A lover of civil liberties. Opposition not to be suppressed, silenced and undermined. An exponent of rights, justice and equality.
- Absolute equality — a misnomer. In a society, there should be reasonable equality and tolerable inequality. Indiscipline in the Indian society. Democracy is in danger. Difficult to choose right persons to represent the people.
- Democracy: the best form of government.
- Seculerism: he was secular. Harmony among different castes, classes and communities. A humanist, a pragmatist.
- Politics not to be influenced by religion. Unhappy with Gandhi's concept of Ram Raj. Not to hate any religion.
- Foreign policy: to be guided by the enlightened self-interest of the country. Historical background, economic interests, cultural compulsions — all these also shape the foreign policy. Gave the Doctrine of *Panchshila.*
- Interest of the nation is to be protected and at the same time it should not ignore the interest of other nations.
- Foreign policy: to promote peace and freedom. There should not be war.
- He condemned the apartheid policy as practised in South Africa.
- Indians settled in foreign countries should be friendly towards the people of those countries.
- Non-alignment: not to enter into military alliances with any country. Issue-based decisions. Independent approach to foreign policy. It is not a negative policy, does not mean neutrality. There was no better or effective alternative to non-alignment.

- Planning: Nehru's visit to Soviet Russia in 1927, impressed by the Five-Year Plans adopted there. His persuasion to Congress governments in 1938 to set Planning Committees in their respective states, inaugurated the era of planning.
- Nationalism: a staunch nationalist, influenced by the concept of cultural pluralism and synthesis, by Tagore's "Synthetic universalism", rejected assimilative–integrative religious approach to nationalism, which was a composite of past achievements, traditions and experiences.
- He rejected British Government's offering of lucrative posts. But some other leaders including S.N. Banarjee gladly accepted them.

12
Subhash Chandra Bose (1897–1945)

INTRODUCTION

A society while encountering a great crisis or passing through an unprecedented upheaval — be it socio-economic or political, or cultural — may collapse because of its disastrous consequences or passes through one of its worst phases of existence characterized by conflict, disturbance, indiscipline, instability, etc. In other words, the situation becomes unbearable and is beyond one's control. The unprecedented turmoil which the society experiences may pose a serious threat to its existence. Helpless, it becomes a silent spectator to what has been taking place around it. Deeply distressed, it earnestly seeks guidance, solace, encouragement, inspiration. At such a juncture are born a few brilliant, self-less and dedicated souls to give a new direction, a new vision to the society for its social, economic and political liberties and emancipation. And certainly and, by all means, Subhash Chandra Bose is one of them. The Indian society looks at him with awe and reverence and feels very much proud of him.

An ardent patriot, a new light of hope for the motherland, a brave, courageous, fearless and indomitable fighter, a powerful and formidable personality, a mystic par excellence, a worthy son of the soil, a legendary figure, he was an ideal hero of the Indian struggle for independence.

EARLY LIFE

Born to Janakinath Bose and Prabhabati Bose on 23 January 1897 at Cuttack, he got his early education in the Protestant European School, managed by the Baptist Mission, from 1902 to 1906 and the Ravenshaw Collegiate School from 1908 to 1913. He passed the matriculation examination in March 1913 and was placed second in the whole University. For higher education, he was admitted into the Presidency College and the Scottish Church College, Calcutta and the Fitzwilliam College, Cambridge. He completed his education in 1916.

During his school days, he was influenced by his Headmaster Basu Beni Madhab Das and also by saints like Swami Vivekananda, Ramakrishna Paramhamsa and Aurobindo. Das shaped his aesthetic and moral feelings. It was Vivekananda and other saints who gave him what he strongly desired. The teachings of Vivekananda appealed his tender mind very much. He learnt from him that one's aim in life should be to attain salvation by rendering selfless service to the mankind. From Paramhamsa, he learnt that both lust and gold be renounced. One attains divinity by renouncing these two things.

DESIRE TO BECOME A SAINT

His close contact and interaction with the saints encouraged and inspired him to choose a path that would take him to his final destination, i.e. salvation, that would free him from all sorts of bondages, that would liberate him from bindings and restraints. As expected, unhappy and distressed, his parents tried their best to restrain him from adopting the spiritual path. The more they did so, the more rebellious he became. Neither his mother's tears nor his father's resentments and admonitions could deter him from pursuing his goal as they had least impact on him. Even though he was unhappy to go against his parents, he was determined to achieve his goal. As a result, he neglected his studies because it would not, he felt, serve his purpose in his life. He pursued with all his sincerity and seriousness his spiritual goal. He was happy and delighted to read the literature on Yoga, Pranayama, Meditation, Concentration, etc. and he practised what he read.

IN PRESIDENCY COLLEGE

In Presidency College, Calcutta, some students misbehaved a Professor. Since he silently watched the incident without any protest, he had to pay a heavy price. The principle, 'Silence is golden', did not work here. He was punished when he was expelled from the college and rusticated from the university. This incident shaped his future political career, gave him a moral strength to confront any crisis with courage, confidence and composure.

SOCIAL SERVICE

Following his expulsion, he devoted his time to serve the society with a missionary zeal. In those days epidemics like cholera and smallpox occurred frequently in Orissa and took a heavy toll of human lives. Victims were left to their fate as doctors were not easily available to treat them. He dedicated himself to their cause, served them with love and affection. He greatly enjoyed this service. With the help of his friends he also disposed off the unclaimed dead bodies by burying or cremating them. This made him happy and gave him tremendous mental peace and satisfaction.

I.C.S. EXAMINATION

On 15 September 1919, he left for England at the behest of his parents to prepare for the Indian Civil Service (I.C.S.) Examination, even though he had a strong disliking for it. During his journey, he had a feeling of the British officials' ill-treatment of the Indians. They were very rough and tough towards them. He reached London on 25 October 1919 and settled down in the first week of November to work at Cambridge. In 1920, he passed the examination and was placed in the fourth position. But this could not make him happy as he could no more serve his people. As a civil servant, he had to simply carry out the orders of the government. He was, therefore, in a dilemma whether to join the I.C.S. or not. It took long seven months to make up his mind. No doubt, the civil service could give him mental comforts, but not mental peace and happiness. It would also deprive him from rendering any service to his country. In other words, the new service would provide him a livelihood but it would not be his life. He would not achieve his cherished goal, i.e. freedom and independence of India. The very idea of working with or under an alien bureaucracy gave him severe pain. The path of Aurobindo was, to him, more noble, more inspiring, more lofty, more unselfish, though more thorny than the path of Ramesh Dutt. He felt that if C.R. Das at a young age could renounce everything and face the uncertainties of life, he could also follow him and might surpass him since he had little worldly cares to trouble him.

HIS LETTER TO C.R. DAS AND S.C. BOSE

Meanwhile, on 23 February 1921 he addressed a letter to C.R. Das requesting him to enrol him as a worker in his gigantic programme of national service. He preferred to work as a Subeditor for the paper "Swaraj" to be set up by Das, besides teaching the junior classes of National College. In another letter to Sarat Chandra Bose, he wrote that he could serve his people and country better not as a bureaucrat but as one of them. Therefore, going against the wishes of his parents and ignoring the advice of many of his friends and well-wishers, he resigned from the I.C.S. on 22 April 1921 after "mature deliberation". He returned back to India on 16 July 1921.

GANDHI AND BOSE

He met Gandhi on 16 July 1921 in Bombay. Least impressed and convinced by his policies and programmes, he did not believe that India could secure independence through non-violence. A pragmatist, a realist and a reactionary, he believed the principle "now" or "never". Unlike Gandhi, he separated means from ends and never thought that bad means would give rise to bad ends. Both were at poles apart because of their approaches to the national struggle. One believed the principle of persuasion and non-violence, while the other had tremendous faith in coërcion and violence as means to achieve the end. Bose never accepted Gandhi as his leader. Desabandhu Chitranjan Das was his inspiration, his ideal. Das' personality, ideals and policies had a tremendous impact on him and he wanted to overthrow the British regime through violence and, if necessary, with foreign aid. To him, Gandhi was an outdated leader with least capacity to deliver the goods.

Bose was unhappy when Gandhi abruptly called off any movement or gave up any programme. For example, Gandhi abruptly called off the Non-cooperation Movement following the Chouri Choura incident on 4 February 1922, which took a death toll of 21 policemen. Gandhi's decision, to him, was an "order of retreat". Strongly criticizing Gandhi's policies, considering him to be "an old and useless piece of furniture", he did not appreciate his dictatorial tendency in concluding the pact with Irwin in March 1931, attending the Round Table Conference (1931) as the sole representative, entering into the Poona Pact in September 1932 and such other acts.

Bose, along with Vallabhbhai Patel, wanted to replace Gandhi as the leader of the Congress. It was because of his misunderstanding with Gandhi, the latter did not support him when he contested for the second time to the office of the President of the Congress. Gandhi preferred Pattabhi Sitaramayya to him. Notwithstanding Gandhi's opposition, Bose was elected to the office as he secured 1,580 votes as against 1,375 votes secured by Pattabhi. Since Gandhi was not happy with his election, he asked him to resign, as he was not fit to hold the office and his plan of action was not acceptable to the party. Bose was forced to resign at the All India Congress Committee meeting held in Calcutta on 29 April 1939. He was also expelled from the party after three months.

FREEDOM

Bose was not satisfied with mere political freedom. He felt that India should win her independence at the earliest. But, at the same time, socio-economic conflict between the landlord and peasant, capitalist and labourer, rich and poor, should be brought to an end. Both the political and social struggle would have to be undertaken simultaneously for the liberation of the country and emancipation of her people.

Like Aurobindo, Bose argued that India should be free from the British regime. He gave a new dimension to the freedom struggle by denouncing Gandhi's argument that independence could be won through non-violence. Averse to the principles of compromise, parliamentarianism and constitutionalism, he attacked Gandhi's policies and methods. Like Aurobindo, he also stressed the importance of force and violence as means to achieve independence. He launched an active propaganda against the British and asked the people to start a mass movement on a wider scale to achieve their goal.

Netaji always believed that freedom and its attainment was an absolute truth. Priority must be given to national freedom followed by democracy and socialism. Freedom was too broad a concept carrying different meanings. But, to Netaji, the meaning of freedom was the most comprehensive as it meant all-round freedom, i.e. freedom for the individual as well as for the society, for the rich as well as for the poor, for all individuals, and for all classes. It implied not only political freedom but also equal or equitable distribution of wealth, abolition of caste and social inequalities, and removal of communalism and intolerance. To some, these goals were a distant dream to be realized. But these were the fundamental aspects which the Indian society must strive for so that India would be free in true sense of the term.

To him, it was not an easy task to secure freedom without sacrifice, without blood, without iron will and strong determination, without dedication and commitment. Once achieved and secured, it would bring glory, progress and prosperity, peace and happiness. Dissatisfied with the Congress programme, he argued that freedom could be achieved with the abolition of the caste system, of social and religious superstitions of all kinds, boycott of British goods, organization of women's associations; propagation of the new programme; organization of peasants and workers as a socialistic programme and of the youth so that they could form volunteer corps to work for the country with perfect discipline.

In his Presidential speech at the All-India Anti-Compromise Conference held in Ramgarh (Bihar), Bose said that the days of imperialism were over and the era of freedom, democracy and socialism had begun. An advocate of national as well as world freedom, it made it his goal to fight against imperialism across the world. India should be made free so that humanity might be saved.

A SOCIALIST

Even though he was not an orthodox Marxist, he said, as President of the Congress session held at Haripura in February 1938 that India's crucial problems like poverty, illiteracy, disease and scientific production and distribution could be effectively solved through socialistic means or measures. National reconstruction or nation-building could be possible only when the social evils like poverty and illiteracy were removed. He argued that feudalism should be abolished, agricultural loans written off, credit made available to poor in rural areas with low interest, cooperation movement extended and agriculture modernized by applying scientific techniques, industrialization should take place on a wider scale under the control of the state and state-ownership of industries be encouraged. The State on the advice of a Planning Commission would have to adopt a comprehensive scheme so that sectors like agriculture and industry should adopt socialistic measures to increase production and appropriation. A protector of the interests of the working classes, he pointed out that socialism might not be the immediate problem for the Indian National Congress, but socialist propaganda was necessary to prepare the country for socialism after securing independence.

A born socialist, his socialism, neither bookish nor borrowed, an outcome of his own environment in which he was born and brought up, his own experience and ethics, was mostly shaped by his spiritual bent of mind, Indian culture and heritage, his family environment, the teachings of Ramakrishna Pararnahamsa and Sri Vivekananda. Compared to other Socialists like Nehru, Gandhi, Jaya Prakash Narayan, Vinoba Bhave, Ram Manonar Lohia, his socialism was moulded purely by Indian environment but not by western thinking.

To him, socialism included and covered justice, equality, freedom, discipline and love. It was not only an economic aspect but also had a political, a social, and above all, a moral dimension. It included all the values which he cherished, and liked to see it established in India.

It was socialism which, to him, could not only attract the attention of the public, but also involve them in large number to make it more and more mass-based. He agreed with Gandhi that leaders should spread the message of freedom among the masses to make them politically conscious so that it would become easier to win freedom. The leaders of different countries, which were once the Colonies, realized the significance of mass participation in launching a successful revolution for ousting the foreigners or the oppressive home-government. But the people required an inspiring and impressive ideology, and an ideal and encouraging leadership. As long as the people remained poor and were exploited and deprived of social justice by their own people, they would have least interest to play any role in the freedom struggle. Steps should, therefore, be taken to bring them into arena of politics by creating a conducive atmosphere.

As the only extremist leader of all-India stature, he firmly believed that socialism, besides being an economic ideology, was also a humanitarian and egalitarian principle. Neither a doctrinaire socialist nor an adherent to any particular school of socialism, he discarded and denounced Gandhism for its extreme spiritualism and did not appreciate Marxism for its emphasis upon materialistic interpretation of life. Gandhi's socialism was Utopian. He looked at it from the perspective of equality. He wrote in the *Harijan*:

> Socialism is a beautiful word...as far as I am aware, in socialism, all the members of society are equal, none low, none high. In the individual body, the head is not high because it is the top of the body nor are the soles of the feet low because they touch the earth. Even as organs of the individual body are equal, so are members of society. This is socialism.

Bose believed that the state and the political parties should play a key role in achieving socialism. But Gandhi rejected this view. To him, Sarvodaya could achieve the basic goals of socialism without the involvement of state as the regulator of the economic and political life of the community. Nehru's socialism was purely western. Criticizing it he wrote to him:

> You call yourself a socialist, sometimes a full-blooded socialist. How a socialist can be an individualist as you regard yourself, beats me. The one is the antithesis of the other. How socialism can ever come into existence through individualism of your type is also an enigma to me.

Bose wanted that production and productivity should go up so that people's standard of living would be high. Steps, therefore, should be taken to modernize industry, agriculture, defence, transport, communication, etc. This would also increase national wealth. As a guild socialist, he favoured the formation of guilds of labour, youths and students. In 1931, he advocated for the foundation of the "Socialist Republic" in India. Though socialism was an universal system, India should adopt a type of socialism something new and original and be suitable to its own conditions. Since the whole world had been experimenting with socialism, she would be a part of such experiment as it would give her a new image, a confidence to achieve her goals; make her progressive and prosperous. He realized that economic freedom would be possible only with political freedom. Food, clothing, education, etc. could be provided to millions only when India would be free and independent.

An advocate of both social and political democracy, he wanted that free India would not be a land of capitalists, landlords and castes. The Samyavadi Sangh would ensure all-round development of the Indians and bring them social, economic and political freedom.

NATIONALISM

Nationalism, a sixteenth century concept, the soul force of a state, is the pride of every nation. Bose, an inspiring and unifying symbol of Indian nationalism, said that in this world everything was subject to decay and destruction, but not ideas and ideals, dreams and thoughts, as they were transmitted from generation to generation. Netaji is no more with us but his beliefs, convictions still continue to influence and inspire us, illuminate and enlighten our path.

His militant nationalism and Gandhi's passive resistance were opposed to one another, both in form and spirit. It was mostly responsible for the split in the Congress in 1939, for the conflict between Bose and Gandhi and even for the former's sensational escape from India. Bose was never convinced that India could be liberated by adopting non-violent means; coercion, but not persuasion, would help in achieving the goal. He honestly felt that the British Government would never surrender or yield to persuasion or moral pressure, or non-violent resistance. It was the human blood that was required to be shed for liberation of India. People of India would be happy if they got independence through non-violence. But India could be free only by resisting the British tyranny with armed might. Freedom gained through it would be the real one. He did not beg for it. He wanted to bargain for it, with its price — blood. It must be got by force. He said to the army: "Give me your blood, I give you freedom". Blood was the price of liberty, and that was the foundation for national unity.

A staunch nationalist, an exponent of Hinduism, he was neither communal nor parochial. To him, the problem of unity was largely a psychological problem. People must be educated and trained to feel that they were a nation. Other factors like language, dress, food, etc. might help unity but could not create it. He always advocated for unity in ideas and action. Unity was a revolutionary movement, a means but not an end in itself, a source of infinite strength whereas superficial unity became a source of weakness. Unity would become an evil, the moment it hampered progress.

Opposed to communal electorate, communal representation and communal reservation, he argued that barriers of wealth, class and caste must be abolished; women must be treated at par with men and there must not be any distinction between the Hindus and the Muslims at election times. He believed that communal representation in the legislatures was a device of divide and rule to perpetuate the British regime in India. So, much emphasis he laid on unity that Humayun Kabir once remarked that Netaji's greatest contribution was to forge national unity in spite of diversities in language, religion, customs and traditions.

More a nationalist than a socialist, believing that the Indian political movement was primarily and essentially a nationalist movement, he rejected any political or economic ideology that did not agree with it as unsuitable and impracticable. Thus nationalism and socialism were practically inseparable.

ROLE IN INDIAN NATIONAL MOVEMENT

"Swaraj is my birthright", said Bal Gangadhar Tilak. Following this, Subhash advocated in 1928 for complete freedom. More progressive than Nehru and Gandhi, he wanted to build up a strong national movement in 1928 itself through an organization like the Independence of India League. He, therefore, requested the people to join the movement in a large scale. True to his spirit and temperament, he was always ahead of the Gandhian thought. A pragmatist, an activist and an extremist — all rolled into one — he argued for a parallel government in the country immediately and for organizing workers, peasants and the youth. Declaring himself an extremist, his demand was: "all or nothing."

On 23 January 1930, he was sentenced to a year's rigorous imprisonment and sent to jail in a case filed against him on 11 August 1929. He was arrested on a charge of sedition for leading a procession on the All Bengal Political Sufferers' Day. He was released from jail on 29 September 1930. In January 1931, he was again arrested and imprisoned, then Mayor of Calcutta, for seven days for visiting a disturbed area in Malda district of Bengal. While leading a procession in Calcutta as the Mayor, he was arrested and sentenced to six months' rigorous imprisonment. He was, however, released on 8 March 1931 under the general amnesty. Dissatisfied with the Gandhi–Irwin Pact (1931) and describing it as a curse, he conveyed his displeasure to Gandhi. He wanted that the Civil Disobedience Movement should be continued with great vigour till the country was made free and declared independent. He was not happy with Gandhi as the latter participated in the Second Round Table Conference as the sole representative of the Congress.

Bose criticized Gandhi for suspending the Civil Disobedience Movement in May 1933 as it exposed the weakness of the principle of non-violence adopted by the Congress and its leader, Gandhi. Hence, his insistence on radical reorganization of the Congress on a new principle and with a new method, and also on change of leadership. Mahatma Gandhi would not go for a programme and a method inconsistent with those principles which he so seriously practised and earnestly cherished. Bose advocated for a total transformation of the Congress. Failing that, a new party would have to be formed within the Congress, composed of all radical elements. Non-cooperation could not be given up, but the form of non-cooperation would have to be changed into a more militant one, and the fight for freedom was to be waged on all fronts.

He was arrested again on 2 January 1932 and imprisoned. Though physically weak, he had a strong will power to live, suffer and serve others. His ill health took him to Europe. He reached Vienna on 8 March 1933 and was admitted into Dr. Furth's Sanatorium. He spent three years in Europe and his activities shaped his future plans, programmes and aspirations for free India. This exile was turning point in his personal life. During his stay in Europe, he fell in love with a German lady, Fraulein Schaekl, whom he married later in 1942. He was blessed with a daughter who is now married happily to an American.

During his exile, Bose gave several talks on the freedom movement in India to enlist the support and cooperation of the foreigners. He visited almost every country in Europe, except the erstwhile U.S.S.R. In Italy, he met Mussolini several times. But in Germany, he was very much disappointed as Hitler did not grant him interviews. He had to wait for a long time for such an opportunity. He returned to India from Europe when he got a message about his father's illness. But his father had passed a day earlier when he arrived in Calcutta. He was asked by the authorities not to leave his house, not to give any interview to any outsider and to handover to the police all books and communications received from any source whatever. He stayed a month with his family members in agony and left for Europe in exile, on 8 January 1935. The Leftists of India invited him to attend the Lucknow Congress Session (1936), to be held under the presidentship of Nehru. He returned to India even though he was warned by the Government of India not to do so. Again he was arrested, but was released from jail on health ground.

He again left for Europe on 18 November 1937 for medical treatment. In Britain, he came to know about his election, in absentia, as the President of the Congress. He left London for India on 22 January 1938 and reached Calcutta on 24 January. The Fifty-first Session of the Congress met on

19 February 1938 at Haripura (Gujarat). In his Presidential speech, he covered various aspects like foreign policy, family planning, British imperialism, socialism. He anticipated many of the problems of free India and warned that the country might be partitioned. He also hoped that the Congress would remain in power after independence. All his predictions came true.

The year 1939 witnessed a storm in the Congress over the issue of election of its President when Bose declared that he would contest the office for the second time. The Congress was virtually divided into two groups, one supporting and another opposing him. As discussed above, he was opposed by the stalwarts like Gandhi, Nehru, Rajendra Prasad and Sardar Patel. Gandhi, the undisputed leader of the Congress, wanted that Nehru should occupy the office though the latter had already been elected to it thrice (1929, 1936, 1937) including two consecutive terms just before Bose (1938). But, Nehru, probably because of this reason, declined the offer. Then Gandhi preferred Maulana Abul Kalam Azad, who politely declined on health grounds. Finally, Pattabhi Sitaramayya was recommended by Gandhi and Bose was asked to withdraw from the contest. Since Bose was nominated by a number of Provincial Congress Committees, he refused to retreat from the battle. Seven members of the Congress Working Committee—Sardar Patel, Rajendra Prasad, Jairamdas Daulatram, J.B. Kriplani, Jamnalal Bajaj, Shankarrao Deo and Bhalabhai Desai—supported Gandhi's nominee. Their arguments were that the President should be chosen unanimously; the same person should not be consecutively elected for the second term unless the situation was an extraordinary one; and the position of the President was just that of a chairman and a symbol of unity of the nation. Even then they would have accepted Bose. But they did not.

It was believed that the British Government and the right wing of the Congress would have a compromise on the federal scheme in the year 1939. Since Bose belonged to the leftist group, he might prove to be a thorn in the way of a compromise. He was, of course, ready to withdraw from the contest if a genuine leftist and an anti-federalist candidate like Acharya Narendra Dev was chosen. He gave his last warning to avoid the contest, otherwise, the blame of the split of the Congress would be on the rightists.

In the presidential election, Bose secured 1,580 votes as against 1,375 votes won by P. Sitaramayya. It was an extraordinary event in the history of the Congress: a success of the leftists over the rightists, of democracy over the autocratic nomination, of definite policy and programme of anti-federation over the prospective compromise with federation. Above all, it was the success of Bose over Gandhi, the uncrowned king of the Congress. Gandhi accepted his defeat. In his words: "The defeat is more mine than his." Bose, however, was still optimistic of winning his confidence. But he failed. The gap between the two widened in due course of time.

On 7 March 1939, the All India Congress Committee met at Tripuri (Madhya Pradesh) under the Presidentship of Bose who was in very bad health. Prior to this meeting, he met Gandhi and requested him to postpone it. But it was turned down and misinterpreted as his lack of confidence in Gandhi and the rightists. Twelve members resigned from the Working Committee. Gandhi also did not cooperate with him as he left for Wardha.

On 10 March 1939, the plenary session of the Congress met and both Gandhi and Bose were absent. Bose's Presidential address was read out by his elder brother Sarat Bose. Maulana Azad presided over the session. In his address, Bose said that national and international situations were in favour of Indians and, therefore, they should start immediately a mass movement.

As expected, Bose failed to win Gandhi's confidence. The latter did not cooperate with him in organizing and reconstituting the Working Committee of the Congress. Nehru and even Rabindra Nath Tagore interfered and requested Gandhi to help him in his task. Bose, finally, had to resign from his office as he was not acceptable to Gandhi. Earlier, he had resigned from the I.C.S. to serve the country. But this time he did so because of Gandhi's autocracy and dictatorship.

THE FORWARD BLOC

Within three days of his resignation, he formed a new bloc called the Forward Bloc within the Congress to rally all the radical and anti-imperialist progressive elements in the country on the basis of a minimum programme. He became its President, Sardar Sardul Singh Caveeshar, the Vice-President and H.V. Kamath, the Chief Secretary.

The First All India Congress of the Bloc was held in Bombay on 22 June 1939 to frame its Constitution and decide its programme. The Constitution made it clear that it was an organization within the Congress and meant for all its leftist members; its goal was complete independence for India and the establishment of a socialist state; assured full religious freedom to its members but opposed tooth and nail, corruption, provincialism and communalism; wanted to give a new shape to the Congress by restoring democracy within it by replacing the authoritarian policy of Gandhi and others. It gave a single common platform to all the leftists (the Congress Socialist Party, the National Front, as the communists called themselves then, the Radical Democratic Party led by M.N. Roy). It also wanted to liberate the Congress from the influence of the vested interests and from the domination of the Congress ministries.

Provoked and upset, the Congress soon met and passed two resolutions to check the activities of the Forward Bloc: first, none from the Congress would offer anything or organize any form of Satyagraha without the sanction of the concerned P.C.C. and, second, any difference between the P.C.C. and the Congress Ministry should be referred to the Parliamentary Sub-Committee of the Congress Working Committee. The open rivalry between the two (Congress and the Forward Bloc) continued. The Congress President, Rajendra Prasad, asked the leftists not to oppose the Congress. Roy's Radical Democratic Party left the

Left Consolidation Committee. This was the first split in the Forward Bloc. Bose could not tolerate it and challenged the Congress resolutions. As expected, the Congress asked him to explain his conduct. He argued that he had every right to express his views on any matter including the resolutions. Dissatisfied, the Congress debarred him from holding any elective office of the Congress for three years from August 1939.

The Second World War broke out on 3 September 1939 when Germany invaded Poland. The Congress Working Committee met to discuss the war problem. Bose was invited to attend the meeting though he was not a member. He asked the members to give an immediate ultimatum to the British Government. But he was ignored by the Committee. Frustrated and disappointed, he convened separately an Anti-Imperialist Conference in October 1939 and asked the Congress to accept his view. Reminding the nation that Britain's difficulty provided an opportunity to India to capitalize the existing situation, he asked the Indians to launch a total struggle for freedom. In the same month the Congress ministers resigned. But Gandhi, unlike Bose, did not feel that the time was ripe for the total struggle. Bose launched an All India Anti-Compromise Movement and convened the All India Anti-Compromise Conference at Ramgarh in Bihar on 19 March 1940 under the joint auspices of the Forward Bloc and the Kishan Sabha of which he was the President.

The Congress Socialist Party (C.S.P.) and the National Front (the Communist Party) did not support him. Instead, they deserted him by coming out of the Forward Bloc. The C.S.P. thought that the time was not yet ripe for the struggle. The National Front criticized the Satyagrahis of the Forward Bloc as "disrupters of unity" and called it the "Fascist Fifth Column".

The Second Conference of the Forward Bloc was held at Nagpur in June 1940 under the Presidentship of Bose. In a resolution, the Block reiterated its aims and objectives that it would be a party within the Congress with mass membership, capture political power as early as possible and reconstruct the national economy on socialist basis. The conference gave a new slogan: "All power to the Indians, here and now". It was the last conference of the Bloc since Bose was arrested in July 1940 and in 1941 he fled for ever from India. After the Nagpur Conference, he met Gandhi in Wardha. This was their last meeting and both expressed their independent views which were poles apart. He left for Bombay from Wardha and stayed there for a few days. He met Veer Savarkar, the veteran revolutionary and the Hindu Mahasabha leader. The latter advised him to escape to Germany.

On 17 January 1941, he mysteriously escaped from India. He wanted to go to Russia via Afghanistan. He believed that since Britain and Russia were the enemies, it would be proper for him to go there and carry propaganda for Indian freedom. But he could not get permission from the Russian embassy in Kabul to go to Moscow, as the latter could not take him into confidence. Then he contacted the German Legation. On 6 February 1941, he went alone there and met Hens Pigler, a minister, who directed him to try through Herr Thomas, a representative of Siemens in Kabul. Thomas directed him to meet the Italian Minister, Alberts

Quaroni in Kabul. Both had a meeting which lasted a whole night. Bose told him about his future action that would make India free, to form the "Government of Free India", create an army called the Indian Liberation Army which would consist of the Indian prisoners of war in Germany and Italy, and install a wireless radio station to carry on propaganda for India's independence. Everything went on secretly.

The Governments of the U.S.S.R., Germany and Italy agreed that Bose would travel across Russia on an Italian diplomatic passport impersonating a clerk at the Italian Legation in Kabul, Orlando Mazetta, on "a courier visa" issued by the Afghan Government. Bose left Calcutta, reached Berlin on 3 April 1941 via Moscow covering the distance by walk within 71 days. He could succeed in escaping from the clutches of British policemen, spies and informers who did their best to catch hold of him. It was the most sensational escapes of history.

Bose made Berlin his headquarters and started his political activities from the hotel Excelsior. In the beginning, he was treated as an uninvited guest and stranger, and considered as a spy. Therefore, he was kept under house arrest for several months. Hitler did not grant him interview for more than a year. They met for the first time on 29 May 1942. The German Government provided the required help to him for undertaking his political activities in Berlin. The "Working Group India" was set up. Bose discussed with German officials on the organization of Free India Centre in Berlin.

The provisional Government of Free India, originally known in Europe as the Free India Centre, started functioning unofficially from October 1941. On 2 November 1941, the Centre was officially inaugurated. There were a few Indian workers, like N.G. Ganpuley, N.G. Swamy, M.R. Vyas, Habibur Rehman. It had all the formalities of an independent government: a flag, a national anthem, a slogan, a national language, etc. The workers of the Centre called him affectionately "Netaji" which became a permanent appellation and honour since then.

Bose not only carried his propaganda programme with all sincerity but also organized the Indian revolutionary army, the Indian Legion, in Berlin to use it in his freedom struggle. There were about 10,000 Indian Prisoners of War (Ps.O.W.) in the camps of Germany and North Africa. He visited in December 1941 many a times the Annaberg Camp in Germany, where the Indian Ps.O.W. were staying. He met them individually, talked to them with all humility, heard patiently their hardships. He consoled and inspired them to join the Indian Legion to fight for the Indian freedom. Within four months, 300 Indian Ps.O.W. joined it. In due course of time, the strength went up.

He was, however, disappointed and frustrated as he could not get much help from the Government of Germany to achieve his goal. Hence he decided to leave Germany for South East Asia. On 8 February 1943, he left Germany and reached Japan on 20 April 1943. This was the end of the second phase of his struggle for freedom, the first being in India from 1921 to 16 January 1941.

In South–East Asia he formed Indian Independence League and constituted the Indian National Army. He became the head of the League and Commander-in-Chief of the Army. His role in South-East Asia constituted the third and the final phase in his struggle for national Independence. He issued slogans like "Chalo Delhi" and "give me your blood, I will give you freedom," etc. By doing so, he could mobilize men, material and other resources to fight against the British imperialism. The Japanese Prime Minister, Tojo, extended Bose all kinds of help so that India could be liberated. Bose was invited on 16 June 1943 to address the Diet (Parliament). He made a historic speech and won the support of its members for the cause of Indian independence.

The I.I.L. and I.N.A. shifted their headquarters to Singapore. On 5 July 1943, first time in military uniform in South-East Asia he took over the command of the I.N.A. with the salute given by the I.N.A. led by the Commander Bhoosle, at the square in front of the city hall in Singapore. That was the proudest day in his life. He left Singapore on 20 July 1943 for Rangoon to attend Burma's independence ceremony to be held on 1 August 1943. He left Rangoon for Bangkok on 4 August 1943 and met the Prime Minister of Thailand, a privilege which was denied to him earlier as he was a revolutionary.

On 21 October 1943, Bose's proposal to set up the Provisional Government of Free India was accepted at a conference held in Singapore. The Government was set up here. He became the chief of the Government. Japan gave it immediate recognition. Germany, Italy, Burma, the Philippines, Nanking, Croatia, Manchukud and Siam recognized it later. On 24th, it declared war on the U.S.A. and Britain. He shifted its headquarters from Singapore to Rangoon on 1 January 1944.

Soon after, he decided to cross the India border as the last phase of the struggle and march to Delhi via Imphal. In this operation (from 15 March to 9 July 1944), Japanese divisions and one I.N.A. division were deployed. But they were defeated by the British army. Shocked and disappointed, Bose wanted to avenge the British Government with the help of Japan and Germany, the axis powers in the Second World War. So, with the help of the Japanese army, he attacked the British from the North–East frontier. But the Manipur operation was not successful. It would have been successful had Dimapur been attacked first. The failure could be attributed to lack of cooperation and coordination among the Japanese Commanders of the three divisions, shortage of supplies, equipment, airplanes, torrential rains, etc.

Germany surrendered to the Allies on 7 May 1945 and Japan on 15 August 1945. Russia declared war against Japan on 8 August 1945.

Netaji left Singapore for Saigon by a plane on the morning of 15 August 1945, accompanied by Colonels Habib-ur-Rahman, Pritam Singh, Gulzara Singh, Majar Abid Hassen, S.A. Ayer, Debanath Das. The party arrived in Bangkok shortly after the official surrender of Japan and left Bangkok for Saigon and from Saigon he along with Habib-ur-Rahman left on 5.30 p.m. on 17 August 1945 for an unknown destination. The plane was overloaded with machine guns and bombs.

Some of them were unloaded when the plane stopped at Tourane. Netaji spent the night at the Morin Hostel. The plane left Tourane at 5 a.m. on 18 August 1945, the last day of Netaji's life. It reached Taipeh at about noon. After lunch and rest for about two hours, the plane took up again at about 2 p.m. Suddenly, a loud explosion was heard and the plane dived to the ground and burst into flames. Seven persons including Netaji were killed. Netaji died in the hospital. Seven persons with minor to major injuries survived. Lieutenant General Shidei and Pilot Takizawa died on the spot and four including Netaji died in the hospital. Netaji, who was admitted in the Nanmon Hospital in Taipeh, enquired about the fate of his friends. He said, "my men are following me and they should be taken care of when they come to Formosa". His last words were "I want to sleep."

He went into 'deep slumber' after involving in a continuous, prolonged, restless and painful struggle aimed at liberating his mother land. He died without any complaint. He died, according to the medical report following the air crash, of "burns of third degree". He died for a noble cause at 8.30 p.m. on 18 August 1945. He was cremated at the Taipeh City Crematorium on 20 August 1945. A life full of sufferings, sacrifices, humiliations, pains, anguish, adventures and restlessness came to a tragic end in a foreign soil. No doubt, after his death, his mortal frame was consigned to flames, but he is immortal and his memory still haunts the Indians. His name would go down in the annals of Indian history as one of the bravest, courageous and dedicated soldiers whose only mission was to see a free and independent India. His death, however, is shrouded in mystery. Indians are not prepared to believe that he is no more.

The reports submitted separately by Shah Nawaj Khan (1956) and G.D. Khosla (1970) have confirmed his death. But every Indian still feels that he is alive and one day he will return. Echoing this sentiment, N. Sanjiva Reddy, the then President of India, remarked while unveiling a colour portrait of Netaji in the Central Hall of Parliament: "I wish I could believe he is alive. Wish he could come amongst us even for one day to inspire us".

WAS BOSE A FASCIST?

Bose, a realist, a pragmatist, sincerely believed that freedom struggle in India should be encouraged and supported by the peoples of the world. He felt that there should be foreign propaganda for arousing world public opinion in favour of Indian freedom. There was no doubt that he was attracted towards the fascist leaders for their 'strong' character. He took no fancy in them. He was happy when Gandhi visited Italy and met Mussolini in 1931. He felt that Gandhi rendered a significant service by visiting Italy. But he wished that Gandhi should have stayed for a longer period in Italy and cultivated more personal contacts with leaders.

In 1934, he argued that there would be a synthesis between communism and fascism and this would be known as Samyavada and India should adopt it and practise it. A vedantic mystic and a believer in the nature of supreme reality, he did not hesitate to subordinate the individual to the state.

He was an extreme nationalist, a militant nationalist. He supported violent techniques for liberation of the country. Violence as a means has been adopted in various countries and it cannot be said that it is the monopoly of fascist countries or a part of fascist philosophy. But Bose's violent struggle appeared fascistic, since he brought the armed help of the fascist powers of Europe and Asia. He could be called a fascist only in this limited sense. Otherwise, there was nothing wrong in soliciting the support and cooperation of the fascist leaders.

He was not a fascist. He never believed the philosophy of fascism, nor sanctioned imperialistic expansion, nor subscribed to the cult of racial supremacy. No doubt, he lived in Germany for two years (1941–1943). He met Hitler and his foreign minister, Ribbentrop and urged them to make a declaration in favour of Indian independence. But, at the same time, he made it clear that the people of India had no love or sympathy for fascism. Ribbentrop refused to make any declaration about Indian independence. Bose could, however, succeed in soliciting support of Mussolini. When he met Hitler and sought his support, the latter refused to make any declaration of India's right to self-determination. To Hitler, India would not be in a position to rule for another 150 years. Angry and annoyed with what Hitler said, he told Vonn Trott in English, "Please tell His Excellency that I have in politics all my life and that I do not need advice from anyone".

Nazism never inspired Bose. Nor was he a Nazi. He simply wanted to take advantage of the international situation so that India could be free. His association with Germany and Hitler rather was a strategy for realizing a goal. No doubt, he hated the British imperialism, but never the British nation. He was against the elimination of the English race. If at all he hated the white race, he would not have appreciated the contributions of U.S.A., Russia, France towards human culture and civilization.

A thinker, a humanist, a rarest of rare personality in contemporary history, he was deeply committed to the cause of national independence. It was alleged that he was in alliance with the Axis Bloc. But the allegation was based on misrepresentation of facts and on concocted stories. He was one of the most outstanding figures of the Indian National Movement who wanted to see India free by the efforts of his countrymen, notwithstanding the fact that he had contacts with Hitler and some other Axis leaders. One who symbolized self-respect and honour and did his best to protect it, would not be even the last person in this world to dance to the tunes of any foreign power. He was certainly not a fascist.

AN ESTIMATE

Subhash Chandra Bose made a significant contribution to the rise and growth of Indian nationalism. A legendary figure, he succeeded in organizing the Indian

National Army, the Indian Independence League, in administering the Andaman and Nicobar Islands, and even in hoisting the independence flag after freeing the Manipur area of India on 18 March 1944.

He was imprisoned for eleven times and spent about nine years in jail, in exile and in detention. During his imprisonment, his health deteriorated much. No other top-ranking leader was subject to British wrath as he was. It was frequent and relentless. Dynamic, a militant fighter for Swaraj, an agitator, a propagandist, an uncompromising fighter, he was more a revolutionary leader than a political philosopher. A brilliant orator, he had an intense capacity for suffering. Except Tilak, no great political leader suffered as much as Bose. A man of action, he was gifted with an analytical mind. His greatness was that he lived and died for a principle, for a cause, for a mission, for a goal. To him, an individual must die, so that the nation might live. He must die so that India might live and might win freedom and glory.

Averse to injustice and slavery, he wanted that India should be free at the earliest from the British regime. He, therefore, fought throughout his life for national freedom with all sincerity and seriousness. To achieve his goal, he maintained his own individuality and adopting his own methods and approaches without any compromise. Even on the death bed, he told Habibur Rahman, who was lying by the side on the ground, to continue the struggle for freedom: "I do not think I will survive this accident. When you go back, tell the countrymen that I fought to the last for the freedom of my country and no power could now keep our country in bondage any longer. They should continue the struggle so that India might be free before long".

A patriot of patriots and second to none in his love for the country and determination to achieve its freedom, he happened to be the most important political leader next to Gandhi and Nehru. In his dedication to the cause of his country, he surpassed all including even Gandhi and Nehru. Outstanding and outspoken as a leader, serious and sensitive to the issues and problems the country faced, he was widely known outside India and ranked next to Gandhi and Nehru. A formidable, impregnable and impressive personality, he overshadowed Gandhi, Nehru and others. Radical and dynamic in his approach, programmes and principles, he sacrificed everything in his life to accomplish his missions. Uncompromising, almost defiant in attitude, he was one of the greatest patriots of the world.

Netaji's whole life was a long, persistent, uncompromising and painful struggle against British imperialism responsible for spiritual degradation, cultural degeneration, dire poverty and political slavery in India. A born democrat, a strong supporter of the principles of liberty, democracy and socialism, he was a perfect gentleman. Once he said he would give up politics and would not remain in the political field even for a single day if he felt that he was no more a gentleman and stooped low by becoming mean and self-centred. But the present politics is no more the profession of gentlemen. It is not even the last resort of scoundrels as it has become the first resort of scoundrels, anti-socials, criminals and mafias, dons and of other destructive and suppressive elements. Power never corrupted him, never made him to think that he was indispensable and infallible. The office of President of the Congres which he occupied without the support of Gandhi and others never made him arrogant. Instead, he earned a good reputation as "one of the silent Presidents of the Congress". An astute politician, a great diplomat, he was well versed in international affairs as he was a close student of international affairs and had personal contacts with international figures. He anticipated correct changes in international affairs. He had a strong belief that India should give right direction and proper guidance to the whole world.

In 1939, Rabindra Nath Tagore admiringly addressed Bose as Desh Nayak (leader of the country) and the latter was also honoured with the title "Netaji" in Germany in 1941. Tagore saw in him a new light of hope for the motherland. In his letter to Bose, he said that he might not survive, because of his old age, in this immortal world to share with him the moments of joy when India would be free in future. He felt happy because Bose had identified himself with his country and made his country's sorrow his own. He blessed him profusely and hoped that he would work hard to attain his goal. Paying a rich tribute to Bose, Nehru said: "Netaji Subhash has set an example of courage and passionate devotion to the cause of Indian freedom which will live long in India's history. Equally important is the way in which he has demonstrated how to wield the different communities in a common unity".

His great slogan "Jai Hind", which strengthened nationalism and national unity, was made extremely popular by the members of the I.N.A. as they use it while greeting one another. Now also Indians use it frequently while greeting others or addressing the audience. Known for his organizational ability and capacity, he lived up to his title "Netaji". He is our pride, our ideal, our encouragement and inspiration. Indeed, he was one of the most luminous stars shining on the horizon of politics. His name is mentioned with much respect, appreciation, and admiration. Occupying a unique place in the history of freedom struggle which hardly any of his contemporaries could have ever imagined to reach or occupy, he is very much among us to encourage and inspire. He belongs to the ages and his loving memory will ever remain fresh in our minds.

POINTS TO REMEMBER

- Subhash Chandra Bose was born on 23 January 1897. Father: Janakinath Bose. Mother: Prabhabati Bose. Early education in an English medium school and the Ravenshaw Collegiate School. Passed H.S.C. Examination in 1913. Higher education in Presidency College. Completed his education in 1916.
- He was influenced by his headmaster and by saints.
- A saint: he wanted to become a saint by going against the wishes of his parents.

- Presidency College: incident of a teacher's humiliation; Bose's silence over it; he was rusticated from the university; it had a great bearing on his life.
- Social service: after expulsion, devoted his time to serve the society. Served the patients, buried the unclaimed dead bodies.
- Passed I.C.S. Examination, but not happy to work as a bureaucrat for the British Government. Aurobindo's influence on him.
- Letter to C.R. Das: to join his gigantic programme of national service; act as Subeditor for his paper "Swaraj". His letter to Bose. He resigned from I.C.S. in April 1921 and returned to India in the same year.
- Gandhi and Bose: Bose met Gandhi in 1921 in Bombay. Least impressed and convinced by him. He did not agree with his plans, policies and programmes.
- Bose was also not happy with Gandhi's indecisiveness. He resigned from the Congress as its President as desired by Gandhi in 1939. He was expelled from the party.
- Freedom: both political and socio-economic freedom were to be secured. Political freedom alone would be meaningless if people were not free socially and economically. Violence to be used as a means to secure the goal.
- People should have freedom in true sense of the term in every sphere. His freedom included abolition of social evils like caste structure, superstitions, boycott of foreign goods, etc.
- A socialist: propagated various socialistic measures.
- His socialism was influenced by his own environment. Socialism was freedom to be mass-based.
- To him, Gandhi's socialism was utopian. Hence, its condemnation. State's role in promoting socialism. He also criticized Nehru's socialism.
- Productivity and production should go up. Industry and defence to be modernized. Increase of national wealth. India should adopt socialism suitable to her socio-economic and political conditions. An advocate of social and political democracy.
- Nationalism: the soul force, the pride of every nation.
- To him, force was the only instrument to achieve independence. "Give me blood, I will give you freedom", he said. He stood for unity in diversity, communal harmony, abolition of barriers of wealth, class and caste.
- He was more a nationalist than a socialist.
- Role in freedom movement: he pleaded for complete freedom in 1928. Set up the Independence of India League. Sent to prison in 1930. His frequent arrests. He was unhappy with Gandhi–Irwin Pact. Unhappy when Civil Disobedience Movement was abruptly stopped by Gandhi and when the latter joined the second Round Table Conference as the sole representative of the Congress.

- Unhappy with the Congress and its leader Gandhi, he stood for a total reorganization of the Congress. His ill health took him to Europe. Met several leaders. Hitler disappointed him. Married to a German. Returned to India.
- His election in absentia, as the President of the Congress in 1938. His reelection in 1939. Gandhi opposed his candidature.
- Bose was ready to withdraw from the contest provided a leftist like Acharya Narendra Dev was chosen.
- Forward Bloc: formed in 1939. Its first All-India Congress was held in the same year. Unhappy, the Congress asked its members not to cooperate with it.
- M.N. Roy's Radical Democratic Party. Left the Left consolidation Committee. Congress passed two resolutions; this made Bose unhappy. He opposed them. Enraged, the Congress debarred him from holding any office for three years.
- In 1939, Second World War took place. Congress Working Committee met. He (Bose) asked its members to give an ultimatum to the British Government. He was ignored. He launched an All-India Anti-Compromise Movement.
- He was arrested in 1940 and left India in 1941 for Germany.
- He met Hitler on 29 May 1942. Initially, he was considered as a spy and kept under house arrest. Made Berlin his headquarters. Free India Centre was inaugurated. It was the Provisional Government of free India. He organized the Indian Revolutionary Army, the Indian Legion. Recruited into it prisoners of war. Germany did not help him as expected. Left Germany and reached Japan in 1943. Set up there the Indian National Army.
- Japan's help to Bose: he set up his Provisional Government. It was recognized by Germany, Japan, Italy, Burma and a few other countries.
- He shifted the headquarters of the Provisional Government from Singapore to Rangoon in 1944. Germany and Japan lost the war. Russia declared war on Japan. He left Singapore for Saigon via Bangkok. He left Saigon for an unknown destination. His plane crashed on 18 August 1945.
- He succumbed to his injuries in the hospital on the same day.
- He was a realist, a pragmatist, but never a fascist. He wanted a synthesis between communism and fascism, known as Samyavada.

13

Madhusudan Das (1848–1934)

INTRODUCTION

A great intellectual, an ardent nationalist, a great leader of the Oriya Movement, a pragmatist, a brilliant speaker, a friend of the poor and downtrodden, he was liberal and secular in his approach. With respect and honour, people addressed him 'kula bruddha' (Grand Old Man). The architect of modern Odisha, he was acclaimed as Cato (Senator Cato of Italy fought for justice and supported the poor, helpless and deprived sections of the society). He opposed all kinds of oppression and exploitation and never supported the Non-cooperation and Civil Disobedience Movements. He firmly believed that socio-economic change could never be brought about by violent means. Progressive in his outlook, he supported the untouchables and appointed a large number of them in his industries. He gave equal importance to all religions. Though a devoted Christian, he was never an orthodox. A strong exponent of Indian nationalism, he did his best to reawaken Odiya nationalism.

EARLY LIFE

Born on 28 April 1848 in Satyabhamapur, a small village of Cuttack district in Orissa, Madhusudan Das was popularly known as "Utkal Gaurab" (pride of Orissa). His father Choudhury Raghunath Das was a Lawyer at Cuttack and also a Legal Adviser of Raja Dibyasingh Deb of Patia. He was deeply influenced by his mother Parbati Devi, a highly religious and spiritual lady. Born and brought up in an orthodox family, he played a very important role in the struggle for independence. An eloquent and fluent speaker, he was a devout Hindu. But the rituals, blind beliefs and superstitions associated with the Hinduism forced him to change his religion and become a Christian.

In 1843, he was admitted into his village school. After completion of his elementary education, he took admission in Middle Vernacular School in Mahasinghpur village in 1857. In 1859, he joined the Cuttack Zilla School for higher studies.

"Morning shows the day", thus goes the adage. The present, shaped by the past, indicates the future. What one would be in future may be predicted on the basis of his present activities. That Madhusudan Das would one day play a great role in awakening the "Oriyas", do a lot for his people and the state, be a great patriot and a man of indomitable spirit and courage, was evident from his activities during his student career in Zilla School. Almost all the teachers and majority of the students of the school were Bengalis and there was an attempt to impose Bengali language in schools throughout the Oriya-speaking districts of Orissa. Das and his friends protested against it. He, therefore, became a target of his teachers and fellow students. Enraged and unhappy, the Headmaster expelled him from the school. But the fact was that Das pointed out a mistake of the Headmaster while the latter was teaching English and explaining a line in the text. This was too much for the Headmaster to tolerate. He could not digest the insult and expelled him from the school on the pretext of his (Das's) misbehaviour.

Deeply hurt and aggrieved, he appealed the Commissioner of Cuttack who gave him a patient hearing, inquired into the allegation and found that the Headmaster was wrong. Therefore, he asked the latter to readmit Madhusudan. This incident reflected the true personality of Madhusudan.

In 1864, he passed the Entrance Examination from the Zilla School. Then he went to Calcutta and got admitted into London Church Missionary Society College for higher studies against the wishes of his father who wanted him to work as a clerk in any government office so that he could later become a Deputy Collector, a powerful and prestigious post. It was during this period he changed his name from Govindaballav to Madhusudan and embraced Christianity. He passed Intermediate Examination in 1867 and got B.A. degree in 1870. After completion of his education, he was appointed as the Headmaster of the Christian Missionary High School at Calcutta. But he relinquished his job and was admitted into the Free Church Institution for higher (M.A.) studies. He was the first Oriya to pass the M.A. Examination with First Class in 1873. Soon after, he married Saudamini Chatterjee, a Bengali Christian Girl, who was one year senior to him in age. He was also the first Oriya to get the Bachelor of Law degree in 1878 from the Presidency College of Calcutta University. Then he joined the Bar in Alipur as an advocate. Meanwhile, his wife's unexpected and sad demise in 1878 was a great shock to him. A widower, he left Calcutta and returned to Orissa. He did not marry again, declining politely but firmly his friends' and relatives' persuasion to do so. Instead of constituting a family, he dedicated his life to the cause of the people.

A LAWYER

He joined the Cuttack Bar as a Lawyer in 1881. At that time the lawyers were mostly Bengalis. Therefore, he was not acceptable to them and was looked upon with contempt. He was so much disliked by them that he was not given any accommodation in the Bar Library. However, the English District Judge Cocklan was very much sympathetic towards him and provided him a separate room so that he could continue his profession. Because of his personality and character, he was later elected as the President of the Cuttack Bar. He became one of the most dignified and renowned advocates of Orissa as well as of India. By dint of his hard work, honesty and sincerity, he could earn name and fame, prestige and reputation in his profession.

UNIFICATION OF ORISSA

With the advent of Madhusudan Das a new era was opened in the socio-economic and political history of Orissa. By education, training and temperament, he was very sensitive to the contemporary issues concerning Orissa and its people. During the British rule, Orissa was much neglected in every sphere as nothing was done for the spread of education, development of means of communication, irrigation, industry, agriculture, etc. She had no political identity of her own at that time. Administratively, the Oriya-speaking tracts remained scattered and formed parts of the erstwhile Presidencies of Madras in the south, of Bengal in the north, and of the Central in the west. Orissa division comprised only three districts of Cuttack, Puri and Balasore and she was merely an administrative unit of the Bengal Province till the new province of Bihar and Orissa was created in 1912. Orissa, therefore, remained as a poor, backward and underdeveloped province throughout the nineteenth century. Even now also in the twenty-first century it is the poorest province in India.

Das was very much convinced that Orissa could not be a developed state unless it was unified under one administration. He was moved by the grinding poverty, humiliation and untold sufferings of the Oriyas living in other provinces. Unhappy with the indifferent attitude of the British Government towards the Orissa Province, he did his best to promote the general welfare of the people. He was influenced by the liberal philosophy of John Stuart Mill. He also studied the unification movements in Italy and Germany. These lessons of history had a deep impact on him. His only dream was to see that Orissa was unified and to achieve this goal he was prepared to do anything. He was one of the first Oriyas to realize that their legitimate interests were being neglected because they remained scattered in different provinces of the British Indian Empire. Therefore, he took keen interest in the political unification of Orissa. He tried for its all-round development. To realize this dream, he joined the contemporary elites as a member of the "Utkal Sabha" (Orissa Association).

The Utkal Sabha was formed in 1871 to promote Oriya language and literature. It met twice a year and the members discussed various aspects like the national life, the local self-government scheme and other welfare measures relating to the Cuttack district. However, it was given a new orientation when Das became its Secretary in 1885 and, subsequently, its President. After that, it laid more emphasis on specific problems of the Oriya-speaking people than on general issues concerning India.

In November 1885, when Sir Richard Thompson, the Lieutenant Governor of Bengal, visited Cuttack, Das demanded that steps should be taken for the all-round development of the Oriyas. Under his dynamic leadership, the Utkal Sabha presented before him the grievances of the Oriya peasantry and their problems concerning irrigation, water cess, etc. It also demanded extension of industries, industrial education, necessity of completing the railway line on the east coast joining Calcutta and Puri, amalgamation of the Oriya-speaking areas, the need for using Oriya language in the courts of Ganjam and Vizagapatam Agency where the Oriya population formed a majority, introduction of remedial measures against droughts and famines.

The Utkal Sabha also selected delegates to attend the annual session of the Indian National Congress. It was, thus, through the Utkal Sabha that the ideas and programmes of the Congress reached the Oriya people in the early years of its inception. Under the leadership of Das, it provided a useful forum for the expression of political views as well as the social problems of Orissa.

Having strong faith in the Indian National Congress, he hoped that it would give due weightage and importance to the demands and aspirations of the Oriyas and do its best to create a separate state for them. In the beginning, he maintained close link with the Congress and hoped that the latter would discuss the problems of Oriyas and help them in carving out a separate state for them. But his hopes were shattered when he found that the Congress was mainly and mostly concerned with India as a whole and it did not bother for a petty issue like formation of Orissa for Oriyas.

He was very much frustrated and this disenchantment motivated him to form a provincial association on the pattern of the National Congress, which would consider the problems of Oriyas and try to solve them. Further, formation of a provincial association with the support of the rulers of native states, officials and non-officials of the native states and common people would go long way in educating the people and making them politically conscious. This would also help a lot in mobilizing the public opinion in right direction. This conviction led him to establish the Utkal Union Conference in December 1903. This gave a new impetus to the Oriya Movement. It held sixteen annual sessions at different places like Balasore, Cuttack, Puri, Sambalpur, Berhampur, Jeypore, Chakradharpur, etc. to discuss important issues. The members gave top priority to the problems like amalgamation of the Oriya-speaking tracts, spread of education, industrialization, mechanization of agriculture through spread of technical training under state patronage, etc. He took personal care to go from place to place to carry on the propaganda work and even on many occasions spent from his own pocket for the survival and success of the conference.

In 1907, he went to England to convince the British public about the necessity of the unification of the Oriya-speaking areas. During his stay there, he met the Members of Parliament, addressed meetings and approached the Press to communicate the feelings and grievances of the Oriya people. He circulated a pamphlet entitled "Unrest in India" highlighting the miserable plight of the Oriyas and succeeded in getting support of the British people for the cause of Oriyas. Lord Curzon also supported the cause of Oriyas in the House of Lords and MacCold Scot took up the issue in the House of Commons. Consequently, Orissa was separated from Bengal and, in 1912, the Province of Bihar and Orissa was formed. Although the formation of the new province was an official recognition of the identity of Orissa, Orissa as a separate province was still a remote dream. Therefore, he launched his movement with more vigour to achieve the end.

The inclusion of the Orissa division and some other Oriya-speaking areas in the newly formed Bihar and Orissa Province did not satisfy the Oriyas. So the Utkal Union Conference under his leadership demanded the merger of all the Oriya-speaking tracts. In December 1917, he brought out a weekly journal titled "The Oriya" in English. In this weekly, he wrote fearlessly on various problems of the Oriyas under such captions as "Industrial Awakening", "Foreign Medical Treatment", "The Jerusalem of the Oriyas", "Orissa Irrendenta", etc.

In 1917, when Edwin Montague, the Secretary of State for India, came to India to study and assess the conditions, he led a delegation and waited upon him. His demand was favourably considered by Montague and Chelmsford and they gave the report accordingly for the creation or re-demarcation of provinces on linguistic basis. This demand for a separate state was endorsed by the Bihar and Orissa Legislative Council. The recommendations of Montague and Chelmsford for the creation of states on the basis of language were also included in the Government of India Act, 1919.

On the whole, it can be said that the Oriyas have a homeland of their own at present not due to the Congress but only because of the tireless efforts of Madhusudan and his Utkal Union Conference.

THE FREEDOM FIGHTER

Das, the maker of modern Orissa, the architect of Oriya Movement, a great champion of the Indian Freedom Movement, chaired a meeting at Cuttack to discuss and approve the resolutions passed in the first session of the All India Congress held at Bombay. After 1885, delegates of the Utkal Sabha regularly attended all the sessions of the Indian National Congress. He evinced keen interest in the Congress organization and influenced the Orissa Association to support fully the cause of the Congress.

For some years, he thought that the Indian National Congress would provide a more effective forum for the amalgamation of Oriya-speaking areas. He, therefore, maintained a close link with the Congress in the early years of its inception. He had a talk with Surendra Nath Banerjee in 1902 who advised him to activate the Congress Movement in Orissa.

In 1905 with the partition of Bengal, the Congress launched an extensive and intensive popular agitation called the Swadeshi Movement. This Movement found its way to Orissa division as well. Das rose to the occasion and called upon the people to use Swadeshi-made goods. He continued his fight for freedom and extended his support and cooperation until that time when the Movement opposed the cause of unification of Orissa.

NATIONALISM

It would be a travesty of truth if it is said that the Oriya Movement headed by Madhusudan Das promoted regional patriotism. It would also be wrong to isolate it from nationalism or national patriotism. While engaging himself for the cause of the Oriyas, he never ignored the interests of India. He always believed that Mother Orissa was an incarnation of Mother India. Doing good to the former must be doing good to the latter. Analysing the factors of nationalism in a broader context, he referred to various instances from the pages of history, while explaining how religion, literature and culture played key role in creating nationalism.

But people might feel that his nationalism was narrow and parochial as he strongly stood for the unification of Orissa. But he was a true patriot and a staunch nationalist. He was, therefore, never opposed to Indian Nationalism. He felt that India was the body and Orissa was one of her limbs. If one organ of the body remained handicapped or underdeveloped, the whole body would be endangered as it could not provide sufficient strength and energy to the whole being. Therefore, all parts of the body must grow uniformly and simultaneously. This was the true spirit of nationalism as advocated and practised by Das.

To Das, Orissa was a colony of a colony and the problems of Oriyas were something quite different from the rest of the country. Not only she was socially, economically and politically backward but also lagged behind other provinces. He wanted that the Oriyas should be united first so that they could contribute to the greater cause of India. Hence, he approached the Congress leaders. But they refused to oblige him as the Indian National Congress was an All India Forum with pan Indian objectives and did not bother about provincial matters. Disappointed and frustrated, he lost his faith in the Congress.

Das' attitude towards the Congress was not appreciated by Gopabandhu Das and other leaders of the Utkal Union Sammilani. Challenging his leadership, they suggested in 1919 that the Conference should merge with the Congress. In the Chakradharpur session of the Sammilani held in 1920, Gopabandhu Das resolved that *Swaraja Prapti* (attainment of freedom), not *Desha Mishran* (merger of Oriya-speaking areas) be the goal of the Sammilani. A moderate politician, Das accepted the suggestion of Gopabandhu Das. But he was not prepared to do so until the unification of the Oriya-speaking tracts under one administration, as they knew it pretty well that he could not realize his goal with the help of the Congress.

Das became a Minister of the Bihar–Orissa Legislative Council on 6 January 1921. After his appointment, he fought for the cause of the Oriya people with great devotion and dedication since rendering service to his people was the sole motive of his life.

ECONOMIC AND SOCIAL VIEWS AND REFORMS

Das, a pioneer among Oriyas in many fields, highlighted various socio-economic issues of Orissa through his Orissa Association. He drew the attention of the Government on the agrarian problems in Orissa. He met high officials in England and appraised them of Orissa's problems including need of the Permanent Settlement. He pleaded that tenants, not Zamindars, should be declared as the real owners of the land. As a legislator, he fought for the abolition of the Zamindari system and the system of absentee landlordism.

He sincerely believed that rapid industrialization of Orissa alone could promote its economy. He was convinced that his country could never progress unless her industries were improved. He was the first Oriya nationalist whose thoughts and ideas were based on a scientific analysis of the economic maladies from which Orissa was suffering. Orissa was famous for its gold and silver works of exquisite delicacy. But because of deliberate and persistent economic policies of a colonial power, these fine native artistic crafts faced a great crisis. To save these precious crafts from ruin, he set up a large factory, Orissa Art Wares at Cuttack in 1897. But it could not survive for long as it incurred huge loss to a tune of one lakh rupees. He was forced to close down his workshop. He encouraged the people to revive the old profession of cottage industry and small scale industry for earning a livelihood.

A strong advocate of rapid industrialization, he suggested the Government to explore the mineral resources of Orissa, impart industrial training to Oriya students, provide them with scholarships for training abroad, so that the economic condition of Orissa could be substantially improved. It was only through his efforts that Sarangdhar Das, Braja Mohan Senapati and Lakshmi Narayan Singh went outside Orissa and abroad for higher technical education. The Utkal Union Sammilani had a special committee to sponsor such projects.

A pioneer of industrialization in modern Orissa, he founded the Utkal Tannery in1905 and formed one Cooperative Weaver's Society to improve the living conditions of a large number of poor but talented beneficiaries. He was the founder of the *Utkal Shilponnati Sabha* to accelerate the growth of industries in Orissa. His service in the field of indigenous industrialization was really praiseworthy. In fact, in the entire Bengal division he was the first person to take positive steps on industrialization.

Salt was an important item of trade in our country in the pre-British days as a large number of people depended on it. He was the first in Orissa to raise the voice against the imposition of Government monopoly over the sale and manufacture of salt in the Allahabad Congress Session held in 1888.

Thus, in various ways, he tried his best to improve the economic condition of the people of Orissa. As a matter of fact, for the establishment and management of Utkal Tannery, he had exhausted all his resources. In 1885, he submitted on behalf of the Oriyas a memorandum to Sir Richard Thomson during his visit to Cuttack. It emphasized the need for (i) expansion of the railways, (ii) development of the industrial training, (iii) medical and nursing training facilities, (iv) appointment of the Oriyas to high posts, (v) planning and development of agriculture, and (vi) amalgamation of areas inhabited by Oriyas.

From 1903 to 1920, the Utkal Union Sammilani held sixteen annual sessions to discuss and pass resolutions on a wider range of issues. Besides political unification, special emphasis was laid on the spread of education which was considered vital by him for the progress of Orissa. It set up a special committee to sponsor meritorious candidates for training outside Orissa and abroad. Due importance was given to the growth of local crafts such as weaving and filigree. He took personal care to go from place to place to carry on the propaganda work in this field. He persuaded the illiterate villagers to strengthen the cottage industry, start spinning and take intensive agriculture. Thus he had a great concern for the poverty of Orissa, and it was his one item agenda to remove it.

Radical and progressive in his outlook, a social reformer, he was an advocate of social reforms like abolition of caste system, child marriage, illiteracy, etc. To make the children educated, he tried to set up schools not only in coastal Orissa but even in the feudatory States. He was in favour of providing physical education and training to the boys serving in jails so that they would be appointed as Physical Training Instructors in schools after completing their jail terms. Thus, he gave much importance to physical education and, in order to encourage it, he founded Orissa Sports Association in 1904. He also took a keen interest in the development of primary education, higher education and technical education.

In the Language Agitation in Orissa, he played an important role by infusing a sense of unity among the Oriya people by writing a series of articles in *Utkal Dipika* under the caption "Banishment of Oriya". While at Bengal, he had struggled hard for introduction of Oriya language in answering Sanskrit papers in the Calcutta University. It was because of his efforts, the University of Madras recognized the Oriya language. He was determined to preserve and protect the identity of the Oriya language and to carve out a separate place for Orissa in the map of India.

A great champion of women's liberation, he advocated for female education and established a Girls' High School at Cuttack in 1908, the first of its kind in Orissa. Spread of female education was his mission in his life and he did his best to accomplish it. He extended all his support to any girl in pursuing her higher education and achieving her goal. He inspired and encouraged Sudhansu Bala Hazra to opt for a legal career. All these were the glowing examples of his real concern and interest for women's education and uplift movements. To him, a nation could not develop without the education of her women. There should be a collective endeavour to spread women's education in India in order to develop the nation. He introduced a resolution in the Bihar–Orissa Legislative Council on 3 November 1921 to provide franchise to women.

A LEGISLATOR

Das had a long and distinguished career as a legislator. He was elected to the Bengal Legislative Council on 14 March 1896. He was its Member up to 1897, again from 1900 to 1902, and from 1908 to 1909. Following the creation of the province of Bihar and Orissa, he served the Legislative Council as a Member for more than a decade, i.e. up to March 1923 when he relinquished the office of Minister of Local Self-Government.

During 1913–1916, he also functioned as a Member of Imperial Legislative Council for a short period. During this period, he drew the attention of the Government that Orissa had never enjoyed the benefits of the British rule.

His speeches as a Legislator reflected his deep concern for the welfare of the people in Orissa. He pressed the Government to appoint qualified Oriyas as Munsifs to transfer the Orissa Salt Department to the administrative control of the Bengal Government from Madras, to establish an agricultural college in Orissa instead of at Sibpur, and not to increase the salt tax. He openly criticized the Bengal Government for neglecting the educational affairs of Orissa and saw to it that a resolution was accepted subsequently in the Council for the establishment of a History Department in the Ravenshaw College. He also suggested that some kind of industrial training should be introduced in the village schools. As a Legislator, he was the first person to demand for the abolition of the Zamindari system. In this regard when the Bengal Tenancy Bill was to be passed by the Bengal Council, he submitted a memorandum to the Lieutenant. Governor of Bengal on behalf of the Orissa peasantry.

He also arranged to establish charitable dispensaries in rural areas and tried to control epidemic diseases.

Following the introduction of the dyarchical system of administration and the enforcement of the Government of India Act, 1919, Lord Sinha of Raipur, the first Indian to be appointed as the Governor of Bihar and Orissa. He appointed Das as a Member of his Council of Ministers and asked him to look after Local Self-Government, Public Health and Public Works. Das assumed his office on 6 January 1921. As the Minister, he introduced two progressive measures relating to Local Self-Government. Considered to be the model pieces of legislation and said to be his most remarkable achievements, these legislations gave a meaning and content to the abstract notion of formal democracy by providing for "recall". Voters cease to have any power to control their representatives if the latter are found to be corrupt, irresponsible and indifferent. They continue to enjoy their office for a full term of five years unless the House is dissolved earlier. They cannot be punished for their inefficiency, misbehaviour and misdeeds. This can be checked if they are held 'responsible' for their misdeeds and taken to task by the voters. One of the best means to achieve this goal is the 'recall' system. Inefficient, ineffective and indifferent representatives should be 'recalled' whenever it was felt necessary. The other remarkable legislation was representation of the depressed classes in the Local Self-Government institutions.

On 7 February 1923, Sir Henry Wheeler, the new Governor of the province wrote a letter to Das stating that the Local Self-Government Act made the districts responsible for the administration of the rural areas. These local bodies were, therefore, required to be constantly guided and advised by the Minister of the Local Self-Government. For an effective control over these bodies and exercising an influence over the honorary workers throughout the province, the Minister should also be an honorary worker, because a salaried official over the heads of thousands of honorary workers would be an anomaly. The Minister could not command respect from them if he draws any salary. Therefore, to ensure the success of the reforms, it was necessary that he should be an honorary worker.

He further argued that the Minister must inspire the members of the Municipalities and District Boards, all local bodies, local authorities and villagers with a patriotic spirit, inculcate in them a genuine spirit of self-sacrifice, a true desire of nation-building and with their cooperation discharge the responsibilities of his office.

In his reply, Das observed that he was willing to work honorarily provided he was allowed to earn a living by practising law. He assured the Governor that his professional work would not hamper his duties as a Minister. He further wrote in his letter: "If I had private means to keep me above the ordinary needs of life, I would not have asked for permission to practise".

On 11 February 1923, the Governor replied to the above letter and observed that it was an absolute impossibility to make the office of Minister of Local Self-Government an honorary one. Dissatisfied, Das resigned from his office on 8 March 1923.

His term of office as Minister in the Bihar and Orissa Government was short, yet it was quite eventful and remarkable.

LIBERALISM

During the first part of the twentieth century, leaders of the Congress believed the British and were quite liberal towards the British Government. Das was also not an exception to it. While at Calcutta, he was associated with the Moderate leaders like S.K. Ghose and S.N. Banerjee, and was very much influenced by their liberal ideas and techniques. He was against the use of violent means to attain the goal. Rather true to his liberal spirit, he tried to attain that through constitutional methods. Liberal in his outlook and approach, he supported the British participation in the First World War in a meeting of the Utkal Sammilani in 1914 on the ground that the Indians being the citizens of the British Empire should support the cause of their Government at least on moral grounds. His liberal and obligatory attitude, his loyalty towards the British Government, did not go in vain because whatever success the Oriya Movement had achieved was only because of the support of the British Government. But, at the same time, his feeling of loyalty should not be construed as slavery. As a matter of fact, he struggled throughout his life against injustice and on many occasions criticized the policies of the British Government, which took little interest in the welfare of the people.

RELIGION

Neither narrow nor conservative in his religious outlook, he had strong faith in the truth of all religions. According to him, religion was a way, which took one towards God and it was through religion only an individual could get his peace of mind. Although during his stay at Calcutta he had embraced Christianity that did not mean that he hated Hinduism, rather he had a great admiration for the Hinduism and its culture. Born and brought up in a conservative Hindu family where he had even witnessed the performance of his grandmother's Sati, he was upset with the Hindu rites, rituals, social rigidities, superstitions and blind beliefs. On the other hand, he appreciated the liberal, rational and humanitarian ideas of Christianity. Therefore, he became a Christian. But his conversion did not alienate him from the mainstream of Indian life and culture as he fought for the privileges of the Raja of Puri and restored the autonomy of the temple. He stood for Hindu–Muslim unity.

DEMOCRACY

In a true democratic spirit, he always represented the hopes and aspirations of the people. He vehemently opposed the bureaucratic administration in India. He was always in favour of a popular administration based upon people's consent. He criticized the I.C.S. Officers, the bureaucrats in India, who ruled the country in an arbitrary manner without having any idea of democracy.

He laid much stress upon self-rule and expressed his view that the problems of the local areas must be resolved by the people themselves. He felt that there was a wide communication gap between the ruler and ruled as the latter was unable to put forth its grievances before the authority. When he was the Vice-President of the Cuttack Local Board in 1887, he found that they were entirely dominated by the Government officials and nominated members. As he had tremendous faith in Self-Government, he tried to convert these local-self bodies into true representative and autonomous bodies.

AN ESTIMATE

Well known for his political sagacity, wisdom, straightforwardness and independent thinking, he never bothered about others' praises and criticisms, appreciations and admonitions; famous for his charity and welfare activities, he left an indelible imprint on the minds of the people. He made it a mission in his life to help the poor and the needy persons. He never disappointed them if they approached him for any help. Large hearted and broad minded, he was quite magnanimous. Even during the last days of his life, when he was not financially sound, he never said 'no' to any one who came to him for his help. He got tremendous peace and was delighted to help others. His ungrudging help made many to stand on their feet and earn a livelihood. He was very much worried about the poor and the oppressed. Moved by the sufferings of the poor peasantry in Orissa, he secured many rights for the tenants when the Orissa Tenancy Act was enacted in 1913.

A versatile genius and a multifaceted personality, he was very strong and determined while doing something for a right cause without bothering about the consequences. It was no small sacrifice on his part to resign from the office of the Minister when he found that it was impossible for him to act consistently with his principles. He never compromised his ideology and principles which he cherished so sincerely and cultivated so assiduously. He readily sacrificed everything for his countrymen. Public interest was the guiding spirit of all his actions. Sense of duty was supreme in his mind.

A renowned educationist, a practical politician, an astute statesman, a man of learning and scholarly attainments, a pioneer industrialist, a successful lawyer, an effective speaker, a powerful writer, and an outstanding personality, Madhusudan Das heralded a new era in the history of Orissa and inaugurated an age of Resurrection and Renaissance in Orissa. He identified himself with Oriyas. He had only one hope to fulfil, one goal to achieve, one task to accomplish, one desire to attain, and one dream to realize. It was the unification of Orissa and its all-round development, progress and prosperity. In all his speeches, he referred to the "Mother in the death-bed". He found "only heaps of dry bones, bones, bones, nothing but bones". He sacrificed all his comforts and luxuries, and neglected his alluring legal career only to serve the people and the society. He undertook the tremendous task of infusing life to his people without any help from any one except the God.

The spiritual background in which he was nurtured and brought up inspired him to work for the cause of the country and the people sincerely and seriously without thinking anything in terms of personal gain. He disliked the idea of personal gain in national service. To him, "life is a race, the world is a racecourse.

Birth is the starting point, death the goal. It should be the aim of one and all to realize the presence of a soul within them, to feel that life was a mission, and the object of life was not the pursuit of pleasure for one's own-self but to seek opportunities and means to make others happy.

His death in 1934 was a great shock, a great loss to the people of Orissa as they lost a towering personality. Born in 1848 and dying at an advanced age, he was beyond all doubt the greatest Oriya of the modern times and was for long justly known as the 'Grand Old Man' of Orissa. A man of principles and of sterling character, a paragon of virtues, an embodiment of ideals, assiduous, straightforward, conscientious and upright, he would go down in the annals of history as one of the greatest personalities whose only mission was to uplift the poor and downtrodden and who rendered a yeomen service to the cause of the people with a remarkable zeal, vigour and persistence till his last breath.

It was he who more than any other Oriya within living memory encouraged and inspired his countrymen to cherish with pride their rich heritage, to give up their inferiority complex and demonstrate their innate strength and vitality. Gifted with talents and an extraordinary capacity to organize, he did his best to transform the Oriya character. The assiduity and earnestness with which he fought for the ideals, and the sacrifice he made for his people, made him immortal.

He was the very personification of the desires and aspirations of the Oriyas for almost half a century from 1882. It has been rightly said that the life history of Madhusudan Das is the history of modern Orissa. A man of varied and useful career, he was a distinguished scholar, an able administrator, a patriot of high order, a man of principles and ideals, a devoted worker, and above all a dedicated soul. He combined in himself three cultures: Oriya, Bengali and European. A man of culture and wide learning, he loved his motherland with all his heart and soul. Being the first Oriya to obtain the highest University degree, he became the first law graduate and an Advocate to join Bar at Cuttack in 1881. He was the life and soul of modern Orissa. His long stay in Calcutta for about fifteen years and his highest education enabled him to emerge as a great leader of the Oriya community. A man of courage, confidence, strength, conviction, integrity, dedication and devotion, he was deeply influenced by the liberal philosophy of John Stuart Mill and the contemporary political movements in Italy and Germany.

A leader of outstanding capacity and calibre, he was deeply moved by the distress and poverty of the Oriyas who had for a long period been suffering from political injustice, social stagnation and economic backwardness. Imbued with a patriotic fervour, he did his best for the unification of Orissa by amalgamating all Oriya-speaking tracts under one administration.

Madhusudan dedicated his whole life for the cause of his motherland. He was the first Oriya to become a Minister and even the first Indian Minister to resign after two years of service. A prolific writer, a versatile genius, he was a practical statesman and a pragmatist. He worked hard to alleviate the distress of the people. He was, therefore, worshipped by the villagers. People felt proud of themselves when they got a chance to see him or came in contact with him. Popularly known as 'Madhu Babu' or 'Madhu Barrister', he is rightly regarded as the 'pride of Orissa' and called with utmost respect 'The Grand Old Man'.

He was, according to Surendra Nath Banerjee, a former President of the Indian National Congress, "a man of great personality, a versatile genius, a successful lawyer, a veteran politician, a great industrialist, the Father of New Orissa and a 'Harischandra' of this age". He further observed:

> I remember the greatness of his soul and his magnanimity that brought him to the brink of worldly ruin. I remember him as an inspiration of souls and as a man who lived on a higher plane than ordinary worshippers.

The motto of his life was "fear no man but God". He raised his voice of protest against all tyrannies and fought "tooth and nail" against all oppressions. A devoted and blessed son of his mother Utkal, he was also a great Indian. He was an Oriya out and out. He gave up his promising and lucrative career in Calcutta when his wife expired and left for Cuttack to serve his soil where he was born. He could inspire men and touch their hearts when he talked. "The greatness of a man shines in his little acts and not in spectacular shows".

Rajendra Prasad, the first President of independent India, while paying glowing tributes to Madhusudan Das, observed that he first met him when he came to preside over the Bihar Students' Conference held at Motihari in 1912. They travelled together on their way to Champaran and the conversation he had with him in the train and on the streamer left an indelible impression on his mind about his (Das') personality and devotion to country. In a long life full of varied activity, he never depended upon others for any financial help. It was a matter of deep regret that the Utkal Tannery on which he spent so much and which he brought up with utmost care like his own child, could not prosper on account of lack of financial support. His public career commenced long before man like Prasad was born and he always chose an original line of his own. When he was a Minister, he visited Chapra and on learning that Prasad was ill, he went to see him and how by the mere touch of his soft fingers, Prasad felt relieved. He was not afraid to speak and do the right thing regardless of consequences.

While unveiling the statue of Madhusudan, Pandit Jawaharlal Nehru remarked that Madhusudan was not only a leader of Orissa, rather he was a great Indian leader who did many pioneering services for the improvement of the Indian soil and economic conditions. He said that he had been hearing Madhusudan's name for the last fifty years. By confining his activities to a particular region of India, he placed an ideal before all other different regions of the country and it was worth emulating.

Aurobindo described Madhusudan as a high spirited and very capable person who roused political consciousness in certain regions of the country and, thus, contributed to the growth of the solidarity and patriotic consciousness of India as a whole.

That Madhusudan was very popular and highly admired is evident from a letter written by Mahatma Gandhi to him. The letter said:

> Dear friend, I have been constantly thinking of you. I am going to Cuttack. I have to put up with you. You will, of course, teach me how to spread the message of the spinning wheel in Utkal.

Even in the midst of the forgetfulness of the nation, Madhusudan, the poet and philosopher, the orator and the spiritual leader of the nation, lives. He lives and is bound to live not only in the hearts of the people of Orissa, but also in the memory of the Indian nation as a whole. His sacrifice to uplift the poor is immense and by no stretch of imagination one can assess it. His efforts in the field of industry were Herculean. His efforts and sacrifices will always inspire and encourage the future generation of Orissa. They have to learn the lessons of fair-play, balance of judgement and toleration, without which no nation can grow and prosper. That was the lesson and motto of his life so worthily spent. His values are to be imbibed and emulated by one and all.

POINTS TO REMEMBER

- Madhusudan Das was born in 1848 in Satyabhamapur. Father: Raghunath Das; an Advocate and a Legal Adviser of Dibyasingh Deb of Patia. Mother: Parvati Devi, highly religious. In 1843, he was admitted into school. His activities in Zilla School: his opposition to imposition of Bengali on Oriyas.
- He was expelled from the High School. He was readmitted. In 1864, he passed the final school examination. Left for Calcutta for higher studies against the wishes of his father. Changed his name and became a Christian. He got his B.A. degree in 1870. He was appointed as Headmaster in a school at Calcutta. Gave up the job and got admitted in M.A. class. First Oriya to get M.A. degree in 1873 and law degree in 1878. Married to Saudamini Chatterjee. Joined the Alipore Bar as an Advocate. Wife expired in 1878.
- A lawyer: joined the Cuttack Bar in 1881. Bengali advocates did not like him. Elected as President of the Bar.
- Unification of Orissa: Orissa was not unified, had no political identity of her own. It had three districts only. Creation of Bihar–Orissa state in 1912. For her development, she was to be unified. Unification would remove her poverty and backwardness. Influenced by liberal philosophers like J.S. Mill and others.
- Orissa's conditions would improve if she was unified.
- He joined the 'Utkal Sabha', formed in 1871 to promote Oriya language and literature. It met twice a year. He became its Secretary in 1885 and

then its President. It sought to promote the interests of the Oriyas and put less emphasis on national issues.

- Sir Richard Thompson, Lieutenant Governor of Bengal, visited Orissa in November 1885. Das presented a memorandum to him, drawing his attention to various problems of Orissa and the Oriyas. Utkal Sabha became a link between the Congress and the people.
- Frustrated, Das wanted to ventilate the grievances of the Oriyas through a provincial association called Utkal Union Conference in December 1903. It gave a new impetus to Oriya Movement. Das' tour to different parts of Orissa. His visit to England in 1907.
- Lord Curzon's support to the Oriyas. People of Britain also supported them. Formation of Bihar–Orissa province in 1912. He brought out an English weekly Oriya in 1917. His memorandum to Montague–Chelmsford.
- Das's support to the Congress through the Utkial Sabha, even though the former did not support the cause of Oriyas.
- Nationalism: he never opposed the Congress. He was never narrow and parochial. He was a patriot, a nationalist. India, to him, was the body and Orissa was a limb. Development of the limb would be the development of the body. He wanted that the Oriyas should be united first and then fight for the country.
- He was challenged by Gopabandhu Das. To the latter, freedom of the country was more important than the unification of Orissa. Madhusudan Das became a Minister in 1921 of the Orissa–Bihar Council.
- Economic and social views, and reforms: he drew the attention of the Government to the problems of Orissa and the Oriyas. He met high British officials. His demands were: the need of permanent settlement, land for the tillers, not for the Zamindars, abolition of Zamindari system, rapid industrialization of Orissa. To save native artistic crafts, he set up Orissa Art Wares in 1897. It was closed down. Criticized monopoly of salt by the Government. Protested against it in Allahabad Session (1888). His memorandum to Richard Thomson.
- Utkal Union Sammilani: held sixteen Annual Sessions (1903–1920). Emphasis on education, encouraged students to go outside the state, promotion of crafts, cottage industry, spinning, agriculture, etc. Abolition of poverty was his one item agenda. He set up schools in different parts of Orissa to promote education. Education to prisoners. His importance to physical education. His role in language agitation in Orissa.
- In 1908, he set up a girls' school at Cuttack. His intention was to promote women education. In 1921, he moved a resolution on extending franchise to women in the Orissa–Bihar Council. He was in favour of women's empowerment and emancipation.

- A legislator: elected to Bengal Council in March 1896. An M.L.C. up to 1897, from 1900 to 1902, and from 1908 to 1909. Elected to Bihar–Orissa Council. Relinquished his post in 1923. He was appointed as a Member of the Council of Ministers in 1921. A Minister of the Local Self-Government. His important measures were "recall" and representation of depressed classes in the Local Self-Government institutions.
- Das did not draw any salary as Minister for Local Self-Government. He wanted to earn a livelihood for himself from law, by practising it. Governor did not accept his proposal. He, therefore, resigned from his office in 1923. A member of the Imperial Council.
- His association with moderate leaders of the Congress. He was against the use of violent means to achieve the goal.
- During the First World War, he supported the British Government.
- Religion: he had faith in the essence of all religions. They provided peace. A Christian. Even then he had love and admiration for Hinduism. But unhappy with its rituals and blind beliefs. Stood for unity of religions.
- Democracy: he represented hopes and aspirations of the people. Against the bureaucrats. For popular administration. Local problems to be solved by the local people. Local government bodies to be true representative bodies of the people.
- Estimate: well known for his wisdom and knowledge. A genius and a multifaceted personality. His only mission was to serve his country and the poor. Never compromised his ideology and principles.
- He was happy to sacrifice everything to achieve his goals; the unification of Orissa and the freedom of the country.
- His death in 1934: a great loss to the country, the nation and the state.
- He was a man of virtues, a great intellect, the life and soul of Orissa, the strength of the Oriyas.
- He was popularly known as 'Madhu Babu' or 'Madhu Barrister'. He was the pride of Orissa.

14

Jayaprakash Narayan (1902–1979)

INTRODUCTION

Victor Hugo once very rightly said: sky is beautiful, ocean is still more beautiful, but soul is the most beautiful. Such a soul was Jayaprakash Narayan. An individual is remembered for his deeds, for his service to the mankind, for his sacrifices and sufferings, and for his dedication and devotion to the noble cause for which he fights with a strong determination and iron will. Such an individual was Jayaprakash, popularly known as J.P. People are born here, live for some time and then leave this world. Hardly they are, except a few, remembered by the posterity, the future generation. After their death, they are consigned to flames or buried and forgotten forever. They become history and are imprisoned in its pages. But J.P. was an exception. Simple and straightforward, he carved out a niche for himself in the hearts of millions and millions of the people who had profound respect, love and admiration for him. An embodiment of virtues, he was a towering personality who liberated India from the "Congress dictatorship" to which Indians were subject during the national emergency proclaimed in India in June 1975. Gandhi freed us from the clutches of British imperialism. But J.P. set us free from the 'Congress bondage'. A humanist and lover of mankind, he was compassionate, and always cherished that people should live in peace, harmony and lead a life of bliss and happiness. He stood for justice, equality and freedom, and symbolized truth, courage and wisdom. He was one of the greatest political thinkers that India produced in the twentieth century.

EARLY LIFE

Born on 11 October 1902 to Harsoodayal and Phool Rani as their fourth child, J.P. led an eventful life in his small village known as Sitabdaria bordering Bihar and Uttar Pradesh. The village was then in Chapra district of Bihar. Now it is a part of the Ballia district of Uttar Pradesh. As his father was a government officer, he always wanted that his sons should also join government service. J.P. was admitted into the village school in Sitabdaria. He left for Patna for higher studies. As a student, he was very brilliant and distinguished himself from others by his sharp intelligence, mature expression and articulation.

Life in school at Patna shaped his future political career. As a student, he came in contact with national activities and national leaders. He was closely associated with Saraswati Bhawan which was frequented by eminent political leaders. He began to think about national problems from an early age. However, he spent most of his time in studies. During his student days, he was daring, dashing, courageous and disciplined. He could even defy the order of his Headmaster. Once the English Headmaster fixed an examination on the day of 'Rakhaee Purnima', not knowing that it was an important day for the Hindus. The Hindu students could not protest against this order out of fear. But Jayaprakash and five other good students did not turn up to the examination hall. The very next day they were asked by the Headmaster to explain their misconduct. Jayaprakash gave him a befitting reply without fear. And for this, he was severely beaten by the Headmaster.

The years between 1914 and 1922 were of much significance for Jayaprakash because of certain memorable events and developments. Mahatma Gandhi returned from South Africa to India in 1915. In that distant land, he was quite successful in protesting against the authorities for their apartheid policy through non-violent means of Satyagraha and non-cooperation. He wanted to repeat the same experiment in his own country. This made him extremely popular as more and more people were drawn towards him. Jayaprakash was not an exception. Gandhi became his inspiration and exerted a tremendous influence on him. Like Gandhi, Jayaprakash also led a simple life dedicated to the cause of the nation.

MARRIAGE

His marriage to Prabhawati Devi at a tender age of eighteen was certainly a significant event for him. It was through his father-in-law Brij Kishore Babu, a well-known nationalist leader of Bihar, he came in contact with some important political leaders of Bihar.

NON-COOPERATION MOVEMENT (1921)

The year 1921 witnessed the launching of the Non-cooperation Movement by Mahatma Gandhi. All national leaders participated in it to oppose the British rule in India. Gandhi and Nehru visited Patna and gave a clarion call to people to participate in the Movement and make it a grand success. Jayaprakash was to sit for his F.A. Examination. Inspired by Gandhi and Nehru he gave up his studies to join the Movement. This was the third significant event in his life. In a way it was the starting point of his long, successful and significant political career. Gandhi called off the Movement because of mob violence and the murder of 22 policemen. Following this event, Jayaprakash continued his studies and passed his F.A. Examination in first class in 1922.

A MARXIST

Jayaprakash went to the U.S. in 1922 for his higher studies. He stayed there for six years without getting any financial support from his family. As a result, he faced a lot of difficulties in maintaining himself and pursuing his higher studies. It was because of this he was forced to change a number of universities, work at different places for his maintenance. He enrolled himself as a student in the universities of California, Iowa, Chicago, Wisconsin and Ohio. Popular among his friends, he developed his contact with some Marxists of America and East Europe. He took a great fancy in Marxism. Influenced by the writings of Anatole France, Ibsen, Gorky and M.N. Roy, he became attracted more and more towards the Marxism and evinced a keen interest in the activities of the America Communist Party. Slowly and gradually his basic interest in science began to decline and he started taking more interest in social science. He deeply felt that India should be developed socially and economically. The problem of socio-economic development could be solved with the help of social sciences. With this view in mind he joined Ohio University so that he could study social sciences. He completed his M.A. in Sociology and wrote a thesis on social variations.

As he had a strong desire to know about the working of the socialist theory, he was advised by his Marxist friends to visit Russia. But he could not do so as he had to return to India in 1929 because of sudden illness of his mother. By that time he had already become a true Marxist, a Marxist by conviction.

He sincerely felt that Marxism would be the best instrument to solve India's socio-economic and political problems and it stood for equality, brotherhood and freedom from all kinds of exploitation. M.N. Roy's interpretation, explanation and exposition of Marxism influenced him very much. Like Karl Marx, he also believed that violence and class-conflict were inevitable phenomena in an industrial or capitalist society. He strongly opposed the system of Parliamentary democracy and the institution of ballot box and party system as they made a mockery of democracy. He stood for nationalization of industries and wanted abolition of landlordism and all sorts of exploitation. He was in favour of distribution of lands among the poor peasants.

He was so much influenced by Marxism that he interpreted the word "freedom" in the light of Marxian philosophy. To him, it meant freedom for all — even the lowliest — and this freedom must include freedom from exploitation, from hunger, from poverty. Like Marx, he never believed that reason and persuasion could bring about any change in socio-economic and political conditions. He had a strong aversion for capitalism as the capitalists were an exploiting class.

DIFFERENCES WITH COMMUNISTS AND THE CONGRESS

No doubt, Jayaprakash was a Marxist. But, he never supported Russian Communism. Rather he hated the Russian Bolshevik Party. With a deep moral revulsion against the state, he strongly condemned the Indian Communists as they made themselves laughing-stocks in India and elsewhere by acting as puppets of Moscow.

During 1930s, he expressed his resentment against the Gandhian techniques since they could not overthrow the British imperialism. He, therefore, advocated revolutionary programmes with radical measures. He was so much against the reactionary leadership of the Congress that he preferred to sail along with communists. He felt that this unity could build up Socialist Movement and unite progressive people in the country against the leadership of the Congress. In other words, he favoured the United Popular Front with the communists to challenge the Congress.

The Congress in its Calcutta Session passed a resolution in favour of full 'dominion status' for India. But in December 1929 Gandhi failed to persuade Lord Irwin to accept and implement it. Soon after Gandhi launched his Salt Satyagraha, the whole nation was awakened, all the people were united by joining the Movement in a large scale. But, surprisingly enough, the Indian communists remained away from the Movement. Unfortunately, they denounced the National Movement as bourgeois and Gandhi as agent of Indian bourgeois. They were guided by the policy laid down by the Third Communist International which was then under the complete control of Stalin. They were dancing to the tunes of Moscow as they were loyal first to Russia and only then to anybody else. When they talked of United Front, it was always a ruse and at best a temporary policy dictated by the exigencies of situation. Their only goal was the Monolithic Communist Rule. They could never think of sharing power with anyone, except as a make-shift with convenient stages. This made Jayaprakash indifferent towards the communists as they were under the influence of Stalin, and drifting away from Marxism. It was because of the policy that the comintern had been following since 1928 the Socialist Movements throughout the world received a severe setback. He, therefore, moved away ideologically from the Soviet Russia and the communists. His hatred for the communists forced him to join the National Movement under the leadership of Mahatma Gandhi. But soon he was disappointed with the Congress as he felt that it could not fight the British imperialism in any manner, nor could it provide a real socialist programme to the Indians. Therefore, he formed the Congress Socialist Party with the help of other disappointed and disillusioned Congressmen having socialist leanings. His party made a significant contribution to the shaping of socio-economic content of the Congress policy. It also gave a new impetus to the freedom struggle.

A SOCIALIST

Jayaprakash, a pioneer of the Socialist Movement and its most renowned theoretician, rightly observed that socialism became an inescapable destination as it ensured and promised social good. Inequality and exploitation, to him, were the most dangerous problems that threatened the stability of a social system. No doubt, every individual has a strong inherent and natural urge to be free and enjoy freedom in every sphere of human life. It is a necessity for one's growth, development and fulfilment of his desires. Without it, he is a slave. Therefore, the state should ensure freedom to all its individuals. But, unfortunately, the poor people do not have that freedom because of glaring inequality between them and the rich class. In other words, freedom is enjoyed by a few individuals who are rich and prosperous. In a society afflicted by inequality, freedom becomes a licence for those who possess it for exploiting the poor, needy and downtrodden. Inequality always proves to be antithetic to freedom and cannot ensure it to one and all.

Jayaprakash argued that socialism ensured equality and equality guaranteed freedom. It wanted to bring to an end exploitation of man, by man, as it was against capitalism, feudalism, private ownership of wealth, etc. It stood for collective ownership of society's wealth. Jayaprakash believed that it was the private property which helped the rich to exploit the poor. But, in socialism, inequality disappeared along with exploitation. Under it, all wealth was held in common and shared equitably. People no longer worked for others. But they worked collectively for their own consumption. Socialism was, thus, a social situation in which each shared his freedom with all.

Jayaprakash published in 1934 a book entitled *Why Socialism.* In this book, he highly praised Joseph Stalin as world-leader of the present Socialist Movement. He believed that in Russia a new social order had emerged and it was free from any kind of exploitation. To him, Russia symbolized economic success. He highly appreciated R. Palme Dutt's work "Fascism and Social Revolution". He not only ridiculed but also denounced Gandhi's theory of trusteeship and his vision of Ram Rajya where the interest of both rich and poor would be protected.

Jayaprakash, a great socialist, an intellectual with a keen insight into the economic forces and factors that influenced and shaped the course of Indian politics, was considered by Gandhi as the greatest Indian authority on socialism. Influenced by British and American socialists, he considered socialism as a complete theory of socio-economic reconstruction and much more than a theory of personal utopian–idealistic ethics. Rejecting the biological or racial inequality of man, he never accepted, unlike Aristotle, the theory or institution of slavery. At the same time, he did not believe the theory of absolute equality among men.

Attributing glaring inequality to the disproportionate ownership and control of the means of production, he urged that all the constraints that prevent economic equality must be removed. He considered socialism to be a theory of planning seeking to bring an all-round development of the society and a harmonious and balanced growth of the whole community. The Fifteen-Point Programme of his socialism was as follows:

1. Empowerment of the people.
2. The state should plan and control its economy.
3. Nationalization of key industries and banks. Insurance should be controlled by the State.
4. State's monopoly over the foreign trade.
5. Cooperatives to be set up in the private sector for production, distribution and credit.
6. Abolition of feudalism and landlordism.
7. Distribution of lands among the poor peasants and farmers.
8. Promotion and encouragement of cooperatives and collective farming.
9. Loans given to poor peasants and workers are to be written-off.
10. Right to work or maintenance is to be guaranteed by the State.
11. 'To everyone according to his needs and from everyone according to his capacity' should be the basis of production and distribution of economic goods.
12. Adult franchise on a functional basis.
13. No discrimination on the basis of caste, community and religion.
14. No discrimination on the basis of sex.
15. Repudiation of the debts of India.

Jayaprakash was so much addicted to socialism that he made it the sole basis of India's freedom and independence. Political and economic organizations of the state should be influenced by the principles of social justice and economic freedom. Development and reorganization of the villages should be made self-governing units and as far as possible self-sufficient. The land should belong to the tillers but not to the Zamindars.

But how could socialism be brought about? Reformism, to him, was not the way to socialism. It was the state which alone could bring about the socialist transformation of society. The first step in this direction would be taking the control of state machinery by socialist leaders. The socialist transformation of social process could be possible only when the community relations were modernized. The state should coordinate this process of society's various community units to bring a harmonious and well-balanced growth of the whole society. The socialist India would have economic and political democracy. Man would neither be a slave of capitalism nor of a party or the state. He would be free and serve the society as this would provide him employment and the means of livelihood but, within limits, he would be free to choose his vocation and situation in life to express his opinion and to rise to his full moral stature with the given opportunities.

A SOCIALIST DEMOCRAT

Jayaprakash believed that Marxism or Leninism would never ensure or expedite social revolution or protect and promote socialism. He had a strong conviction that if changes could be brought about in a society through peaceful means, it would be futile and counter-productive to adopt violent means. He also realized that socialism and freedom went together, one supplementing another. Rejecting the theory of dictatorship of proletariat, he strongly argued that power should not be captured through forcible means. It would be still worse if it was done by majority as it happened in Russia.

The Soviet experience made it clear to Jayaprakash that elimination of capitalism and nationalization of industries might not give rise to socialism. In Soviet Russia, a new social order emerged when the communists came to power. Unfortunately, there existed inequality, absence of freedom, injustice, exploitation and the growth of a new class of bureaucratic rulers. All these were against socialism.

He argued that violent overthrow of capitalism would breed contempt, hatred and cruelty. After a careful analysis, he concluded that dictatorship of proletariat would not be a means to transform capitalism into socialism. Social changes must come through conscious revolution involving the masses instead of violent revolution. Socialism did not mean negation of capitalism nor should it pass through dictatorship. Centralization of political and economic power would be an antithetic to socialism.

Even though he revised his views about Marxism, he still considered it to be the most perfect instrument of social change. He was terribly agitated when the Soviet Russia was attacked by Germany in 1942. After his escape from Hazaribagh Jail, he tried to organize Guerrilla Movement against the British rule. He was imprisoned again in September 1943. And this sealed the fate of the underground Movement. He was in jail up to 1946. His imprisonment changed his perception about Marxism as he developed a strong aversion towards it and came out of the jail as a convinced social democrat.

In 1948, he was no more an orthodox Marxist. He moved very close towards Gandhi and appreciated his socio-economic and political ideas. He rejected the theory that the state was the only instrument of social good. If it was considered so, a regimented society would emerge to curb freedom of the people. They would be mere cogs in a human machine. Such a society was denounced by him. This indicated his complete faith in democratic socialism. He was convinced that socialism would not mean anything without democracy. In the Patna Session of the Congress in 1949, he said that Gandhiji tried to evolve a new method of social change. He preached a new set of values to lift up our public life from the morass in which it had fallen. This should not be criticized as surrender to Gandhism as there was nothing wrong in it. To him, democratic socialism should be one's mission in his life, the philosophy of his life. It did not merely mean solving the problem of bread and butter.

In 1950, at Madras Session of the Socialist Party he made an emphatic statement on the theory of democratic socialism. To him, socialism was not merely anti-capitalism, nor statism. Nationalization of industries and collectivisation of agriculture were important aspects of socialist economy, but in themselves they were not socialism. The aim of Socialist Movement was not mere overthrow of capitalist order and establishment of a party dictatorship, but the creation of a society of free and equal people, a society based on certain values of human and social life, values which could never be sacrificed in the name of theory of the party line.

A Socialist State should seek to have certain basic values. Decentralization of political and economic power was a must to ensure socialism. The goal of a Socialist State could be and should be achieved through democratic means. Thus, he made a synthesis between Marxism and Gandhism.

SARVODAYA

Vinoba Bhave's Bhoodan Movement and Sarvodaya left a deep impact on Jayaprakash. He was convinced that the Movement would bring a lasting solution to the land problem in India. It was a kind of revolution without any reference to power. In 1954, the Sarvodaya workers had their annual conference at Bodh Gaya. Addressing the Conference, he declared that he would devote himself to the cause of the Bhoodan and Sarvodaya. Disappointed with the failure of the Socialist Party in 1952 General Election to the Lok Sabha and disgusted with the way he was looked upon with suspicion by some of his friends when he had negotiations with Nehru, he gave up practical politics. He said, Bhoodan was the beginning of all-round social and human revolution; human because it aimed at changing man along with society. It was an application of a general scale of Mahatma Gandhi's non-violent technique of revolution. Bhoodan was a great mass movement of conversion and the creation of a new climate of thought and values of life.

Jayaprakash was very much convinced that Sarvodaya as a means of achieving the end was more effective and original than the traditional socialist methods. This would certainly bring the social revolution. Emphasizing the importance of Sarvodaya, he said in 1957 that socialism as understood today could not help the mankind in achieving the sublime goals of freedom, equality, brotherhood and peace. But it certainly promised them that it would take them closer to these goals than any other competing social philosophy. But unless it was transformed into Sarvodaya, it might not achieve these goals. He was very much confident that socialism would play a key role in future. He decided to withdraw from Praja Socialist Party and power politics not out of disgust or of any personal frustration, but because it became clear to him that politics could not deliver the goods, the goods being the same old goals of equality, freedom, brotherhood, peace, etc.

It was because of Sarvodaya's inspiration, influence and impact on him, he dedicated his whole time to its cause. At Sakhodevra, a village bordering Gaya and Munghir in the State of Bihar, he founded an ashram which became the centre of his activities. Though he led a simple life in his ashram totally devoted himself to the cause of people and the society, he was criticized by self-centred, corrupt and dishonest politicians. So this was the reward he got from his so-called friends and political parties.

India lives in villages. But, unfortunately, the towns and cities have received more attention. Efforts have been made to promote and develop them. J.P. wanted that villages should get proper attention from the government. He believed that Sarvodaya would be an effective means of social transformation.

Modern science made our life more comfortable by providing all sorts of amenities. But, at the same time, people had to pay a heavy price for it. Reduced to the status of a machine, their life became purely mechanical. As they had become materialists seeking after external comforts and luxuries, they had forgotten their "own-self", their true mission, their goals and the purpose of their life. They were no more spiritual. As a result, they lost their mental peace. No more they led an integrated life. No doubt, communism and socialism emphasized the social and economic aspects of human life. But, at the same time, they neglected its ethical and spiritual aspects. While one aspect of human life had been overemphasized, another vital aspect completely ignored. Jayaprakash touched every aspect of human life as he wanted an integrated development of human life. Taking the modern man to task for his lust and greed, he very rightly observed:

> In such a restless society violence and war would be endemic. All values of life would be subordinated to this over-mastering desire for more. Religion, art, philosophy, science would have to serve that one aim of life: to have more and still more. Equality, freedom, brotherhood would all be in danger of being submerged in a universal flood of materialism.

Hence, steps should be taken to control bodily appetites of man. He should have his moral development. All the human qualities should blossom in him. Socialism sought to achieve this through Sarvodaya.

SELF-RULE AND SARVODAYA

Jayaprakash was a strong critic of parliamentary democracy and party politics as almost all the political parties, to him, were power-seekers. Their only aim was to capture power through dubious means. During the time of elections, they, gave false assurances to the people. Double-standards, dishonesty, treachery, fraud, force, etc. were the instruments that brought them to power. Politics failed to deliver the goods, the goods being the great ideals of equality, freedom, brotherhood and peace. The present democracy and party system failed miserably to develop the strength and initiatives of the people and to help them in establishing their self-rule and manage their affairs themselves.

Jayaprakash felt that the present flaws and deficiencies found in the body politic could be removed if the people's self-rule was established. Parliamentary democracy was to be replaced by something new, something different. The process must start from the bottom. A programme of self-rule and self-management must be started and implemented in a non-partisan manner. It was with this view in mind, Gandhi wanted to abolish the Congress as a party after independence and turn it into a non-partisan Lok Sevak Sangh. Vinoba Bhave had also such a mission to undertake. Jayaprakash also felt that the state was becoming an instrument of exploitation by suppressing individual freedom. State, to him, was a Leviathan trampling down the human freedom. Then what was the remedy for such a situation? Jayaprakash found an answer in Sarvodaya. The remedy lay in creating and developing a socialist living through the revolutionary endeavour of the people rather than establishing socialism with the help of the state. In other words, the remedy was to establish people's socialism rather than the state socialism.

Sarvodaya, to Jayaprakash, was people's socialism. He advised the political parties to enforce people's voluntary socialism. Power and party would not have any place in such kind of people's socialism. There should be a band of dedicated workers who must teach and train the people in the art of self-reliance and self-control.

The present society, mostly run by oligarchs and bureaucrats, should be changed and transformed. The prevailing conditions did not allow the people to live like brothers. Unfortunately, the socialists also in the name of science, production, efficiency, standard of living and other "hallowed shibboleths", accepted this "whole Frankenstein of a society" — lock, stock and barrel, and hope, by adding public ownership to it, to make it socialist. Such a society could not adopt socialism. Sarvodaya ensured a right socialist society.

TOTAL REVOLUTION

There should be a revolution to make the people empowered. It is evident from history that revolutions that occurred at different times in different places to liberate the people from bondages were not fully successful as power did not percolate to the grass-roots level. People could not become their real masters. The real power was exercised by their so-called representatives and bureaucrats. There were revolutions: governments were overthrown and the power-structure was changed, the relationship between the rulers and the ruled underwent drastic change. But though the structure of the elites changed, the real power could not be enjoyed and experienced by the people as they were oppressed by their 'rulers'. They had least significance in the political system as they did not have any role to play in it except casting their votes on the day of polls.

If his integral scheme of sevenfold revolutions scheme would really be implemented, it would certainly promote an integrated development of the individuals, as well as cultural creativity, moral autonomy and spiritual liberation. In his book *From Behind the Bars in Independent India*, he said that total revolution was a combination of seven revolutions — social, economic, political, cultural, ideological or intellectual, educational and spiritual.

Total revolution as a concept has been interpreted differently. Authoritarians mean it as a total planning and total war, the radicals as integral humanism, the physicists talk of field theory and law of complementarity. It, however, means an integral transformation of man and society. It is a society which makes everyone's life rosier without allowing him to have hangovers of any sort. It is an ideal and perfect society which ensures to one and all a balanced and harmonious growth and which is free from all evils. In such a society, there would be no discrimination, harassment, deprivation, humiliation, suffering, poverty, inequality, injustice, unemployment, untouchability, social segregation, economic exploitation, political violence, corruption, nepotism, bribery, suppression of human rights, enjoyment of special privileges, etc.

Jayaprakash strongly argued that political life should remain pure. Political actors should declare their assets periodically, not hold any office for more than two terms, be "called back" (recall) by the people when they lost the latter's confidence and faith. They should not be arbitrary, arrogant, dishonest and must try to operate within the legal and constitutional limits. He asked the police and army not to obey the unconstitutional and illegal orders of the authorities.

Educational institutions should not be polluted by nasty politics and power-hungry politicians. Primary education should be made compulsory. Universities should be the centres of learning, research, planning and training.

The society should be free from crimes; science humanized, virtues taught and cooperation encouraged. People should imbibe aesthetic and ethical values of life and be enriched with moral ideals and standards. Total revolution aimed at reinforcing such motivational determinants.

TECHNIQUES OF TOTAL REVOLUTION

The techniques of total revolution were as follows: persuasion, non-cooperation, civil resistance and civil disobedience, strikes, direct takeover and management and running of enterprises, mobilization of youth and student power, counter bureaucratic pressures and routinization.

AN ESTIMATE

A dedicated leader of the Indian freedom struggle, he was influenced by *Bhagwat Gita*, Swami Satyadeva, natural sciences, the Marxists like Abram Landy, the writings of M.N. Roy and Gandhi. A nationalist and socialist (1929–1953), he laid stress on radical ideological programmes for the socio-economic reconstruction of the society. Unhappy with the developments in the Soviet Communism, he renounced Marxism and embraced the philosophy of Sarvodaya.

A freedom fighter, a national hero, a crusader, a pragmatist, a socialist, a political thinker, Jayaprakash was popularly known as 'Loknayak'. His writings from 1954 to 1977 clearly indicated that he was thoroughly aware of socio-economic problems of the country. His dominant theme was to emancipate the people from all sorts of bondages.

His philosophy addressed to both: the ruthless competitive individualism and the aggressive totalitarianism. He emphasized 'Lokniti' (people's ethics) and preferred it to 'Rajniti' (government's rules). Opposed to parliamentary democracy, party system and ballot box, he stood for something new that would give a new lease of life to the people and for a co-responsible sharing community.

A great mass leader, he favoured a world community as this could be a challenge to "organized militarism, racial ethnocentrism, imperialistic virulence and totalitarian ravages". The community should be based on a moral foundation. His involvement in freedom struggle took a heavy toll of his life. He was the architect of Indian Socialist Movement, its great leader. He strived his best to bring about a solution to all the problems of the country. He championed the cause of liberation of Tibet and Bangladesh.

A great revolutionary and a profound humanist, the total revolution phase of Jayaprakash's life (1974–1979) revealed the wide and vast dimensions of his charismatic personality. He appeared as a strong and powerful leader to rekindle the energies of the youth for India's Second Freedom Movement and economic reconstruction. He dominated the political scene as a mighty colossus.

One of the greatest defenders of democracy, he had to pass through severe ordeals when he was thrown into prison in 1975. He had to pay a heavy price for his efforts to liberate India from the clutches of totalitarianism. His death in 1979 was very sad, premature and tragic. He is no more with us. But his revolutionary fervour, sacrifice, simplicity, self-amalgamation, noble idealism, etc, made him immortal and he will continue to inspire the future patriots and intellectuals of India for all times to come.

POINTS TO REMEMBER

- Simple, straightforward, an embodiment of virtues, a towering personality, J.P. liberated Indians from "Congress dictatorship". A humanist, a lover of mankind, he was compassionate and fought for truth, liberty and justice. He was one of the greatest political thinkers of the twentieth century.
- He was born on 11 October 1902. His father was a government officer. Left for Patna for higher studies. Here he came in contact with national leaders. He thought about the national problems at an early age.

- He was brave, courageous and outspoken. Once he opposed and defied the Headmaster. Gandhi was his inspiration and strength.
- Marriage: married to Prabhawati Devi at the age of 18. His contact with leaders through his father-in-law Brij Kishore.
- Non-cooperation Movement: launched in 1921 by Gandhi. J.P. gave up his studies, did not appear at the F.A. Examination and joined the Movement. He passed the F.A. Examination in 1922.
- A Marxist: he left for the U.S. in 1922. Stayed there up to 1928. No help from his parents. Faced a lot of difficulties. Changed universities. His contact with Marxists. His liking for Marxism. His interest in the activities of the America Communist Party.
- His interest in science declined. He took more interest in social science as it would solve India's socio-economic problems.
- He passed M.A. in Sociology. Wanted to visit Russia to study socialism and its practice there. Returned to India in 1929 as a true Marxist. Tremendous influence of Marxism on him.
- Differences with Marxists: though he was a Marxist, he never supported Russian Communism. He condemned the Indian communists as they were the puppets of Soviet Russia. In 1930, he opposed Gandhi's techniques. Favoured revolutionary methods. He preferred communists to the Congress leaders including Gandhi. Congress demand — dominion status — not accepted by Lord Irwin.
- Gandhi's Salt Satyagraha Movement: Communists did not cooperate with Gandhi. They condemned him by calling him a "bourgeois". They were controlled by Stalin. Their only goal was the Monolithic Communist Rule.
- He formed the Congress Socialist Party. He was disappointed with both the Communists and the Congress.
- A socialist: socialism was the final destination.
- Freedom: a licence to exploit the poor. Inequality an antithetic to freedom. Socialism ensured equality and equality guaranteed freedom. Stalin, to him, was the greatest leader and Russia symbolized economic success. Socialism would change the image of the world and remove inequality and exploitations. Gave a Fifteen-Point Programme of socialism.
- Socialism was made the sole basis of India's freedom. Social justice and economic freedom should influence political and economic organizations. Villages to be made self-governing and self-sufficient units. Land to belong to the tillers.
- India: a Socialist State with economic and political democracy.
- A socialist democrat: revolution was not the answer to the existing problems. Power not to be captured by violent means.

- He was unhappy with what happened in Russia. Capitalism should not be forcibly thrown away. Marxism, to him, would be the most perfect instrument of social change. His escape from Hazaribag jail. Arrested again in 1943 and in jail up to 1946. Developed hatred against Marxism.
- He moved away from Marx to Gandhi. Democratic socialism should be one's mission, a way of life, but not to be a mere means to solve the problem of bread and butter.
- In a Socialist State, there should be decentralization of political and economic power. Its goal to be achieved through democratic means. J.P.'s synthesis between Marxism and Gandhism.
- Sarvodaya: its tremendous impact upon J.P. It would be a lasting solution to land problems. His disappointment with 1952 general election results. Bhoodan — a great mass Movement.
- Sarvodaya: to bring a revolution, more effective than socialism and socialist methods in achieving the goal. Socialism to be transformed into the Sarvodaya. Left the P.S.P.
- He set up an Ashram at Sakhodevra and led a simple life. In spite of his dedication, he was criticized by corrupt politicians.
- India lives in villages. Steps to be taken for their development. They are to be made self-sufficient. This can be possible through Sarvodaya.
- Impact of matter and materialism on human life: over the years, he became a seeker after the matter that gave him maximum pleasure. Spiritual aspect of life was completely ignored. J.P. favoured an integrated development of human life.
- Every one led a restless life in modern society as he wanted to have more and more of everything that provided him pleasure, prosperity and happiness.
- Self-rule and Sarvodaya: J.P. — a critic of Parliamentary democracy. Political parties were power-seekers.
- To improve the political system, self-rule be restored. People's socialism, not state socialism, be the goal. Sarvodaya was people's socialism. Here power and party had no place.
- Total revolution: to make the people empowered. Revolutions took place in different places at different times. They were incomplete and imperfect as power did not flow or percolate into the hands of the people at grass-roots level.
- Total revolution is a total planning and total war. It is an integral transformation of man and society. It is interpreted differently. It ensures a society free from evils and assures of a balanced growth.
- Political life to remain pure, leaders to declare their assets periodically, not to hold any office for more than two terms, be "recalled", police and

army not to obey illegal and unconstitutional orders of the government. No politics in educational institutions. Primary education be made compulsory.

- Techniques of total revolution: persuasion, non-cooperation, civil resistance, etc.
- A dedicated worker, a freedom fighter, a nationalist, a socialist, he strived for socio-economic uplift of the society. Popularly known as Lok Nayak. Preferred "Lokniti to Rajniti". He was opposed to ballot box, party systems, parliamentary democracy. Arrested in 1975. Died in 1979. A tremendous source of encouragement and inspiration to the future generations of India.

15

Gopabandhu Das (1877–1928)

INTRODUCTION

An ardent nationalist, a profound humanist, an astute politician, an eminent journalist, a dedicated worker, a paragon of virtues, Gopabandhu Das was the Father of the National Movement in Orissa. He was its torchbearer, inspiration, guide and soul. Popularly known as the 'Utkalmani' (Gem of Orissa), he was a true representative of Gandhi in Orissa. That one could be so complete, so noble, so perfect, so good, so self-sacrificing — one might not believe this unless one made an objective analysis of his life and achievements. A patriot among patriots, a man of action, an institution by himself, he was perhaps the most outstanding personality of Orissa in the twentieth century. He could be compared with Madhusudan Das. Both of them could be said to be the founders and architects of modern Orissa and rendered significant contributions to its development.

EARLY LIFE

Gopabandhu was born on 9 October 1877 in Suando, a small village in Puri district of Orissa. His father was Daitari Das. His mother, Swarnamayee Devi, passed away a few days after his birth. He grew under the tender influence of his widowed aunt Kamla Devi. She shaped his life to a great extent. Quite at an early age he started composing poems and contributed articles and poems to literary magazines.

Gopabandhu passed his B.A. Examination in 1904 from Ravenshaw College, Cuttack. In 1906, he became a law graduate from Calcutta University. Working as a Legal Assistant to Madhusudan Das and Gokulanand Choudhury, he joined the Mayurbhanj State Service as the State Pleader in 1909 and continued to work in the same capacity up to 1912. After the death of Maharaja Sri Ram Chandra Bhanj Deo, he left Mayurbhanj in 1912 and started his legal practice first at Cuttack and then at Puri. Legal practice or profession might have been his livelihood but rendering of selfless service to the society was his life.

MARRIAGE

Quite at an early age of twelve he got married in 1899 when he was a student of Upper Primary School. Early marriage was then the prevailing custom in orthodox families. But he was not destined to lead a happy married life. In 1906, he lost his wife. He was very unfortunate as he lost his mother soon after his birth, his father during his school days, his wife after six years of marriage and his only son when he was reading in college. During this time, he also lost his companion and inspirer Muktear Ram Chandra Das. It is very sad to mention that the news of his success in the Law Examination and his wife's death reached him at the same time. Both his domestic life and student career came to an end when he was quite young.

After the sad and premature demise of his young and charming wife, he politely but firmly declined his friends' and relatives' requests to go for second marriage. He sincerely felt that the institution of marriage and family was one of the greatest obstacles and hindrances to serve the society and people. Madhusudan Das, who did not marry again after his wife's death and dedicated himself to the cause of the people, was his ideal, inspiration.

INFLUENCES

Religion

Religion and scriptures tremendously influenced him. Born in a devout Hindu and an orthodox Brahmin family, he was brought up in such an atmosphere that from an early age he started appreciating Indian culture and civilization. He regularly read Oriya *Bhagabat* of Jagannath Das and the *Bhagabat Gita*. Secular in his approach, he was never a sectarian.

Personalities and Literature

During his school days at Puri, he came in close contact with Muktear Rama Chandra Das, a man of impeccable character and integrity, and unquestioned patriotism. The latter was his political master and source of inspiration. But both of them accepted Pandit Harihar as their ideal.

He was deeply influenced by the works of Edmund Burke, Mazzini and of the utilitarians. Like Burke, he had tremendous love and reverence for the society. He agreed with Mazzini that the nation was divinely ordained and had a mission to accomplish. He shared the utilitarians' strong belief and unbounded faith in human progress and democracy.

Indian philosophers and saints like Vivekananda, Dayananda, Aurobindo and Tilak influenced him very much. The heroic deeds of Mazzini and Garibaldi inspired him a lot.

He evinced a keen interest in the literature, particularly that dealing with revolutions like French and Italian.

Events

Certain events that took place at Puri had a decisive impact upon him when he was quite young and also influenced his political career. Once there was an outbreak of Cholera during the Cart Festival of Lord Jagannath. The administration miserably failed in handling the situation. The disease took a heavy toll of human lives. The Public Health Department was so callous that even it did not remove the dead bodies lying on the roads.

Visibly moved by the situation, Gopabandhu organized a volunteer corps—"Puri Seva Samiti" (Puri Service League) — which rendered yeomen service during the epidemic.

He remained for one year in Calcutta to complete his law course. He was terribly shocked when he saw in his own eyes the wretched and humiliating conditions of the Oriya labourers. He did his best to improve their economic conditions. He encouraged them to form associations as this would empower them. He set up night schools to teach them the rudiments of the Oriya language. He organized them, united them, educated them, and made them aware of their rights and duties. This went a long way in securing for them a position of respectability in Calcutta.

SWADESHI MOVEMENT

During his stay in Calcutta, the Swadeshi Movement was in full swing following the partition of Bengal by Lord Curzon in 1905. Gopabandhu was influenced by this Movement. His contact and acquaintance with revolutionary leaders like Khudiram and Sashibhusan Raychoudhury made him a patriot. Though he hated the terrorism and the terrorists he, however, did not criticize the ideal of terrorism. The Swadeshi Movement enkindled the fire of patriotism in him and developed in him a thirst for national freedom.

A LEGISLATOR

Gopabandhu was initially reluctant to become a legislator. But motivated, goaded and inspired by Madhusudan Das the 'Grand Old Man' of Orissa, he contested the election for the only one seat allotted to Orissa from the Local Bodies Constituency. In 1917, he was elected to the Bihar–Orissa Legislative Council and served the House for four years (1917–1920). The office provided him an opportunity to articulate the grievances of the people of Orissa, who were worst affected by natural calamities like floods and droughts. He demanded for a permanent solution to this problem. He also pressed that the people of coastal Orissa should have freedom to manufacture salt free of duty for their own consumption.

As a legislator, he was very powerful and assertive. Even his worst critics admired him for his eloquent and forceful presentation of views on different subjects. He was solely responsible for the opening of M.A. course in English and LL.B. course in Ravenshaw College. Credit also went to him for his efforts in establishing an Engineering School at Cuttack and a Sanskrit College at Puri.

A JOURNALIST

Gopabandhu was a pioneer in the field of journalism in Orissa. His keen interest in this field dated back to his school days when he felt the importance of a newspaper to highlight the problems of Orissa and inform and educate them on various aspects. It was because of his strong influence and persuasion, Sashibhusan Rath started the first Oriya daily newspaper, *The Asha*, in Berhampur town in 1913. Gopabandhu edited the paper and wrote its editorials till 1919. Meanwhile, he had started publishing a magazine called *The Satyabadi* in 1915. This he did to promote Oriya literature and culture. He, however, felt the need and importance of a newspaper of his own. With this, he hoped to educate and inform the people. His wish, his dream and his desire materialized when *The Samaja* appeared as a weekly from Sakhigopal on 4 October 1919. Choosing a very right and appropriate name for his paper, he dedicated it to the people and through it he served the society. He was its Editor till his last breath. As a journalist, he was superb and unparallel.

Reflecting Gopabandhu's ideology and philosophy, the "Samaj" played a significant role in reconstruction of social order in Orissa and in the freedom struggle of India. It became a daily after his death.

A POET

Gopabandhu was an eminent and celebrated poet. His writings and poems, which reflected his philosophy, included *Abakash Chinta* (Thoughts of Leisure), *Kara Kabita* (Prison Poem), *Go Mahatmya* (Greatness of Cow), *Dharmapada* (The Story of Dharmapada) *Nachiketa Upakhyana* (The Story of Nachiketa), *Bandira Atmakatha'* (Autobiography of a Prisoner). Some of his poems like *Abakash Chinta*, *Kara Kabita*, etc. revealed his philosophy. Through his writings, he brought to limelight the untold miseries and sufferings of the people, exposed the indifference of the authorities towards their problems, pressed for the fulfilment of their demands.

A NATIONALIST

Nationalism: A Psychological Aspect

People living within a defined geographical territory, speaking the same language, professing the same religion, and sharing the same sentiments and culture constitute a nation. Nationalism is a psychological aspect of man and it is deeply rooted in his subconscious mind. It is a common belonging, a common way of life and culture. To Gopabandhu, it is a religion and nation is the manifestation of God on earth. Here he was deeply influenced by Mazzini and others. Thus, he had a religious approach to politics.

PARTICIPATION OF THE YOUTH

He strongly believed that unification of Orissa would be a must. He called upon the people to develop strength, courage and manhood. They had to make themselves prepared to sacrifice whatever was demanded from them. Influenced by Hinduism, he believed that a nation suffered because of its sin. And it had to work hard for its own redemption. Glorifying the past culture and heritage of Orissa, he said that throughout India the Oriyas alone in the past understood that humanism, not parochialism, was the goal of nationalism. Oriya nationalism consisted of universal love and fullness of life. It was not selfish, lifeless or interested in inactive life. It was not based on desire for conquest or bloodshed. Deep religious devotion and full faith in God were its foundation and equality, fraternity and liberty its watchwords.

Gopabandhu urged upon his people to cultivate the virtues of self-reliance, unity, cooperation brotherhood, courage, etc. They must achieve something by dint of their merit and hard work but should not depend on one's mercy and sympathy. He awakened the Oriya nation. For him, it was more important than the movement aiming at the unification of Orissa. Once the Oriyas were awakened, the Oriya nation would exist and grow.

Along with Harihar Das, Nilakantha Dash, Godavarish Mishra and Krupasindhu Mishra, Gopabandhu Das dedicated himself to the cause of Oriya nationalism. They felt that at that time the Oriyas had nothing, either wealth or power, or even collective effort. The Oriya nation existed only in past achievements. He strongly believed that national resurrection could be possible only when the energy of the youth was harnessed and directed in proper channel. He, therefore, gave them a clarion call to come forward, dedicate themselves to the cause of nation, and be prepared to undergo hardships and difficulties, face hazards, and sacrifice anything and everything to rebuild the nation.

SATYABADI SCHOOL

Gopabandhu sincerely felt that education should spread among the people as this promoted their nationalism. In this regard, his first step was to set up a school at Satyabadi in 1909. The aim was to produce young men of strong moral fibre, make them fit to face the battle of life and inculcate into them values of life, pride in their national heritage and love for their nation. Efforts were made at Satyabadi to bring about an all-round development in young men — the future of the country.

Gopabandhu and his friends believed that the social emancipation of people should precede their political freedom. Steps should be taken to remove the social evils from the society as they had polluted it, perverted its people and prevented the development and growth. In the Satyabadi School, students were not discriminated on the basis of caste, wealth, religion, etc. Community living and dining had immediate impact on the society around the school as it seriously challenged orthodoxy and conservatism.

The Satyabadi School was not merely an academic institution set up to fulfil the educational needs of the young men of the time, it did its best to awaken the national consciousness, to rouse the nation to its destiny, and to inspire it with the spirit of freedom.

LANGUAGE

To Gopabandhu, language was at the root of thought and civilization. The unity of language ensured the unity of thought. As such the civilization could not but be one and homogenous. Linguistic unity promoted and fostered national identity. Gopabandhu and other nationalists of Orissa strongly believed that the national existence of the Oriyas depended on the Oriya language. Gopabandhu in his address to Utkal Sammilani asked the Oriyas to remember that the destruction of Oriya language would mean the destruction of Oriya nationalism. The problem of language was now a problem of life and death for the Oriyas.

ORIYA NATIONALISM: NOT PAROCHIAL

Gopabandhu firmly believed that Oriya nationalism was not opposed to Indian supranationalism, rather strong Oriya nationalism helped the growth and realization of the latter. He was never parochial, nor local in his approach. He rather encouraged the Oriyas and urged upon them to join the freedom struggle. He attended for the first time the Calcutta Session of the Indian National Congress in 1906. However, he did not show any interest in the Congress until 1920. The callousness and indifference of the British Government towards Orissa and its problems made him very unhappy. Oriyas were struggling for unification of Orissa. But their demand was completely ignored by the Government and the Congress.

Gopabandhu strongly criticized the Government for its indifference to the famine that took a heavy toll of human lives in Orissa. He was convinced that the Government would not do anything to protect the interests of the Oriyas. Therefore, with all sincerity and seriousness he plunged himself into the freedom movement. He no more wanted that Orissa should remain itself aloof from the freedom movement. He argued that when India marched ahead in the national movement, it was unwise for Orissa to remain aloof; for by such dissociation from the main stream of national struggle, Orissa stood to lose very much.

The Congress at its Nagpur Session in 1920 adopted a resolution for the formation of the provinces on the basis of language. But, unfortunately, in 1903 the Congress at its Madras Session had adopted a resolution that went against the interests of Orissa. The 1903 resolution certainly stood as a barrier between the Congress and the people of Orissa. The 1920 resolution, however, destroyed this barrier. The Utkal Sammilani met under the Presidentship of Gopabandhu at Chakradharpur in 1920 and passed a resolution *inter alia* that the aims and objectives of the Indian National Congress be accepted as those of Utkal Sammilani.

The movement for the unification of Orissa, as a result, suffered a great setback and the same for national independence gained momentum in Orissa. The Oriya Movement was relegated to background.

An ardent nationalist, Gopabandhu denounced national egotism as this would terribly affect national life. Unlike Hegel, he never deified the state. He never believed that "it is the march of God on earth". Having faith in the reality of nation, he stood for a healthy type of nationalism. To him, a nation existed to promote the welfare of the people. Emphasizing the fundamental human values, he said that the full development of nationalism was not possible within a narrow confine. An individual might belong to any nation. It was immaterial whether he belonged to this nation or that nation. There was nothing to be worried as it did not have any bearing on him. He felt that first of all he belonged to God and then to the nation. Since all were the children of God, they were equal and must live like brothers. Equality and fraternity were the fundamental principles which guided our conduct and influenced our behaviour.

Nationalism, to Gopabandhu, was never opposed to universalism, rather it fulfilled it. Nationalism was the river and the universalism was the ocean. The former got submerged in the latter. Therefore, he asked the Oriyas to remember that they were first human beings, next Indians, last of all, Oriyas. Unless they maintained and followed this sequence, the progress of the nation would be at stake. Every individual had a personality of his own and this unfolded only in a social milieu. Similarly, the personality of the Oriya nation could find its full and complete expression in the arena of a broader nationalism and through universal humanism.

SOCIO-ECONOMIC AND POLITICAL IDEAS OF GOPABANDHU

State

To Gopabandhu, the state was positive, not an evil, nor even a necessary evil. A means to an end, it sought to promote the welfare of the people in all aspects — social, economic, political, cultural, ethical, etc. and brought about an integrated development in them. Invested with huge powers, it strived to secure their economic prosperity, moral welfare and cultural advancement. By providing a proper climate, it promoted their political orientations, made them politically conscious, inducted them into political culture and made them conscious of their rights and duties. It helped them to realize their best. It was their protector, their guide. It created a climate so that a nation existed, grew and realized its potentialities.

In the economic sector, the role of the state was quite significant. It should strive to promote and strengthen the economy of the nation. It should see that people should not starve as poverty destroyed their potentialities and killed the prospects of a nation. It should, therefore, have power to regulate the economy of the nation so that people would lead a good life. Gopabandhu stood for a mixed economy. He argued that economic initiative should be undertaken both by the individuals as well as the state. He did not like rigid individualism or extreme collectivism.

The state should encourage the cooperative movement as it played an important role in the economic reconstruction of the society. Besides, it had also an educational impact upon the people. Emphasizing the importance of the cooperative movement in promoting the welfare of the people, Gopabandhu said that cooperative societies would help in containing the individual acquisitiveness and sublimating selfishness in the individual and, in the long run, usher in a society based on economic prosperity, moral trust and social solidarity.

Dharma

Like Gandhi, Gopabandhu also laid much emphasis on Dharma without referring to any religion or sect. It was a way of life, a mode of living. It meant truth, right action, virtue, a code of customs and traditions, righteousness, etc. It had social, religious and political implications. Derived from the Sanskrit word *dhri*, it meant to sustain, to nourish, to uphold, to support, or to keep in balance, etc. As a philosophical concept, it meant a moral order which constituted the foundation of the whole universe. As a political concept, it was comprehensive as it embraced the life of man in its entirety. It regulated human conduct in every sphere of life.

Dharma was the basis of the state in ancient India. The King treated his subjects like his own children and the latter considered him to be their patron and protector. The King and his subjects lived like a family. All of them were duty-conscious. The ruler was prepared to sacrifice everything for the welfare of his subjects. Far from being selfish, egocentric, dishonest and arbitrary, he was always a benevolent ruler and was, in true sense, of the people and for the people, if not by the people. He identified himself with his subjects. The latter had also tremendous love, respect and admiration for the former. The ruler was just like the head of the family. This showed that religion influenced politics. Gopabandhu attributed the present political degeneration to non-observance of Dharma.

Democracy

Gopabandhu was aware that "power corrupts, and absolute power corrupts absolutely". When authority became absolute, people lost their liberties and freedoms. State absolutism grew at the expense of individual's liberty. Believing in the capacity of the people to liberate themselves from all sorts of bondages, he strongly argued that public opinion alone would keep the government under check. No government could deliver its goods unless it enjoyed the moral support of its people. They could be effective and play a decisive role in the political system if they were strong, united and courageous. Like Gandhi, Gopabandhu also believed that India lived in villages. Hence steps should be taken to develop them and make them self-sufficient and self-governing. Villages should be the basis of democracy. The ideal democracy is a federation of more or less self-sufficing and self-governing village communities. Gopabandhu wanted them to function as integral units of the state and contribute to the unity and strength of the nation. Every village should have a panchayat as it had both democratic and educational values. The panchayat system made the people politically conscious, provided them an opportunity to participate in the political process, and inducted them into political culture. Gopabandhu was very much particular about the growth of such institutions. In ancient India, emphasis was laid on duties. Everyone was to perform certain duties towards his family, community, village, society, state, etc. Proper discharge of duties gave him tremendous satisfaction. But degeneration started when emphasis was laid on rights. Gopabandhu criticized the doctrine of rights in spite of his faith in democracy. He argued that the idea of duty is deeply rooted in the Indian tradition whereas the concept of rights had been borrowed from the West. Emphasis on rights would bring disaster and disorder, and disrupt the social process. No doubt, he recognized the importance of certain rights like freedom of speech and expression, of movement, of association, etc. At the same time, he warned that rights would have no significance without corresponding duties.

Socialism

It appeared from his writings that Gopabandhu was a staunch socialist. He was very much pained to see inequality among the people. He was very much distressed to see the deplorable conditions of the workers who worked very hard and endangered their lives, some died while working in factories, some were buried alive while working in the mines, some died of diseases. Certainly, it was the labour of these labourers that created wealth. But they were deprived of it and it was pocketed by the industrialists. Marx found an answer to this problem in his dialectal materialism, class struggle, dictatorship of the proletariat, etc. Gandhi found the same in trusteeship. But Gopabandhu relied upon a divine plan which would help in setting up a classless society. He was not a socialist in the traditional sense as he hardly went through any literature on socialism, nor was he probably aware of any socialist movement taking place in any part of the globe. His socialist ideas were the product of his deep conviction in spiritualism.

Cottage Industry

Like Gandhi, Gopabandhu also made the village economy the key to the economic development of the nation. Village economy should not be subordinated to that of the cities. The latter should not be allowed to grow as centres of economic activity. Setting-up of big industries should be preceded by the revival of cottage industries. For this purpose, model factories should be started in central places in the rural areas and artisans and aspirants for trade should be given proper training. He attributed economic degeneration of the society to the decay of cottage industries.

Untouchability

The Indian society, which was once ideal and value-based, has become corrupt and polluted. It had been ridden with certain evils like inequality, injustice, deprivation, untouchability, child marriage, sati, rigid caste structure, etc. Gopabandhu strongly denounced untouchability. Though he was brought up in an orthodox and conservative Brahmin family, his cook was always a non-Brahmin. In his Satyabadi School, community living and common dining were strictly observed. There was no difference between the Hindus and 'untouchables'.

Mere criticism of untouchability would not solve the problem. Attacking the social order or crying hoarse against it was also not an answer. So deeply it had been rooted that legal measures alone would not also eradicate it. The goal could be achieved only with love and sympathy. Gopabandhu rightly said that the Hindus should change their attitude towards the untouchables. They must accept the latter as their equals and work for their uplift with love. He relied upon divine plan which would unfold itself in future and bring into existence a classless society.

Widow Marriage

Gopabandhu was deeply hurt when he found the society ridden with blind beliefs and superstitions. Widows were not allowed to remarry. Expressing his deep anguish over it, he said that there could not be one principle for men and another for women. This was unnatural; nature could not tolerate it any longer. It would, therefore, be a sin if widow marriage was opposed. Posterity would never forgive us if natural justice was denied to them.

Criticizing the Pandits for their resistance to social changes, Gopabandhu observed that no social evil could be removed by law alone. It was to be strongly resisted by the people themselves. As the proverb went, example was batter than precept. So those leaders who were educated and rich to guide the society must introduce social changes by setting examples so that others would be inspired to follow them.

Education

Gopabandhu said that education could bring social change. Unhappy with the western education as it produced parasites, he argued that education should reflect the national spirit and sentiments, fulfil the national needs and aspirations, and be based on history and culture of the nation and imparted in the regional language. Vocational education and manual activity were highlighted by him. They should be an integral part of education.

Education, Gopabandhu said, developed human potentialities, shaped one's personality and promoted one's dignity, freedom and character. It sought to achieve what was called harmonious development of the individual. It helped him to realize the very essence of life. It was because of this, he said very rightly that it should be widely diffused among the people. Primary education should be made free and compulsory.

It was the duty of the state to make people educated. But it should have no control over education. There should be freedom for education. Education, an instrument of social change, a key to healthy social growth, a force to generate a silent social revolution, the foundation of a just social order free from exploitation, inequality, casteism and communalism, ensures equality, liberty, fraternity and dignity of labour.

Political Obligation

The state existed to promote good life and helped individuals to realize their best selves. Hence their obligation to it. But, to Gopabandhu, no authority — whether political or social — could claim unconditional obedience from the people. Consent of the individuals or public opinion was the basis of the state. It was the moral impulse of the people, their conscience, their conception of 'good' that legitimized the authority and validated its laws. They should be watchful of the activities of the state and its laws. At the same time, he warned them not to be sensuous, not to indulge in self-gratification but to work for the realization of the good of the society. Like other Indian philosophers, he subordinated law and government to the rule of Dharma. He firmly believed in the existence of the moral order independent of and superior to the political authority and affirmed his faith in the moral will of the individual that influenced his political obligation.

Utkal Sammilani

The Utkal Sammilani or Utkal Union Conference was set up in 1903 with a view to fight for the cause of unification of Orissa. Gopabandhu extended his full support and cooperation to this cause. At that time Oriya-speaking areas remained scattered in other provinces like Madras, Bihar, Central Provinces and Berar (now known as Madhya Pradesh), etc. His association with Sammilani began right from its very inception. He attended its first conference held in 1903 at Paralakhemundi as a student leader. His speeches and writings revealed his tremendous love for his state and people. Significantly, he gave a new dimension to the activities of the Sammilani. Earlier, it was considered to be a regional organization with a local or parochial approach. But Gopabandhu broadened its base. He strived hard to integrate regional loyalty with nationalism. His constant efforts resulted in bringing the Indian National Congress to Orissa. He became an active link between these two.

The idea that the Sammilani should be a part of the national movement by integrating itself with the Congress was not palatable to many leaders of the Sammilani. They apprehended that by this the latter would lose its identity, deviate from its path and might not attain its goal, that is, the unification of Orissa. But Gopabandhu strongly denounced those who subscribed to such a view. He asked them to rise above localism or parochialism and join the national stream. It would be undesirable and also harmful if Orissa remained isolated from the national struggle for independence. Asking the people not to be narrow and rise above all pettiness, he urged them to join the national movement, to sail along the current of nationalism, and be prepared to pay a heavy price for it. In the process, they might lose their identity, but need not be worried about it. They should dedicate themselves to the cause of Indian nationalism.

A liberalist, a humanist, he was dedicated to the cause of Orissa as well as of India. He did his best for the merger of the Sammilani with the Congress. But all his efforts ended in dismal failure when he joined along with his friends the Non-cooperation Movement launched by Gandhi in 1921. Following this, the Sammilani ceased to function anymore as a political organization as it relapsed to its earlier stand of non-political character. Thereafter, he snapped all his connections with Sammilani and continued to work as a devoted and dedicated congress worker for the rest of his life.

AN ESTIMATE

A man of indomitable spirit, strong faith and deep commitment; a great apostle of nationalism; an ardent humanist; a lover of mankind, Gopabandhu was a noble soul. A political saint, he symbolized truth. An epitome of knowledge and wisdom, he sacrificed all his comforts and luxuries for the sake of the society. His only mission in his life was to serve the people without any selfish motive. He wept for others when he saw them affected by any disease or natural calamity. Braving cold and spine-chilling winter, incessant rain, hot summer, he served the poor, ignorant, needy, victims, downtrodden, sick and ailing, old and diseased. He symbolized the truth and stood for service. It might not be exaggerated to say that Gopabandhu and dedicated service were synonymous. He strongly believed that work was worship and, therefore, completely identified himself with it. Even now, also, we call someone 'Gopabandhu' if we find him working sincerely for others without any *mala fide* intention.

A reformer, an idealist, an individualist, a revolutionary, a rebel, an altruist, a secular, Gopabandhu mixed politics with religion. To him, end never justified the means. He believed just the opposite: means justified the end. A visionary but, at the same time, a pragmatist, Gopabandhu made himself immortal, never to be forgotten, but always to be remembered with respect, love, admiration and reverence. He will continue to be a perennial source of inspiration for those whose only mission is to work for others without any expectations.

Every individual, by nature, is more or less acquisitive, aggressive, possessive, greedy, lustful, selfish, and egocentric. He is a grabber, but not a giver. But certainly there are some exceptions to this and Gopabandhu was one of them, a flower of mankind.

POINTS TO REMEMBER

- A patriot among patriots, a man of action, a paragon of virtues, Gopabandhu was born in Suando on 9 October 1877. Father: Daitari Das. Mother: Swarnamayee Devi, who died soon after his birth. His aunt Kamala Devi brought him up.
- In 1904, he passed B.A. Examination and Law Examination in 1906. A Legal Assistant to M.S. Das, joined Mayurbhanj State Service as State Pleader in 1909. Returned to Cuttack in 1912, started his legal profession there.
- Marriage: he got married when he was only 12 years old. His wife died in 1906. He lost his father, mother, wife and son when he was quite young. He did not marry again.
- Influence of religions, personalities, literatures, etc. Influence of Muktear Ram Chandra Das, Edmund Burke, Mazzini and of the utilitarians. Influence of Vivekananda, Dayananda, Aurobindo, Tilak and others.
- Events: epidemic like cholera that broke out in Puri, working conditions of the Oriya labourers in Calcutta. He organized them and educated them.
- Inspired and influenced by Swadeshi Movement, by revolutionary leaders like Khudiram.

- A legislator: reluctant to become a legislator. Elected in 1917 to Bihar–Orissa Legislative Council. The Government to help the poor and the destitute.
- A powerful legislator. Responsible for opening of M.A. in English, LL.B. course in Ravenshaw College, and also an Engineering School at Cuttack and a Sanskrit College at Puri.
- A journalist: A pioneer in the field of journalism. His influence on Sashibhusan Rath to start the first Oriya Daily, *the Aasha*, in 1913. Edited it up to 1917. Published a magazine *The Satyabadi* in 1915.
- He started his own newspaper *The Samaja*, a weekly in 1919.
- A poet: an eminent poet. His poems reflected his philosophy, his attitude towards the problems the Oriyas faced.
- A nationalist: nationalism is a psychological concept. It is a common belonging, a common way of life and culture, a religion. A nation is the manifestation of God.
- Youth participation: participation of youth was a must for achieving the goal. He urged upon the people to be virtuous. He awakened them so that they could be united and Orissa unified.
- Satyabadi School: set up a school at Satyabadi in 1909 to make the people educated and virtuous.
- Social emancipation to precede political freedom. To remove social evils from the society. No discrimination in the school.
- Language: played an important role in promoting unity and identity.
- Oriya nationalism was not parochial. Gopabandhu attended the Calcutta Session of the Congress in 1906. Least interest in it as it did not take any steps for the unification of Orissa.
- Government's indifference towards Orissa famine made him unhappy.
- 1920 Nagpur Session of Congress adopted a resolution for the formation of the provinces on the basis of language. The Utkal Sammilani appreciated it and extended full support to the National Congress. He stood for Nationalism and universalism — not opposed to one another.
- State: positive, not an evil, nor even a necessary evil, a means to an end, promoted the welfare of the people and brought an integrated development in them.
- State to control economy for the welfare of the people. He was opposed to rigid individualism and extreme collectivism. Cooperative movement to be encouraged. Its importance in economic reconstruction of the society.
- Dharma: it was the basis of the State in India. The king and subjects lived like a family. King was just like their father and they were his children. Religion influenced politics.

- Democracy: power corrupts. If authority became absolute, people lost their rights. India lived in villages. They should be made self-sufficient and autonomous.
- Concept of right: a western concept, concept of duty — an eastern value.
- Gopabandhu was a staunch socialist. He was distressed to see the dismal and painful conditions of the workers.
- He was not a Marxian socialist. He was highly spiritual. His socialism was influenced by his deep conviction in spiritualism.
- Cottage industry: village economy is the key to economic development of the nation. No overemphasis on urban economy. Revival of cottage industries.
- Untouchability: social values declined. His cook was a non-Brahmin. The problem of untouchability to be handled with sympathy. Law alone could not solve the problem. What was required was the attitudinal change towards the 'untouchables'.
- Widow marriage: he favoured widow remarriage.
- Education: an agent of change. Opposed western education.
- Political obligation: Will, not force, is the basis of the state. The state should be guided by the consent of the individuals or the public opinion. People should shun all their luxuries. People to work for the welfare of the state.
- Utkal Sammilani: set up in 1903 for the unification of Orissa. He strongly supported the cause. He broadened its base.
- Orissa should be a part of freedom struggle. He snapped his ties with the Sammilani.

16

Bhimrao Ramjee Ambedkar (1891–1956)

INTRODUCTION

A great jurist, an eminent lawyer, a powerful and influential political leader, a messiah for weaker sections of the society, Bhimrao Ramjee Ambedkar (B.R. Ambedkar) carved out a place for himself in Indian politics. Born at Mhow near Indore in the erstwhile Central Provinces of the British India on 14 April 1891, he lost his mother Bhimbai when he was only five-year-old. Thereafter he was brought up by his aunt Mira Bai. His father Ramji Sakpal and grandfather Maloji Sakpal were influenced by the teachings of Kabir, a great and renowned saint. Bhakti Movement had also a tremendous influence on them, though both of them worked in military force.

A social reformer and revolutionary, Ambedkar was born in a Mahar family. As an untouchable, he had to bear the onslaught of the upper castes, face worst humiliation from his classmates and digest them with all humility. Pain, anguish, bitterness, sufferings, torture, humiliation — all these became a painful part of his life. As the untouchables were socially ostracized and segregated, they had developed a strong hatred towards the caste system and Ambedkar, as an untouchable, was not an exception to it. He made it a mission in his life to abolish the caste system and give a new image to the Hinduism or, if necessary, give it up and embrace a new religion. This he did when he, along with his followers and friends, embraced Buddhism and became a Buddhist.

Ambedkar had his early education at Satra. In schools, he was not allowed to sit with his classmates who belonged to upper castes. His teachers did not touch him, nor his books as this would pollute their body and mind. He had to pass through great ordeals as a student in his schools. This had a strong impact upon his personality.

After graduating from Elphinstone College, Bombay in 1913, he got a fellowship from the Gaekwad of Baroda and was admitted into the Columbia University, New York and he got his Ph.D. degree in 1916. The topic of his doctoral thesis was "The Problem of the Rupee".

With the financial assistance from Chatrapati Shahu Maharaj of Kolhapur, he pursued his higher studies in London School of Economics and got his D.Sc. degree in 1923. It was a rare privilege on his part to be a student of two prestigious academic institutions. It was also a unique distinction for him when he completed his Bar at Law in London.

His exposure to Western education and values, and the fight against racism in the West, shaped his personality and gave him enough courage and strength to launch a 'war' against the caste system in India.

MARCH TO THE TANK

Soon after his return from abroad, Bhimrao dedicated himself to the cause of the untouchables. It was rather the only agenda in his life to protect and promote their interests. He fought for them, for their liberation, for their emancipation, for their freedom. To make them conscious of their rights, of their place and position in the society, of their plight and sufferings and of means and measures to redress them, he convened a meeting on 27 March 1927 at Mahad, a Tehsil town in Kankan. Attending in large numbers, the delegates demanded that the caste system should be abolished from the society. On 28th, he asked them to march to the public tank to fetch water from it.

The march was undertaken to test the effectiveness of a Resolution passed in the Bombay Legislative Assembly in August 1926, throwing open all the public places to all irrespective of their colour, caste, sex and religion and not preventing any one on these grounds from making use of the same. A bold resolution, it aimed at removing untouchability from the social system and establishing equality among all in the society. It also directed the Municipalities and District Boards to take steps to abolish untouchability.

As expected, the above incident provoked the caste-Hindus. Apprehending that the untouchables might forcibly enter into the temple to destroy its sanctity, they protested against the action of Ambedkar and his followers. A battle ensued between the two groups. Outnumbered, weak and helpless, the untouchables left the scene.

The incident compounded the intensity of hatred and bitterness between the untouchables and the Hindus. The former felt insecure, helpless. Denial and deprivation made them more and more aggressive and assertive, and provided them enough strength to fight against injustice and inequality. Feeling their pulse and sharing their feelings, Ambedkar wrote an article in 'Bahiskrit Bharat', a Marathi periodical, demanding justice for them. He further wrote that the day would come when there would be equality, liberty and freedom for all. He felt that the untouchables would certainly achieve their goal, and if they failed to get their dues, they would certainly give up Hinduism and embrace a new religion. In fact, he along with his followers embraced Buddhism on 14 October 1956. Once they gave up Hinduism, they would no more be worried about temples and idols. But, initially, he was confident that untouchables would win the 'war' though they might lose some battles.

Ambedkar, along with his followers, became a Buddhist because he preferred Buddhism to other religions like Sikhism, Islam, Christianity, etc. for three reasons. First, Buddhism stood for compassion and non-violence both in words and deeds. It was an international religion and also a part of Hinduism, of Indian culture. It stood for freedom, equality, liberty and fraternity. He did not live long after his conversion as he died on 6 December 1956.

In another attempt to challenge the caste system, the untouchables met in large number at Mahad on 25 December 1927. They wanted to enter into the tank forcibly to fetch water. But the situation took a different turn when they burnt a copy of *Manusmriti*, a sacred text of Hindus, written by Manu, the lawgiver and a great saint. Ambedkar strongly criticized Manu for all kinds of evils in the society. To him, Manu was responsible for inequality and injustice found in the social system. He discussed it in detail in an issue of 'Bahiskrit Bharat', dated 3 February 1928. By burning the sacred text, the 'untouchables' sent a message that they would no more tolerate any kind of oppression perpetrated upon them by the Hindus. This incident could be compared with the burning of garments, manufactured in Great Britain, by the Indians in India during the freedom struggle.

MAHAD SATYAGRAHA WITHDRAWN

The Mahad Satyagraha launched by Ambedkar to achieve the goal — to fetch water from the Mahad public tank — could not be fulfilled as it had to be withdrawn on the request of district administration which apprehended that there might be law and order problem unless the Satyagraha was withdrawn. While withdrawing the Satyagraha, Ambedkar very forcefully said that one day they would certainly capture the public tank and they would not rest until the goal was achieved.

ENTRY INTO THE TEMPLE

The untouchables made another attempt under the leadership of Ambedkar, to make a forcible entry into the Kalaram temple at Nasik. Their attempt, however, ended in dismal failure as it was strongly resented by the temple authorities.

Distressed and disgusted, angry and annoyed, Ambedkar and his followers changed their religion and embraced Buddhism. Failure to achieve the goal forced them to give up Hinduism. Not only he changed his religion but also wrote a book entitled *Who Were the Shudras*?

SECOND MARRIAGE

After the death of his first wife, he married to a Saraswat Brahmin girl. It is said that he did so to take vengeance against the Brahmins.

POLITICAL ROLE

Ambedkar's political role and activities centred round mostly the untouchables—their development, their progress and prosperity, etc. He made it his only programme in his lifetime and made it the only goal to achieve, the only mission to accomplish, the only dream to realize. No other leader has done so much for their cause as Ambedkar has done in the living memory of the mankind. He dedicated his whole life for their cause, served them with full devotion. Whatever platform he got to speak, he spoke about them, their sufferings and sacrifices; articulated their demands, put forth their grievances.

During the Round Table Conferences held during 1930–1932, Ambedkar forcefully argued in favour of a separate electorate for the untouchables, besides demanding a separate identity for them. In the Second Round Table Conference (September—December 1931), he had a confrontation with Gandhi since the latter rejected his proposal and threatened that he would go on fast unless it was withdrawn. Pressure was mounted upon Ambedkar to withdraw his proposal and he had to withdraw it with much pain and anguish.

But, at the same time, nobody wanted to ignore him and hurt his sentiments by throwing to dustbin his proposal. To satisfy him it was decided to allow certain reserved seats for untouchables. This compromise was known as the Poona Pact of 1932.

The Pact was put to severe test during the 1937 Assembly elections held across the country. Ambedkar's Independent Labour Party fared well in the elections by winning 11 of 15 reserved seats in the Bombay Legislature. But it did not do well outside the Bombay Presidency. Even the untouchables rejected him by supporting the Congress. The latter won 70 of 150 reserved seats in the country as a whole. This shows that Ambedkar was not a popular leader even among the people of his own caste or class.

The Second World War changed the course of Indian politics. Great Britain was involved in War and became a member of the Allied Group to fight against the Axis powers. Taking advantage of the situation, the Congress demanded from the British Government that it should promise to grant independence to India soon after the War was over. But the Government kept quiet without making any promise. As expected, the Congress became much worried and expressed its resentment by asking the Congress governments, which were in power in various provinces, to resign. And they did so.

But, Ambedkar, on the other hand, supported the British Government with an intention that the latter would take care of the untouchables soon after the War was over. In lieu of his support to the Government, he got a reward from the latter when he was inducted into the Viceroy's Executive Council as a Member to look after the Labour. And in that capacity he tried to develop a new industrial policy. He criticized the Congress for putting in demands before the British Government while she was fighting against her enemies.

After assuming the office, the Labour Party in Great Britain decided to hold elections in India. In the elections held in early 1946, the Congress did very well by sweeping the polls, while Ambedkar's Scheduled Castes Federation tasted its defeat. It shows that he was not that popular among the dalits as he himself or for him others claimed. The Congress won a comfortable majority in the elections and formed the Government at the Centre. It remained in office till the first general elections held in 1951–1952. Soon after Independence, Ambedkar joined the Government headed by Nehru and became the Minister of Law.

In 1946, Ambedkar was elected as a Member of the Constituent Assembly and subsequently was elected as the Chairman of the Drafting Committee set up to frame the Constitution. It was certainly a herculean task. But he did it with all his sincerity and dexterity. His hard work, commitment and devotion to his job earned him the title "Father of the Indian Constitution". This shows his skill and a strong grasp over the subject matter.

As the Minister of Law, he introduced the Hindu Code Bill since he wanted that women should have also equal property rights and there should be a uniform civil code. But it could not see the light of the day as it was opposed by certain powerful leaders of the Congress. Disappointed and distressed, he resigned from the Cabinet on 27 September 1951 and his defeat in 1951–1952 general elections to Parliament saw the end of his active political career.

SOCIAL AND POLITICAL IDEAS

Caste Classification: A Hindrance to Progress and Prosperity

In the earlier periods of Indian history, quite a few saints, seers and sages attained divinity, realized God, reached the pinnacle of glory by rendering significant contributions to literature on Indian ethics and religion. They gave solace to the mankind during their distress, knowledge and wisdom to those who deserved them. In true sense of the term, they were the "friends, philosophers and guides" of the society. Some of them, notwithstanding their high status, position and eminence in the society, hailed from very humble origins and belonged to low castes. Some of them were illegitimate children while some were said to be the mental-born children ('Manas Putra') of Lord Brahma. For example, Vasistha was the son of a prostitute. Vyasa, who classified the Veda under four categories, was an illegitimate son of Matshyagandha, a fisher-woman. His father Parasara, was a great sage. She was an unwed mother. Narada is said to be the son of a maid servant in his previous birth. Similarly, Agasthya was born in a jar, possibly indicating his illegitimacy. Saints like Sanaka, Sanatana, Sananandan, Sanatkumar and Sanat Sujata, Pulaha, Pulastya, Kratu, Angira, Atri, Marichi are the mental-born sons of Lord Brahma. It is believed that either the ancestry or parentage of the mental-born children of Brahma is either unknown or all of them belonged to humble origins. Whatever may be the case, the fact remains that their merit, not their origins, brought them glory and eminence, conferred on them distinctions. But emergence of caste system threw the society into a great turmoil marring its peace, progress and prosperity and tearing the social fabric apart.

Caste system, a slur on the system, a blot in the social structure, is solely responsible, as many believed, for all kinds of discord, disharmony and degeneration in the society. It has, therefore, been strongly condemned and denounced by Kabirism, Sikhism, Buddhism, the Brahma Samaj, the Arya Samaj. Swamy Vivekananda was also against this deadly evil and predicted that the future belonged to untouchables, backward, oppressed and suppressed ones. His predictions came true. Now they are a force to be reckoned with.

Lord Buddha, said to be an Avatar (reincarnation) of God, denounced Brahmins for their arrogance, ignorance, etc. They were also mischievous, superficial, mean, narrow and selfish, spoiling the sanctity and purity that once characterized a society. Challenging their supremacy and teaching them proper lessons, He categorically said that Brahmin was not the most important caste as it was claimed by them. Kshatriyas were said to be superior to the Brahmins.

Gandhi gave equal importance to all castes and wanted the emancipation of Harijans and 'untouchables'. Like Buddha and Gandhi, Ambedkar also wanted to bring an all-round development of the dalits (the 'suppressed' men).

Invasion of India

It is believed that Aryans invaded India. Historians do not agree on it. Some believe that the Aryans defeated the Shudras and drove them away into jungles or enslaved them, while others do not subscribe to this view. Supporting the latter, Ambedkar argued that the Shudras were neither dark-skinned aboriginals nor ever enslaved by the Aryans as they too were the Aryans who belonged to the Kshatriya solar dynasty. Following a bloody battle between Vasistha and Shudas, the king of Shudras, and the defeat of the latter, they were enslaved. Over the years, they became degraded and lost their Kshatriya status.

Ambedkar considered the Vedic king Shudas, son of Devadas Atithigua, a Shudra on the basis of Mahabharat Shantiparva (Chapter LX). The Brahmins, to him, were responsible for the degradation of the Shudras by not performing thread ceremony for them.

Classification of Castes

As said earlier, Ambedkar was highly critical of classification of castes as it was solely responsible for social and economic degradation of the society. This could be set right if untouchables were given more and more space in the society and its administration.

During the days of Second Round Table Conference, Ambedkar contemplated that Untouchables should be separated from the mainstream of the Hindu society. He also demanded a separate electorate for them. His proposal was strongly opposed by Gandhi and others. The latter never wanted any kind of disruption in the organic structure of the Hindu society.

A progressive and rational thinker, an activist, an optimist, a great humanist and opposed to myths, superstitions and blind beliefs, Ambedkar strongly believed that division of labourers, not division of labour, was certainly bad. Caste division produced the former. This also led to the fragmentation of the Indian proletariat.

He had different attitudes towards the Brahmins and the Brahminism. Holding the Brahmins and the texts written by them solely responsible for all sorts of degeneration in the society, he tried to give an impression that he was not against the Brahmins but against the Brahminism which negated the spirit of liberty, equality and fraternity. In this sense, Brahminism permeated the whole society and the Hindu order, undermining social and civil rights and denying the privilege of inter-dining, inter-marriage and use of public wells, public schools, public conveyances, public restaurants to the Shudras. What a great shame?

RELIGION

Ambedkar was not an atheist though his ideas were influenced by Western values. He had strong faith in religion since it was the life force, the soul force that gave everyone strength and sustenance; that inspired and encouraged everyone. Being the best 'friend, philosopher and guide' to everyone unless one denounced, discarded and discredited it, it was universal in nature since it was applicable to all countries, all peoples, all races, and all times. A faithful servant but a bad master, it worked wonders when applied with care and caution. Its proper interpretation would be highly beneficial to the society, but its improper analysis would destroy the mankind, annihilate the civilization and culture. Maximum blood had been shed in its name and found to be one of the most severe and destructive forces in the society. Instead of fomenting communal conflagration, it must establish peace and ensure security to one and all. It should not encourage exploitation or oppression or suppression. The characteristics of religion, to Ambedkar, were as follows:

1. Governing principle of every society.
2. Rational in approach.
3. Ensuring liberty, freedom and rights to one and all, and
4. Not to sanctify poverty.

Ambedkar was so much fed up and disgusted with the Hinduism that he never considered it as a religion because it did not possess the aforesaid characteristics. Arguing that it should change from a 'religion of rules' to a 'religion of principles', he said that religion should have one textbook, its priests should not be hereditary, but appointed by the government, and the latter should decide their number, supervise their activities and prescribe standards for them.

Ambedkar wanted that Hinduism should undergo a drastic change for its sophistication, acceptance and access. The functions assigned to the 'untouchables' and their 'no entry' into public places like hotels, tanks, schools, etc. made him very unhappy. He, therefore, strongly criticized the Brahmins for not allowing them to read scriptures and texts of the religion, or learn Sanskrit as this would have certainly enabled them to know many things about Hinduism. The Shudras and untouchables would have been severely punished had they tried to read them. Except Brahmins, others were not allowed to utter Mantras or perform rituals like initiation, Gayatri, daily sacrifices, etc.

Ambedkar expressed his resentment as everything in the Hindu society centred around caste. Everything was caste-bound and caste-centred. It determined one's status, position in the society. Efficiency and merit were sacrificed at the altar of the caste. He observed:

> Caste has made public opinion impossible. To a Hindu, public opinion is his caste. His responsibility is only to his caste. His loyalty is restricted to his caste. Virtue has become caste-ridden, morality has become caste-bound. There is no sympathy for the deserving. There is no appreciation of the meritorious.

Considering Hinduism as nothing but Brahminism and treating it as a false religion, Ambedkar said:

> The religion which regards the recognition of man's self-respect as sin is not a religion but a sickness. The religion which allows me to touch a foul animal but not a man is not religion but madness. The religion which says that one class may not acquire wealth, may not take up arms is not a religion but a mockery of man's life. The religion which teaches that the unlearned should remain unlearned, that the poor should remain poor is not a religion but a punishment.

Ambedkar did his best to bring about reforms in Hinduism so that it could be more and more acceptable to more and more number of people including untouchables and dalits. Because of oppression and suppression, the latter had a strong hatred against the religion and its 'protectors'. He, therefore, tried to persuade them to take care of the dalits and untouchables by allowing them to use public places. But, unfortunately, all his efforts to give a new image to Hinduism ended in dismal failure. Overtaken by frustration and disappointment, he gave up Hinduism and, as said earlier, became a Buddhist. Because Buddhism opposed Brahminism and ensured dignity, justice, status, equality and liberty to one and all and professed its faith in non-violence and compassion. He asked his followers and friends to change their religion (Hinduism) and accept any other that would give them equality and dignity, space and status in the social system. He felt it was his sheer misfortune that he was born as a Hindu. But he would certainly not die as a Hindu, because he had every right to change his religion. Finally, he did so to teach a lesson to those who humiliated the 'untouchables' and dalits in the name of protection and perpetuation of the Hinduism.

SOCIAL DEMOCRACY

To Ambedkar, social democracy, which gave importance to equality, justice, dignity, etc., preceded or should precede political democracy. It was because of this, the former was more important than the latter. Political democracy would not have any meaning in the absence of social democracy. The latter gave the former a meaning, a purpose, and a direction. People could live without political democracy, but they would certainly suffer if social democracy was denied to them. The latter would go a long way in preventing the society from becoming oppressive and arbitrary. Indian society, to Ambedkar, needed both social democracy and political democracy. The latter, but not the former, could wait. Untouchables and dalits suffered because society oppressed the weaker sections of the society. He had a strong conviction that it would not progress and prosper if it failed to establish social democracy and encouraged oppression and exploitation. He observed:

> There must not be an oppressed class. There must not be a class which has got all the privileges and a class which has got all the burdens to carry. Such a thing, such a division, such an organization of society has within itself the germs of a bloody revolution, and perhaps it would be impossible for democracy to cure them.

Ambedkar strongly argued that both political democracy and economic democracy should rest on social democracy, giving maximum importance to social democracy, and it was the substructure on which both political democracy and economic democracy rest. The success of social democracy depends upon the reconciliation of conflicting interests through compromise and understanding. There should not be stratification of castes in a society. Once it takes place, social democracy will be in danger.

Ambedkar was in favour of parliamentary form of government. The presence of a strong and powerful opposition would help in strengthening the latter. A strong opposition would bring the government into right track and check it from becoming arbitrary and authoritarian. In democracy, the legislature must control the executive and there should be an independent judiciary to control both the executive and the legislature and keep them within their limits.

A government may be democratic in form, but in spirit it may not be so unless the people have an attitude to remain democratic in mind. To Ambedkar, democracy was more than a social system; an attitude of mind, a philosophy of life.

STATUS OF WOMEN

As women constitute half of the human race, they have a right to live, grow and flourish. They must be given a space in every field so that they can enjoy their rights and freedoms. A society, to Ambedkar, would degenerate and never be perfect if they were denied and deprived of their dues. Attempts to ignore them, undermine them, underestimate them would have disastrous consequences for the society. He attributed all the sufferings and miseries of women to Manu and his writings. It seems he was very much obsessed with the development of women and untouchables and for every lapse found in the society he held Brahmins responsible. It seems he was not objective in his approach and very much narrow and prejudiced while interpreting the scriptures.

He was for empowerment of women. They must be equal with men and should not be considered inferior in any way to men. Their education, their growth and development, their status and position — all these would go a long way in strengthening the society as well as the democracy. Democracy cannot be successful unless women's participation was ensured.

Ambedkar rightly said that the progress of the society depended upon that of women. He urged them to educate their children and never to suffer from inferiority complex. To promote their status, he introduced the Hindu Code Bill while he was the Minister of Law, the Government of India.

SOCIALISM

Economic inequality is one of the worst social evils that has destroyed social harmony, torn apart the social fabric, impeded the economic progress, brought imbalances in the social sector, and damaged the sensibilities of the poor, backward and exploited ones. One of the distressing consequences of exploitation, indifference and inefficacy, it is said to be a bane, a monster spreading its tentacles to eat away the very vitals of the society. A major source of clash, conflict, and confrontation, it has thrown the system into a great turmoil and posed a great threat to its security and integrity.

Distressed at the living conditions of millions of the poor, backward and poverty-stricken people, Ambedkar advocated for economic democracy. He was very much convinced that unless people were economically sound and free from bondages like slavery, political democracy would be meaningless and of no use to them. Steps, therefore, should be taken to remove economic inequality. He urged upon the state to intervene and adopt effective measures to curb the evil. Concentration of wealth in a fewer hands should be discouraged as it would certainly prevent exploitation.

State socialism is, therefore, a must. Interfering in the activities of the rich and the industrialists, the state should ask them to improve the conditions of the workers working under them by giving them more wages, and facilities like health, education, leisure and recreation, transport and communication, etc.

Advocating for nationalization of economy, Ambedkar argued that state socialism should be made an integral part of the constitution so that it would be seriously implemented for the betterment of the poor and downtrodden.

As said above, he was always for the welfare of the workers. As a matter of love for them, he kept the title of his political party "The Indian Labour Party". The Party always stood for bringing out a great change in their living conditions. He allowed them to go on strike to achieve their goal. He did not consider it a crime though he described it as a 'civil wrong'. Strongly criticizing the Industrial Disputes Bill, he said that it had made the workers slaves. They were exploited by the rich and the industrialists, and the latter never suffered from any guilt complex. As said above, he was a Member in the Viceroy's Executive Council and, in that capacity, he looked after interests of the labour and the workers. In this regard, he took several initiatives to improve the status of industrial workers. He recommended for compulsory conciliation or arbitration which, he thought, would certainly improve the conditions of the workers. He always stood for their cause. He wanted that reasonably minimum wages should be paid to them.

To him, agriculture should be under the control of the state and cultivation collectivized on democratic basis. Agriculture should be treated as an industry run by the government. Workers, landless, poor and backward — all of them should actively engage themselves in agriculture.

He wanted to include social and economic rights in the chapter on 'Fundamental Rights'. But he could not as powerful leaders of the Congress opposed it. Therefore, he wanted that all should be engaged in collective farming.

To Karl Marx, economics influenced the course of history, and it constituted the substructure while the rest like social, political, cultural, etc. the superstructure. But Ambedkar, unlike Karl Marx, had a different view. To him, social relations, but not economics, shaped the course of history and constituted the substructure, while economics and politics constituted the superstructure. Demanding for the abolition of caste system, he hoped that changes in favour of 'untouchables' would certainly take place and be brought through constitutional means.

SOCIAL DEMOCRACY

By nature and temperament, in his attitude and approach, by his thinking and perception, Ambedkar was a democrat. Social democracy and political democracy were his goals, though he laid much emphasis upon the former. The latter would collapse and become non-existent without the support of the former.

A victim of oppression and humiliation, Ambedkar vehemently protested against the caste system. Democracy would be a dismal failure if caste inequality perpetuated in the society. To the oppressed and the suppressed ones, democracy would have no meaning and it would be of no use to them. He said that there must not be an oppressed class. There must not be a class to enjoy all the privileges and a class to bear the burden of the society. Such a thing, such a division, such an organization of a society had within itself the germs of the bloody revolution, and perhaps it would be impossible for democracy to cure them.

To Ambedkar, political democracy and economic democracy should rest upon social democracy. Stratification of the society on the basis of caste was a great curse to the society. Democracy would be successful only when conflicting interests were reconciled and existence of various groups was tolerated.

Political democracy could be successful if opposition was tolerated and encouraged. There must be at least two major political parties to contest the election; one of them would win it and the other one would lose the game. Elections, to him, were to be held at regular intervals. Three branches of the government, namely, executive, legislature and judiciary were to function within their jurisdiction as prescribed in the Constitution itself. An independent judiciary would be a boon and blessing for the successful functioning of democracy.

The success of democracy depended upon the attitude of the people. Democracy would be reduced to a farce if the people were not oriented towards it. To him, it was more than a social system; an attitude of mind, a philosophy of life.

AN ESTIMATE

A man of great intellect, knowledge, wisdom and vision, Ambedkar gave his mind, heart and soul to the cause of untouchables. His action and his words centred round freedom of untouchables and freedom for untouchables. His dream was the liberation of the poor and downtrodden from all bondages and restrictions that impeded their progress, denied their legitimate claims and deprived them of their dues. He wanted a society that would ensure liberty, equality and justice to one and all; that would give a guarantee that there would be no suffering, miseries and pains.

A man of courage and conviction, he did not hesitate to challenge the supremacy of Gandhi. He confronted him at the Second Round Table Conference. Opposed to caste system, he challenged Hinduism that was responsible for its perpetuation.

A true friend of labourers, a philosopher who laid emphasis upon the emancipation of women, a crusader, a feminist, he fought for the removal of social contradictions. On 25 November 1949, while moving a motion for the adoption of the Constitution, he said: "On the 26 January 1950, we are going to enter into a life of contradictions. In politics, we will have equality and in social and economic life we will have inequality". Whatever he said six decades back still holds good.

POINTS TO REMEMBER

- B.R. Ambedkar was born in Mhow near Indore. Father: Ramji Sakpal. Grandfather: Maloji Sakpal. Mother: Bhimbai. Influence of Kabir and of Bhakti Movement on the family.

- He was a Mahar (Scheduled Caste). Upper caste people tortured him as he was born in a low caste. His only mission was to abolish the caste system. Disgusted with its rituals, restrictions and reservations, he gave up Hinduism and embraced Buddhism.
- His early education at Satara. His humiliation as a student. This had a strong bearing upon his personality.
- Got his Ph.D. in 1916 from Columbia University, New York, U.S.A. and D.Sc. from the London School of Economics. Completed Bar-at-Law at London. Impact of western education on his personality.
- March to the tank: he convened a meeting on 27 March 1927 at Mahad. Decision was taken to march to the tank and bring water from it, to test the effectiveness of the Resolution passed in the Bombay Legislative Council in August 1926. Clash between the Hindus and the untouchables was apprehended.
- Ambedkar was disgusted with rituals and superstitions found in the Hinduism. Unless these were removed from the religion, Hinduism would become pervert. He threatened to change his religion unless it was brought on right track.
- Untouchables met at Mahad on 25 December 1927 and decided to get water from the public tank. Burnt a copy of *Manusmriti* written by Manu. Ambedkar strongly criticized Manu for all kinds of social injustice. Mahad Satyagraha withdrawn because the district administration felt that there would be disturbance unless the situation subsided.
- Entry into the temple: untouchables' forcible entry into the Kalaram Temple at Nasik. A failure because of strong protest by the temple authorities.
- Second marriage: he married to a Brahmin girl after his first wife's death.
- Political role: his political activity centred round the untouchables. He was deeply committed to them and their cause.
- In the Round Table Conference, he demanded a separate identity, a separate electorate for them. It was, however, withdrawn. He was forced to withdraw his proposal. Certain seats were 'reserved' for untouchables.
- Poona Pact of 1932. His political party's (Independent Labour Party) fate in the 1937 elections. The voters preferred the Congress to him.
- Second World War: Ambedkar's policy was opposite to that of Gandhi. He supported the British Government, but Gandhi made it conditional. He was duly rewarded by the British Government. Defeat of Ambedkar's party in 1946 elections.
- He did a splendid job as a Member of the Constituent Assembly, as the Chairman of the Drafting Committee, and as the Minister for Law. His Hindu Code Bill was strongly opposed by many in the Congress. He

resigned from the Cabinet. He was defeated in the 1951–1952 general elections. End of his political career.

- Social and political views: (i) caste system: many saints and seers attained divinity even though they belonged to low class and humble origins. Caste system was criticized by many including Vivekananda, Lord Buddha and Gandhi. To Buddha, Kshatriyas were superior to Brahmins. Like Buddha and Gandhi, Ambedkar also wanted to bring an all-round development of the dalits. (ii) Invasion of India by Aryans. Historians do not support it. Following the defeat of Shudras at the hands of Vasistha, the Shudras were degraded and lost their original status.
- Classification of castes: caste classification was responsible for degradation in the society. Untouchables were separated from the mainstream. He demanded a separate electorate for them. It was not acceptable to Gandhi and others.
- He opposed Brahminsm, but not the Brahmins.
- Religion: not an atheist. Religion provided one the strength.
- Religion could be both useful and harmful. He set certain rules to be followed by everyone. The nature of religion should be changed. He expressed his anger and resentment as everything was caste-centred and caste-bound.
- He felt that it was a curse for him to have been born as a Hindu.
- Social democracy: it preceded political democracy; it gave a meaning to political democracy. Without it, no society would progress and prosper.
- He supported the parliamentary form of government. Legislature to control the executive. Judiciary should be independent.
- Status of women: They must be given a space in every field. A society degenerates if women are deprived of their dues.
- He attributed sufferings of the society to the writings of Manu.
- Socialism: economic inequality was a great evil. Its consequences were disastrous.
- Steps to be taken to curb economic inequality. Concentration of wealth to be discouraged. State socialism a must. Economy to be nationalized.
- His political party: "The Indian Labour Party". It was for protecting the interests of the workers. Minimum wages to be paid to them. Social and economic rights to be declared fundamental rights.
- He did not agree with Karl Marx who argued that economics influenced the course of history.

17

Sir Sayyed Ahmed Khan (1817–1898)

INTRODUCTION

A great Muslim leader with a modern outlook and scientific approach to issues and problems confronting the contemporary society in general and the Indian Muslim community in particular, a powerful personality vibrant with a noble desire to uplift his community by making its members literate and educated, dynamic and progressive, forward and ambitious, Sir Sayyed Ahmed Khan rendered a significant service to his society. What Raja Ram Mohan Roy did to Hindus, Khan did the same to the Muslims. Well known for his learning and piety, he commanded respect from Ulemas of his time who accepted him as their leader. He did his best to "purify" Islam by restoring its original purity. He also denounced the un-Islamic practices that had crept into the Muslim community.

It may be noted that though the western education suffered much from numerous flaws and deficiencies, it had, by all means, a positive impact upon the Indians, particularly those who were exposed to it. A new elite class emerged. Committed, it took a vow to liberate India from the British regime. Apart from it, others being exponents of Indian culture and thought, did something to usher in a new era—an era of socio-cultural renaissance. They were Raja Ram Mohan Roy, Swami Dayanand Saraswati, Swamy Vivekanand, Swamy Ram Krishna Paramhamsa, Keshav Chandra Sen, Mrs. Annie Besant and a few others. Sir Sayyed Ahmed Khan did the same work for the Muslims.

A strong supporter of modern education, he wanted to give a new image to Koran. It was because of this his friends called him a heretic. He did his best to bring a synthesis between the old system and the new system of education. Education should be modern, secular and Islamic.

TAHZIBUL AKHLAQ (SOCIAL REFORMER)

Sayyed brought out a monthly journal Tahzibul Akhlaq (Social Reformer) in which he propagated the importance of social reform. Founder of Mohammedan Educational Conference, he made the people aware of social reforms, modern education and general economic and intellectual progress. It was painful for him to see the plight of the Muslims as they were poor, backward, illiterate and ignorant. They also suffered from arrogance and false pride. Hence, they lagged behind, could not prosper.

LIFE AND CAREER

Born on 17 October 1817, Khan started his career as a clerk in the East India Company in 1837. Later, he changed his job. He became a Munsif in 1841 at the age of twenty-four. He worked in Delhi courts during 1846–1854. His forefathers had held high offices under the Mughals.

The First War of Independence (1857) had a great impact upon him. Inspired and influenced, he wrote a very famous book entitled *The Causes of the Indian Revolt*. His work had a tremendous influence upon A.O. Hume. He suffered at the hands of the rebels and helped the British against them.

He visited England during 1869–1870. During his stay there he was very much influenced by liberal ideas. As a consequence, he defied orthodox hostility and declared that modern learning was neither forbidden by the Koran nor dangerous to the faith it taught. To make the Muslim education "modern and liberal", he set up schools in different places where he was posted. He strongly felt the influence and relevance of western education. He made Aligarh the centre of his activities.

To westernize the Islamic education, he set up a Translation Society in Ghazipur for the translation of scientific books. He set up in Aligarh a school on 24 May 1875 and soon it developed into the Mohammedan Anglo-Oriental College and its foundation stone was laid by Lord Litton in 1877. He was very much confident that modern education would ensure jobs to them.

It may be noted that Muslims did not take much interest in the western education. But later, they changed their mind as they believed that it was the western education that would provide them jobs in the Government service. Revivalism was, therefore, need of the hour and this was provided by the Wahabi Movement and the personality of Sayyed Ahmed Khan. Wahabi Movement was brought to India by Sayyed Ahmed of Raibareli (UP). He preached *jehad* (a holy war) against the Sikhs of Punjab who illtreated the Musalmans, prevented them from fulfilling their religious obligations and desecrated their places of worship.

In 1877, a conference was held in India to find out doctrines and notions which could be acceptable to most of the people in India. He along with Keshab Chandra Sen, Swamy Dayanand and others attended the meeting. But it ended in failure as the idealism that inspired the conference could not take any concrete shape.

Posts Held

In 1878, Lord Dufferin appointed him as a Member of the Public Service Commission. He was also a Member of the Viceroy's Council (1878–1882), a Member of the Indian Legislative Council and the Central Provinces.

A LOYALIST

Khan was a great loyalist of the British Government. He believed that Muslims' loyalty to the Government would bring them rewards, benefits and benedictions. He wanted to win the heart of the Government by extending it the community's support and cooperation. And for this he was prepared to face the consequences. He, therefore, congratulated the Government for introducing the Self-Government Bill in 1883 for imparting training to the Indians in the field of Self-Government. This reflected Government's greatness and magnanimity. But at the same time he objected to the introduction of the elective element in Indian politics. For this extreme loyalty to the Government, he was known as "a loyalist of the loyalists".

THE CAUSES OF THE INDIAN REVOLT (1857)

In 1858, Sayyed wrote a book entitled The Causes of the Indian Revolt in Urdu. It was later translated in English by Colvin and Graham in 1873. He attributed the causes of the revolt to total absence of Indians in the legislative bodies. They were denied to participate in the legislative process. There was not a single Indian in the legislature. The people, therefore, did not get any opportunity to ventilate their grievances before their representatives. The British Government also did not have any liking for the Indians. Indifferent to developmental activities of the people and ignorant of their difficulties, the Government was always concerned with its own welfare and development. It treated them like slaves or servants. Its indifference to the problem of the people created a barrier between the rulers and the ruled. And day by day it got widened. It was, therefore, high time for the Government to give a chance to the people to participate in the legislative process. Other causes responsible for the revolt were as follows:

- The enactment of laws which went against the traditional values of the people.
- The Government was not aware of the real desires and aspirations of the people.
- The principles of good governance were ignored by the Government.
- The bad management of the army.

Sayyed drew an inference from the revolt that the ruler and the ruled should stay together in peace so that the society would grow, develop and prosper. There should be perfect harmony and understanding between them.

POLITICAL IDEAS

An ardent patriot, Sayyed sincerely felt that the Hindus and the Muslims breathed the same air, drank the same water, ate the same fruits that the Mother Earth gave to them. Therefore, they should live together, die together for the sake of the country. Since they belonged to the same nation, they should have sympathy, love and goodwill for one another. India, to him, was like a newly wedded bride having two beautiful and shining eyes and these eyes were the Hindus and the Muslims. If they remained together in peace and harmony, her eyes would be beaming with joy. But if they quarrelled with one another and if they harboured hatred, ill-will and animosity against one another, her eyes would become squinted or even partially blind.

As a patriot, he supported the Illbert Bill which sought to eliminate discrimination against the authority of the Indian judges.

But like any other Muslim leader, he also changed his mind and became suspicious of the Congress. He asked his people not to support it. He, as a strong advocate of their well-being, argued that instead of joining politics, they should concentrate on education. For the sake of promoting education among the Muslims, he founded the Educational Congress in 1858.

Posing a challenge to the Congress and with a view to prevent the Muslims from joining it, he established the United Indian Patriotic Association in August 1888 with the help of Raja (king) Siva Prasad of Varanasi, and the Anglo-Oriental Defence Association in 1893, a loyalist Association encouraging the Muslims not to join any political agitation that would undermine or challenge the authority. But all his sincere efforts to keep all the Muslims away from the Congress miserably failed.

CONCLUSION

Like any other Muslim leader, Sayyed also had a keen interest in uplifting the Muslims from poverty and backwardness. His main concern was their all-round development. Their good health, sound mind, better socio-economic status, their safety and security, etc. mattered him much. Like John Stuart Mill, he also felt that the minorities would be or might be suppressed or repressed by the Hindu majority. Majority tyranny was intolerable to him as it would crush or suppress the interests of the minorities.

A leading pioneer in the advancement of modern education for the Muslims, he was a great promoter of enlightenment.

During the early part of his career, he took part in the national awakening. His position on the two great political issues of the 1870s—the Illbert Bill and Civil Service Reform—was the same as that of Hindu nationalists. Initially, an exponent of Hindu–Muslim unity, he later urged Muslims to assert their separateness. He felt or believed that the freedom movement had, over the years, become more and more Hindu-centric and the day would come when the Muslims would be completely margianlized and ignored. The widening gulf between the Hindus and the Muslims was also appreciated by the British Government as it suited them to perpetuate their rule. Their policy "divide and rule" was a great success because of lack of understanding between two major communities. When two 'cats' quarrelled, it was the 'monkey' who got maximum benefits by exploiting the situation to his own advantage.

Sayyed advised the Muslims to remain aloof from the Congress organization and the freedom movement—as he sincerely felt that it would be an instrument of Hindu domination.

POINTS TO REMEMBER

- Sir Sayyed Ahmed Khan (1857–1898) hailed from a rich and renowned family. His only mission was to uplift the Muslims who were poor and backward, illiterate and ignorant.
- He visited England and was impressed by western education.
- A supporter of western ideology and liberal ideas, he wanted to modernize the Koran and the Muslim education. This would give name and prestige to them and ensure government jobs. He defied orthodox hostility. To westernize education, he set up a Translation Society. He set up various schools and colleges in different parts of the country.
- What Raja Ram Mohan Roy did for the Hindus, Sayyed Ahmed Khan did for the Muslims. A great reformer, he published one monthly journal *Tahzibul Akhlaq* (Social Reformer).
- Initially, he was a nationalist. But later, he became a "communal" as he concentrated all his attention on his own community—its progress and development. He asked the Muslims not to join the Congress and advised them to support the Government.
- He established the United Indian Patriotic Association in August 1888.

18

Muhammad Ali Jinnah (1876–1948)

INTRODUCTION

A staunch nationalist during the earlier days of freedom struggle; an apostle and ambassador of Hindu–Muslim unity; a close friend and follower of his contemporary freedom fighters like Dadabhai Naoroji, Bal Gangadhar Tilak, Gopal Krishna Gokhale; a private secretary to Naoroji (1906); a great admirer of Gokhale, an ardent champion of Muslims; Muhammad Ali Jinnah, the "Muslim Gokhale", would go down the annals of Indian history as a great leader who was largely, if not solely, responsible for the division of India into two nations—Pakistan and Hindustan. But for him, a theocratic state of Pakistan might not have emerged in 1947. He was born in Karachi on 23 December 1876 and also died in Karachi on 10 September 1948.

A NATIONALIST

Jinnah was a nationalist as is evident from the fact that not only he described in May 1915 Gopal Krishna Gokhale as a great political saint, a master of the Indian finance and the greatest champion of education and sanitation, but also strongly defended his Education Bill in 1912 when it was vehemently opposed by Harcourt Butler. Jinnah argued that great and renowned teachers could be appointed, sky-high buildings constructed with money, but the question was whether the Government of India wanted to spend money on education for the poor, illiterate and ignorant Indians. Spending three crore rupees was not a big problem for it. It was the duty of every civilized government to make the people conscious of their rights and duties, encourage them to play an important role in decision-making process, allow them to occupy a space in the system so that they can make their presence felt. Hence, the importance of education and everyone should, therefore, be educated.

That Jinnah was a nationalist is also evident from the fact that efforts were made in 1925 to establish peace and harmony between the Hindus and the Muslims, which was very often marred by communal riots. With a motive to achieve this goal, Maulana Muhammed Ali, the then President of the Congress, convened on 21 and 22 November 1924 in Bombay an All-Parties' Conference. The Conference appointed a Committee of fifteen representatives of all political parties to prepare a scheme of Swaraj, including a communal settlement, and to report not later than 31 March 1925. A scheme was devised to promote unity between the two communal groups. As a result, communal riots ceased for some time. Jinnah at this Conference said that he did not go there "to say what the Muslims wanted, but he was there to sit with the Hindus as a coworker". He appealed to all the delegates to put their heads together not as Hindus or Muslims but as Indians. This was his love for his country where he was born and brought up. This was his spirit of nationalism that was very much distinct in his thought and action. He called himself an Indian first and a Muslim second. But, with the passage of time, he became parochial to achieve a narrow and selfish communal end, i.e. formation of Pakistan. He converted himself from a "Nationalist Muslim" to a "Muslim Nationalist".

A LIBERALIST

Jinnah was a liberalist. It is evident from his address to the Constituent Assembly of Pakistan on 11 August 1947. He told his people that they were free, absolutely free to go to mosques and temples or any other place of worship in the state of Pakistan. They might belong to any religion, caste or creed and this had nothing to do with the fundamental principles that they were all citizens and equal citizens in the state. This should be the guiding principle. He assured his people that in course of time Muslims would cease to be Muslims and Hindus as Hindus. It was not from the perspective of religion but from the point of view of politics.

A CONSERVATIVE

It is significant to note while he was a political liberalist, he was, at the same time, a conservative from the economics perspective. Having faith in Islamic theory, he strongly criticized the western economics responsible for all kinds of problems facing the mankind. Only a miracle could save it from the disaster the world confronted. Neither it could provide justice to the mankind, nor could it resolve the clash, conflict and confrontation that had taken the world under its grip.

Jinnah held the western economic system responsible for the outbreak of two World Wars. The history of War(s) was the darkest chapter in the history of mankind. No government could make its people happy if it adopted such type of economic systems. He urged upon his people to shape their own destiny and adopt an economic system based on true Islamic concept of equality of mankind and social justice. They would be fulfilling their missions as Muslims and give to humanity the message of peace which alone could save it and secure its welfare, happiness and prosperity.

AN EXPONENT OF PAKISTAN

Jinnah was not religious. A shrewd politician, a product of contradictions and confusions of Indian nationalism, he along with other Muslims continued to support the Congress to oust the British imperialists from the Indian soil. But once it was made clear that India would be free very soon, the Muslims started getting panicky, which was unfounded, as they thought they would be suppressed by the Hindu majority. The Muslim leaders and intelligentsia, therefore, started propagating that Muslims should get a separate state for themselves. Inspired and encouraged, Muslims started supporting Jinnah and other leaders for their ideology.

ELECTED TO IMPERIAL LEGISLATIVE COUNCIL

In 1910 and 1916, Jinnah was elected to the Imperial Legislative Council by the Muslim electorate of Bombay (now Mumbai). A brilliant Parliamentarian, he made powerful speeches on Gokhale's Elementary Education Bill, the Transfer of Ships Registration Bill and the Indian Criminal Law Amendment Bill. He supported the Indian Defence Force Bill and did not oppose the Press Bill.

ALL-INDIA MUSLIM LEAGUE

Following the partition of Bengal on 7 July 1905, there was a spontaneous outburst of anger and resentment among the public in the province of Bengal and elsewhere. The Congress condemned the partition and launched the Swadeshi Movement. Earlier, it had made certain demands: direct representation of Indians in the House of Commons; their appointment in the Council of the Secretary of State and in the Executive Councils in India; and Self-Government for India on the pattern of the self-governing British colonies. All these had a great impact upon the Government.

The atmosphere was quite disturbing and day by day it started deteriorating. The whole country came under the grip of a political storm, forcing every one to watch it with anxiety. At this critical juncture, Lord Gilbert Minto assumed the office as the Viceroy of India in November 1905. Worried and agitated, he faced the challenges with courage and confidence. To achieve his goal, he successfully devised a scheme to create rifts between the Muslims and the Congress. He won the game when the All-India Muslim League was formed on 30 December 1906 with three objectives:

1. To promote among Indian Muslims feelings of loyalty towards British Government.
2. To protect the political and other rights of Indian Muslims and place their needs and aspirations before the Government, and
3. To promote friendly feelings between Muslims and other communities.

That a Government, whose ministers, viceroys and bureaucrats claimed to be so highly educated, civilized and advanced, could be so nasty, mean, selfish or self-centred, as is evident from the above move, was beyond any Indian's imagination. Formation of the League laid the foundation stone of an independent theocratic state, called Pakistan, on the north-west border of India.

LEAGUE OPPOSED THE AGITATION FOLLOWING THE BENGAL PARTITION

The Muslim League organized under the bureaucratic encouragement to isolate the Muslims from the national movement, strongly opposed the agitation launched by the Congress following the partition of Bengal.

BENGAL PARTITION: ITS REACTION

While Minto and Lord John Morley, the Secretary of State, and *The Times* newspaper published from London extolled the virtues in Muslims and praised them for their efforts in forming the League, Ramsay Macdonald, a British statesman, strongly criticized it for sowing the seeds of discord between the Hindus and the Muslims by conferring special favours upon the Muslims.

JINNAH DENOUNCED LEAGUE'S DEMAND FOR SEPARATE ELECTORATE

The leaders of the League put forth, after careful and serious deliberation, the demand for separate electorate for the Muslims. It was "a matter of life and death" for them. They achieved their goal when separate electorate was introduced in the 1909 Act. Following this, they became more serious about protecting the interests of the Muslims. While the Congress was fighting against the Government, the League showed its loyalty towards the British monarchy. Unhappy with such attitude of the League, the nationalist Muslims urged the Muslims to support the Congress and other Indians as there was no difference between their interests and those of the Congress. Badrauddin Tyabji and Rahmat Ullah Sayani advised them to support the Congress. Jinnah (then a staunch Congressman) denounced the separate electorate as "the obnoxious virus introduced into the body politic of India with evil designs".

BENGAL PARTITION ANNULLED AND LEAGUE'S NEW CONSTITUTION

On 2 December 1911, the Bengal partition was annulled. It was a great setback to the Muslims. They felt that they were ditched by the Government as it never took them seriously. The honeymoon period between them (League and the Government) was also over. Ditched, disappointed and dejected, the Muslims developed a feeling of distrust towards the Government and wanted to have an understanding with the Congress. The first step was taken in this regard in December 1912 when some young Muslims wanted that the League should meet in Calcutta to consider the adoption of a new Constitution for it. Jinnah attended the meeting though he had earlier refused to join it as it was purely a communal organization. In the meet a constitution was drafted and accepted. The goal of the Congress was declared as its own. Such attitudinal change of the League was highly appreciated by the Congress when it adopted a resolution to that effect in December 1913 in its meeting held at Karachi.

Jinnah and his friends took some steps in promoting and maintaining communal harmony between the Muslims and the Hindus. They requested the office bearers of the League to hold its meeting at Bombay in December 1915 at the same time and at the same place the Congress was going to have its session. Madan Mohan Malaviya, Sarojini Naidu, Gandhi attended the meeting. Both decided to work together in preparing a common plan on post-war reforms and in pressing its adoption by the British authorities. They set up a joint committee in this regard. The joint scheme of reforms was as follows:

1. In the Central Legislature, one-third of the Indian elected members should be the Muslims.
2. The principle of separate electorate for Muslims was accepted, and
3. The minorities were also given the right of vetoing any legislation concerning their community if they were opposed to it.

CONGRESS–LEAGUE PACT

The aforesaid scheme became the basis of a pact between the Congress and the League a year later. In December 1916, both the parties held their annual sessions at Lucknow in 1916 and accepted the scheme almost in full.

PACT HAILED

Bal Gangadhar Tilak and others hailed the pact as a significant step towards national solidarity, while it truly laid the foundation of Pakistan thirty years later.

JINNAH JOINED THE HOME RULE LEAGUE

Annie Besant and Tilak founded the Home Rule League on 1 April and 28 April 1916 respectively, with an objective to attain the Home Rule or Self-Government within the British Empire by all constitutional means and educate and organize the public opinion in the country towards the attainment of the same. Jinnah joined the League immediately after the internment of Besant and her two associates.

INDIA'S FREEDOM NOT A DISTANT DREAM

Like Gandhi and other Congress leaders, Jinnah was also in favour of India's independence. While addressing the Muslim League in 1917 as its President, he argued that the Government should make it clear that the Self-Government for India was not "a mere distant goal", but the definite aim and objective of the Government to be given to the people within a reasonable time. This shows his deep involvement in the freedom struggle and his desire to set the country free in the nearest future.

JINNAH LEFT THE CONGRESS

The strained relations between the Hindus and the Muslims had an adverse impact upon the relationship between the Muslim League and the Congress. Both could no more work together against the British Raj. In 1913, the League, on the advice of the Congress leaders, adopted Self-Government as its goal. On 8 September 1920, it also accepted Gandhi's non-cooperation programme and formally became a party to the struggle against the British rule. But it could not, because of its composition and character, take direct action against the Government. The struggle on behalf of the Muslims was carried by the Central Khilafat Committee. Because of Gandhi's successful programme the League became defunct. Its annual session could not be held in 1923 for want of a quorum. Following the abolition of Caliphat by the Turks themselves, the Central Khilafat Committee received a severe jolt and the League became free to take decisions on its own. Once again, it became close to the Congress. Jinnah, even after joining the League in 1913, took active interest in Congress politics. Several times he acted as a link between the League and the Congress. But he did not appreciate Gandhi's non-cooperation programme. When in December 1920 the Congress in its Nagpur Session adopted it, Jinnah left the Congress forever. He was terribly shocked when he came to know that workers resorted to violence during the non-cooperation movement. Suspicious of Gandhi's following, he declared that the new leader drew his principal support from the inexperienced youths and the ignorant and the illiterate. So saying, he withdrew from the Congress. He accused Gandhi of turning the Congress into an instrument for the revival of Hinduism and of wishing to establish the Hinduraj in the country.

A MEMBER OF THE MUDDIMAN AND SKEEN COMMITTEES

In 1924, Muddiman Committee was appointed to examine the working of the Government of India Act, 1919. Besides Jinnah, other Members were: Sapru, Paranjape, Sivaswamy Iyer. He signed the minority report which proposed termination of the diarchy. He was also a Member of the Skeen Committee which examined the problems of Indianization of the Indian army.

JINNAH REJECTED THE NEHRU REPORT

Lord Birkenhead, who left the India Office in October 1928, had a poor impression about the Indian leadership. He believed that since the Indians were divided on the basis of caste and religion, they were unfit to run the Government. As the gap between the Hindus and the Muslims could not be bridged up, the Congress and the Muslim League would never be able to reach an understanding with regard to the future set-up of the governmental system, and to produce "an agreed constitution" for India. He always doubted their efficacy and efficiency. Birkenhead's opinions and feelings deeply hurt the sentiments of Indian leaders cutting across caste, religion, region, etc.

In view of the above developments, the Muslim League in its meeting held at Calcutta recommended "Hindu–Muslim unity on the lines laid down by the Unity Conference. In its annual session held in December 1926 at Madras, the Congress also directed its Working Committee to convene an All India All Parties' Conference for the purpose of drawing up a Constitution for India, acceptable to all parties, and thereby meet the challenge of the Secretary of State. The CWC accordingly invited a number of organizations and the All Parties' Conference met at Delhi in February and March 1928 to discuss the questions of a Constitution for India on the basis of "Full Responsible Government", with special reference to communal problems. The progress was, however, marred by communal discord.

The Congress met again on 19 May 1928 in Bombay. By then, there was a wide gap between the Congress and the Muslim League. Instead of recording the failure, the Conference appointed a small Committee with Motilal Nehru as its Chairman, "to determine the principles of the new Constitution for India and draft a report thereon". The Committee was asked to submit its report before 1 July 1928.

The Members of the Committee were: Sir Immal Ali and Shuaib Qureshi (Muslims), M.S. Aney and M.R. Jayakar (Mahasabha), G.R. Pradhan (non-Brahmin), Sardar Mangal Singh (The Sikh League), Tej Bahadur Sapru (Liberal) and N.M. Joshi (Labour). Jawaharlal Nehru, then General Secretary of the Congress, was nominated as Secretary of the Committee.

The Committee, unlike the authors of the Congress–League Pact of 1916, made no concession to the Muslim standpoint on the question of separate electorates. It discarded the separate electorates, and allowed joint or mixed electorates. The only communal safeguard should be "reservation" of seats, and this should only be afforded to the Muslims and not to any other community or group except the non-Muslims in the North–West Frontier Province. Nor should seats be reserved for Muslims where they were in a majority, but only at the Centre and in the Provinces in which they were in a minority. The right to contest other than reserved seats should be conceded but no "weightage" should be allowed.

JINNAH'S FOURTEEN POINTS

The Nehru Report evoked mixed response from the Muslims. The Nationalists among them like Maulana Azad, Dr. Ansari, T.A.K. Sherwani supported it wholeheartedly. Sir Mohammed Shafi and his followers adopted a non-possumus (we cannot—a form of refusal) attitude. Another group, led by H.H. Aga Khan, wanted to secure for the Muslim Community all the possible advantages. The group felt that the Nehru Report repudiated the Lucknow Pact of 1916 regarding "weightage" and "separate electorate", and that the Hindus were determined to secure power for themselves. Jinnah led the fourth group of Muslims.

Notwithstanding his disliking for the Congress and its policies adopted under the leadership of Gandhi, Jinnah was a strong follower of the principle of Hindu–Muslim unity and cooperation, peace and harmony. As said above, he was, till late 1920s, a liberal Muslim. He desired to become "The Muslim Gokhale". Sarojini Naidu, a distinguished Congress leader, described him as "the ambassador of Hindu–Muslim unity". He was of opinion that the destiny of Muslims was linked with the rest of Indian population.

In December 1927, the Muslim League held its session in Calcutta. Jinnah advocated a nationalistic point of view, and reiterated his view points that he was in favour of joint electorate and the Delhi proposals sponsored by him.

Jinnah left for England and returned six months later. He was distressed to find the Muslims divided on the provisions of the Nehru Report. He did his best to bring unity among them. He convened All-Parties Conference to meet in Delhi on 31 December 1928 and invited Aga Khan to preside over. But Khan was very much opposed to the Nehru Report as he believed that its hidden agenda was the dominance of the Hindus over the Muslims. Repudiating it, Jinnah, however, said that both the communities would have to work together to achieve the common goal, i.e. freedom from foreign dominance, without any prejudice or bias against one another. They should feel that they had common goals to achieve and they should give up all their differences and keep themselves united and bound by common values and traditions. The progress and prosperity of the country depended upon their mutual love and understanding. Since they had a common goal, since their destination was the same, they should live together, work together and march together. Otherwise, they might not achieve their goal. Their mutual support and cooperation would ensure the unity and integrity of the country.

Nothing was achieved in the meet because of rigid attitude of different Muslim groups. It was, therefore, adjourned to a later date. However, the process should be over by the end of May 1929. Jinnah was authorized to meet representatives of various groups to discuss their view points and give a shape to it and present it before the next session.

After a lengthy and fruitful discussion with the leaders, Jinnah prepared a draft taking into account their diverse views. Main points of the Draft were as follows:

1. India should go for a federal set-up and provinces should enjoy the residuary powers.
2. They should enjoy a uniform measure of autonomy.
3. Minorities should be adequately and effectively represented in all legislatures and elected bodies in every province without reducing the majority in any province to a minority or even equality.
4. The representation of Muslims in the Central Legislature should not be less than one-third.
5. Separate electorates should continue and there should be representation of communal groups. However, it shall be open to any community at any time to abandon its separate electorate in favour of joint electorate.
6. No territorial redistribution should, in any way, affect the Muslim majority in the Punjab, Bengal and the North–West Frontier Province.
7. All communities should enjoy full liberty of belief, worship and observance, propaganda, association and education.
8. No bill or resolution or any part thereof should be passed in any Legislature or in any other elected body if three-fourths of the members of any community in that body opposed it as being injurious to the interests of that community.
9. Sind should no more be a part of Bombay Presidency.
10. Reforms should be introduced in the North–West Frontier Province and Baluchistan on the same footing as in other provinces.
11. Muslims be given adequate representation in all the services of the State subject to the requirements of efficiency.
12. There should be adequate constitutional safeguards for the protection and promotion of Muslim culture, education, language, religion, personal laws and charitable institutions, and for their due share in grants-in-aid given by the State.
13. At least one-third members of the cabinet, either Central or Provincial, should be the Muslims.
14. While bringing any change in the constitution, the Central Legislature should seek the help and cooperation of the States constituting the Indian federation.

CIVIL DISOBEDIENCE MOVEMENT AND JINNAH

When Gandhi launched the Movement, Jinnah, on behalf of the League, declared that they refused to join the Movement because it was not a Movement for complete independence of India, but for making the 70 million Muslims of India dependent on Hindu Mahasabha.

Following his lead, a bulk of the Muslims remained aloof from the Movement. Nevertheless, some Nationalist Muslims, under the leadership of Khan Abdul Gaffar Khan (better known as Frontier Gandhi), Azad and a few others, made common cause with the Congress, and courted arrests and suffered at the hands of the Government.

DR. IQBAL, RAHMAT ALI AND JINNAH

While the Muslim League posed a great challenge to the Congress—its programmes, policies and actions, Dr. Iqbal and Rahmat Ali did their best to motivate, inspire and encourage the Muslims to leave the Congress and join the League and fight for the cause of Muslims. They found Jinnah to be "hard-headed, strong-minded, aggressively anti-nationalist, unwilling to make compromise and fanatic about the theory that the Hindus and the Muslims were two different nations".

SIKANDAR KHAN AND JINNAH

Jinnah firmly believed that creation of Pakistan would solve the communal problem. After the Lucknow Session (1936) of the Muslim League, Jinnah entered into a pact with Sir Sikandar Hayat Khan, leader of the Unionist Party and Premier of Punjab, and the latter declared that he would extend his cooperation to the League in the provincial elections. Jinnah toured the whole country to propagate the League's point of view.

ELECTIONS OF 1937 AND JINNAH'S FALSE ALLEGATIONS

Intensely depressed by the Hindu–Muslim differences, Jinnah settled in London to practise at the British Bar. League leaders like Iqbal, Liaquat Ali Khan requested him to return India so that their goal could be achieved. They succeeded in converting him from a "Nationalist Muslim" to a "Muslim Nationalist". In October 1935, he returned India, became the President of the League and did his best to revitalize it. In April 1936, he convened a special session of the League in Bombay and the decision was taken to fight the elections in Provinces under the new constitutional framework. A campaign for separation and anti-Hinduism was also launched by the League.

Jinnah, according to Nehru, accepted the leadership of the Muslim League not because he really believed in Islam or Pakistan, but because it was a policy which would win him easy attention and secular power and also because that would give him a chance to lash back at Gandhi and those Congress leaders who snubbed him.

Jinnah along with his friends and followers always alleged that Muslims were ill-treated by the Hindus. But all these allegations were baseless, devoid of truth and ill-motivated. For example, following the enactment of the Government of India Act, 1935, elections to the eleven provincial assemblies were held in February 1937 and Congress won an overwhelming victory. It secured absolute majority in five major provinces and was the single largest party in four. It was only in the Punjab and Sind that the Congress did not achieve comparable success.

Of the total 1585 seats, the Congress won 711, with clear majority in five Provinces—United Provinces, Central Provinces, Madras, Bihar and Orissa. In Bombay Presidency, Bengal, Assam and NWFP, the Congress emerged as the biggest single party, and in the Punjab and Sind, it was in a comparatively smaller minority. Of 175 seats in the Punjab, the Congress won only 18, and out of 60 seats in the Sind, the Congress secured only 7. In Bombay, the Congress got 86 out of 175; in Bengal 54 out of 250; in Assam 33 out of 108; and in NWFP 19 out of 50.

When the Congress accepted office, a Parliamentary Board was formed to supervise the work of the minorities and give them general guidance on policy. The Board consisted of Sardar Patel, Dr. Rajendra Prasad and Maulana Abul Kalam Azad. The latter was in charge of the parliamentary affairs in several provinces, viz., Bengal, Bihar, UP, Punjab, Sind and the Frontier. Every incident which involved communal issue came up before Azad. Highly responsible and conscious of his duties, he observed that all the allegations levelled by Jinnah and his friends were absolutely false. He would have certainly gone through them if there had been an iota of truth. Azad was also prepared even to resign if necessary on an issue like this. Levelling false allegations reflects one's immature and imperfect personality. Jinnah undermined his own personality by lowering the image of the Congress.

JINNAH CHANGED HIS STAND

Following the 1937 elections, the Congress launched a programme to keep contact with the Muslims. Jinnah was not happy with such development. Instead, he put forward a proposal suggesting fifty–fifty share of power between the Hindus and the Muslims, between the Muslim India and the 'Non-Muslim India'.

Earlier, he, however, argued that people in India should remain together in peace and harmony as it would certainly ensure the unity and integrity of the country as well as progress and prosperity of its people. But with the change of time, he changed his mind and argued that the Congress as well as the Hindus would dominate others including the Muslims and other minorities. Giving highly emotion-charged slogans like "Congress tyranny" and "Hindu domination", he claimed that the Muslim League was the sole representative of the Muslims in India. Criticizing the Hindus and the Congress being solely their representatives, he promulgated his "Two-Nation Theory" at the Lahore Session (1939) of the Muslim League.

JINNAH: APPREHENSIVE ABOUT COUNTRY'S FUTURE

About the future of country, Jinnah argued in March 1940 that India would be granted Dominion Status and this would be in accordance with Westminster Statute of Great Britain. India would become a democratic society and the power would pass on to the political party securing majority of votes in the elections. He, however, expressed his apprehension about the suitability of such type of government in India being highly heterogeneous in nature. Unless it was taken into account, the future of the country would be bleak and dark.

Jinnah was also against the adoption of a federal form of government, as practised in Canada and Australia, for India. It would be certainly a futile, useless and unproductive exercise. He argued that the British people forgot the religious wars between the Catholics and the Protestants notwithstanding their disastrous consequences. No other incident(s) including the World Wars witnessed or experienced such ravages and destructions as the religious wars in Great Britain and Europe. Things, however, changed. Religion, to them, became a personal matter, an affair between man and God. But this could not be the case in Hinduism and Islam as these religions were definite social codes which governed not so much man's relation with his God, as man's relation with his neighbour. They governed not only his culture but every aspect of his socio-economic and political life.

JINNAH'S ELEVEN DEMANDS

It may be noted that the communal programmes and pronouncements of the Hindu Mahasabha and of the Muslim League widened the gap between them. Instead of working together to achieve the common goal, i.e. 'Independence', they were divided on communal passions. To ease out the tensions and reach at an understanding the Congress leaders like Gandhi, Bose, Nehru met Jinnah. In response to their talks, he presented on 9 October 1938 eleven demands to Congress which, inter alia, meant that Congress should "withdraw all opposition to the Communal Award, give up the song Bande Mataram, not interfere with the Muslims' practice of cow-slaughter and, above all, should recognize the League as the one and the only representative organization of the Indian Muslims. But his demands were rejected by the Congress. Jinnah gave a great blow to the Congress–League unity as all the doors for a settlement were closed. Gandhi's efforts to patch up with Jinnah also failed.

JINNAH REITERATED THE PARTITION OF INDIA

On 10 October 1938, Jinnah while presiding over the Sind Provincial Muslim League declared that India should be divided into Hindustan and Pakistan. The goal was set: it was no less than the division of the country. The ball starting rolling till it reached its destination in 1947. The year saw the emergence of Pakistan.

JINNAH'S CONDITIONAL SUPPORT TO GREAT BRITAIN

During the Second World War, Jinnah extended conditional support of the League and the Indian Muslims to the British Government. In return, he expected that the latter should take them seriously and allow them to grow and prosper. He declared 2 December 1939 as the "Deliverance Day"—a relief from the Congress rule which "at last ceased to function".

The Muslim League in its Lahore Session (1940) passed a resolution seeking the partition of India as it was the only solution to the Indian problem. On 10 January 1941, he appealed in Bombay to Hindus to approach the partition issue with fresh minds as it would enable both the communities to live in peace.

JINNAH AND THE CRIPPS MISSION (1942)

He pursued the matter of partition of India when Sir Stafford Cripps visited India on 22 March 1942 to give some "concessions" to India in respect of its independence. Cripps visited with a motive to break the political deadlock, make an offer of Dominion Status after the War to the people of India "in the most impressive manner". Along with Sir Feroz Khan Nooh, Jinnah wrote a letter to Cripps stating that if Britain did anything to sacrifice the interests of Muslim India, great harm would be done to its war efforts, and that if HM's Government wanted to secure free and equal partnership of the Muslims, the demand for Pakistan should be accepted.

JINNAH AND THE CONGRESS RESOLUTION (1942)

Unhappy with the Congress' Quit India resolution adopted on 14 July 1942, Jinnah appealed the Muslims to remain calm and quiet and asked the Congress leaders not to picket, harass or interfere with Muslims. He condemned the campaign as it was aimed at forcing Congress demands "at the point of bayonet". He declared that if these demands were conceded to pacify and appease the arrogant attitude of Gandhi and his party Congress, it would involve the surrender of all Muslim Rights. He made a fervent appeal to the Hindus to stop this internecine civil war before it was too late. It was because of Jinnah, the League maintained an attitude of "benevolent neutrality" towards the government.

JINNAH REITERATED HIS PARTITION PROPOSAL: GANDHI'S DESIRE TO MEET HIM

On 11 October 1942, Jinnah reiterated the partition proposal when he said:

> We, the Muslims of India, are determined to attain our national freedom and independence by establishing our own independent sovereign states in the north-western and eastern parts of this subcontinent which is our homeland and where we are in a majority.

He called it "a matter of life and death". He said: "Either we achieve Pakistan or we perish". Three weeks later, he again said: "To Congress or Hindu India, Pakistan is anathema. To Muslims of India, it is an article of faith". In his interview to Herbert Mathews, the correspondent of The New York Times on 6 February 1943, he said: "The north-western and the north-eastern states of Pakistan would be connected by a corridor running along the northern borders of the United Provinces and Bihar".

Jinnah again reiterated India's partition in 1943. On the occasion of the Twenty-fourth Session of the League held on 24–28 April 1943, he invited Gandhi to negotiate with him to settle the Congress-League dispute on the basis of Pakistan. He strongly alleged that the Congress did not want to change its policy either vis-à-vis the Government or the League. Gandhi, who was inside the jail, wanted to meet Jinnah but he was not allowed by the Government. Jinnah argued that it was Gandhi who did not write him any letter. Had he written, the Government would not have dared to prevent his letter from reaching him. He alleged that Gandhi's letter was designed only "to embroil" the League "into clash with the British Government and to seek his own release" so that he would be free to do what he pleased thereafter. Jinnah was critical more of Gandhi and other Congress leaders than of the authorities.

Jinnah argued that Hindu–Muslim differences could be resolved with the division or break-up of the country. His argument was not acceptable to many Muslims and their organizations like Jamait-e-Ulema, the Ahrars and the Ittihad-e-Millat. On 4 October 1944, he told the correspondents and reporters of London News Chronicle in an interview: India should be divided into two sovereign countries—Hindustan and Pakistan. Pakistan should include the whole of North-West Frontier Province, Baluchistan, Sindh, Punjab, Bengal and Assam as sovereign Muslim territories. Pakistan should tolerate the Hindu minorities and Hindustan the Muslim minorities.

Jinnah was very much apprehensive whether the Hindus would allow a Pakistan to emerge, whether they would reconcile themselves to Muslims' complete independence.

THE RAJAGOPALACHARI FORMULA

The Cripps Mission failed in 1942. Disappointed, Chakravarti Rajagopalachari, a Congress leader from Madras, sincerely felt that the only way to break the communal deadlock was to accept the League's demand for a separate state. At his behest, the Madras Assembly passed a resolution to this effect. It was then sent to the All India Congress Committee for consideration. The Congress President Maulana Azad vehemently protested against it. Gandhi also did not support it. The rank-and-file of the Congress also opposed it. Unhappy, Rajagopalachari resigned from the Congress Working Committee.

In 1943, while Gandhi was in jail, Rajaji discussed with him a scheme which would serve as a basis for a settlement with the League. In 1944, Gandhi was released from jail. Rajaji communicated his formula to Jinnah, saying that it had Gandhi's "full approval". Though Gandhi approved the formula, he later made it clear that he really did not believe in it, and that what he wanted was some form of self-determination for Muslims in a United India.

The Rajagopalachari Formula went much beyond this. It endorsed the League's Lahore Resolution and, in return, it demanded its support for India's independence and its cooperation to the Congress in the formation of a provisional interim government. 'Contiguous districts' would be demarcated in the north-west and east of India, wherein the Muslim population is in absolute majority. Here plebiscites would be held 'on the basis of adult suffrage' in order to decide the issue of separation from Hindustan. Any transfer of population would be 'on an absolutely voluntary basis'.

Jinnah turned down the formula. He was not satisfied with the offer of "a maimed mutilated and moth-eaten Pakistan". He wanted full six provinces. As far as the franchise was concerned, he said that Muslims alone should be entitled to vote for partition. The Hindu population in the disputed areas did not count. However, he wanted to discuss the issue with Gandhi.

JINNAH–GANDHI TALKS FAILED

During July–August 1944, Gandhi made correspondences with Jinnah on the basis of Rajaji's proposal. But the latter remained non-committal. He then sought an interview with Jinnah and left for Bombay on 9 September 1944. The talks were "free and friendly". During his discussions with Gandhi, Jinnah vehemently argued that Muslims were a nation. But the talks broke down on the issue of Pakistan. In his letter to Gandhi on 15 September 1944, he said that the Muslims and the Hindus were two major nations by any definition or test as a nation. India with a population of one hundred million had its own distinctive culture and civilization, language and literature, art and architecture, names and nomenclature, sense of values and proportion, legal laws and any moral codes, customs and calendar, history and tradition, aptitudes and ambitions. In short, Muslims had their own distinctive outlook on life. By all standards and canons of International Law, "We are a nation." On 8 October 1944, Jinnah proclaimed: there was only one realistic way of resolving Hindu–Muslim differences. This was to divide India into Pakistan and Hindustan. Gandhi's move to resolve differences with Jinnah failed.

GANDHI'S UNDUE IMPORTANCE TO JINNAH

Gandhi gave undue importance to Jinnah. He overrated and overvalued him. Jinnah would not have become what he became, had Gandhi not overestimated him. All this inflated his ego. To Azad, it was one of the greatest blunders of Gandhi as it finally led to the partition of the country. Soon after his release from jail in 1943, Gandhi wanted to strengthen the relationship between the Congress and the Muslim League. In this connection, he wanted to meet Jinnah. By doing so, he, in the words of Azad, committed a great political blunder as it gave a new and added importance to Jinnah who acquired a new image, a new personality, a new status in politics. But, unfortunately, the situation was later exploited by him (Jinnah) and the Muslim League.

Gandhi's attitude towards Jinnah was, from the very beginning, peculiar. Following his separation from the Congress, Jinnah lost much of his popularity. So to say, he became a zero in Indian politics. When his popularity was on its decline, Gandhi came to his, rather unconsciously, rescue. It was largely Gandhi's acts of omission and commission that made Jinnah great and brought him to limelight and gave a status which he did not deserve, nor had he ever enjoyed before. Gandhi's interaction with Jinnah transferred the latter's personality from golden zero to a supreme hero. It may be noted that a large section of Muslims did not have confidence in Jinnah's leadership, his policies and principles. But when they found him to be a blue-eyed baby of Gandhi, they also started taking him seriously, thinking that Jinnah must be 'great', otherwise, Gandhi might not have called him great. They also, like Gandhi, admired him. Many Muslims took special interest in Jinnah and developed a feeling of awe and reverence towards him. They also believed that he would be the best protector and promoter of their interests as they would gain much in the communal settlement.

It was Gandhi who first gave currency to the title Qaid-i-Azam or great leader as applied to Jinnah. He had a lady follower who was foolish but well-intentioned. She was Antus Salam. She had seen in some Urdu papers a reference to Jinnah as Qaid-i-Azam. When Gandhi used to address letters to Jinnah in some connections she told him that since Urdu papers called Jinnah Qaid-i-Azam, he should also follow them by addressing Jinnah Qaid-i-Azam. Without giving a second thought to the consequences of his action, Gandhi addressed him as Qaid-i-Azam. This letter was published in the press. When Indian Muslims saw this news item, they felt that Jinnah must have been a great leader in the true sense of the term, otherwise Gandhi might not have addressed so.

When in July 1944, Maulana read this news about Gandhi's meet with Jinnah in Bombay, he told his colleagues that Gandhi committed a great political blunder. Instead of bringing any solution to India's problems, it would compound them, aggravate them. Later developments confirmed the apprehensions of Maulana Azad. Jinnah made political capital out of Gandhi's attitude towards him and strengthened his position without rendering much to the cause of freedom struggle. He exploited his relationship with Gandhi.

THE SIMLA CONFERENCE (1945)

From the very beginning of the Second World War, the people of the US were in favour of India getting her independence. Because they felt unless she became independent and as long as she remained as a colony she could not take an independent decision. She also could not support the Allied Powers against Axis Powers in the War. After the Pearl Harbour Crisis, the US joined the War and became directly involved in it. President Roosevelt asked Churchill several times to grant freedom to India. As a result, Britain took some steps to meet the demands of the Americans. With the visit of the Cripps Mission to India (1942), it was felt that India would be granted her "Independence" very soon. But the Mission failed.

On 14 June 1945, L.S. Amery, Secretary of State for India, stated in the House of Commons that full scope would be given to India to decide about the War as a free nation. Both the Congress and the Muslim League would be asked to form the Government. In this regard, a Round Table Conference was convened at Simla on 25 June 1945.

The Working Committee of the Congress met on 24 June 1945 and decided to press for the following points:

1. The relation between the Viceroy and the Executive Council should be made categorical. Whether the unanimous decision of the latter would be binding on the former? Whether the Viceroy be allowed to exercise his veto power?
2. The position of the army should be defined. There should not be any barrier between the people (and their leaders) and the army.
3. The British Government had pushed India into the War without consulting her. The Congress strongly criticized it. If there was a settlement and a new Executive Council formed, it must have the right to refer the question of India's participation in the War to the Indian Legislative Assembly.

India would participate in the War against Japan not as a result of a British decision but by a vote of her own representatives.

The Simla Round Table Conference was attended by several prominent delegates including Presidents of the Congress and the Muslim League as well as representatives of Scheduled Castes and the Sikhs.

When members started discussing the issues in the Simla Conference, the differences between the Congress and the Muslim League cropped up on different aspects including the composition of the Executive Council. Jinnah demanded that Congress could nominate all the Hindu Members, but all the Muslim members must be nominated by the League. Congress did not accept it.

The Conference reassembled on 26 June 1945. But its members dispersed before lunch so that the delegates could confer among themselves. Jinnah expressed his desire to talk to the Congress. Maulana Azad nominated Pandit

Govind Ballabh Pant to negotiate with Jinnah. They held prolonged discussions without any result.

The Simla Conference marked a breakwater in Indian politics. It saw the failure on the part of leaders to reach an understanding not on any political issue but on a communal issue that divided different Indian groups.

During the Second World War, it became evident that India would get her freedom without delay. Congress had gained immensely in prestige and strength. Jinnah had also now become the leader of the Muslims and of the League. He exploited to his full advantage any difference, even the smallest one, between the Congress and the Government. He remained silent when discussions on issues like transfer of power were held between the Congress and the Government and also when negotiations failed, Jinnah condemned both the parties and used to say that since the negotiations failed, there was no need for the Muslim League to give any opinion on the British offer. This was what he did during the August offer in 1940 and the Cripps proposals of 1942. The Simla Conference presented him with a new situation that he had never faced before.

In the Simla Conference, Jinnah forcefully argued that neither the Congress should function as a national organization nor it should retain any national character. It should function as a communal organization. His argument was that it should nominate only Hindu members to the Executive Council. But neither Jinnah nor the Muslim League had any right to prevent the Congress from nominating members belonging to the minority groups. The strength of the Hindus would be proportionately reduced with the selection of members from minority communities. Jinnah did not have any business to argue that the Congress should nominate only the Hindu members.

Both the Congress and the Muslim League submitted a panel of five names each to Lord Wavell. But the latter raised their strength from five each to nine each. The list which Lord Wavell himself prepared included four names in addition to the five names each of the Congress and the Muslim League. One of them was a representative of the Sikhs, two of the Scheduled Castes and the fourth was Khizir Jayat Khan, the Premier of Punjab. Jinnah reacted violently to the suggestion that there would be two Muslims in the Executive Council who were not his nominees.

The Simla Conference ended in failure: the reason was not any political issue but communal in nature.

JINNAH AND CABINET MISSION PLAN (1946)

The Cabinet Mission Plan of 1946 was the first British proposal that directly admitted the possibility of independence. This possibility became a reality within two years of time. None could believe that things could move so swiftly. End of the Second World War, coming of Labour Party into power in Great Britain, the US' insistence that India should get freedom—all these expedited the process of making India 'free'.

The Mission consisted of three ministers of the new British cabinet: Lord Petrick Lawrence, Sir Stafford Cripps and A.V. Alexander. As the British Government was eager to grant independence, it decided to hold discussions on the framing of a constitution, setting up a constitution—making body, and appointing a new Executive Council.

The Mission favoured an undivided Union of India consisting of all the British provinces and Princely States. The idea of Pakistan was rejected. The Mission made concrete proposals for the setting up of a Constituent Assembly, and formation of an interim or provincial government. Both the Congress and the Muslim League accepted the Mission's Proposal with reservations. While the Congress agreed to join the Constituent Assembly, the Muslim League backed out. Frustrated, it wanted to take direct action and 16 August was fixed as Direct Action Day. Peaceful demonstrations were held at different places to show to the world that Muslims were one and united.

The situation, however, took a different turn. Hindu–Muslim clash marred the atmosphere, taking a heavy toll of lives and properties. The communal madness or frenzy that saw killings of thousands of innocent people and the worst orgies of violence came to normal because of tremendous efforts on the part of Gandhi.

On 12 August 1946, Lord Wavell asked Nehru, as the leader of the largest party, to form an Interim Government. Nehru submitted twelve names and offered five portfolios to the Muslim League which declined the offer. On 2 September 1946, the Interim Government was sworn in. The absence of the League in the Ministry was a severe setback. Nehru, therefore, requested Jinnah to propose the names of five persons for the ministry. On 13 October 1946, the latter agreed. Among the new Ministers was Liaqat Ali Khan, who was given the important Finance portfolio. Khan abused his position by rejecting or modifying every proposal that came up for consideration. Though he was in the Government, he was always against it. The administration came to a standstill.

The Muslim League members refused to take part in the Constituent Assembly. It even went to the extent of demanding its dissolution.

Meanwhile, Lord Wavell was replaced by Lord Mountbatten. The latter reached India on 22 March 1947. Though he was instructed to work for a United India, he realized, after consulting leaders of different parties, that partition was inevitable. Though Congress leaders stood for a United India, Jinnah felt that Muslims must have a separate state for themselves.

Jinnah's desire was fulfilled with the inauguration of Dominion of Pakistan in Karachi on 14 August 1947, 'a day of sorrow' for India.

CONCLUSION

Born in Karachi and died in Karachi, Muhammed Ali Jinnah had only one agenda in his life, i.e. the creation of a state for Muslims. Initially, he was a devout nationalist. But later, he became communal. He felt that the Muslims being minority would be suppressed by the Hindus who constituted the majority. It was this fear that goaded him to demand a separate state for Muslims. He achieved his goal in 1947 when Muslims got Pakistan, a new state, a new homeland that would ensure a new hope, a new confidence, a new strength.

It was decided that the Indian Dominion would come into existence on 15 August 1947. The Muslim League decided that Pakistan should be constituted a day earlier on 14 August. There was an unpleasant incident even about the birth of two dominions. According to the convention, a dominion could choose its own Governor-General and many dominions had appointed their own nationals to this post. India was, therefore, free to choose an Indian to this highest office of free India. She, however, decided that it would be better not to make a sudden change and felt that the appointment of Lord Mountbatten would help in maintaining continuity of polity and administration. It was also thought that in the initial stages, there would be one Governor-General for the Dominions and any change could be carried out later. It was generally thought that Pakistan would be influenced by the same considerations.

India accordingly announced that Lord Mountbatten was her choice for the Governor-General. She also expected that the Muslim League would also select him, but at that moment the League caused a surprise by proposing that Jinnah should be appointed the first Governor-General of Pakistan. And he became the first Governor-General of Pakistan.

"The proposition that communalism has a logic of its own and, if not checked in its early stages, inevitably develops into its 'higher' stages, is illustrated by the life history of Muhammad Ali Jinnah". His case shows how communalism is an inclined plane on which a constant slide down becomes inevitable unless countersteps are taken. Once the basic digits of communal ideology are accepted, the ideology takes over a person bit by bit, independent of the subjective desires of the person. This is how a person who started as the "Ambassador of Hindu–Muslim Unity" ended up by demanding Pakistan" and finally became its first Governor-General.

POINTS TO REMEMBER

- Jinnah was a nationalist, a liberalist, a conservative. He was not religious.
- Elected to the Imperial Legislative Council. A brilliant parliamentarian.
- Jinnah opposed the Muslim League's demand for separate electorate. He did not join it in the beginning of its formation. He branded it as a communal organization.
- His attempt in maintaining and promoting communal harmony.
- He joined the Home Rule League. Sincerely wanted India's independence.
- He joined the Muslim League in 1913 and left the Congress in 1920.
- A Member of the Muddiman and Skeen Committees.

- He rejected the Nehru Report. His 14 points.
- His false allegations against the Congress and its leaders. He always developed a fear that Hindus would dominate the Muslims.
- His conditional support to the British Government during the Second World War.
- His only aim was to see the creation of an Independent state for the Muslims.
- He strongly opposed the principles, policies and programmes of the Congress.
- His dream was realized when an independent state was created for Muslims in 1947.

19

Lala Lajpat Rai (1865–1928)

INTRODUCTION

A formidable personality, a powerful leader, a learned scholar, a gifted orator, a prolific writer, a versatile genius, an effective political actor endowed with wisdom and foresight, and a "dangerous revolutionary", Lala Lajpat Rai was the greatest man, next to Ranjit Singh, ever produced by the State of Punjab. Popularly known as the "Lion of Punjab", he was the founder of the Servants of People Society. A brave and courageous freedom fighter dedicated to the nation and its freedom, he rendered significant service to the nation during its freedom struggle.

An author of outstanding works like *Unhappy India* (which he wrote in response to Catherine Mayo's Mother India), *National Education, Young India* (1916), *England's Debt to India, The Political Future of India* (1919), *The United States of America: A Hindu's Impressions and a Study*, he published some tracts like *The Fight for Crumbs*, *A Call to Young India*, *An Open Letter to Lloyd George* and *Self-determination for India*. He also wrote small biographies of Sri Krishna, Ashoka, Shivaji, Swamy Dayanand, Gurudatta and *The Story of My Deportation* (1908), etc.

A national hero endowed with an indomitable spirit and courage, a staunch nationalist, a great social reformer, he commanded both awe and reverence from his associates, friends and followers. Founder of the Indian Home Rule League in the US (16 October 1916) and the Indian Labourers Association, he left an indelible print on the sands of time. Founder of the Tilak School of Politics, he spread the message of Swaraj across the country. Founder of three papers, *The Punjabee*, *The Bande Mataram* (in Urdu) and *The People* (in English), he also wrote his autobiography.

Born on 28 January 1865 in Jagaraon in the Ludhiana district of Punjab, he left his mortal frame for his heavenly abode on 17 November 1928. In 1883, he opened a new chapter in his life by joining the Jagaraon Bar as an advocate. Then he shifted to the Hissar Bar and then to Lahore Bar in 1892. By dint of his hard work and honesty, sacrifice and sincerity, dedication and devotion, he carved out a place for himself in the arena of politics as well as in his profession. Influenced and inspired by the Arya Samaj, he was selfless, fearless and service-oriented.

His close contact with Lala Saindas and Pandit Gurudatta Vidyarthi enkindled in him the fire of patriotism. A prominent member of the DAV College (Lahore: June 1896), a dynamic and revolutionary leader, a biographer of Garibaldi (1892–93) and of Mazzini (1895), he was profoundly influenced by the works and deeds of Mazzini and Garibaldi and inspired by the book *Life and Teachings of Mazzini*, he translated Mazzini's Duties of Man in Urdu.

Initially, an admirer of Sayyed Ahmed Khan, Lala's father Munshi Ramachandra changed his mind when the Khan became "communal". Frustration and disappointment forced him to publish an open letter against Khan in the paper *Kohinoor*. In 1877, he came under the influence of Swami Dayanand Saraswati.

Lajpat Rai also read Sayyed Khan's book *The Causes of Mutiny*, and his journals *Social Reformer* and *Aligarh Institute Gazette*. Unhappy and enraged with his views, he published in the press letters strongly criticizing his views. His open letters to Khan could be compared to the Letters of Junius. Publication of letters helped him to make an entry into politics. In 1888, three years after the formation of the Congress, he joined the organization. Attending its Allahabad Session, he distributed copies of his "Letters to Khan" among the delegates.

VISIT TO THE UK AND THE US

Within a short period he became very popular among the members of the Congress. In 1905, he along with Gokhale, left for England as a Congress delegate to articulate the grievances of Indians before the public. They went there to persuade the authorities to give up their proposal to partition the Bengal. But they failed. They were ignored and their submission was rejected by an imperial power. Their requests were turned down. From the UK Rai made a short trip to the US for three weeks.

BANARAS SESSION OF THE CONGRESS (1905)

The beginning of the 20th century witnessed a new phase in the political life of India. It was the emergence of militant leadership in Congress. The new leaders of the movement were Bal Gangadhar Tilak, Bipin Chandra Pal and Lala Lajpat Rai, the "Lion of Punjab". Denouncing the Congress policy of the past fifteen years as "political mendicancy", condemning the peaceful and constitutional methods as "useless" and acclaiming the virtues of direct action and forceful activity, they did their best to influence the course of the Congress movement by giving it a new orientation. Striving their best to make it more active and dynamic, they preferred some political agitations so that the presence of the Congress as an organization would be felt. But they were not supported by the moderate leaders like Dadabhai Naoroji, Surendra Nath Banerjee, Pherozeshah Mehta, Gopal Krishna Gokhale who were committed to their policy of gradual socio-political reforms, and the remaking of India largely in the image of the West.

Rai and his associates including Tilak presented their programme (Boycott, Swadeshi and National Education) in the Banaras Session of the Congress held in 1905 for adoption. Rai told the Congress that the British bureaucracy was too busy with their own affairs, that the British press was unwilling to champion Indian aspirations, and that it was hard to get a hearing in England. He observed that if "the Indians really cared for their country, they would have to strike the blow for freedom themselves, and that they would have to furnish unmistakable proofs of their earnestness". He acted as a conciliator between the President (of the session) Gopal Krishna Gokhale and Bal Gangadhar Tilak, an extremist.

RAI'S DEPORTATION

The year 1907 was a crucial year for India. Following Curzon's assumption of office as Viceroy, the political atmosphere was surcharged with full of tension. The Morley–Minto partnership failed to assuage the Indian feeling. Early in May 1907, the Government of India received information from Sir Denzil Ibbetson, the Lieutenant-Governor of Punjab, on Punjab's political situation which was "exceedingly serious" and "exceedingly dangerous". The Editor of the *Punjabee*, a nationalist paper, stirred up feelings in Lahore. Tension also prevailed in Rawalpindi, Ambala, Ferozepur, Multan and other towns. The most disconcerting feature of the unrest was that it had a great bearing upon the rural areas and the ruralites. Lower rank revenue officials resorted to strikes by not collecting revenues. Carriages and other conveniences were denied to officers on tour. Policemen were being pilloried and forced to quit the service of an alien government.

Sir Denzil was convinced that the brain behind the agitation was Lajpat Rai of the Arya Samaj. His minute was received in Simla on 3 May 1907 by the Central Government. Within ten days, Regulation III of 1818 had been resurrected from the dusty State Archives and applied to the "dangerous revolutionary", Lala Lajpat Rai, who was, along with Sardar Ajit Singh, taken in a special train (bypassing Calcutta) to Diamond Harbour where the steamer Guide was waiting to carry him to his ultimate destination—Mandalay gaol in Burma.

NAGPUR SESSION OF THE CONGRESS

After his release on 7 September 1907, the New Party of the Nationalists wanted to make Rai the President of the forthcoming Nagpur Session of the Congress. But he withdrew from the contest as the moderates opposed his candidature.

VISITED THE UK, THE US AND JAPAN

In 1914, he visited England along with other Congress delegates including Bhupendra Nath Basu, Jinnah and others. From there, he went to the US. He stayed there for five years. However, during this period he visited Japan for six months.

CONGRESS SESSIONS HELD AT CALCUTTA AND NAGPUR

Lala presided over the Calcutta Session of the Congress held during 4–9 September 1920. In a resolution, the Congress strongly criticized the Majority Report of the Hunter Committee and did not agree with its findings and recommendations. Gandhi urged the Congress to adopt the policy of "progressive non-violent and non-cooperation" until the wrongs were righted and Swaraj (self-rule) was established. Lala, Gangadhar Tilak, Madan Mohan Malaviya, Mrs. Besant, Motilal Nehru, Chittaranjan Das and Bipin Chandra Pal opposed Gandhi's resolution. The resolution was, however, adopted by 1886 delegates, while 884 delegates rejected it. It came up for approval before the annual session of the Congress held at Nagpur. The opponents of the resolution secretly met before attending and participating in the session. Chittaranjan Das brought 250 delegates from East Bengal and Assam at a cost of ₹36,000 from his own pocket to undo what had been done in Calcutta. But Gandhi won and his critics including Lala lost the battle.

RAI ARRESTED

In mid-November 1921, the Prince of Wales visited India officially with an intention to congratulate the people for supporting the Government during the War period. But he was shown black flags wherever he visited. The Government took drastic action on a comprehensive scale. Lala was arrested.

LEFT THE CONGRESS

Disillusioned with the philosophy of Gandhi, Lala left the Congress in 1922, joined the Swaraj Party and became its Deputy Leader in the Central Legislative Assembly in 1925. Party's 'walkout' from the House and its preparedness to sanction concessions to Muslims made him unhappy. As a result, he resigned from it and along with Madam Mohan Malaviya formed the National Party which achieved stupendous success in the elections.

RE-ELECTED TO THE CENTRAL ASSEMBLY

In 1926, he was re-elected to the Central Assembly. He attended the Eighth International Labour Conference held at Geneva as the representative of Indian labourers.

SELF-GOVERNMENT TO SWARAJ

Opposed to Simon Commission and the Public Safety Bill of the Government, Rai, however, initially supported the colonial form of Self-Government. But later, he demanded Swaraj (full dominion status) in 1928.

LAHORE PROCESSION (1928) AND DEATH OF LALA

On 30 October 1928, Lala led a procession in Lahore boycotting the Simon Commission. Presiding over a large gathering, Lala gave a fiery and provocative speech. When the Simon Commission arrived at Lahore, the police beat up a crowd which was demonstrating in front of the railway station. Rai received two blows on his chest. He succumbed to his injuries on 17 November 1928. His unexpected and tragic death sent a wave of humiliation and indignation throughout the country. Its consequences were diametrically opposite: on one hand, the demonstrators intensified their demonstration and boycott and, on the other, the Government became more and more vindictive towards the demonstrators.

Rai's death provoked the young dynamic and brave leaders who considered it a great and direct challenge to them. And so, on 17 December 1928, Bhagat Singh, Azad and Rajguru assassinated at Lahore, Saunders, a police official involved in the lathi-charge on Lala Lajpat Rai. The assassination was justified as follows:

> The murder of a leader respected by millions of people at the unworthy hands of an ordinary police official ... was an insult to the nation. It was the bounden duty of young men of India to efface it. We regret to have had to kill a person but he was part and parcel of that inhuman and unjust order which was to be destroyed.

A NATIONALIST

A staunch nationalist, Lala firmly believed that every nation including India was free to decide its own course of action, its own culture, its own preferences. Any amount of interference in this regard would be unjust. India should do its best to lay the foundation of a strong independent political life. Consent, not force, should be the basis of the state.

In *Young India* (1916) he not only discussed the history of national movement but also interpreted it brilliantly. To him, British never conquered India by sword and bloodshed but by conspiracy, treachery and secret machinations. The 1857 Revolution was both political and national. A deep and powerful force, it was nurtured by sacrifice of the freedom fighters. Favouring a parliamentary form of government, he always argued that Indians were partially matured and fit to be members of representative institutions. Nationalism as a force could not be suppressed. More its suppression, greater would be its momentum and strength. More the British Governors and Viceroys resorted to violent means to suppress it, more it became powerful. It could not be suppressed.

Laying emphasis upon liberty, the essence of democracy; declaring that 'independence' should be the goal of India; criticizing the government policy of economic exploitation of the Indians and denouncing the denial and deprivation of their dues, Lala wanted an integrated development of the people. No more they should be misguided by any biases, caste and racial prejudices. No more there should be exploitation, inequality, humiliation, torture, oppression, etc. He wanted the uplift of the masses.

SOCIALISM

On 20 February 1920, he returned from the US. Thereafter, he started propagating and popularizing socialist ideas. The preface of his book *The Arya Samaj* was written by Sidney Webb, a famous socialist. He never wanted the capitalists and landlords to be more powerful than what they were.

Unhappy with the contemporary society, its functioning and organization, its cruelty and barbarism, he encouraged workers' participation in the management of the industries. The First President of the Indian Trade Union Congress, he wanted that India should send its delegates to International Labour Organization. Urging upon the intellectuals to take care of the labourers, criticizing the British liberals for their hypocritical imperialism and capitalism, he asked the Indians to keep more faith in the British Labour Party.

Exploitation, to Rai, must be brought to an end. If it continued and people were allowed to suffer, communism would be the order of the day. Equality, liberty, freedom, rights—all these would keep communism at a distance.

Lala did not subscribe to Marx's view that capitalism would give rise to or bring in dictatorship of the proletariat. Even if it was true, he never wanted that capitalism should grow and strengthen its roots in India. Socialism or Bolshevism would be more dependable and reliable.

HINDU IDEOLOGY

During the First World War, Lala was in the West and there he wrote a famous book, *The Arya Samaj*, in which he said that the Arya Samaj should be more tolerant and universalistic in nature. Attached to Punjab Arya Samaj during his early career, he strongly criticized the Pundits like Lekharam and Gurudatta as they were fanatic and dogmatic. He never appreciated their dogmatic fanaticism.

The religion that gave strength and sustenance to people should be protected, promoted and preserved and that which was dysfunctional or harmful should be criticized, condemned, discarded and discouraged. There should be a perfect reconciliation between the ancient culture and modern institutions. A society should have both. It should be both modern and conservative, progressive and dynamic. An Arya Samajist, he was under the influence of ancient culture and traditions. One should not move away from the past by abandoning culture, tradition, values, etc. To him, divorce from religion would be a risky affair. Old values had still their relevance. Religion along with ancient culture, tradition and values gave a purpose and meaning to one's life. Modern civilization might have made his life more comfortable. But religion provided him peace and happiness and made him moral and spiritual, promoted his socio-economic development. To him, a true follower of religion should be free from biases and prejudices and be rational and objective.

His stay in the West developed in him a comprehensive approach to life. He sincerely felt that there should be perfect synthesis between the East and the West. He believed that it was high time to discontinue and discard the philosophies of Manu, Narada and Apastamba. He never admired a dull uniformity or rigid monotony. While criticizing Dickinson, he maintained that the East had a great degree of unity in the field of "religious ideals, intellectual norms, social patterns of behaviour and artistic criteria". Nevertheless, he wanted that the East should imbibe the spirit of the West and adopt and assimilate her intellectual achievements. He had a strong liking for western philosophies and its institutions. Bertrand Russel and John Dewey exerted a tremendous influence upon him.

Lalaji always, like any other Congress leader, favoured unity and cooperation between the Hindus and the Muslims. At the same time, unlike other Congress leaders, he never wanted that the interests of the Hindus should be affected or jeopardized. Some Congress leaders argued that since the Muslims were in minority, they should be given certain concessions, benefits or privileges. He never agreed with them.

As the President of the Hindu Mahasabha (1925), he presided over its Calcutta Session and laid down the following policies and programmes: To organize Seva Samitis (Service Centres); popularize Hindi; set up gymnasiums for imparting physical training to the young Hindus; persuade reconversion to Hinduism; organize Hindu Mahasabha regularly and throughout the country; provide help to the riot victims (only the Hindus); request the managers of the Hindu temples to allow the halls for holding meetings to discuss the matters of socio-economic interest; promote understanding among the people belonging to different religions; represent communal interests of the Hindus in all political controversies; encourage Hindu boys to launch industries; improve the socio-economic conditions of women and promote understanding between Hindu agriculturists and non-agriculturists.

Lala considered the existing caste structure and system a slur, an evil, a challenge, a problem, a hindrance, an obstacle to growth and development of the society. Hence it required immediate attention.

A supporter of Nehru Report and an opponent of the communal electorate, he, however, suggested that Punjab should be divided into the Western Punjab with Muslim majority to be governed by the Muslims, and the Eastern Punjab to be governed by the Hindus and Sikhs.

CONCLUSION

A great leader of modern India, a "dangerous revolutionary", a man of strong determination and iron will, he rendered significant contributions to the mankind through the Arya Samaj. His deportation in 1907 and his death in 1928 were the epoch-making events in the history of modern Indian nationalism.

A dedicated worker with a commitment to the cause of the nation and its people, he was an eminent social reformer. Aware of socialism, capitalism, bolshevism and labour organization, he was a pioneer in propagating socialist ideas in India.

He was not a political theorist or philosopher in true sense of the term. But he was thorough in sociology, political science, economics, etc. His range of knowledge in these fields was encyclopaedic. His contributions to India were superb and he did a very splendid job by joining the freedom struggle of India.

Lala Lajpat Rai, better known as "Lion of Punjab", did for the Punjab what Bipin Chandra Pal and Bal Gangadhar Tilak did for Bengal and Maharashtra respectively. A patriot, an educationist, a social worker, a religious reformer, an effective journalist and a leading member of the Lahore Bar, he was the leader of the Arya Samaj Movement in the Punjab and did a very good job by providing relief to the people from the rut of anachronistic rituals. An effective public speaker, a powerful leader of militant nationalism, he had the capacity for rousing the indignation of the masses and producing thrilling effect upon their minds.

POINTS TO REMEMBER

- Born in 1865 in the State of Punjab, he was rightly called as the "Lion of Punjab".
- Founder of the Servants of People Society, a prolific writer, a staunch nationalist, a great social reformer, he was the founder of the India Home Rule League and of the Tilak School of Politics. He spread the message of the Swaraj.
- He opposed the writings of Sayyed Ahmed Khan, joined the Congress in 1888 and became very popular in the organization. Visited the UK and the US in 1905.
- Banaras Session of the Congress (1905): Rift between the moderates and extremists was resolved. The latter placed their agenda before the Congress.
- He was deported in 1907.

- Nagpur Session of the Congress in September 1907: Withdrew from the contest to the office of President.
- Congress sessions at Calcutta and Nagpur.
- He was arrested in November 1921 during the visit of Prince of Wales to India.
- Left the Congress in 1922 out of disgust.
- He was re-elected to the Central Assembly.
- Lahore procession and death of Lala in 1928.
- A nationalist: India to decide its own fate, determine its own culture, take its own action without any interference from any quarter. The 1857 Revolution was both political and national. Favoured a parliamentary form of government. Nationalism as a force could not be suppressed. Wanted to have an integrated development of the people.
- A socialist: Unhappy with the existing conditions in the society. Encouraged people's participation in the management of the industries. Against exploitation. Opposed Marx's views.
- Hindu ideology: He asked the Hindus to be more tolerant and universalist. Religion, if it was true in spirit, would give protection to one and all. It should reconcile ancient culture with modern institutions. It should be modern and conservative. No one should be away from it. Philosophies of Manu, Narada and Apastamba be given up. He was the President of the Hindu Mahasabha.
- Criticized the existing caste structure.

20

Ram Manohar Lohia (1910–1967)

INTRODUCTION

A powerful exponent of socialism, a strong advocate of decentralized economy, an effective and eloquent speaker, Ram Manohar Lohia played an important role in freedom movement. An outspoken critic of Nehru, he did not appreciate his non-alignment policy. A promoter of Hindi as a national language, he was convinced that India would remain backward unless English was replaced by Hindi and other regional languages. Instrumental in holding the Asian Socialist Conference in 1953 in India, he rendered significant contributions to the growth and progress of socialist movement in India.

In 1952, as the President of the Congress Socialist Party, which was formed in May 1934, Lohia made a fervent plea to make socialist thought more and more Gandhi-centric or Gandhianized. Unlike Communists, he preferred small industries, small machines so that there would be maximum use of labour force with minimum capital investment. Unhappy and dissatisfied, his critics criticized him in Panchmarhi Socialist Convention held in May 1952 for his ideas. In June 1953, Ashok Mehta propounded a theory called "Political Compulsions of a Backward Economy" and argued that since the Congress had become more and more 'socialist' in nature, there should be greater cooperation between the Congress and the Praja Socialist Party. Lohia, as a counterpoise to it, offered his 'equidistant theory'. As his socialism had been greatly influenced by Gandhian thought, he felt that the socialists were maintaining almost equidistance from the communists and the Congress. He urged the Praja Socialist Party not to enter into any alliance with the Congress but, if necessary, it should be ready to have electoral adjustments with either the communists or the Congress.

The Socialist Party was formed in December 1955 and Lohia became its first Chairman.

POLITICAL AND SOCIOLOGICAL IDEAS

History

Like Aristotle, Lohia also said that history always moves in a cyclical way but never in straightlinear direction. In the course of cyclical movement, a country may reach its zenith in respect of its civilization, scientific development, etc. Then it takes a U-turn and faces the worst crisis. It goes down to the nadir, to rise, perhaps, again. The exponents of the cyclical theory of history are Sorokin, Spengler, Northrop, etc. Earlier, India was rich, highly developed and advanced. It used to attract students from outside. But now it has taken a U-turn.

Asian Socialists should be Original

Lohia always stressed that the Asian socialists should be original in their thinking and initiative. It is not the western ideology, but the existing socio-economic conditions in Asia that should influence their writings. While writing they should not forget that the Asian society had been slowly emerging from the past social order: despotism and feudalism. The history of a society is often influenced by religion, caste, class, etc. as it is full of biases and prejudices. Another weakness of Asian society was the emergence of a new class of bureaucrats and technocrats.

Corrupt Leaders

Flaws and deficiencies in a system have given rise to the emergence of such leaders who have exploited the poor, helpless and innocent people to their maximum advantage. Self-centred, narrow, mean and irrational and unscientific in their approach and outlook, they try to acquire and perpetuate themselves in power by all means. To them, end justifies the means. They maintain themselves in office through demagogic and theatrical social philosophy.

Four-pillar State

An exponent of a four-pillar state, he observed that in this system, the village, the mandal (the district), the province and the central government all retain their importance and are integrated in a system of functional federalism. In such a state there should be no district magistracy.

Decentralized Socialism

Lohia was an advocate of decentralized socialism. This implies small machine, cooperative labour and village government. Averse to mounting unemployment, he was in favour of small unit machine as a remedy against capitalist concentration.

Poverty

He strongly believed that the problem of poverty could be addressed by the state by adopting a Thirteen-point programme. The state should take steps to:

- lower the prices on the basis of parity between agricultural and industrial prices;
- adopt austerity measures (income or salary should not exceed one hundred rupees per month);
- encourage the invention and manufacture of small unit machines;
- take over the sick industries;
- appoint an impartial and independent anticorruption commission;
- allow tillers to have full control over the land they cultivate; possession of land to be within a range of 12½ and 30 acres of land; wrong entries in Patwaris registers to be rectified;
- recruit food army for the cultivation of one crore acres of new land;
- decentralize the administration and economy so as to achieve the four-pillar state;
- undertake housing programme and other economic activities to provide full employment;
- setup polytechnics, high schools and cultural activity centres;
- old adult franchise elections in unrepresented areas, i.e. merged states and unions;
- maintain world peace and cooperation; every nation should be free and independent and it should enjoy rights; there should be socio-economic equality among nations; and
- recruit volunteer bands for agriculture, irrigation, road-making and the like.

NEW SOCIALISM

Declaring the orthodox and organized socialism as a dead doctrine and a dying organization, he argued that there should be a New Socialism and outlined a six-point plan for it. To him, in the fields of income and expenditure, maximum equalitarian standards should be maintained. Nationalization of resources, organizations, institutions, etc. would go a long way in this regard. It would be an important measure to achieve the goal. Resources were to be tapped and harnessed so that standards of living could be raised.

WORLD PARLIAMENT/INDIVIDUAL'S FREEDOM

An exponent of World Parliament elected on some sort of adult franchise, a powerful advocate of democratic freedoms, he strongly argued that every individual should be absolutely free to lead a private life and no interference from any quarter could be tolerated. A Gandhian in true spirit, he was always of the opinion that people can resort to collective civil disobedience for the protection of their rights.

ON INDIA'S ECONOMIC AND HISTORICAL DYNAMICS

India should be a socialist society. This was his only mission and goal. This could be realized through civil disobedience. Dissatisfied with the functioning of the Congress as an organization as it was under the control and influence of capitalists, landlords, bourgeoisie and other vested interests, he wanted to achieve his goal through Gandhian means.

Peasants being the victims of the landlords, zamindars and rich class, should be 'liberated' from their bondage. India's prosperity and progress depended on their socio-economic conditions. If they were happy, the nation would be happy. Otherwise, not. Therefore, all kinds of suppressions should be suppressed, protested and resisted.

OPPOSED CASTE STRUCTURE

He fought tooth and nail against the caste structure. He denounced it, condemned it. A socialist society could be built up if backward castes combined with poor elements found in the upper castes. He had a strong conviction that unless the Shudras, Harijans and the tribals were emancipated and given a space to play an active role in the socio-economic and political system, India would never progress.

CRITICIZED INDIAN ECONOMY

He was opposed to ostentatious display of wealth. He reprimanded those who indulged in luxury. He did not hesitate to speak with courage and confidence that the average income of thousands of India's teeming millions was less than three *annas* a day. His bold and fearless statement exposed the hollowness, ugliness and emptiness of the Indian economy.

ABOLITION OF LAND REVENUE

He boldly said that land revenue on uneconomic holdings should be abolished. It was a revolutionary slogan given by an outspoken, brave and courageous leader. Land revenue on unprofitable holdings would, if not abolished, give a severe blow to the poor peasants and increase their insurmountable difficulties.

ENGLISH LANGUAGE TO BE REPLACED

People called Lohia a mad fellow, a maniac, an eccentric when he argued that the English language, the symbol of domination and exploitation, should be replaced by Hindi and other regional languages in public institutions.

CONGRESS TO BE REPLACED

For the first time he argued in 1966 that the Congress which ruled the country, both in the states and at the Centre, should be replaced by non-Congress opposition parties by forming coalition governments. But it was not taken seriously. However, his prediction came true when in 1967 coalition governments led by non-Congress parties were formed in various states. It shows he had a hunch, a premonition, an intuition. He diagnosed the Indian dynamics with precision and correctness.

INDIA AND PAKISTAN TO FORM A CONFEDERATION

He also argued that India and Pakistan should form a confederation. He attributed the formation of Pakistan to some old and ailing leaders of the Congress who had a lust for power. They were more interested in acquisition and perpetuation of power than in maintaining the unity and integrity of the country. He also attributed the formation of Pakistan to shrewd and cunning diplomacy of the British Government which always wanted a divided India on the basis of religion. The rift between the Hindus and the Muslims was a boon for the British as it gave them a space to perpetuate themselves in power for a longer period. British diplomacy succeeded in creating a wedge between the Hindus and the Muslims in the Indian subcontinent.

Lohia felt that Gandhi should not have yielded for the creation of Pakistan. Since its formation could not be outdone, a confederation between India and Pakistan could be formed for the sake of stability and progress of the two countries.

A passionate and fearless fighter for freedom in every sphere of life, he took steps to liberate Goa in June 1946. He also initiated a movement against the Ranas of Nepal.

INDIAN CULTURE

Lohia had his own interpretation of Indian culture. To him, Vasistha and Parsuram symbolized caste orthodoxy, while Valmiki and Viswamitra were the champions of liberal and open philosophy. While Lord Rama stood for moderation and restraint, Lord Krishna, to him, was "a thief, a liar, a cheat, a killer". His opinion on Lord Krishna was unwarranted and undesirable. This must have hurt the sentiments of millions and millions of the devotees of Lord Krishna. Casting aspersion upon a person who is regarded as Lord was not at all wise on his part to do so. To him, Lord Siva is the symbol of infinity. In modern times, Nehru, to him, typified the tradition of Vasistha while Gandhi belonged to the tradition of Ram. One should not give much importance to what Lohia said on God, sages and seers.

CONCLUSION

While Narendra Deva and Jaya Prakash Narayan were influenced by Marx and his philosophy, Lohia was more Gandhi-centric, Gandhi-oriented. He leaned heavily on Gandhism.

He made a significant contribution to socialist thought. He gave it a new look and made it Indianized. He wanted an integrated and wholesome development of the society as well as of the individual. He was strongly opposed to any lopsided development. He criticized caste structure, oppression of peasants, formation of Pakistan, the self-centred politicians, heavy industries, land revenue system, etc.

POINTS TO REMEMBER

- An exponent of socialist thought, an advocate of cottage industries, Lohia played an important role in freedom struggle.
- He criticized Nehru's foreign policy. A promoter of the Hindi as a national language, he wanted the abolition of English as a language in India.
- He criticized caste structure, exploitation of peasants, formation of Pakistan, narrow-minded politicians, etc.
- Congress as an organization to be abolished.
- Non-Congress parties to form governments in various states.
- Depended heavily on Gandhian philosophy.

21

Vinayak Damodar Savarkar (1883–1966)

INTRODUCTION

A man of action and vision, a fearless fighter and revolutionary, an ardent and outstanding patriot, a great and extraordinary nationalist, Vinayak Damodar Savarkar was a towering personality in Pre-Independent India. Daring and dashing, brave and courageous, outstanding and outspoken, he never hesitated to call spade a spade and never compromised his principles. By nature and nurture he was a great, a perfect, a just and an upright Hindu who understood the basic tenets and principles of Hinduism. The essence and spirit of Hinduism used to 'flow' through his verses. History of India would have been different and Indian politics would have taken a different shape and Savarkar been duly recognized for his significant contributions to the Indian freedom struggle.

LIFE SKETCH

Born on 28 May 1883 in Bhagpur, a tiny village in the Nasik district of Maharashtra, Vinayak Damodar Savarkar, a born patriot and revolutionary, lost his mother Radhabai in 1892 and his father Damodarpant in 1898 (9 September). His elder brother Ganesh looked after the family. In 1898, the British hanged the Chapakar brothers in Pune for killing a British officer. This incident deeply stirred the emotional feelings of a young man. This agitated him, enraged him, hurt his sentiments. Angry and annoyed, he took a vow in 1898 before the family deity to wage armed revolt against the British regime. And to achieve his goal, he founded Mitra Mela, a servant revolutionary society on 1 January 1900. He entered into wedlock with Yamuna Mai on 1 March 1901. He was blessed with a daughter

(Prabhat by name) on 7 January 1925 and a son (Viswas) on 17 March 1928. He passed Matriculation examination (19 December 1901) and soon after he was admitted in Fergusson College, Pune on 24 January 1902. He passed his BA examination in December 1905. In May 1904, he founded a revolutionary organization called Abhinav Bharat and organized in November 1905 a public meeting in Pune to burn foreign clothes.

LITERARY ACTIVITIES

As he got a scholarship, he left for London in June 1906. On 10 May 1907, he celebrated the Golden Jubilee of Indian War of Independence, 1857. Inspired by the role played by Mazzini in the unification of Italy, he wrote a book *Joseph Mazzini* in June 1907. It was later published by Babarao Savarkar. He wrote another one *Indian War of Independence*, 1857 in 1908. It was secretly published in Holland. Copies of the book were secretly smuggled into India. It was a huge success. It made the people proud of their soldiers and provided a fresh perspective on a war that was till then merely seen as the outcome of disgruntled Indian soldiers serving the British Government. Its second edition was published in the US by the Indians and third edition by Bhagat Singh. Its Punjabi and Urdu translations were a tremendous success, while its Tamil translation almost became a mandatory reading for soldiers of Subash Chandra Bose's Indian National Army as a majority of them were Tamilians from South East Asia.

REVOLUTIONARY ACTIVITIES

In London, he organized the students and advocated an armed struggle to bring to an end the British rule in India. He called the Sepoy Mutiny the First War of Independence, a terminology the Indian Government accepted after Independence of India. Because of his involvement in revolutionary activities, he came in contact with other revolutionaries like Madam Cama, Lala Hara Dayal and Madan Lal. Notwithstanding his involvement, he passed Bar-at-Law examination in May 1909, but he was not allowed to practise law.

ARRESTED

In March 1910, he was arrested for his revolutionary activities when he reached London from Paris and sent to India to face the trial. He escaped through the port-hole of SS Morea on 8 July 1910 when it berthed at Marseilles (France). He swam a great distance in the cold water to reach the shore. He had earlier told his friends including Madame Bhikaji Cama to meet him at Marseilles. But they arrived late. Since he did not know French, he could not speak the French police that he was a refugee. He was arrested and handed over to the British Government. He was tried in India and sentenced to life for fifty years on 24 December 1910.

He was again awarded transportation for life on 31 January 1911. He was the only person in the history of the British Empire to have received it twice. On 4 July 1911, he entered the Cellular Jail, Andmans. He spent most degrading and difficult days in jail as he was sent to rigorous imprisonment for fifty years. He was placed in solitary confinement while other leaders enjoyed more facilities and privileges. They were released when they fell ill or someone in their family fell ill. But Savarkar was not allowed to such luxury. In 1920, Vithalbhai Patel, elder brother of Vallabhbhai Patel, demanded his release. Nehru and Gandhi also supported it. But it was ignored by the government. On 21 May 1921, he along with his elder brother were brought back to the mainland of India and he spent his days (1921–1923) in Alipore (West Bengal) and Ratnagiri (Maharashtra) jails.

RELEASED

On 6 January 1924, he was released on conditions that he would not leave Ratnagiri district, which was not very far from Mumbai, till 1937 and not to participate in politics. After his release from the internment, he joined the Tilakite Democratic Swaraj Party and later the Hindu Mahasabha to infuse his own revolutionary fervour and heroic will.

ASSOCIATION WITH HINDU MAHASABHA

Soon after his conditional release from internment he became active in the Hindu Mahasabha (founded in 1915), which sought to protect the interests of Hindus. Radically different from the Congress, the Hindu Mahasabha had its own followers who had a strong belief in Hindutva or who were opposed to Gandhi and the Congress. He was elected as President of Akhil Bharat Hindu Mahasabha at its Nineteenth Session at Karnavati (Ahmedabad) on 10 December 1937. He was continuously re-elected to the same post for the next seven years.

PRESIDENT OF NATYA SAMMELAN AND SAHITYA SAMMELAN

Besides being a patriot, a revolutionary, Savarkar was also a littérateur. It was because of his contribution to literature, he was elected as President of Marathi Sahitya Sammelan on 15 April 1938. Recognizing his literary talents, the University of Nagpur conferred Honorary D.Litt. on him on 14 August 1943. On 5 November 1943, he was also elected President of Marathi Natya Sammelan at Sangli.

LOST HIS FAMILY MEMBERS

As said above, he lost his parents when he was quite young. It was a grave shock and irreparable loss to him. But, it seems, it could not satiate the hunger and thirst of the Lord of Death. As he needed more and more and, therefore, demanded more and more from Savarkar and the latter had to satiate Him by losing his elder brother Babarao on 16 March 1934, his younger brother Narayanrao Savarkar on 19 October 1945 and his wife Yamuna on 8 November 1963.

ARRESTED AGAIN

Loss, deprivation, denial, arrest, imprisonment—all these very closely followed him and became his close and lasting friends, never to isolate him. He faced another ordeal when he was arrested under the Preventive Detention Act on 5 February 1948 after Gandhi's murder. However, he was acquitted on 10 February 1949. But he was again arrested and detained in Belgaum jail on the eve of arrival of the then Pakistani Prime Minister Liaquat Ali Khan in Delhi.

ABHINAV BHARAT DISSOLVED

Savarkar dissolved his revolutionary society Abhinav Bharat in May 1952 following India's Independence in 1947. The Hindu Mahasabha, headed by him, never supported the Quit India Movement launched in August 1942. He also asked Hindus to help the British in their effort against Germany and Japan. Critics argue that it was more a strategy than a policy adopted by him. This might help him in selecting more Hindus for imparting military training. And this might have been turned against the British later. Apart from him, the Muslim League and the Communists also did not support the Quit India Movement.

GODSE AND APTE ARRESTED

Following Gandhi's assassination in 1948, Nathuram Godse and Narayan Apte were arrested. They were well known to Savarkar as they visited him frequently. His house was, therefore, stoned by the public. He was arrested but later set free for lack of evidence.

DEMISE IN 1966

Too much hard work and commitment took a heavy toll of his life. Tired, exhausted and restless, he badly needed rest for some time. God was probably kind enough to him when he was admitted into hospital on 29 May 1963 for a fracture in his leg. But he recovered soon and was discharged. But after a lapse of two years, he was taken seriously ill in September 1965 and on 1 February 1966, he took a decision to fast unto death. On 26 February 1966 at 10.30 a.m. at the age of 83, he passed away. The light was off. An era often characterized by violence came to an end. His demise was a great loss to the country. On 27 February 1966, his cremation took place at the electric crematorium. The final salute was given by 2500 uniformed Swayamsevaks of the Rashtriya Swayam Sangh and millions of admirers across the country.

INTERPRETATION OF INDIAN HISTORY

In his book, *Six Glorious Epochs of Indian History* (published in 1971), Savarkar said that Indian History contained six glorious epochs. They were:

- First, the Maurya Empire set up by Chandragupta with the assistance of his great teacher Chanakya. Without any strong background, he founded with his own efforts his empire mightier even than that of Alexander himself.
- Second, the triumph and victories of King Pushyamitra who destroyed the Greek power in India.
- Third, Vikramaditya who annihilated the might of the Sakas.
- Fourth, Yashodharma of Malwa who defeated the Huns at Mandasore in 528 A.D. and captured the powerful and cruel Hun leader Mihiragula.
- Fifth, the foundation of the Maratha power as a powerful counter-blast to the might of the Islamic forces in India. Maratha leaders believed in the aggression against the enemy. Mere defence was not their policy, and
- Sixth, successful removal of the British from India and getting freedom for the country.

While making a brilliant exposition of Indian history, Savarkar glorified with much passion and zeal the Vedic Hinduism. At the same time, he strongly opposed virtues like pacifism, generosity, forgiveness, etc. as these were against the achievement of goal through violence. He praised Medhatithi for his brilliant comments on Manu's monumental work Manu-Smriti, and for his views on expansion of the empire; admired Vidyaranya for his views on liberalism; extolled the virtues of Shivaji who established the independent empire and reconverted Palkar and Nimbakar who were forcefully converted into Islam; criticized the Hindus for tolerating "foreign rulers" who invaded India, plundered its property, killed its innocent people and enslaved those who survived their wrath. Devoid of virtues like sympathy, goodwill, sacrifice, cordiality, compromise, understanding, etc., they were cruel, selfish and arrogant.

Savarkar highly praised the Marhata power for challenging the Muslim regime and accepting "Swadharma and Swaraj" as its two fundamental ideals which they cherished.

Calling the Sepoy Mutiny (1857) as the First War of Independence and praising those who participated in it, he argued that the fear of "greased cartridges" and the annexation of Oudh might have been its minor and immediate causes. But it was, in fact, the result of suppression.

Quoting others, he said that the term 'Sepoy Mutiny' did not mean that it was the Sepoys only who participated in it. It was by no means merely a military mutiny. Several factors like military grievances, national hatred and religious fanaticism were responsible for it. The Meerut Sepoys found, in a moment, a leader, a flag and a cause and the Mutiny was transformed into a revolutionary war. When they reached Delhi, they had all "unconsciously seized one of the great critical moments of history and converted a military mutiny into a national and religious war". Assuming a new dimension in 1857, the Mutiny became the rebellion of a whole people.

THEORY OF HINDUTVA

Opposing the concept of absolute non-violence, Savarkar strongly believed that violence has no place if the world is good, peaceful and where saints and angels rein the supreme. But when there are thousands of wicked ones, where there are full of contradictions and maladies, righteous violence can be resorted to as a means to achieve an ideal. Unless there is a kingdom of God where good souls dwell, unless and until a new era—era of perfect peace and love—ushers in, it would be a sin if violence is given up as a means to achieve the goal. But once there exists a kingdom where virtues play a dominant role, it would be a great sin to apply violence to achieve a cause, however noble it may be. He observed:

> So long as that divine age has not arrived, so long as the highly auspicious end remains only in the lines of saintly poets and in the prophesies of the divinely inspired, and so long as, even to make that state of universal justice possible, the human mind has to be busy eradicating sinful and aggressive tendencies, so long rebellion, bloodshed and revenge cannot be purely sinful.

Savarkar, therefore, admired those who adopted violence to vindicate justice, establish the truth, promote equality, guarantee liberty and achieve fraternity. He wrote:

> We do not hold the justice which gives the death sentence responsible for bloodshed but rather the injustice which is taken to the gallows. Therefore, the sword of Brutus is holy. Therefore, the "Baghanakha" (tiger's nail) of Shivaji is sacred. Therefore, the bloodshed in the revolutions in Italy is of fair fame. Therefore, the beheading of Charles-I is a just deed. Therefore, the arrow of "William Tell is Divine". He had full faith that justice must triumph in the end. But because every Hiranyakashipa has the Narasimha, because every Dushashana has his Bheema, because every evil-doer has his avenger, there is still some hope in the heart of the world that Injustice cannot last.

India as a nation has its cultural and organic solidarity. Strongly subscribing to the theory of Hindu Resurrection, he powerfully argues that Hinduism is certainly superior to other religions, and firmly believes that Hinduism should undergo both moral and social regeneration. It should be concerned with various and otherwise different aspects like "life after death", "salvation", "rebirth", "existence of heaven and hell", "existence of God", etc. But so far as the materialistic aspect is concerned, the Hindus are a nation bound by a common culture, a common history, a common language, a common country and a common religion. There can be development among them if they consolidate their interests and responsibilities. Fellowship and community feeling should replace their pervasive isolationism.

A Hindu is he who regards this land of Bharatvarsha, stretching over from the Indus to the Seas, as his Fatherland as well as his Holyland. It is the cradle land of his religion. There are three criteria which make someone a Hindu. First, he should have an intense love and attachment for his country which extends from the Sindhu river to the Brahmaputra and from the Himalayas to the Cape Comorin. Second, the racial or blood bond or the *jati*. A Hindu is one who inherits the blood of the race "whose first and discernible source could be traced to the Himalayan attitudes of the Vedic Sapatasindhu". It is evident from history that the Hindus have developed a physiognomy and racial features over the centuries and these are in some respects different from those of Germans, Chinese or Ethiopians.

It is only the Hindus and to some extent the Jews who belong to a racial unit. No other religion can claim this status. A Hindu marrying a Muslim may lose his caste but not his Hindutva. He may be an orthodox or heterodox. He may believe any theoretical or philosophical or social system which is indigenous and founded by a Hindu. He may lose his sect but not his Hindutva—his Hinduness—because it is determined by blood which gets transmitted from generation to generation. Therefore, one who loves his Fatherland and inherits the blood of the race that has evolved, can be said to possess two of the most essential requisites of Hindutva.

A Hindu is being known by his culture, the third criterion. He feels proud of it. It is a set of values which regulate, determine or control his behaviour; a feeling, an attitude, an impression born out of common language, common history, common geography, common achievements and failures, common expectations and anticipations, common religion, common art and architecture, common rituals and festivals. Those who give up Hinduism and accept Christianity or Islam can never be called as Hindus, because they no more subscribe to the culture of Hindus. The converted Christians and Muslims eat beef, criticize Hindu God and deities, do not take 'Prasad' offered to them.

Obviously, Hindutva is more comprehensive than Hinduism, while the latter has religious significance and covers rituals, etc., the former includes the social, moral, political and economic aspects. It transcends the Hinduism. It is not merely a concept of organic socio-political unity. It is something more than that; an embodiment of essential elements of nationalism; an organic socio-political body knit together by three bonds of territorial belongingness, blood or birth and culture. It is a programme for action. All these forces that create discord and division are to be controlled so that there can be unity and understanding among them. All the barriers that separate the Hindus must be demolished. Intercaste marriage will go a long way in this regard. It will remove caste barrier. Jains,

Sikhs, Buddhists, Arya Samajists and Brahma Samajists are to be treated as Hindus.

Savarkar argued that Hindutva and nationalism are not antithetic. They go together. Rationalistic and scientific, Hindutva is not a narrow creed and it stands for humanism and universalism.

Opposed to the policy of appeasement to Muslims, he was confident that Swaraj could be achieved without their support to the freedom struggle. It would, therefore, be better if they voluntarily participated in the freedom struggle.

HINDU–MUSLIM UNITY

The human world has been divided, according to the Muslim theology and theoretical politics, into two groups: the Muslim land and the enemy land. While the former is inhabited entirely by the Muslims or is ruled by the Muslims, the latter is just the opposite. A faithful Muslim becomes intolerant of the latter and his only mission or his only goal is to conquer all the enemy lands and their rulers. He wants to convert the entire enemy land into the Muslim land. He feels more happy if he converts the Hindus into Muslims.

A faithful Muslim's love for the Muslim mankind is unique as it transcends all barriers; geographical, territorial, historical, etc. Territorial patriotism is something unknown to them. He may be staying in India among his friends and relatives, but thinking about Mecca and Medina. Needless to say, he treats India and every non-Muslim Indian as his enemies.

An Indian Muslim, to Savarkar, hardly loves India. Rarely, he shares with its sorrows and sufferings. He feels shy of identifying himself with a country where he is born and brought up. It is because the country's majority of the population are the Hindus and it is not ruled by Muslims. He is not loyal to India, nor has any commitment towards it. He always looks up to Mecca and Medina and develops an extra-territorial allegiance. He is moved more by events in Palestine than that concerns India as a nation. He is worried more about the well-being of the Arabs than the well-being of their Hindu neighbours and countrymen in India. He conspires with any one any number of things to bring India under the Muslim rule.

A Muslim theologian has maximum hatred for the Hindus. To him, Christians and Jews are after all "Kitabis", having holy books partially in common. But Hindus are totally "Kafirs", and as a consequence their land Hindustan is pre-eminently "Enemy Land" as long as it is not ruled by Muslims or all Hindus do not embrace Islam. This is, to Savarkar, the religious mortality of all Indian Muslims.

Consequently, political and cultural mentality of the Muslims is essentially anti-Hindu and is bound to be so as long as they continue to be the Muslims and "faithfuls". They are always conscious of the fact that they entered India as conquerors and subjected the Hindus to their rule. But they have forgotten that they were bitten by the Hindus in a hundred battlefields in India. In the long run, the Hindus freed India from the Muslim yoke and re-established Hindu-Pad-

Padshahi. Muslims know that they are a powerful minority and their population has been growing every day.

Muslims want that Urdu should be the national language even though crores of them living in India and elsewhere do not speak it or understand it. It can claim no more merit than Hindi which is the mother tongue of more than twenty crore people and easily understood by more than ten crore people. "While the Arabian language itself on which Urdu is fed is deemed outlandish by Kemal and the Turks in the land of the Khaliphas itself, the Muslims expect some twenty-five crore Hindus to learn it and adopt it as their national language".

The Muslims insist on the adoption of the Urdu script as the national script, without bothering about the oldest script "Nagri". Kemal discarded the Arabian script itself as it was not suitable to the present day needs. The Nagri is more scientific, more amenable to printing. Yet the Urdu script must be, to them, the national script and the Urdu the national language. The only reason for this is that they consider Urdu as their cultural asset. Therefore, to make room for it the culture of Hindus and other religions must go to dogs.

The Muslims do not tolerate the song "Vande Mataram". It is reduced and shortened because of lack of unity amongst the Hindus. But they are not satisfied even with abridged portion. Even if the whole song is dropped, they would treat the very words "Vande Mataram" quite insulting to them.

SCHOOLS OF THOUGHT

Gandhian School

Savarkar discusses various schools of thought concerning the Hindu–Muslim unity and the solution provided by them. According to the Gandhian school of thought, it was the British Government that created the rift between the two communities. It would be over soon after the departure of the British from India. Left to themselves, the Muslims are good, gentle, polite and never indulge in any anti-national activities. Neither they are against the Hindus nor do they have any ulterior designs against them. Even the Frontier tribes like the Moplas, the Muslims of Bengal or Sindh who indulged in horrible outrage against Hindus have no taste for such activities. They were rather compelled to indulge in such activities by the British Government. Hindus and Muslims will live together peacefully once the British leave the country or do not interfere in their affairs.

A pertinent question can be raised here. Did the British instigate the Mohammedans, Kasims, Gazanis, Ghoris, Allaudins and Aurangzebs to torture the Indians, to eliminate them, to slaughter them and to butcher them? The rift between the Hindus and the Muslims is a pretty old one. Before the arrival of the British into India, the Hindu–Muslim conflict was not there. This is what the Gandhian school believed. But it is not the case. It dates back to several centuries. This is a historical and cultural conflict and the legacy was handed down to us by centuries of a cultural, religious and national antagonism between the Hindus and Muslims.

Common Origin Theory

This theory argues that Indian Muslims were once upon a time the Hindus. Conversion took place at different points of time, during the reign of different rulers. They are close to Hindus because they speak the same language and belong to the same race. Hence, they could be easily persuaded to acknowledge this homogeneity and even the blood relation with the Hindus and to merge themselves into a common National Being. Muslims should be reminded of this fact and an appeal be made to them to do the needful.

To Savarkar, such kind of thought is to be pitied, because the Muslims know about it pretty well. Hindus are also aware of this. But the difference lies in the fact that while Hindus feel proud of their culture, language, race, religion, etc., the Indian Muslims want to forget it as they hate it and do not like to be reminded of their past. They want to get rid of it. Some of them fabricate the history and genealogies to connect their origin with Arabians or Turks; they are trying to create a separate language for themselves and graft it as best as they can on the Arabian stock; they have been severely criticizing the Hindu family names such as "Tambe" and "Modak" which in parts like the Kokan convert-Muslims still bear and replace them by Arabian ones. They have been striving their best to remove every trace which may remind them of having once something in common with the Hindu stock. Indian Muslims will not be at peace until every Hindu becomes a Muslim or pays zizia to the Muslim ruler.

They have a strong aversion for the terminology "Hindustan" as it emits a very bad smell to them. They do not tolerate the term.

Theory of Appeasement

This theory believes that the mistrust that exists between these two communities can be removed if the demands of Muslims are met.

Theory of Economics

The last school of thought is the force of economics as an important factor influencing the course of history. There will be better understanding between the two communities if their economic conditions improve.

But economics is not everything. Man does not live by bread alone. Human nature is a constituent of several aspects like racial, cultural, national, etc. Therefore, any attempt to interpret the human history in the light of economics would be one-sided and incomplete. It means that he has no other urge in him except hunger. Besides hunger, the problem of bread, man has other appetites as fundamental as that, sensual, intellectual, sentimental, some natural, some acquired, some personal, some social and his Being is a complex one; so also in his history. Man has a stomach but the stomach is not man. It is, therefore, superficial to suggest that economics would address or solve all the problems—cultural, national, religious, racial, etc.—facing the country as a whole. No doubt, it plays an important role in human interaction. But it does not mean that factors other than it will be completely ignored. Hence, steps should be taken to improve the economic conditions of both the communities.

THE REAL SOLUTION

The Hindu–Muslim conflict is neither a simple thing nor the creation of the third party. It may be attributed to differences in race, culture, language, religion, etc. It is a legacy handed down to us by centuries of cultural, religious and national antagonism between the Hindus and the Muslims. The day the Hindus made the Muslims feel that without their support it would not be possible to achieve Swarajya, that day it was made impossible to have an honourable unity between the Hindus and the Muslims.

It is the greatest irony that the majority community bends its knees before the minority community and requests the latter to lend its helping hand so that it would not be doomed to death. Aware of this weakness of the majority community, the minority community feels happy as it does not help or cooperate with the majority community so that the latter's doom will be expedited. This will help it to establish its supremacy and political sovereignty.

Unity can be possible if everyone, irrespective of his status, standing, calling, colour, race, sex, etc. is treated on equal terms with others. "One individual, one vote", this principle should operate. Hindus constituting the majority should not claim any specific privileges or facilities for themselves. Rather they should ensure certain rights to the minorities. But it is unfortunate that all the Muslim states are united against the Hindus. They hate them.

The Hindus should, therefore, no more trust the Muslims. No blank cheque should be given against them, explaining their virtues and good qualities. India will be free soon. Consequently, its people will also be free. Hindus want freedom because they will be free and become their own masters. Unless India is free, the Indian Muslims cannot be free and will continue to remain as slaves. The Hindu formula for Hindu–Muslim unity is only this:

> If you come, with you; if you don't, without you; and if you oppose, in spite of you; the Hindus will continue to fight for their Freedom as best as they can.

CONCLUSION

A nation should remember its leaders, statesmen, poets, litterateurs, philosophers and others for their sacrifice, for their contributions towards its liberation and development. It should cherish their memories by celebrating their birthdays, etc. to inspire the future generations. But it is unfortunate neither a country nor its people, nor its leaders do remember them in true sense of the term, do anything to commemorate their memories in true spirit. The least that it (India) does is to garland their statues on their birthdays. Their statues are also not properly maintained. Most of them are defaced. In fact, the immortal souls that one day adored this country are forgotten, neglected and ignored. Veer Savarkar is not an exception.

The self-centred politicians of India have deprived him of his dues. He was never against the Muslims, but he was certainly opposed to the policy of appeasement towards them. This was solely responsible for the partition of India. He strongly criticized Nehru and Gandhi for their role in this regard and also opposed Golwalkar, the then Head of the Rastriya Swayam Sevak Sangh, for his role during the massacre of Hindus. He kept quiet while Hindus were mercilessly butchered, silently watched the perpetration of the worst crimes and did not do anything to prevent such ghastly events. Neither he nor the RSS supported Veer Savarkar and the Hindu Mahasabha who were opposed to the partition of the country.

One may call rose by any name. But it will have the same fragrance. Similarly, one may ignore the sun and the moon. But they will always be emitting their light to remove darkness. Veer Savarkar may be ignored or undermined. But he shines and will continue to shine in the arena of politics as long as there is wind and the fire.

POINTS TO REMEMBER

- Life Sketch:
  - Date of Birth: 28 May 1883. Village: Bhagpur. District: Nasik. State: Maharashtra.
  - Parents: Damodarpant (father), Radha Bai (Mother).
  - Brother: Ganesh.
  - Wife: Yamuna Mai. Son: Viswas. Daughter: Prabha.
  - Influence of Chapkar brothers' hanging. Decided to fight against the British. Set up revolutionary societies.
  - Passed HSC. Exam. in 1901 BA in 1905.
  - Went to London for higher studies in 1906.
  - Important literary works: "Joseph Mazini" and "Indian War of Independence".
  - Arrested for his revolutionary activities (1910). Awarded transportation for life twice (1911).
  - Spent a number of years in jail.
  - His association with Hindu Mahasabha.
  - Arrested after Gandhi assassination.
  - Death in 1966.

- Interpretation of Indian History:
  - Made a brilliant exposition of Indian history.
  - Praised the Marhata power.
  - Called Sepoy Mutiny as the First War of Independence.
- The Theory of Hindutva:
  - Opposed to the concept of absolute non-violence.
  - Violence often can be preferred to non-violence.
  - In a society where there is rampant corruption, violation of law, rules and procedures, there violence is required to bring order.
  - Hinduism is superior to other religions.
  - Clearly distinguishes terms like Hindu, Hinduism and Hindutva.
- Hindu–Muslim Unity:
  - Muslims hate Hindus. They do not share their feelings.
  - They are fanatics. Their love transcends all barriers.
  - They do not tolerate Vande Mataram.
- Schools of Thought:
  - Gandhian
  - Common Origin Theory
  - Theory of Appeasement
  - Theory of Economics

22

Mahatma Jyotirao Govindrao Phule (1827–1890)

INTRODUCTION

A prominent social reformer, a renowned activist, a great thinker and above all a noble 'Soul', Jyotirao Govindrao Phule did his best to bring in positive changes in the spheres of education, agriculture, caste system, social position of women, etc. in the 19th century. He is admired and remembered for his selfless service to educate women and low caste people. Respectfully addressed as "Mahatma", he lead a movement against the existing caste structure, revolted against the domination of the Brahmins, and fought for the rights of the peasants and others belonging to low castes. The first Hindu to set up an orphanage for the unfortunate children, he was a prolific writer, brilliant scholar, eminent philosopher, fearless editor and a daredevil revolutionary.

LIFE SKETCH

Born on 11 April 1827 in Satara district of Maharashtra, his father Govindrao was a vegetable vendor at Poona. He lost his mother when he was only nine months old. Since his father and uncles were 'Mali' by caste, they were known as florists. It was because of their caste and profession, they were called as "Phule" (Florist).

Though intelligent, he was poor. Grim poverty was a strong barrier to his studies. He had to give it up quite at an early age. He assisted his father and uncles by working in their farms. Impressed by his talents, a Muslim and a Christian neighbour persuaded his father to send him to school. He was admitted in the Scottish Mission's High School, Poona in 1841. There, he met Sadasiv Ballal Govinde, a Brahmin who became one of his best friends and remained close to him throughout his life. At the age of thirteen, he was married to Savitribai. He completed his schooling in 1847.

MOVEMENT

The year 1848 was a crucial year for him, a turning point in his life. An event relating to his participation in his friend's (a Brahmin) marriage function and the insult and humiliation meted out to him by family members of his friend—left a deep impact upon his life. His joining the marriage procession as a member of bridegroom's party was not to the liking of his friend's father and others. Humiliated and insulted, he left the procession and took a vow to set right the caste structure which was 'derailed' because of arrogance and complex of a few upper caste people.

The aforesaid event laid the foundation stone of a new era—an era free from caste prejudices and biases, social inequality, caste-based exploitation and humiliation, untouchability, etc. He dedicated his life to the cause of *dalits* who were deprived of all their rights as human beings.

Thomas Paine's book *The Rights of Man* had a tremendous influence upon him. He strongly felt that all the problems of *dalits* could be solved if right and proper education was provided to them. Education was the key to their survival, success and enlightenment.

He had also a strong conviction that women should have a voice in the society, a power to influence the decision-making process and revolt against injustice, deprivation and exploitation. His stress on women education impelled him to establish in 1848 the first girls' school in India. His wife, who was educated by him, played a key role in this regard.

His efforts in making the *dalits* and women educated and conscious of their rights were strongly condemned and denounced by orthodox Brahmins. Furious at his activities, they accused him of vitiating the norms and regulations of the society. Many considered him to be an agent acting on behalf of the Christian missionaries. Firm, courageous and fearless, Jyotirao remained committed to his goal. Interestingly, he was strongly supported by some Brahmin friends. But for them, his "Movement" might not have been successful.

Criticizing and condemning the attitudes of orthodox Brahmins and others belonging to upper castes, he called them 'hypocrites' and campaigned against them for their authoritarianism and urged upon the peasants and "proletariat" to defy the restrictions imposed upon them.

In 1851, Jyotirao established another girls' school and asked his wife to teach the students. He also set up a number of schools for girls and an indigenous school for the lower castes, especially the *Mahars* and *Mangs*.

Moved by the plight of the poor widows and their children, he established an orphanage in 1854 to provide shelter to them. In fact, it provided shelter to many young widows belonging to upper castes.

Jyotiba felt that a new society or social system could be created to ensure liberty, equality, freedom, rights, fraternity, etc. and this could be possible only when blind beliefs and superstitions were given up. The old social system, which encouraged and protected old, obsolete blind-beliefs and superstitions, should be replaced by a new one having strong faith in those phenomena which were rational. He condemned things like belief in God, astrology, fate, rituals, sacredness, God-men, etc. as these were absurd and irrational. To him, religious books and sacred texts were never created by God. It would be better if they were analysed scientifically but not accepted blindly. They should not be put into practice without any proper analysis. He criticized the priests as they were solely responsible for all kinds of social evils and disorder.

To him, God never wrote the Texts (religious scripts). If at all he wrote, why did he write in Sanskrit, a language which was understood only by few people in India? He further asked: if there was only one God, who created this entire world? It was one's ignorance and prejudice that made him to believe that Scriptures and Texts were divine-oriented. All religions were men-made and all Texts written by men and the intention behind such writing was to perpetuate the blind beliefs and keep the 'Shudras' and other backward people under their (authors') control.

Every Text, every Scripture, every Religion has a value system. But it is purely temporary in nature. It loses its relevance, validity and importance in due course of time. It is not universal.

Religion, an instrument for exploitation, a paradise for Brahmins, could be interpreted in any way by them. And their interpretation was final. It was certainly ridiculous. It was not religion but removal of economic exploitation that mattered.

SATYA SHODHAK SAMAJ

Jyotirao strongly believed that Brahmins were solely responsible for all kinds of social oppression and suppression in the society. The laws were made in such a manner that it helped them to 'enslave' the 'Shudras'. Disgusted with the existing laws and regulations, he formed the Satya Shodhak Samaj (Society of Seekers of Truth) on 24 September 1874 to set the 'Shudras' free from the domination of the Brahmins. He became its first President and Treasurer. Any one could be a member of it. As a result, some Jews also were its members. In 1876, its strength was 316. In 1868, Jyotirao decided to construct a common tank outside his house for common man's bath. He also wished to dine with all regardless of their caste.

After the formation of the Samaj, his wife Savitribai became the head of the women's section which included ninety female members. She also taught tirelessly the girls. Deenabandhu Publication, the mouthpiece of the Samaj, played an important role in its movement. After the demise of Jyotiba in 1890, his sincere and devoted followers spread the message of the movement in the remotest parts of Maharashtra. Shahu Maharaj, the ruler of Kolhapur Princely State, gave a lot of financial assistance to the Samaj. As a non-Brahmin party, it dedicated itself to the cause of *dalits,* women, etc. and did its best to remove superstitions.

DEATH

After a prolonged, ceaseless and continuous struggle against the Brahmins, their tyranny against the *dalits*, Jyotirao Govindrao Phule passed away on 28 November 1890.

CONCLUSION

A dedicated and devoted 'Soul', Phule spent his whole life to uplift *dalits*. He laid the foundation of a new society where there would be no more exploitation, humiliation and torture against any one, particularly the *dalits* and the women. He ignited the spark, lit the fire that started engulfing the whole society. It enkindled a passion for a new social order that would protect equality, liberty and rights of every *dalit*. His relentless revolt against arrogance, obduracy and meanness of the Brahmins made him a 'Mahatma'. A significant figure in the social reform movement, he developed an impeccable sense of social justice. He was not critical of British rule in India as it gave India a new notion of social justice. A pioneer of anticaste movement, he was the first *dalit* to start a chain of girls schools at Pune in 1850s. Founder of a fondling home to take care of unwanted children, he set up a shelter home for neglected widows and an orphanage for the poor women. Opposed to child marriage and 'Sati' system, he favoured widow remarriage. Because of his contributions to the upliftment of the *dalits*, poor, women, destitute, orphans, widows, etc. he became a legend and pioneer of social transformation and *dalit* liberation in is lifetime.

Opposing idolatry, denouncing the *Chaturvarnya* system (caste system), propounding rational thinking and rejecting the need of a Brahmin priestly class as educated and religious leaders, Jyotirao did not regard the Vedas as sacrosanct.

Phule called Shivaji a 'destroyer' of Muslims who were a degenerative force like the Brahmins. The True inhabitants of India were the Astiks but not the Brahmins. The latter were outsiders to Hindustan. He did not like the casteists of Tamil Nadu using Rama as a symbol of oppression of Arya conquest.

Some of India's first modern feminists were closely associated with Phule. They were: his wife Savitribai Phule; Pandita Ramabai, a Brahmin lady who created a sensation in the liberal reforms movement; Tarabai Shide, a non-Brahmin who wrote a book on gender inequality; and Muktibai, a fourteen-year-old baby girl, who became famous for writing an essay on social oppression of the Mang and Mahar castes.

It is because of his popularity, place and positionin in the society, the Crawford Market in Mumbai and an agricultural institution are named after him. The latter is called Mahatma Phule Krishi Vidyapeeth set up in Rahuri in Ahmednagar district of Maharashtra.

POINTS TO REMEMBER

- A great social reformer, an activist, a revolutionary.
- Born on 11 April 1827 in Maharashtra. A 'Mali' by caste.
- Poverty—a great barrier to his studies. Encouraged, he was admitted in Scottish Mission's High School in 1841.
- Sadasiv Ballal Govinde—a Brahmin—was his best friend.
- Savitribai was his wife.
- 1848—a crucial year. His participation in his friend's marriage function. Humiliated. It was a turning point in his life.
- His dream was to set up a new society—free from caste-related biases and prejudices.
- Thomas Paine's book *The Rights of Man*. Its influence upon him.
- *Dalits* to be educated for their empowerment.
- He set up the first girls' school in India in the year 1848.
- His efforts in making women and *dalits* educated were strongly criticized.
- Set up an orphanage in 1854.
- A new society to emerge with liberty, equality, rights, etc.
- No faith in concepts like God, God-men, fate, rituals, etc.
- Sacred Texts and Epics were not the creation of God. They should be scientifically analysed, but not to be blindly believed.
- Priests—responsible for social evils and disorder.
- Religions—made by men; Texts (sacred)—written by men. They are not divine-ordained.
- Founded Satya Sodhan Samaj to uplift the Sudras.
- His relentless struggle against the Brahmins for the upliftment of the *Dalits* earned him the title "Mahatma".

Bibliography

Ambedkar, B.R., *What Congress and Gandhi have done to the Untouchables*, Bombay: Thacker and Co., 1945.

______, *Who were the Shudras*, Bombay: Thacker and Co., 1945.

______, *Pakistan or Partition of India*, Bombay: Thacker and Co., 1945.

Appadorani, A., *Indian Political Thinking in the Twentieth Century from Naoroji to Nehru: An Introductory Survey*, Calcutta: Oxford University Press, 1971.

______, *Documents on Political Thought in Modern India*, Bombay: Oxford University Press, 1973.

Azad, Maulana Abul Kalam, *India Wins Freedom,* Hyderabad: Orient Longman, 1959.

Bakshi, S.R., *V.D. Savarkar,* New Delhi: Anmol Publications, 1994.

Baral, J.K., *Indian Political Tradition,* Kolkata: Macmillan, 2004.

_____ (Ed.), *Madhusudan: The Architect of Oriya Nationalism,* Cuttack: Vidyapuri, 2003.

Bipin Chandra, *India's Struggle for Independence,* New Delhi: Penguin Books, 1989.

_____, *Colonialism and Nationalism in Modern India,* New Delhi: Orient Longman, 1979.

Bose, Nemai Sadhan, *The Indian National Movement: An Outline,* Calcutta: Firma KLM, 1982.

Bose, Sisir Kumar (Ed.), *Netaji and India's Freedom,* Calcutta: Netaji Research Bureau, 1975.

Bose, Sisir Kumar (Ed.), *Subhas, Through Congress Eyes*, Allahabad: Kitabistan, 1938.

_____, *The Indian Struggle (1920–42)*, Bombay: Asia Publishing House.

_____, *The Indian Struggle (1935–1942)*; Calcutta: Chakravarti, Chatterjee & Co., 1952.

_____, *An Indian Pilgrim or Autobiography of Subhas Chandra Bose (1897–1920)*, Calcutta: Thacker, Spink & Co., 1948.

_____, *The Indian Struggle (1920–34)*, Calcutta: Thacker, Spink & Co., 1948.

Brecher, Michael, *Nehru: A Political Biography,* London: Oxford University Press, 1959.

Bright, Jagat S., *Important Speeches and Writings of Subas Chandra Bose*, Lahore: The Indian Printing Press, 1947.

Das, H.H., *Subhas Chandra Bose and the Indian National Movement*, New Delhi: Sterling Publishers, 1983.

_____ and Sasmita Das, *The National Movement in India*, Delhi: Renaissance, 1988.

Das, Naba Kishor, *Utkal Gaurab Madhusudan*, Bhubaneswar: Utkal University Press, 1999.

Dasgupta, H., *Subhash Chandra*, Calcutta: Jyoti Prakashalaya, 1946.

Dash, Surya Narain, *Deshaprana Madhusudan*, Cuttack: Grantha Mandira, 1988.

Dash, S.C., *Pandit Gopabandhu: A Biography*, Cuttack: Grantha Mandira, 1964.

Datta, Bhupendra Nath, *Vivekanand: Patriot–Prophet*, Calcutta: Navbharat Publishers, 1954.

Desai, A.R., *Social Background of Indian Nationalism*, Bombay: Popular Prakashan, 1982.

Devagirikar, T.R., *G.K. Gokhale*, Delhi: Government of India Publication Division, 1964.

Donager, Wendy and Smith, Brian K., *The Laws of Manu*, New Delhi: Penguin Books, 1991.

Dube, M.P., "Jawaharlal Nehru—A Profile", in M.P. Dube (Ed.), *Jawaharlal Nehru – Legacy and Legend*, Kumaun University Publication.

Edwards, Michael, *The Last Years of British Rule*, London: Allied, 1963.

Fischer, Louis, *The Life of Mahatma Gandhi*, New York: Collier Books, 1973.

Gandhi, M.K., *Satyagraha*, Allahabad: Navjivan, 1951.

_____, *An Autobiography or the Story of My Experiments with Truth*, Ahmedabad: Navjivan, 1957.

_____, *Democracy: Real and Deceptive*, Allahabad: Navjivan, 1961.

_____, *Gandhi's Correspondence with the Government (1944–47)*, Ahmedabad: Navjivan, 1959.

Ghose, J.C. (Ed.), *The English Works of Raja Rammohan Roy*, Vols. 1, 2 and 3, Calcutta: Srikanta Roy, 1901.

Ghose, Shankar, *The Renaissance to Militant Nationalism in India*, Calcutta: Allied Publishers, 1969.

Ghose, Shankar, *The Western Impact on Indian Politics (1885–1919)*, Bombay: Allied Publishers, 1967.

_____, *Political Ideas and Movements in India*, New Delhi: Allied Publishers, 1975.

Gordon, Leonard A., *Brothers Against the Raj: A Biography of Sarat Chandra and Subas Chandra Bose*, New Delhi: Penguin Books, 1990.

Gupta, D.C., *Indian National Movement*, Delhi: Vikas, 1970.

Heehs, Peter, *India's Freedom Struggle (1857-1947): A Short History*, Bombay: Oxford University Press, 1988.

Hibbert, Christopher, *The Great Mutiny: India 1857*, Harmondsworth: Penguin Books, 1982.

Jayaprakash Narayan, *Why Socialism*, Banaras: Jnanamandal Press, 1936.

_____, *A Picture of Sarvodaya Social Order*, Tanjore: Akhil Bharat Sarva Seva Sangh, 1955.

_____, *From Behind the Bars in Independent India*, Calcutta: Samajwadi Yuva Janasabha, 1976.

_____, *Kranti Ka Adhunik Prayog*, Patna: Janta Prakashan, 1954.

_____, *Swaraj for the People*, Varanasi: Akhil Bharat Sarva Seva Sangh, 1961.

_____, *Towards Struggle in Yusuf Meherally* (Ed.), Bombay: Padma Publications, 1946.

_____, *Towards Total Revolution*, Bombay: Popular Prakashan, 1978.

Jog, N.G., *In Freedom's Quest: Life of Subas Chandra Bose,* New Delhi: Orient Longman, 1969.

_____, *Lokamanya Bal Gangadhar Tilak*, New Delhi; Publication Division, Government of India, 1970.

Joshi, V.C., *Raja Rammohan Roy and the Process of Modernization in India*, Delhi: Vikas, 1975.

Khan, Shah Nawaj, *My Memories of INA and Its Netaji*, New Delhi: Rajkamal, 1946.

Kuber, W.N., *Ambedkar: A Critical Study*, New Delhi: People's Publishing House, 1979.

Lohia, Ram Manohar, *Will to Power and Other Writings*, Hyderabad; Navahind Publication, 1956.

_____, *Towards the Destruction of Castes and Classes*, Hyderabad; Samajvadi Prakashan, 1958.

Lohia, Ram Manohar, *Marx, Gandhi and Socialism*, Hyderabad: Navahind, 1963.

_____, *Bharat, China and Uttari Simayen*, Hyderabad: Navahind, 1963.

Majumdar, R.C., *On Rammohan Roy*, Calcutta: The Asiatic Society, 1972.

_____, S.K., *Evolution of Netaji: The Warrior–Prophet of India*, Calcutta: Netaji Reserch Bureau, 1969.

Mehta, V.R., *Foundations of India's Political Thought*, New Delhi: Manohar, 1996.

Mohanty, Surendra, *Kulabrudha*, Bhubaneswar: Lark Books, 1990.

_____, *Satabdeer Surya*, Cuttack: Lark Books, 1986.

_____, Madhusudan Das, New Delhi: National Book Trust, 1972.

Moraes, Frank, *Jawaharlal Nehru: A Biography,* Bombay: Jaico Publishing House, 1978.

Nanda, B.R., *The Nehrus: Motilal and Jawaharlal,* London: George Allen and Unwin, 1962.

Nehru, Jawaharlal, *An Autobiography*, London: John Lane, The Bodley Head, 1936.

_____, *The Discovery of India*, Calcutta: The Signet Press, 1946.

_____, *The Unity of India*, London: Lindsay Drummond, 1941.

_____, *Glimpses of World History*, London: Lindsay Drummond, 1938.

_____, *Soviet Russia*, Allahabad: Law Journal Press, 1928.

_____, *A Bunch of Old Letters*, Bombay: Asia Publishing House, 1960.

_____, *Letters from a Father to His Daughter,* Allahabad: Kitabistan, 1938.

Padhy, K.S., *Indian Political Tradition*, Berhampur: Taratarini Pustakalaya, 1997.

Pal, Bipin Chandra, "Rammohan as Reconstructor of Indian Life and Society", *Calcutta: Municipal Gazette*, 22 December 1928.

Panda, Dola Govind, *Political Philosophy of Gopabandhu Das*, Cuttack: Grantha Mandira, 1980.

Pantham, Thomas, "The Socio-Religious and Political Thought of Ram Mohan Roy", in Thomas Pantham and Kenneth L. Deutsch (Eds.), *Political Thought in Modern India*, New Delhi: Sage, 1986.

Parvate, T.V., *Bal Gangadhar Tilak*, Ahmedabad: Navjivan Publishing House, 1956.

_____, *Gopal Krishna Gokhale*, Ahmedabad: Navjivan, 1956.

Patabhi Sitaramaya, *History of Indian National Congress*, Vol. 1, Bombay: Padma Publications, 1946.

Patnaik, Surasingha, *Madhusudan Das: The Pride of Nation*, Cuttack: Priyadarshi, 1991.

Philips, C.H. and Wainright, M.D., *The Partition of India*, London: George Allen & Unwin, 1970.

Rai, Lajpat, *The United States of America: A Hindu's Impressions and a Study*, Calcutta: R. Chatterjee, 1916.

_____, *Young India*, New York: B.W. Huebsch, 1917.

_____, *India's Will to Freedom*, Madras: Ganesh & Co., 1921.

_____, *The Call to Young India*, Madras: Ganesh & Co., 1921.

_____, *The Political Future of India*, New York: B.W. Huebsch, 1919.

_____, *The Arya Samaj*, London: Longmans Green & Co., 1915.

_____, *The Problem of National Education in India*, London: George Allen & Unwin, 1920.

_____, *England's Debt to India*, New York: B.W. Huebsch, 1917.

Rajendra Prasad, *India Divided*, Bombay: Hindu Kitabs, 1947.

Ray, B.N., *Traditions and Innovation in Indian Political Thought: Politics and Vision*, Delhi: Ajanta Publications, 1998.

Ray, B.N. and Rajat, K., "Introduction" in V.C. Joshi (Ed.), *Rammohan Roy and the Process of Modernisation in India*, Delhi: Vikash Publishing House, 1975.

Rolland, Romain, *Life of Vivekanand*, Alroora: Advaita Ashram, 1953.

Roy, M.N., *Reason, Romanticism and Revolution*, Calcutta, 1955.

_____, *India in Transition, Documents of the History of the Communist Party of India*, Delhi: People's Publishing House, 1971.

_____, *Nationalism: An Antiquated Cult*, Bombay: Padma Publications, 1944.

_____, *New Humanism: A Manifesto*, Calcutta: Renaissance Publishers, 1947.

_____, *Planning in India*, Calcutta: Renaissance Publishers, 1944.

_____, *Ram Mohan: His Life, Writings and Speeches*, Madras: G.A. Natesan & Co., 1923.

Sarkar, Sumit, *Modern India* (1885–1947), Delhi: Macmillan, 1983.

_____, "Ram Mohan Roy and the Break with the Past" in V.C. Joshi (Ed.), *Ram Mohan Roy and the Process of Modernisation in India*, Delhi: Vikas, 1975.

_____, *Tanika, Hindu Wife, Hindu Nation*, New Delhi: Orient Longman, 2001.

Savarkar, V.R., *Hindu Rastra Darshan, A Collection of the Presidential Speeches*, Bombay, 1949.

Selected Speeches of Subas Chandra Bose, New Delhi: Publications Division, Government of India, 1962.

Sethi, R.R., *The Last Phase of British Sovereignty in India*, Delhi: S. Chand & Co., 1958.

Shahni, T.K., *Gopal Krishna Gokhale*, Bombay: R.K. Mody, 1929.

Sharma, J.S., *A Descriptive Bibliography of Nehru*, Delhi: S. Chand & Co., 1965.

Sharma, S.R. (Ed.), *Netaji: His Life and Work*, Agra: Shivlal Agarwala & Co., 1948.

Sinha, Sachidananda, *A Short Life-Sketch of Jawaharlal Nehru*, Patna: Law Press, 1936.

Smith, Donald Eugene, *Nehru and Democracy*, Calcutta: Orient Longmans, 1958.

Speeches and Writings of G.K. Gokhale, Madras: G.A. Natesan & Co., 1920.

Sri Aurobindo, *The Ideal of Human Unity in the Human Cycle, The Idea of Human Unity* (and) *War and Self-Determination*, Pondicherry: Sri Aurobindo Ashram, 1962.

_____, *The Spirit and Form of Indian Polity*, Pondicherry: Sri Aurobindo Ashram, 1962.

Varma, V.P., *Modern Indian Political Thought*, Agra: Laxmi Narayan Agarwal Educational Publishers, 1961.

_____, *The Political Philosophy of Mahatma Gandhi and Sarvodaya*, Agra: L.N.A. Educational Publishers, 1959.

Zacharias, H.C.E., *Renascent India: From Ram Mohan Ray to Mohandas Gandhi*, London: George Allen & Unwin, 1933.

Zakaria, Rafiq (Ed.), *A Study of Nehru*, Bombay: Times of India Publications, 1960.

Name Index

Subject Index